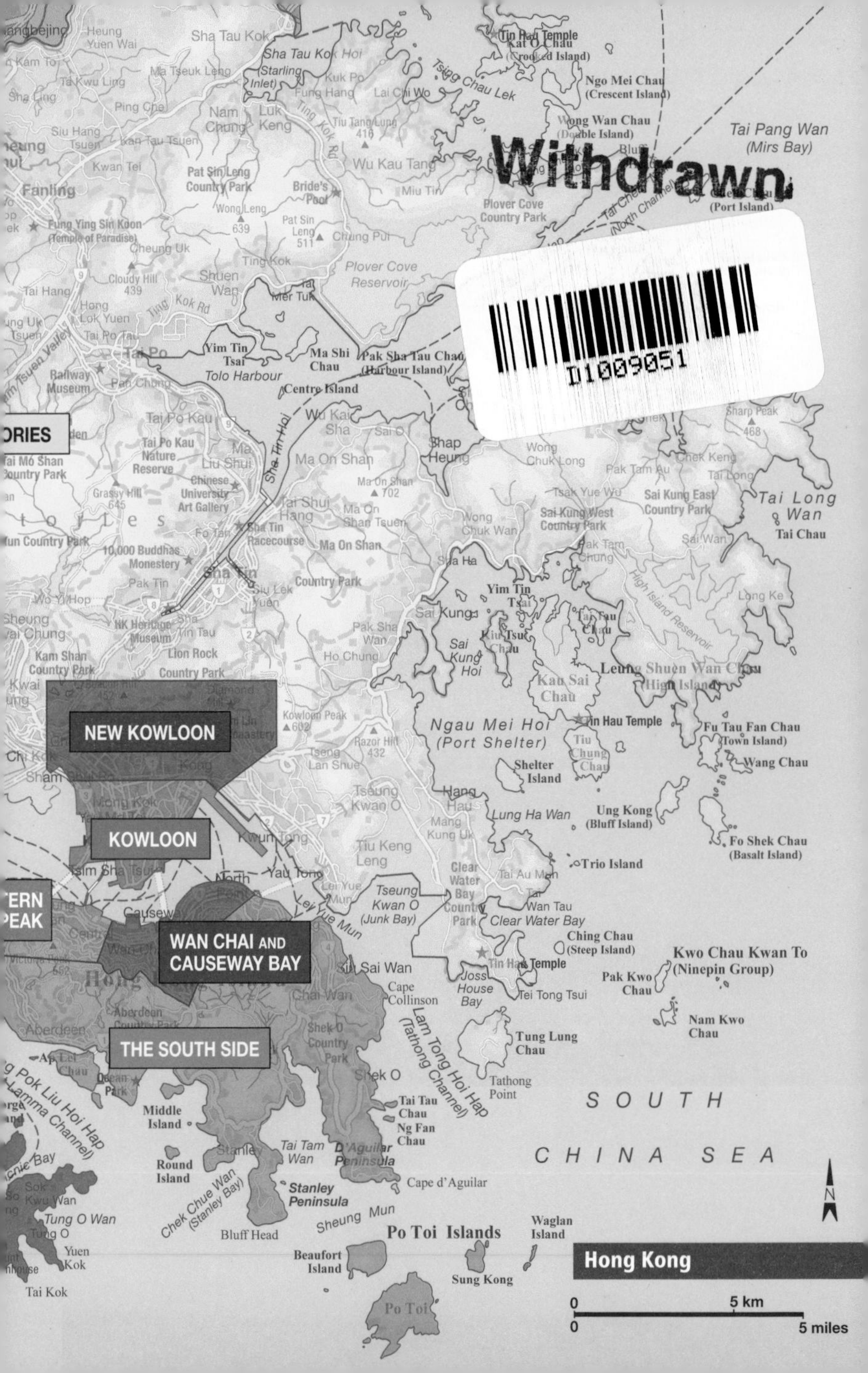
Hong Kong
NEW KOWLOON
KOWLOON
WAN CHAI AND CAUSEWAY BAY
THE SOUTH SIDE
Sha Tau Kok
Sha Tau Kok Hoi (Starling Inlet)
Tin Hau Temple
Kat O Chau (Crooked Island)
Ngo Mei Chau (Crescent Island)
Wong Wan Chau (Double Island)
Tai Pang Wan (Mirs Bay)
(Port Island)
Tsing Chau Lek
Kuk Po
Fung Hang
Lai Chi Wo
Ma Tseuk Leng
Ta Kwu Ling
Ping Che
Nam Chung
Luk Keng
Ting Kok Rd
Tiu Tang Lung 416
Wu Kau Tang
Kwan Tei
Fanling
Pat Sin Leng Country Park
Bride's Pool
Miu Tin
Wong Leng 639
Pat Sin Leng 511
Chung Pui
Plover Cove Country Park
Fung Ying Sin Koon (Temple of Paradise)
Cheung Uk
Ting Kok
Plover Cove Reservoir
Cloudy Hill 439
Shuen Wan
Tai Mei Tuk
Tai Hang
Hong Lok Yuen
Tai Po Tau
Tai Po
Yim Tin Tsai
Ma Shi Chau
Pak Sha Tau Chau (Harbour Island)
Tolo Harbour
Centre Island
Railway Museum
Pan Chung
Tai Po Kau
Wu Kai Sha
Sai O
Shap Heung
Sha Tin Hoi
Tai Po Kau Nature Reserve
Ma Liu Shui
Ma On Shan
Chinese University Art Gallery
Ma On Shan 702
Sharp Peak 468
Wong Chuk Long
Chek Keng
Pak Tam Au
Tai Long
Tsak Yue Wu
Sai Kung East Country Park
Tai Long Wan
Tai Chau
Grassy Hill 645
Tai Shui Hang
Ma On Shan Tsuen
Sha Tin Racecourse
Ma On Shan Country Park
Wong Chuk Wan
Sai Kung West Country Park
Pak Tam Chung
Sai Wan
Fo Tan
10,000 Buddhas Monastery
Sha Tin
Siu Lek Yuen
Sha Ha
High Island Reservoir
Pak Tin
Wo Yi Hop
Yim Tin Tsai
Long Ke
Sai Kung
HK Heritage Museum
Sha Tin Tau
Pak Sha Wan
Kiu Tsui Chau
Tai Tau Chau
Sai Kung Hoi
Kam Shan Country Park
Lion Rock Country Park
Ho Chung
Leung Shuen Wan Chau (High Island)
Kau Sai Chau
Kowloon Peak 602
Ngau Mei Hoi (Port Shelter)
Tin Hau Temple
Fu Tau Fan Chau (Town Island)
Razor Hill 432
Tseng Lan Shue
Tiu Chung Chau
Wang Chau
Shelter Island
Sham Shui Po
Mong Kok
Hang Hau
Tseung Kwan O
Lung Ha Wan
Ung Kong (Bluff Island)
Mang Kung Uk
Kwun Tong
Fo Shek Chau (Basalt Island)
Tiu Keng Leng
Tsim Sha Tsui
Yau Tong
Clear Water Bay Country Park
Tai Au Mun
Trio Island
North Point
Lei Yue Mun
Tseung Kwan O (Junk Bay)
Tai Wan Tau
Clear Water Bay
Causeway
Central
Ching Chau (Steep Island)
Kwo Chau Kwan To (Ninepin Group)
Victoria Peak 552
Hong Kong Island
Siu Sai Wan
Tin Hau Temple
Pak Kwo Chau
Joss House Bay
Tei Tong Tsui
Cape Collinson
Chai Wan
Nam Kwo Chau
Aberdeen Country Park
Aberdeen
Lam Tong Hoi Hap (Tathong Channel)
Tung Lung Chau
Ap Lei Chau
Shek O Country Park
Ocean Park
Shek O
Tathong Point
Pok Liu Hoi Hap (Lamma Channel)
SOUTH CHINA SEA
Middle Island
Tai Tau Chau
Ng Fan Chau
Stanley
Tai Tam Wan
D'Aguilar Peninsula
Round Island
Cape d'Aguilar
Sok Kwu Wan
Chek Chue Wan (Stanley Bay)
Stanley Peninsula
Tung O Wan
Tung O
Sheung Mun
Bluff Head
Po Toi Islands
Waglan Island
Yuen Kok
Beaufort Island
Sung Kong
Tai Kok
Po Toi
N
0 5 km
0 5 miles

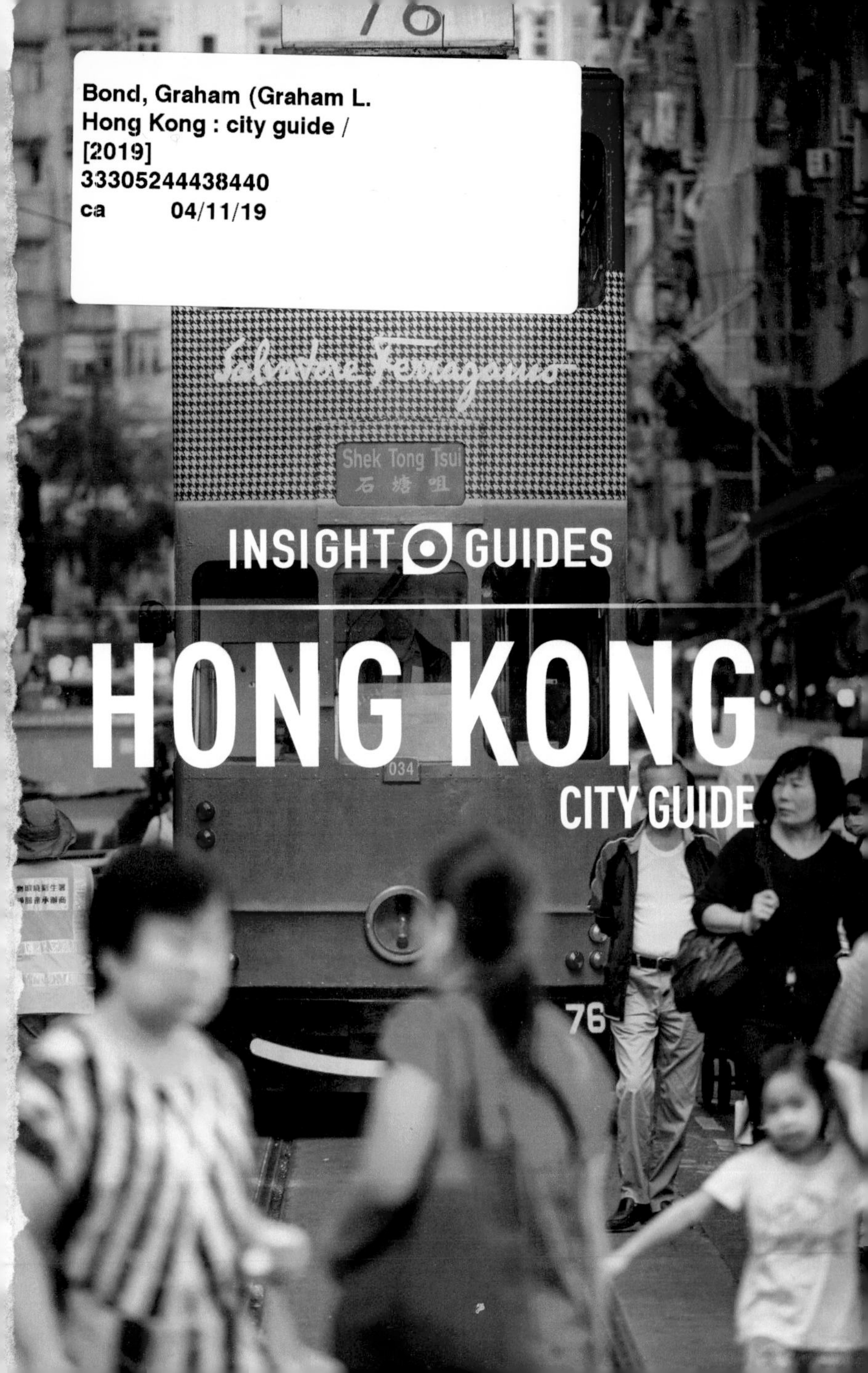


INSIGHT GUIDES

# HONG KONG

## CITY GUIDE

# Walking Eye App

## YOUR FREE DESTINATION CONTENT AND EBOOK AVAILABLE THROUGH THE WALKING EYE APP

Your guide now includes a free eBook and destination content for your chosen destination, all for the same great price as before. Simply download the Walking Eye App from the App Store or Google Play to access your free eBook and destination content.

### HOW THE WALKING EYE APP WORKS

Through the Walking Eye App, you can purchase a range of eBooks and destination content. However, when you buy this book, you can download the corresponding eBook and destination content for free. Just see below in the grey panels where to find your free content and then scan the QR code at the bottom of this page.

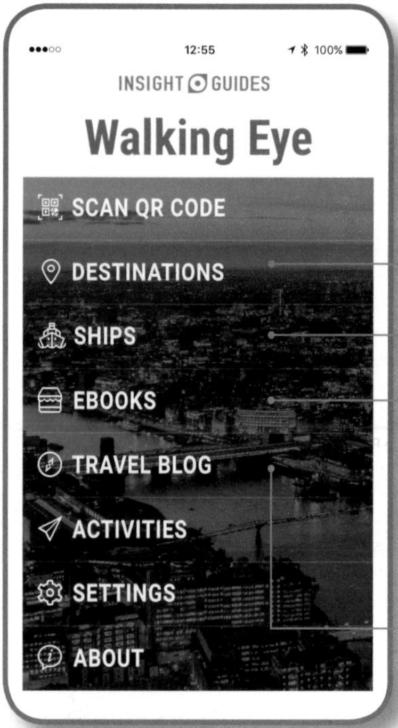


**Destinations:** Download your corresponding essential destination content from here, featuring recommended sights and attractions, restaurants, hotels and an A–Z of practical information, all for free. Other destinations are available for purchase.

**Ships:** Interested in ship reviews? Find independent reviews of river and ocean ships in this section, all available for purchase.

**eBooks:** You can download your free accompanying digital version of this guide here. You will also find a whole range of other eBooks, all available for purchase.

**Free access to travel-related blog articles** about different destinations, updated on a daily basis.

## HOW THE DESTINATION CONTENT WORKS

Each destination includes a short introduction, an A–Z of practical information and recommended points of interest, split into 4 different categories:

- Highlights
- Accommodation
- Eating out
- What to do

You can view the location of every point of interest and save it by adding it to your Favourites. In the 'Around Me' section you can view all the points of interest within 5km.

## HOW THE EBOOKS WORK

The eBooks are provided in EPUB file format. Please note that you will need an eBook reader installed on your device to open the file. Many devices come with this as standard, but you may still need to install one manually from Google Play.

The eBook content is identical to the content in the printed guide.

## HOW TO DOWNLOAD THE WALKING EYE APP

1. Download the Walking Eye App from the App Store or Google Play.
2. Open the app and select the scanning function from the main menu.
3. Scan the QR code on this page – you will then be asked a security question to verify ownership of the book.
4. Once this has been verified, you will see your eBook and destination content in the purchased ebook and destination sections, where you will be able to download them.

Other destination apps and eBooks are available for purchase separately or are free with the purchase of the Insight Guide book.

GET IT ON Google Play

Download on the App Store

# Contents


## Introduction
The Best of Hong Kong ............ **6**
The Hong Kong Way............... **17**
Hong Kong's People .............. **19**

## History
Decisive Dates....................... **26**
The Story of Hong Kong......... **31**

## Features
Culture and Society ............... **48**
Where Food is an Art............. **57**
Chinese Medicine.................. **67**
The Performing Arts............... **77**
Business and Money............. **82**

## Insights
**MINI FEATURES**
The last governor................... **44**
Chinese arts and crafts ......... **55**
The animal parts trade .......... **70**
Hiking in the hills ................. **180**
Macau's casinos.................. **206**

**PHOTO FEATURES**
Dim Sum ................................ **64**
Beliefs and Superstitions...... **72**
Modern Architecture.............. **86**
The Star Ferry...................... **116**
Horse-Racing....................... **126**
Shopping............................. **152**
Hong Kong's Festivals ......... **162**
Hong Kong's Wild Side ........ **182**
Theme Parks........................ **192**

## Places
Introduction ........................... **93**
- Central, Western and The Peak................................. **97**
- Wan Chai and Causeway Bay................. **119**
- The South Side................ **131**
- Kowloon .......................... **139**
- New Kowloon .................. **156**
- The New Territories ......... **167**
- The Outlying Islands........ **184**
- Macau ............................. **197**
- Shenzhen and the Pearl River Delta ............. **215**
- Guangzhou....................... **220**

## Travel Tips


**TRANSPORT**

Getting there....228
- By air....228
- By rail....229
- By sea....229

Getting around....229
- Public transport....229
- Macau transport....231

Regional Transport....231
- By boat....231
- By helicopter....232
- By rail....232

**A-Z**

Accommodation....233
Addresses....234
Admission charges....234
Age restrictions....234
Budgeting for your trip....234
Climate....234
Crime and safety....235
Customs regulations....235
Disabled travellers....235
Embassies & consulates....236
Emergency numbers....236
Etiquette....236
Health and medical care....236
Internet....237
Left luggage....237
LGBTQ travellers....237
Lost property....237
Maps....237
Media....237
Money....237
Opening hours....238
Postal services....239
Shopping....239
Smoking....239
Student travellers....239
Telephones....239
Time zone....240
Toilets....240
Tourist information....240
Visas and passports....241
Weights and measures....241

**LANGUAGE**

Tones....242
Pronunciation....243
Numbers....243
Common words and phrases....243
Nouns....243
Questions....243
People....243
Adjectives....243
Taxis....244
Health and emergencies....244
Food and drink....244
Glossary....244

**FURTHER READING**

Fiction....246
History and current affairs....246
Nature/walking guides....246
Macau....246
China....246
Other Insight Guides....246


## Maps


Hong Kong....94
Central and Western Districts....98
Victoria Peak....114
Wan Chai and Causeway Bay....120
Hong Kong Island....128
Kowloon....144
New Kowloon....157
New Territories East....168
New Territories West....179
Lantau....187
Macau....200
Pearl River Delta....212
Shenzhen....219
Guangzhou....222
Hong Kong Street Atlas....247
**Inside front cover** Hong Kong
**Inside back cover** Pearl River Delta

# THE BEST OF HONG KONG: TOP ATTRACTIONS

**With its vibrant Chinese culture, superb food, exciting nightlife, shopping and one of the world's most dramatic settings, there is an awful lot to see and do in Hong Kong. This brief introduction sketches out some of the highlights.**

◁ **The Outlying Islands.** In complete contrast to the crowded urban areas, Hong Kong's 230 Outlying Islands – such as Lamma – are largely rural, and lack buildings over three storeys tall. Most also lack roads. There are some beautiful beaches and great hiking. See page 184.

▽ **Tsim Sha Tsui and Yau Ma Tei.** Quintessential Hong Kong: shops, restaurants, crowds and neon everywhere. Temple Street Night Market is a great place to get acquainted with the local vibe, but watch out for fake merchandise! See page 139.

△ **The Star Ferry.** Take in the superb harbour views aboard one of these appealingly old-fashioned vessels. At HK$2.50 for the upper deck, this is one of the world's great travel bargains, and a must for all visitors to Hong Kong. See page 116.

▷ **Hong Kong Island views.** Like nowhere else on earth, the urban strip along the north coast of the island is a mass of skyscrapers wedged against tall green mountains. See pages 97 and 141.

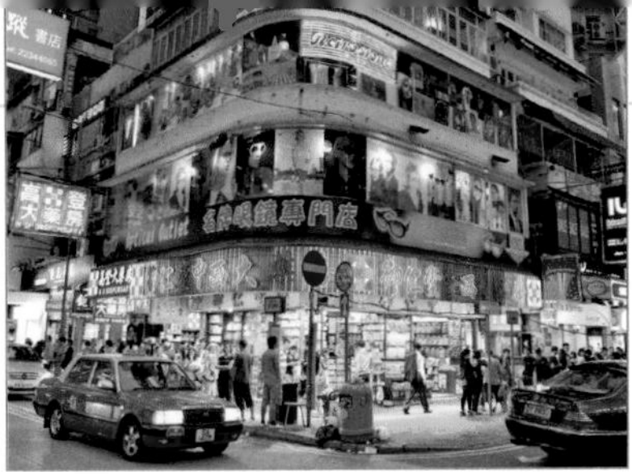

△ **Wan Chai and Causeway Bay.** Two of Hong Kong's most dynamic and colourful neighbourhoods, crammed full of bars, restaurants and shops. See page 119.

△ **The Peak.** Gaze down from these wooded heights and take in one of the world's greatest vistas, accessed from Central by the Peak Tram – an attraction in itself. There are some wonderful walks from the tram terminus. See page 113.

▽ **Happy Valley.** Encircled by twinkling apartment blocks, the Happy Valley horse racing track is a fantastic amphitheatre of sporting and cultural drama. The astonishing gambling passions of locals are on display most Wednesday nights, September to July. See page 123.

△ **Man Mo Temple.** Hong Kong's most atmospheric temple – all clouds of pungent incense and mysterious statues looming out of the darkness. See page 108.

△ **Hiking in the hills.** A surprisingly high proportion of Hong Kong is covered by country parks, largely uninhabited tracts of land consisting of big grassy hills and patches of woodland. The Sai Kung area in the eastern New Territories is one of the most attractive, and is well-endowed with fabulous hiking trails. See pages 180 and 175.

▷ **Po Lin Monastery.** A spiritual retreat high in the mountains of Lantau. The Big Buddha statue draws the crowds, and the area can be accessed by cable car from Tung Chung. See page 185.

# THE BEST OF HONG KONG: EDITOR'S CHOICE

**An overview of the best family attractions, festivals, walks and other free highlights, plus the Hong Kong essentials – eating, shopping and nightlife – as selected by our editor.**

## ONLY IN HONG KONG

**Light fantastic.** The nighttime view from the Peak, so breathtaking that it borders on the spiritual. See page 114.
**Red sails in the sunset.** Catch a ride on the *Aqua Luna* junk, which crosses the harbour every afternoon (https://aqualuna.com.hk). For a budget option, grab a drink-to-go from a convenience store and take a ride on the Star Ferry. See page 116.
**Cultural insights.** The Hong Kong Tourist Board (HKTB) runs free talks and tours where local experts share their knowledge on subjects ranging from Chinese medicine and feng shui to t'ai chi. Most require advance booking. See page 240.
**Escape the city.** Few cities in the world have such easy access to beautiful, empty countryside with lofty hills and good beaches. See page 182.

*The Aqua Luna.*

## BEST DINING

**Seafood feast.** Take a ferry over to Lamma or Cheung Chau and gorge yourself on delectable seafood at one of the islands' open-air restaurants.
**Dim Sum.** Don't miss out on this Hong Kong speciality.
**Be adventurous.** Try some of the more unusual local delicacies, such as snake soup or the unappetising-sounding "thousand-year eggs".
**Cosmopolitan choice.** Hong Kong is hard to beat for sheer quantity and choice of restaurants from all corners of the globe. Quality is generally high.
**For more on Hong Kong's culinary scene, see page 57.**

*Dim Sum is served in wicker baskets.*

## BEST FOR FAMILIES

**Ocean Park.** Always a hit with families. Attractions include rides for all ages – there is a thrilling rollercoaster – plus aquariums and performing dolphins. See page 133.
**Disneyland.** This has naturally become a must-visit for kids. See pages 188 and 192.
**The Peak.** Appealing to visitors of all ages, with the exciting Peak Tram, amazing views (best after dark for kids) and Madame Tussauds to boot. See page 113.
**Outlying Islands.** The ferry ride, the seafood and the beaches make for an enjoyable day out. See page 184.
**Science Museum.** This has the usual hands-on interactive exhibits to entertain and educate. Nearby, find the Space Museum with its IMAX cinema. See page 147.
**Jumbo Kingdom floating restaurant.** A trip to Aberdeen's finest always seems to go down well with children. See page 132.
**Ngong Ping 360.** The cable car is great for children, and, once at the top, the Big Buddha won't disappoint either. See page 186.

*Exotic sea life at the Ocean Park.*

## BEST SHOPPING

**Smart shopping malls.** Seek out Armani, Dior and co. See page 102.
**Grimy markets.** At the other end of the scale, Hong Kong's street markets are worth a visit for local colour and, of course, that fake Rolex you have always promised yourself. See pages 149 and 152.
**Antiques.** Don't expect bargains, but the shops along Hollywood Road are full of interesting chinoiserie. See page 108.
**Electronics.** People tend to think of Nathan Road's "Golden Mile", but while there is no denying the abundance, prices can be keener elsewhere. Citywide chains Broadway (www.broadway.com.hk) and Fortress (www.fortress.com.hk) are reliable options.
**Clothing bargains.** Hong Kong has everything from 5-star luxury to factory outlet stores – and obliging tailors. See pages 239 and 155.

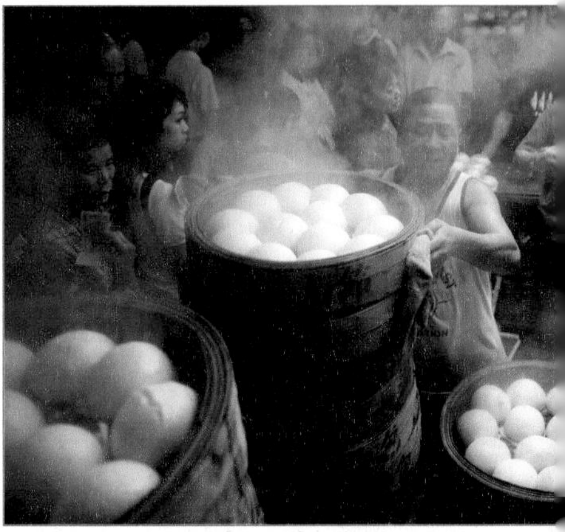

*Bun Festival on Cheung Chau Island.*

## BEST FESTIVALS

**Chinese New Year.** This is the time to see dragon dances, firecrackers and a truly breathtaking firework display over the harbour. See page 162.
**Bun Festival.** Stilt-walkers and colourful costumes descend on Cheung Chau. See page 189.
**Dragon Boat Festival.** This takes place in early summer, with dragon boat races at locations around Hong Kong. See page 162.
**Mid-Autumn Festival.** With its lantern parades and moon cakes, this festival is best experienced at Victoria Park. See page 162.

*Cat Street merchandise.*

## BARGAIN HONG KONG

**Junk trip.** For just HK$160, take a trip around the harbour on an old Chinese junk. https://aqualuna.com.hk.
**Free museums on Wednesdays.** All day Wednesday, every Wednesday. Applies to most major museums in Hong Kong.
**WiFi.** Numerous cafés (and some restaurants and bars) have free WiFi access for customers. Free government WiFi spots are also located at hundreds of premises across the city, including public libraries, food markets, government buildings and major parks. See page 237.
**Local phone calls.** These are free in Hong Kong (also, mobile calls are very cheap). If you need to make a local call you can ask in a shop and they will probably let you use their phone. See page 11.
**Horse racing at Happy Valley.** Admission fee is a nominal HK$10, great value for what can be an exhilarating night out – although of course it can work out very expensive... See page 126.

*Hong Kong Racing Museum in Happy Valley.*

*The MacLehose trail covers much of the New Territories.*

## BEST WALKS – URBAN AND NON-URBAN

**Kowloon waterfront to Kowloon Park.** Admire the famous skyline, then head north via subways to the heart of Tsim Sha Tsui – Nathan, Peking, Hankow roads and Kowloon Park. See page 141.
**Star Ferry Pier (Central) to Lan Kwai Fong.** Iconic skyscrapers show the way on this short trip through Central's financial heartland to Lan Kwai Fong, Hong Kong's glitziest drinking den. The trip can be made at bustling street level or via the sci-fi elevated walkway. See page 98.
**Central/Western back streets.** Explore the area around Staunton Street, hub of the lively SoHo nightlife area, then return downhill to the authentic Chinese atmosphere around Gage, Graham and Peel streets. See page 105.
**The Peak Trail.** The circular route along Lugard and Harlech roads is an easy but spectacular stroll. Some more strenuous hikes can also be enjoyed from here. See page 115.
**MacLehose Trail.** Take your pick of walks along this 100km (62-mile) trail running across the New Territories. Highlights are Tai Long Wan, a beautiful beach at the eastern extremity, and Tai Mo Shan, the SAR's highest peak. See pages 180 and 175.
**Tai Po Kau.** One of the largest remaining forests in the New Territories. Watch out for monkeys. See page 171.
**Lantau.** To escape the Big Buddha crowds, follow any of several trails leading into the peaceful grassy hills around. See page 184.

## BEST NIGHTLIFE

**SoHo (SOuth of HOllywood Road).** This area adjoining Lan Kwai Fong has really taken off over the past few years, with lots of trendy bars, clubs and restaurants. See page 106.
**Wan Chai.** More down-to-earth than the Central nightspots. The main hub is focused on Lockhart and Jaffe roads. See page 120.
**Lan Kwai Fong.** Long-established nightlife hub in the heart of Central, with a wide range of restaurants and bars – packed at weekends. See page 103.
**Tsim Sha Tsui.** A mix of touristy and local bars and restaurants, with clusters in the streets between Peking and Haiphong roads, and on Knutsford Terrace. A new nightlife zone is developing around Minden Avenue east of Nathan Road. See page 143.

*Lan Kwai Fong nightlife.*

*The iconic view of Hong Kong from Victoria Peak.*

## BEST FREE VIEWS

**ifc2.** The Hong Kong Monetary Authority building's 55th-floor Information Centre has stellar views back towards the forest of high-rises in Central. See page 98.
**Central Plaza.** Hong Kong's third-tallest building offers the island's most expansive skyscraper view from its wonderfully untouristy 45th floor. See page 121.
**Bank of China Tower.** A public viewing deck occupies a corner of the 43rd floor of this landmark building with views over the skyscrapers of Central and beyond to Kowloon. See page 101.
**Lugard Road.** The views from this pedestrianised street are hard to beat, especially the majestic night-time vista with its soundtrack of chirruping cicadas. See page 115.

## MONEY-SAVING TIPS

### Octopus Card
Recommended for anyone who is staying more than a day or so, this stored-value card costs HK$150 (which includes a refundable $50 deposit; unused credit is also refundable). It can be used on almost all forms of transport, as well as to buy museum tickets, and even items in convenience stores. You can top up the credit (up to HK$1,000) at MTR stations and convenience stores. Tel: 2266 2222 or visit www.octopuscards.com.

### Museum Pass
Available from HKTB visitor centres and participating venues, the annual museum pass costs only HK$50 and allows unlimited access to seven of Hong Kong's top museums. Pays for itself with just a few museum trips, and also entitles holders to 10 percent off purchases at museum shops and cafés.

### Mobile phones and phone cards
If you are staying for a few days and need to make local calls on your mobile, invest in a SIM for your phone, sold in 7-11 convenience stores for around HK$100. Another worthwhile purchase if you are calling abroad from Hong Kong is a phone card – the kind that gives you an access number. These can provide you with up to 5 hours calling time to the UK and US for only HK$50, and can also be used on your mobile.

### Miscellaneous
In restaurants, ask for filtered tap water rather than bottled mineral water. Taxis are quite cheap, but costs can add up quickly – try to avoid rush hours and cross-harbour tunnel routes as far as possible.

*Incense coils are featured at many temples.*

*Trams in Central.*

超級宴會廳

*Dim sum is a Hong Kong speciality.*

# THE HONG KONG WAY

**Few cities ignite the senses as does Hong Kong, offering an intoxicating blend of tradition and modernity, and colonial history alongside a vibrant Chinese culture.**

Hong Kong pulsates with the visual energy of a fireworks display. It resonates to the din of a dim sum restaurant's peak hour. Mesmeric in a multitude of ways, at times chaotic, intriguing, puzzling, endlessly exciting and in parts possessed of an astounding alternative beauty, Hong Kong is a place that precipitates the strongest emotions. More than one visitor has noted that this must be one of the Earth's acupuncture points.

*Hong Kong's seafood is very fresh.*

Hong Kong is fuelled and inspired by constant immigration, from mainland China, from elsewhere in Asia and from the four corners of the world, with more than 7.3 million souls simultaneously focused on top dollar and bottom line in an area rather smaller than the English county of Berkshire and less than half the size of the American state of Rhode Island. Cosmopolitan yet integrally Chinese, Hong Kong's inhabitants are defined by what's written on their business cards. Off duty, they may go shopping, play tennis and basketball on courts perched atop skyscrapers, or pinball their way between the bars and clubs crammed hugger-mugger in the numerous nightlife zones; everyone here is all too aware that Time's winged chariot doesn't so much hurry near as overtake on the inside lane.

*Lockhart Road by night.*

Hong Kong took an extended bath in the limelight at the end of the 20th century, with a dignified return to Chinese sovereignty in 1997 which marked the end of a colony, an era and an empire. It's all history now. Hong Kong is a Special Administrative Region (SAR) of China, with a key role to play in the spectacular growth of the Chinese economy, although it remains markedly different from the mainland: the "one country two systems" pledge is clearly working, despite concerns and protests over certain issues. Within this framework, Hong Kong's peculiar, cosmopolitan blend of Chinese and Western, and its prosperity, continue to thrive.

For the first time, though, it is facing real competition from its neighbours. The economic revolution in the Pearl River Delta has catapulted entire new cities like Shenzhen onto the world map. And Macau's former lackadaisical ambience has been transformed by the arrival of a dozens of glitzy casinos which pull in more patacas than those in Las Vegas. Does the former Crown colony have the stamina to keep up? The smart money is saying: you bet.

*Chinese chess is only vaguely similar to its Western counterpart.*

# HONG KONG'S PEOPLE

**Outsiders may see Hong Kong's people as materialistic and sometimes brusque. But there are reasons for this, including an obsession with success.**

The people of Hong Kong are variously described as being the most business-minded, materialistic, competitive and restless population on the planet. Few other cities have such a complex, unsettled history. It is a place that moves at lightning speed because time is money, and every minute costs. Though it can sometimes infuriate, life in Hong Kong is addictive, and even those who have escaped to more peaceful places – vowing never to return – have been drawn back like iron filings to a magnet. Even the most jaded visitor usually finds something seductive about it.

Hong Kong's 7.3 million people are packed into just 1,103 sq km (426 sq miles), and certain areas have some of the world's highest population densities. During rush hour, overwhelming crowds of commuters squeeze themselves into trains and buses. Lunch hour is a feeding frenzy, as thousands of office workers dash for restaurants, jostling and barging their way into tiny noodle shops and delicatessens. Elbowing strangers, jumping queues and honking horns in traffic jams (often complemented by deafening construction sites and roadworks) are unavoidable features of daily life here.

As a major trading port situated on the fertile Pearl River Delta, Hong Kong has long been a magnet for immigrants in search of a better life. New arrivals continue to flood in from China and overseas, all sharing one dream: to make money quickly and to enjoy spending it. This continual injection of new blood is part of what gives Hong Kong its excitement and intensity.

For those seeking a settled, peaceful existence, Hong Kong will be a hard slap in the face. This place resounds with rags-to-riches tales of entrepreneurs who built up their business empires from scratch, and this promise of success is in the minds of almost every immigrant who heads here.

*Family shopping at Graham Street Market.*

## Local identity

Hong Kong is, and always has been, Chinese. In spite of more than 150 years of colonial rule, the Chinese, who make up about 92 percent of the population, never had a sense of allegiance to the British Crown. Those of the older generation, who originated from elsewhere, often identified with their home provinces or towns in China rather than Hong Kong.

On the whole, however, local Chinese are more inclined to view themselves as Hong Kong citizens rather than Han Chinese. This sense of identity has increased in the post-handover years, along with what could be termed an embryonic civic pride – Hong Kongers no longer regard their city simply as somewhere to live and make money, with an eye to moving on somewhere else as needs dictate. Greater political and even environmental awareness – examples include the campaign to halt further reclamation of the harbour – are symptoms of a maturing city growing in confidence and sophistication. It is in part due to the fact that the local population is ever more likely to have been born and raised here, and that they are part of what is likely to become the world's largest economy within a generation.

## Ethnic groups

Hong Kong's original inhabitants (see page 31) settled in what is now the New Territories and outlying islands. Sometimes referred to as the **Punti** "people of the earth", they were mainly farmers. In the 13th century, Kublai Khan's Mongol hordes swept south into China, destroying the Song dynasty and pushing Han Chinese farmers southwards from the mainland into Hong Kong. The Tang clan settled in the fertile Shek Kong Valley, where they established a cluster of walled villages including Kat Hing Wai in Kam Tin (see page 179). They were followed over the centuries by various other families, forming the so-called "Five Great Clans": the Tang, Hau, Pang, Liu and Man. These people developed trade in salt, pearls, ceramics and fishing, and farmed the fertile river valleys.

*Western sports such as basketball are popular in Hong Kong.*

Meanwhile, the **Hakka** ("guest people") migrated southwards in waves from central China. As later arrivals they made the best of the more hilly land in the eastern New Territories.

For centuries a sprinkling of **Tanka** "boat people" have lived on junks in places like Tai O and Aberdeen, harvesting pearls and making salt. Legend has it that the Tanka are the descendants of the 5th-century general, Lu Tsun, who revolted against the emperor; after his death, his people were persecuted and deemed unworthy to live on land.

The Tanka's boat-based communities also attracted the **Hoklo** people, who originate from the area around Fuzhou (Fujian province) and were traditionally fishermen and manual labourers. Today all fishing communities celebrate the sea goddess Tin Hau's birthday on the 23rd day of the third moon, sailing in elaborately decorated fishing boats to her temples to pray for protection at sea.

### THE CANTONESE LANGUAGE

The Cantonese language often sounds harsh and argumentative to unaccustomed ears, but its humour, slang and interspersed English words make for lively conversation. Cantonese is also centuries older than Mandarin (putonghua), the official language of China, which evolved later in the courts of Mongol emperors during the Yuan dynasty (1271–1368). Therefore, the original rhythms and sounds of classical Tang- and Song-dynasty poetry are probably closer to modern-day Cantonese. On a day-to-day level Cantonese is a bawdy language: quite innocent-looking individuals swear like troopers, and people are often brutal when commenting on other people's appearance and delight in puns and double entendre.

Locals sitting on a bench.

These ethnic groups remained remote from the Chinese, and later British, imperial authorities all the way through to the 1950s.

## The Cantonese

This mix of "indigenous" people is now comprehensively outnumbered by the Cantonese, who trace their roots back to other areas of Guangdong province. Traditionally regarded as a rebellious, ungovernable people given to spontaneous action if angered, they have always been mistrusted by emperors and regimes. The Nationalist revolution, which toppled the Qing dynasty in 1912, was instigated by a Cantonese, Dr Sun Yat-sen, and Guangzhou became the centre for the Nationalist Party, the first modern political party in China. The Chinese Communist Party founded the Peasant Movement Training Institute, their first school, in Guangzhou in 1922, and Mao Zedong is said to have developed his theory of peasant revolution while working in the city.

For over a hundred years, from the latter part of the 19th century to the present day, the port of Hong Kong has been the destination of migrants, some of whom stayed in the farming villages of the New Territories or the urban centres of Kowloon or Central and Western. Many headed further afield to the US, Australia or Southeast Asia. Never was the push and pull of migration more evident than during and after the Japanese Occupation and following the end of the Chinese Civil War. Arrivals from Guangdong remained the majority, but in the late 1940s large numbers of refugees from Shanghai, the former commercial centre of China, fled to Hong Kong when the communists took over. Many foreign firms also relocated their Chinese headquarters to Hong Kong. The Shanghainese community settled in North Point on Hong Kong Island, and the businessmen among them were quick to use their capital, know-how and pool of labour to set up factories.

The Chiu Chow (Shantou) people from further up the Guangdong coast, also renowned for their business acumen, clung together in powerful clan networks, and settled in Sai Ying Pun and Kowloon City.

Friends talk over noodles.

## Population explosion

For much of the 1950s, '60s and '70s, illegal immigrants continued to outwit the battalions of the People's Liberation Army (PLA) and Chinese coastal gunboats, which cooperated with Hong Kong's security forces. By 1980 this influx, combined with a high birth rate, had pushed Hong Kong's population to 4 million (see page 37).

These decades of population growth coincided with Hong Kong's rapid industrialisation, a time when factories were desperate for labour. During the early 1950s many people lived in squatter huts, then later in newly built government housing blocks in Kowloon, which preceded the vast new town developments (today more than half of Hong Kong's citizens live in new towns in the New Territories).

In the New Territories, farming was in decline, unable to provide sufficient employment for the typically large families living there. Throughout the 1950s, the UK's policy to recruit unskilled workers from its colonies drew thousands of young men from these rural communities. Many of the founders of British Chinese takeaway restaurants were part of this exodus.

## The Right of Abode

As China opened up in the 1980s, a growing number of Hong Kong men, typically new migrants, married mainland Chinese women, creating a new social problem of divided families. Dad lived and worked in Hong Kong while Mum and the kids stayed in Guangdong, visiting only occasionally. After 1997 many of these dependent children, now grown up, sought to claim Right of Abode in Hong Kong, causing fierce debate over residency rights. Initially the Hong Kong Court ruled in their favour, but with Hong Kong concerned that this would instantly grant residency to around 300,000 mainland Chinese, the government in Beijing was asked to rule on the matter, and the interpretation of the Right of Abode was subsequently altered.

Since then, anyone from mainland China who is coming to Hong Kong from China to reunite families is given priority in the quota of new arrivals allowed. Nowadays, the number of

*Boarding a tram.*

*An elderly resident.*

*A school outing in PoHo.*

mainlanders allowed to settle has been increasing – from 25,000 a year in the late 1980s to 54,750, or 150 per day, in 2013. However, tens of thousands of Hong Kong men marry mainland women every year and a 2001 court ruling that anyone born in Hong Kong was entitled to residency led thousands of pregnant mainland women arriving at Hong Kong maternity wards in the advanced stages of labour. This became one of the hot topics around the 2012 legislative elections, with the winning chief executive, Leung Chun-ying, banning mainland mothers from scheduling birthing appointments in 2013. This is one of the primary reasons that resentment against mainlanders still smoulders in parts of Hong Kong society.

Many of these mothers plan to send the children to Hong Kong for schooling, often while mothers, and sometimes fathers too, remain in Guangdong to work; this is creating a new range of social problems and difficulty in adjustment. Today, many new arrivals from the mainland are still derided as *ah tsan* (country bumpkins) and are the butt of jokes in soap operas, despite the fact that they share the same heritage as most Hong Kong residents.

## Expatriates in Hong Kong

Hong Kong's cultural diversity is largely a result of the many different foreign nationals who have made their home here, either

### POPULATION FACTS & FIGURES

Hong Kong's population passed the 7 million mark in 2009 and at the last census, in 2016, stands at 7.34 million. It means that each square kilometre of its territory is home to an average of 6,777 people (17,230 per sq mile) – making it one of the world's most crowded places. Locally born residents form the majority of the population (61 percent), with 31 percent having been born elsewhere in China. Cantonese is spoken by 96 percent, but 45 percent can speak English and 40 percent Mandarin. There are also over 200,000 speakers each of Hakka, Chiu Chow, Hokkien (Fukien) and Shanghainese. At 83.74 years, life expectancy is among the world's highest, while infant mortality rates are among the lowest.

*Shopping at the Temple Street Night Market.*

temporarily or permanently. Indeed, the 6 percent of the population that is not Chinese have made valuable contributions to cuisine, arts, culture and religion in Hong Kong, while assimilating local customs and traditions. Hong Kong grants permanent residency and the right to vote (albeit for a limited number of seats in Legco) to all – with the exception of domestic helpers – who have lived here legally for seven years continuously, but only those with Chinese parentage will be granted a Hong Kong SAR passport (see box).

American, Australian, Canadian, South African, British and other European expatriates – *gweilo* ("ghost person" or "foreign devil") as they are known in Cantonese – make up the majority of the foreign business community, numbering around 36,000. (It is worth noting that the term *gweilo* is in such common use that it is not generally taken to be offensive. However Cantonese slang for people from the mainland, and anyone with a darker skin, is generally derogatory.) During British rule, expatriates were often given preferential treatment in the workplace, commanding much higher salaries than the Chinese. Today, these inequalities are less apparent. Nonetheless, in recent years Hong Kong has tried to focus on attracting skilled professionals through various schemes. It grants working visas to more than 210,000 non-Chinese professionals each year,

## DUAL IDENTITY

After the 1984 Sino-British agreement to return Hong Kong to China, and the events in Tiananmen Square in 1989, a new type of migration emerged in the territory. Between 1990 and 1997 some 300,000 are thought to have left Hong Kong, travelling mainly to Canada, Australia and the United States. The price of securing a foreign passport meant sacrificing businesses, family and friends, and starting from scratch in an alien country. Many of the émigrés then returned to Hong Kong after establishing permanent residence overseas, shuttling back and forth annually to retain their status in both places. Many enter the SAR (see page 27) and China with their Hong Kong ID card, but use their foreign passport when travelling farther afield.

*Busy chefs at Little Bao.*

*Fresh fish at the market.*

and has a special scheme targeting mainland professionals.

There are increasing numbers of Asian expatriates and overseas-born Chinese living as expatriates in Hong Kong. The Japanese business community has played a quiet but important role in commerce in Hong Kong and China, and there are some 2,000 Japanese companies and almost 14,000 Japanese residents in the SAR.

One of the more established foreign communities in Hong Kong comprises the descendants of early merchant traders and soldiers who followed the Union Jack from the Indian subcontinent to Hong Kong: Indians – including many Sikhs and Parsees, as well as Sri Lankans, Pakistanis and Bangladeshis. Their descendants, many of whom speak fluent Cantonese can only be granted HKSAR passports if they can prove Chinese blood or jump through a tough series of hoops. Up to 8,000 were granted British passports in a last-minute ruling in 1996.

A few thousand ex-Gurkha troops, who once served in the British army, are now working as security guards in Hong Kong, and many of their locally born offspring use their right to permanent residency to work in Hong Kong too.

Hong Kong's largest ethnic groups are Filipina and Indonesian domestic helpers. Over 200,000 each year enter on strict employment visas that stipulate they must live-in with their employers and work six days a week. A minimum monthly wage of HK$4,310 (US$556) is in force. This enables both parents in many Hong Kong families to work full time and care for children and elderly relatives.

Most domestic helpers remit the bulk of their pay home to support their own children through schooling and to provide for their extended families. Come Sundays and public holidays, thousands of Filipina helpers gather in Central to meet friends, while the growing Indonesian community tends to gather near Victoria Park in Causeway Bay.

# DECISIVE DATES

**c.4000 BC**
The first stone-age settlements are established on the south China coast.

**1557**
Portuguese traders establish a colony at Macau.

**1685**
Emperor Kangxi allows limited trade in Guangzhou (Canton). Ships begin arriving from the British East India Company.

**1773**
British traders unload 1,000 chests of opium in Guangzhou.

**1799**
China's opium consumption reaches 2,000 chests a year, forcing Beijing to ban the drug, which then drives the trade underground.

*Emperor Kangxi.*

**1834**
The British East India Company loses its monopoly on the opium trade to other European nations.

**1839**
China appoints the anti-opium viceroy, Lin Zexu, to clean up drugs in Guangzhou. He confiscates some 20,000 chests of opium from the British. Hostilities mount until November, when British ships blow up four Chinese junks, sparking the first Anglo-Chinese War, which became known as the First Opium War.

**1840–1**
Negotiations between China and Britain break down, and the British fleet attacks Guangzhou and occupies the city's forts. The two sides agree on a preliminary resolution (the Convention of Chuen Pi), which cedes the island of Hong Kong (population 5,000) to the British. But neither government is happy with the terms and both refuse to ratify it.

**1842**
The Opium War ends and British possession of Hong Kong is confirmed by the Treaty of Nanjing, which cedes Hong Kong Island to Britain "in perpetuity". Sir Henry Pottinger becomes the first British governor of Hong Kong.

## Colonial period

**1856–60**
The Chinese cede Kowloon and Stonecutter's Island "in perpetuity" to Britain. But hostilities continue, culminating in the Second Opium War.

**1862**
A Sino-Portuguese treaty grants Macau colonial

*Hong Kong harbour in 1800.*

status similar to Hong Kong's.

**1898**
Britain forces China to lease the New Territories, including the outlying islands, for 99 years.

**1911**
Dr Sun Yat-sen overthrows the Qing dynasty and establishes the Republic of China.

**1912**
Emperor Puyi abdicates, signalling the end of Imperial China.

**1932**
The Chinese Communists declare war on Japan.

**1941**
On Christmas Day the British surrender Hong Kong to the Japanese.

**1945**
World War II ends and the British resume control of Hong Kong. China's civil war between the Communists and the Nationalists (Guomintang) resumes.

*Sir Henry Pottinger, the first governor.*

**1949**
The Nationalists are defeated and flee to Taiwan. The Communists found the People's Republic of China (PRC).

**1953**
With tens of thousands of people arriving each month, Hong Kong's population hits 2.2 million, but many are living in squatter camps. The Shek Kip Mei fire leaves 53,000 homeless. Public housing policy is fast-tracked.

**1966**
Cultural Revolution begins in China, spilling over into Hong Kong with riots over a price increase in the first-class Star Ferry fare.

**1971**
Sir Murray MacLehose becomes the first Hong Kong governor to be appointed from the British diplomatic corps.

**1972**
Opening of the first cross-harbour tunnel. Hong Kong population hits 4 million.

**1973**
The first new town, Tuen Mun, is completed.

**1974**
The Independent Commission Against Corruption (ICAC) is set up to stamp out crime and corruption.

*Sun Yat-sen.*

**1976**
Death of Mao ushers in a new era for China.

**1978**
Under Deng Xiaoping, China starts to reform its economy and open its doors to the world.

**1979**
Hong Kong's US$1 billion Mass Transit Railway (MTR) opens.

**1982**
British Prime Minister Margaret Thatcher visits Beijing and Hong Kong to begin discussions on Hong Kong's future. China decides to develop Shenzhen, a small town on Hong Kong's northern border, into a Special Economic Zone (SEZ).

## Handover countdown

**1983**
China reveals its plan for Hong Kong to become a Special Administrative Region (SAR) after 1997. Under the proposed terms, Hong Kong will keep its own capitalist system, judiciary and police, and

the leading official will be a Hong Kong Chinese. The Hong Kong dollar is pegged to the US dollar at a rate of 7.8.

*The Japanese arrive, 1941.*

**1984**
The British Ambassador to China and the Chinese Vice Foreign Minister initial "A Draft Agreement on the Future of Hong Kong", ending two years of acrimony. The Hong Kong government starts to plan for the territory's administration in the years running up to 1997.

**1985**
Britain and China ratify the Sino-British Joint Declaration. The colony holds its first election for the Legislative Council (Legco), drawing criticism from China, which insists that any political changes not accepted by Beijing will not be respected after the handover.

**1988**
The proposed Basic Law, Hong Kong's post-handover constitution, is published.

**1989**
One million people take to the streets to protest against the Tiananmen Square massacre. Forced repatriation of Vietnamese boat people begins.

**1991**
Beijing and London announce an agreement regarding the new airport.

**1992**
Hong Kong's 28th and last British governor, Chris Patten, arrives in the territory and proposes political reform. The move draws attacks from Beijing.

*Chris Patten at the Handover ceremony in 1997.*

**1994**
Legco passes Patten's proposed electoral reforms. China and UK continue to squabble.

**1997**
China resumes sovereignty on 1 July, Tung Chee-hwa is appointed chief executive (CE) and Hong Kong becomes an SAR. The stock market dives in response to the Asian economic crisis.

## Post-handover

**1998**
Voters go to the polls to select a third of the seats

on Legco. Hong Kong International Airport at Chek Lap Kok opens. Asian economic crisis worsens. First known human case of bird flu virus kills six people.

**1999**

The rule of law is undermined as government asks Beijing to overturn the Court of Final Appeal's ruling on the right of abode. Typhoon York kills two and injures over 500. China resumes sovereignty of Macau.

**2003**

The deadly SARS virus spreads to Hong Kong, killing 299. Economic recovery stumbles. On 1 July, over half a million people join a march to protest against proposals for national security laws ("Article 23"). The government backs down and shelves the plans indefinitely.

*The SARS outbreak caused panic in 2003.*

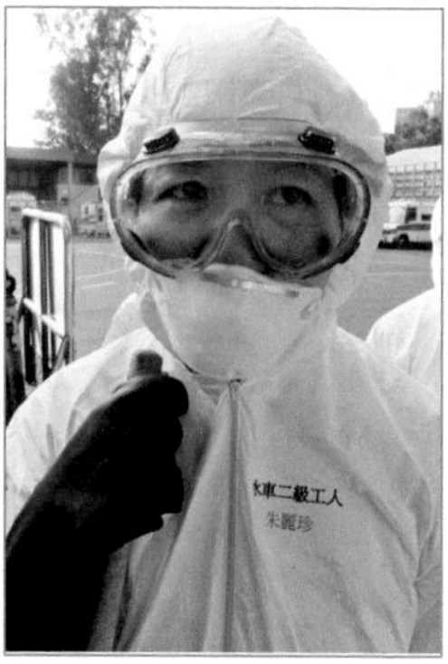

*Protester during the "Umbrella Revolution".*

**2004**

Mainland tourist arrivals boom and economic recovery begins. Up to half a million protestors again march on 1 July, calling for more democracy and local control.

**2005**

Tung Chee-hwa resigns and is succeeded by Donald Tsang, a career civil servant with a finance background.

**2006**

As travel restrictions on the mainland continue to ease, Chinese visitor arrivals hit 13.6 million.

**2007**

An election committee appoints Donald Tsang as CE until 2012.

**2008**

Hong Kong hosts equestrian events for the Beijing Olympics. In September, SAR-wide elections are held for half the seats on Legco.

**2012**

A new-look chief executive election sees Leung Chun-ying become Hong Kong's most senior official. After weeks of protests, the new government abandons plans to force Hong Kong schoolchildren to sit Chinese "patriotism" classes.

**2014**

Mass protests, including mass civil disobedience, are staged to pressure Beijing to introduce universal suffrage (Umbrella Revolution).

**2017**

Carrie Lam, a Beijing-supported candidate, becomes chief executive. The election remains indirect (by the Election Committee and not by public vote).

**2018**

Typhoon Mangkhut strikes in September, causing widespread damage. The Hong Kong National Party becomes the first political party to be banned since Hong Kong's return to China.

*Laundry hanging across the streets, 1941.*

# THE STORY OF HONG KONG

**Initially regarded by the British as an ill-chosen gain of limited value, Hong Kong soon became an important part of the Empire – and one that was only reluctantly relinquished.**

To most people, Hong Kong's history starts with the Opium Wars in the 1840s. However, archaeological studies have uncovered evidence of human habitation along this stretch of the southern Chinese coast dating back some 6,000 years.

Most of the excavated stone tools, pottery and other artefacts have been found preserved in coastal areas, suggesting a strong dependence on the sea. Bronze appeared in the middle of the second millennium BC, and weapons and tools such as axes and fish hooks have been excavated from local sites. There is evidence, too, in the form of stone moulds from the islands of Chek Lap Kok, Lantau and Lamma, that the metal was worked locally. Rock carvings, most of which are geometric in style, have also been discovered around Hong Kong Island and on some of the smaller islands.

An increasing number of people from the mainland came to settle in the region during the Qin (221–206 BC) and Han (206 BC–AD 220) dynasties. Coins of the Han period have been found in Hong Kong, and a brick tomb was uncovered at Kowloon's Lei Cheng Uk (see page 161) with a collection of typical Han tomb furniture. Other findings included pottery and iron implements. Little has been discovered from the next 1,000 years, but engraved writings, coins and celadon pottery suggest strong links with the Chinese Song dynasty during the 13th century. The many Ming-style blue-and-white porcelain works discovered on Lantau suggest increasing contact with the mainland during the Ming (1368–1644) and Qing (1644–1911) dynasties.

*Early colonial buildings on the harbour, 1856.*

## The coming of the Europeans

The West began to show an interest in China and Asia during the 15th and 16th centuries due to the increased trade in products such as silk and tea. The Portuguese were the first to arrive, trading with China at various points along the coast and establishing a settlement at Macau in 1557. The British, on the other hand, did not appear in force until the latter part of the 17th century.

In 1685, Emperor Kangxi, who reigned when the Qing dynasty was at the peak of its power, opened Guangzhou for limited trade. Ships began arriving from the British East

*Nineteenth-century opium addicts.*

India Company stations on the Indian coast, and soon Hong Kong, with its deep-water harbour, began to establish itself as a trading hub. Fifteen years later the Company, the world's largest commercial organisation, received permission to build a storage warehouse outside Guangzhou.

### EARLY TRADE WITH EUROPEANS

To begin with, in the early 18th century, trade with Western countries was in China's favour. Traders paid huge amounts of silver for fine Chinese tea and silk products, for which there was great demand in Europe. Tough terms were imposed on foreign traders, considered to be barbarians. They could only live in restricted areas in Guangzhou. They could not bring in arms, warships or women. Learning the Chinese language was forbidden, and traders also had to put up with the Chinese system of royalties, bribes and fees. Furthermore, local merchants were appointed by the emperor to keep an eye on foreigners.

## The opium trade

After more than a century of trading with China, the East India Company tried to balance its increasingly expensive purchases by developing its profitable sale of opium to the Chinese, mostly shipped from their colonies in Bengal. By the beginning of the 19th century there were already millions of addicts in China, and the country was paying for its spiralling drug habit with silver specie, disastrously depleting the national treasury. Clearly, from a Qing perspective, something had to be done.

Alarmed at the increasing outflow of silver, the emperor Jiaqing banned the drug trade completely in 1799. In 1810 he went further, announcing: "Opium is a poison, undermining our good customs and morality. Its use is prohibited by law." But neither foreigners nor Guangdong merchants were willing to give up the profitable business, and they resorted to smuggling. By 1820, the trade had grown to 30,000 chests annually.

Jiaqing's son, Daoguang, continued to issue edicts after he came to the dragon throne in 1820, but to no avail – the British weren't listening, and nor, apparently, were the opium addicts. Accordingly, in 1838 Daoguang dispatched Lin Zexu, the formidable Governor-General of Henan and Hubei, as his commissioner to impose Qing anti-opium legislation on the unruly foreign traders in Guangzhou. To the fury of the Westerners – at whose head stood the British – Lin confiscated and destroyed more than 20,000 chests of opium and blockaded the port to foreign shipping. Lin also wrote to Queen Victoria, asking why the British prohibited opium imports into their own country, but forced it on China. "Was this a morally correct position?", the commissioner asked rhetorically.

Lin's letter was never delivered to the queen, although it was published in *The Times*. And while it may have given liberal anti-opium campaigners in Great Britain pause for thought, it raised no sympathy at all with the opium merchants of India and Canton, who loudly demanded compensation for their lost opium, and pressed for military retaliation. This came in 1840, with the arrival of warships and soldiers from India. European military superiority ensured the First Opium War (1840–42) was short, sharp and one-sided. The British seized control of Guangzhou. Intimidated, the Qing commissioner, Qi Shan, who had replaced Lin, agreed in January 1841 to the Convention of Chuen Pi, which ceded Hong Kong Island to Britain. On 26 January 1841, the British flag was raised at Possession Point on Hong Kong Island, and the island was officially occupied. Five months later, British officials began selling plots of land and the colonisation of Hong Kong began.

*The name "Hong Kong" is derived from the Cantonese Heung Gong, which means "fragrant harbour". In the past, sandalwood incense was produced around what is now Aberdeen, and the scent drifted out to sea.*

Neither China nor Britain was happy with the terms of the Chuen Pi agreement, however. The Chinese government and its people saw the loss of a part of its territory as an unbearable humiliation, and Qi Shan was ordered to Beijing in chains. The British government, particularly Lord Palmerston, the irascible Foreign Secretary, was unhappy with Hong Kong, which he contemptuously – and famously – described

*The British demand the opening of China's ports.*

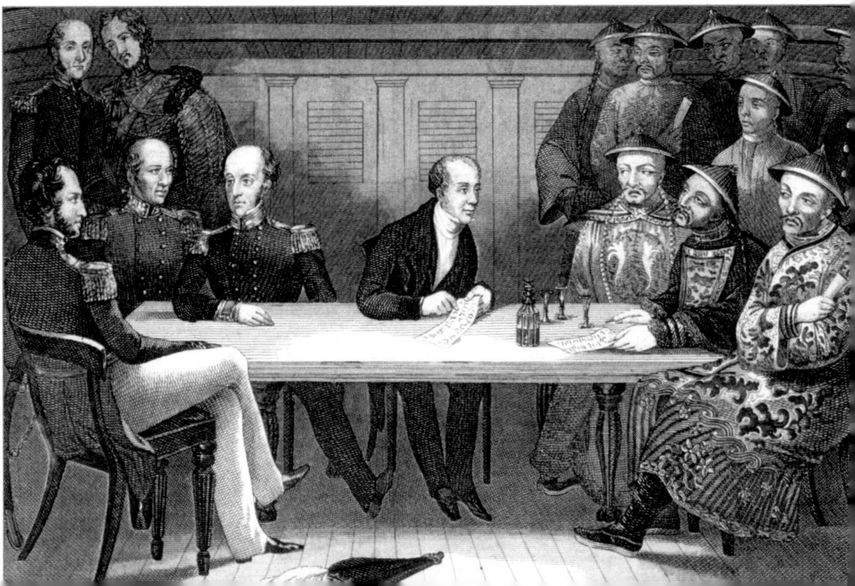

*Hong Kong became a British colony in three stages: Hong Kong Island (1841–2) was followed by the Kowloon peninsula (1860), then New Kowloon and the New Territories were leased for 99 years (1898).*

as "a barren island with barely a house upon it", and refused to accept it as an alternative to a commercial treaty.

Blaming Captain Charles Elliot of the Royal Navy for failing to make full use of the troops sent to China, Palmerston replaced him with Sir Henry Pottinger, Hong Kong's first governor, in August 1841. Pottinger soon realised Hong Kong's potential future, even though Britain had treated it as just another pawn in ongoing negotiations with the Chinese. He encouraged long-term building projects and awarded land grants.

After Shanghai fell in 1842, the Qing authorities sued for peace, and the Treaty of Nanking was signed in August, formally transferring Hong Kong Island to the British "in perpetuity" (the Chuen Pi Convention of the previous year had not been signed and so was never accepted as an official agreement by the British). As well as awarding the British 21 million ounces of silver in compensation for the opium seized three years earlier, the treaty also opened five "Treaty Ports" to foreign shipping and residence including Guangzhou, Xiamen and Fuzhou, Ningbo and Shanghai. Suddenly China was exposed to a new and troublesome "enemy at the gate". Subsequently, with the silting of Macau's harbour and the weakening of Portuguese power in Asia, Hong Kong began its growth into one of the greatest port cities the world had ever seen.

## The early colonial period

In its early days, the new British colony grew slowly, but further Anglo-Chinese conflict was soon to change this. In 1856 a dispute over the interpretation of the earlier treaty led to the outbreak of the Second Opium War, and during the two-year conflict, many companies in Guangzhou transferred their offices to Hong Kong, considerably strengthening the fledgling colony. China, weak with a corrupt

*Storming the fortress at Xiamen (Amoy) in 1841.*

government, lost again. By the summer of 1858, allied British and French troops had advanced far to the north, forcing the Chinese government to sign the Treaties of Tianjin (Tientsin). The terms gave foreigners the right to send diplomatic representatives to China and travel freely throughout the land.

Hostilities were renewed the following year when Chinese soldiers fired on the first British envoy to China as he made his way to the court in Beijing. Fighting continued until 1860. The British consul in Guangzhou secured the perpetual lease of the Kowloon peninsula all the way north to what is now Boundary Street, including Stonecutter's Island.

By this time, other countries – Russia, France, Germany and Japan – were waking up to the importance of having easy access to China. Not to be outdone by the British, they began to make similar incursions to secure footholds all along the Chinese coastline. In 1862, a Sino-Portuguese treaty gave Macau a colonial status similar to that of Hong Kong. A second treaty in 1887 confirmed it as a Portuguese colony in perpetuity.

The British were concerned that their territory in Hong Kong was vulnerable to attack from the north, and wished to gain control of the mountainous area north of Kowloon as far as the Shenzhen River. In 1898 they got their way, securing the lease of what became known as the New Territories (as well as some 230 islands) for a period of 99 years. There was later regret at having signed this treaty, which only leased the land, while Hong Kong Island and the Kowloon peninsula were British in perpetuity. (It would later be impractical for Britain to keep Hong Kong Island and Kowloon when the New Territories lease ran out in 1997.)

At first, Chinese warships were allowed to use the wharf at Kowloon City, and Chinese officials were permitted to remain in office. However, a year later, the British took over the city completely. The New Territories was declared a part of Hong Kong, although it kept a separate administrative body from the urban area. Under a laissez-faire style of British rule, Hong Kong people were left alone to concentrate on their businesses.

During the late 19th and early 20th centuries, the colony developed rapidly, becoming a magnet for immigrants and a centre of trade with Chinese communities abroad. Several public-service companies were established, including the Hong Kong and China Gas Company in 1861, the Peak Tram in 1888 and the 137km (85-mile) Kowloon-Canton Railway (KCR) in

*A panorama of Victoria Harbour from 1860.*

*The Prince of Wales is carried in a Chinese litter through the streets en route to Government House, 1922.*

1910. The paucity of land for building due to the steep terrain meant that land-reclamation projects got under way as early as 1851. In 1904, the first land reclamation was completed in what is now the area of Chater, Connaught and Des Voeux roads. In 1929, another reclamation project was completed in Wan Chai. Today around 6 per cent of Hong Kong's land has been reclaimed from the sea.

## Turbulent times

From the beginning of the 20th century, China experienced a series of political upheavals. In 1900, a peasant uprising known as the Boxer Rebellion seriously challenged the authority of the creaky and corrupt Qing government, which collapsed for good a few years later. In 1911 Sun Yat-sen established the Republic of China. (Although Sun Yat-sen travelled to Hong Kong many times to enlist support for his cause, his revolution did not have much impact on the British colony.)

Between 1920 and the late 1940s life in China was dominated by conflict. The long-running civil war between Mao Zedong's Communist Party (founded in 1921) and the Nationalists (Guomintang), led by Chiang Kaishek, divided the country. The Japanese invasion in 1937, and World War II, brought terrible suffering. In December 1941 Japanese troops attacked Hong Kong from the north; Allied forces withdrew from the New Territories and Kowloon to Hong Kong Island. After 18 days of fighting, the British forces surrendered on Christmas Day. The Japanese Occupation lasted for three years and eight months, during which time all British and Allied nationals were interned in camps and two-thirds of Hong Kong's Chinese population fled to China.

During the occupation, Hong Kong's trade virtually stopped, the currency lost its value

*The divide between the British colonial administrative and business districts (Central) and the Chinese commercial "bazaar" areas (Western) were well established by the 1860s and can still be discerned today.*

and food supplies were limited. Chinese guerrillas fought against the invaders in the New Territories, and villagers helped foreigners to escape. Under an agreement between Japan and Portugal, Macau became neutral territory, and some Europeans found refuge here during the war.

In August 1945, after the Japanese surrender, the Royal Navy arrived in Hong Kong to re-establish British rule over a battered colony with a population of just 600,000.

## Post-war Hong Kong

After the war, Hong Kong Chinese who had escaped to those mainland areas beyond Japanese control returned in large numbers. China's civil war, which resurfaced in 1946 soon after the Japanese surrender, drove more people – including affluent Shanghai entrepreneurs, shipping magnates and property tycoons – into the British territory. By 1949, the population had swelled to 2 million.

In October 1949, Mao Zedong declared the establishment of the People's Republic of China, and the defeated Nationalists fled to Taiwan. The United Nations imposed an embargo on trade with China, with serious consequences for Hong Kong's economy. A shift to manufacturing proved its saviour, with the hundreds of thousands of refugees providing cheap labour for textile factories set up by Chinese entrepreneurs.

With hundreds of thousands of people living in squatter camps, a series of fires culminated in the1953 Shek Kip Mei fire, which left 53,000 homeless and led the colonial government to fast-track its public housing policy. Soon the first high-rise new towns were being planned and developed.

By the 1960s the textile and garment industries accounted for more than half of the colony's exports. The manufacture of plastic toys also became important. At the same time, the situation in China was becoming ever more desperate, with famine bringing another wave of immigrants to Hong Kong. This time the numbers were alarming, and the colonial government tried desperately to keep them out. For most of the Hong Kong population, the standard of living continued to rise during the 1960s, in stark contrast to their relatives on the mainland.

During the Vietnam War in the late 1960s and early 1970s, US Navy vessels, en route to or from Vietnam, were a familiar sight in Victoria Harbour, and American soldiers headed to bars and nightclubs of the Wan Chai and Tsim Sha Tsui for R&R.

At this time, China was ravaged by the Cultural Revolution, and the turmoil drifted into Hong Kong, where tensions erupted into a series of disturbances in the mid-1960s, and also to Macau where Red Guards waged a propaganda war with posters and slogans, calling on the Chinese residents to start a revolution. The chaos almost paralysed the economy, but by the end of 1967, the unrest had been more or less quelled.

## 1970s and 1980s

Starting in the late 1970s and continuing through the 1980s, Hong Kong's economy developed at an amazing pace, as it expanded its

### REFUGEES AND MIGRANTS

For much of the 20th century, Hong Kong was a place of refuge from the chaos in China. The civil war of the 1930s brought large numbers of refugees from southern areas, but this paled in comparison with the influx that took place between 1945 and 1950, when more than 1.5 million Chinese flooded south. This expanded the supply of cheap labour, though a significant number of émigrés were savvy businessmen, notably from Shanghai. Seen as modern-day rivals, Hong Kong and Shanghai share a deep affinity, born of this post-war influx, and many aspects of modern Hong Kong culture can be seen as a continuation of a Shanghai culture that existed before 1949 and the Communist revolution.

After 1950, regulations were introduced to limit numbers, yet throughout the 1960s and '70s people continued to arrive at the Lo Wu border post, desperate to escape poverty. Some succeeded, but after numbers shot up between 1978 and 1980, the door was firmly shut. The focus then switched to the Vietnamese boat people, arriving by sea and housed in refugee camps until forced repatriation in the 1990s. Post-1997, movement between the PRC and the SAR is controlled, but fluid. For more on immigration, see page 21.

role as an entrepôt with its neighbours and as China's trading partner. This was made possible by greater stability in China, and the rapid economic advance there due to Deng Xiaoping's pragmatic policies. Hong Kong began to play a vital role as China's window to the world and the world's gateway to China. An increasing number of local businesses began investing in factories in the PRC, where labour and raw materials were cheaper.

To keep pace with economic development, infrastructure was improved, and the territory was transformed into a modern, efficient and cosmopolitan city. The government increased its investment in education, housing and other social welfare projects. An efficient civil service system introduced by the British government played a major role in the economic boom, aided by the Independent Commission Against Corruption (ICAC), set up in 1974.

By the 1980s, the Hong Kong government enjoyed near-complete autonomy from London, and even had the power to conclude certain negotiations with foreign powers. The colony regularly negotiated its own economic agreements with other countries, and was admitted into several international financial institutions, such as the Asian Development Bank.

## Anxieties and the build-up to dialogue with China

Amid all the prosperity, however, was an inescapable anxiety over the future, with the 1997 expiry of the 99-year lease on the New Territories looming large. By the early 1980s, life in Hong Kong was dominated by the issue of its return to China. Most of the local population would have preferred to stay under British rule rather than embrace the communist regime. Although they were unhappy with the fact that British companies and expatriates had enjoyed privileges in business and in government positions, people appreciated being able to compete in a free market. Having escaped extreme poverty or, in some cases, political persecution, they feared going back to the communist system. But their destiny was not in their own hands.

China had always maintained its stance that it would take back Hong Kong when the time was "ripe". By the early 1980s, the moment seemed to have arrived, and Beijing became intent on expunging 150 years of humiliation.

## Negotiating the return

Margaret Thatcher's visit to Beijing in 1982 formally launched the discussion on what would happen to Hong Kong after the 99-year lease on the New Territories, nine-tenths of the colony, expired in 1997. The reaction to the news that the colony's future was being negotiated was typical of Hong Kong – the local stock market nosedived.

In September 1984, after two years of often acrimonious negotiations, Britain and China came to an agreement, the Joint Declaration, which formally agreed the return of the colony to China in 1997. The Declaration stipulated that Hong

### FUNDING THE NEW AIRPORT

At the start of the 1990s it seemed that barely a day went by without some wrangling between Britain, Hong Kong and China over who was to foot the bill for the hugely expensive new airport under construction at Chek Lap Kok, off the coast of Lantau Island.

To boost the economy and restore confidence battered by the Tiananmen Square massacre, the Hong Kong government announced it would build a new airport, scheduled for completion in early 1997 at an estimated cost of HK$78 billion. China attacked the scheme, insisting that it should be consulted because its future SAR government might be saddled with debt.

Government representatives paid many visits to Beijing to win approval for the project, all the time trying not to appear as if they were grovelling. China was unrelenting. Finally, in 1991, Beijing and London announced that an understanding had been reached, although – like the 1984 Sino-British Agreement – its conclusion was without Hong Kong's participation. China gave its support for the airport in exchange for fiscal guarantees and a place on the airport authority's board.

Almost two decades on, it all appears to have been worthwhile – Chek Lap Kok is universally acclaimed as one of the world's most efficient airports, and plays a large part in Hong Kong's continuing success.

*Margaret Thatcher meets Deng Xiaoping in 1982 to discuss the Sino-British Joint Declaration.*

Kong's way of life would remain unchanged for 50 years, that the territory would become a Special Administrative Region (SAR) and continue to enjoy a "high degree of autonomy" – except in foreign affairs and defence – and that China's socialist system and policies would not be imposed. As Deng Xiaoping put it, "Horses will keep racing, and nightclub dancing will continue."

Plans were drawn up for Hong Kong's administration in the years running up to 1997. Key points included elections to the Legislative Council (Legco), the District Boards and new Regional Councils. Beijing soon appointed a committee of 59 members, only 23 of whom were from Hong Kong, to draft the mini-constitution – known as the Basic Law – for the SAR. In military matters, Britain announced it would phase out its garrison, while China said the People's Liberation Army (PLA) would be stationed in Hong Kong after the handover.

During Hong Kong's first Legco elections in 1985, initiated by the British, 24 of the 56 members took their places through indirect elections. Out of a total population of 5.5 million at the time, only 70,000 people were eligible to vote under Hong Kong's restricted system of indirect elections. Of that number, only 47,000 registered to vote and only 25,000 actually went to the polls. Nevertheless, this election started a debate about whether the Hong Kong government would allow open elections to take place in 1988, as had been promised.

## The democracy question and the brain drain

By the late 1980s, China was beginning to worry about the territory's fledgling attempts

> *Although China refused Portugal's offer to return Macau in the mid-1970s for fear of destabilising Hong Kong, circumstances had changed by the 1980s. Now China's leaders began thinking about getting Hong Kong back.*

at democracy. Beijing's top man in the territory, Lu Ping, insisted that Britain was deviating from the Joint Declaration and arousing fear and anxiety amongst Hong Kong's people. Amid the political tension, however, Hong Kong's economy continued to thrive.

The British government wanted direct elections to be held before 1997. Increasingly irritated, Beijing eventually declared that political changes not consistent with the Basic Law would be nullified in 1997. Deng Xiaoping added that universal suffrage might not be beneficial for Hong Kong.

In June 1989, the Chinese government crushed a pro-democracy demonstration centred in Beijing's Tiananmen Square. Horrified by the brutality, 1 million people took to the streets in Hong Kong to protest.

The massacre exacerbated the Hong Kong brain drain, with large numbers leaving the territory annually in the next few years. At the end of 1989, Britain said it would grant British citizenship to just 225,000 Hong Kong Chinese before Hong Kong reverted to China. In 1990, about 60,000 of Hong Kong's most accomplished professionals moved overseas (often to secure passports), mainly to Canada and Australia. Britain called on its allies to accept Hong Kong immigrants; the United States amended its immigration laws to increase Hong Kong's quota to 10,000 annually until 1994 and 20,000 thereafter. The Hongkong & Shanghai Bank (HSBC), the territory's largest, moved its HQ to Britain, generally seen as reflecting the company's lack of confidence in Hong Kong's future.

*Martin Lee, pro-democracy politician.*

## Direct elections

London tried to keep earlier promises of democratic reform without provoking China's displeasure at free elections for Legco. Pushed by budding political awareness among its citizens, the Hong Kong government agreed to speed up the process, saying it would put 18 seats up for direct elections in 1991.

After numerous consultations, the two governments agreed in early 1990 that members elected to Legco in 1995 would serve until their term ended in 1999, two years after the handover, and that they would be among the 400 people who would select Hong Kong's first post-1997 handover Chief Executive. China later reneged

*Street demonstrations following the deaths at Tiananmen Square in 1989.*

*Free speech (anti-Article 23) protests, July 2003.*

on the agreement after Governor Chris Patten carried out electoral reforms against Beijing's wishes; China replaced the elected Legco with a Beijing-appointed provisional legislature.

In June 1991, Hong Kong's new Bill of Rights backing the "rights and freedoms" guaranteed in the 1984 Sino-British Agreement became law, despite China's insistence that the move was against the principles stated in the Basic Law, Hong Kong's post-handover constitution.

The first direct elections in Legco's 150-year history took place in September 1991. For the first time, the incumbent government faced opposition and the potential of legislative defeats from the opposition under barrister Martin Lee. China, in a not-too-subtle move, advised voters to take candidates' "attitudes toward the mainland" into account when casting their votes. The comment was widely interpreted as a call to vote for the pro-Beijing candidates and not those of the pro-democracy camp represented by Lee's United Democrats. Unimpressed, voters demonstrated their independence by giving 15 of the 18 seats up for direct election to pro-democracy candidates.

## Patten and the handover

In April 1992, Britain's Conservative Party chairman Chris Patten was named Hong Kong's last governor – the first time a politician instead of a diplomat had been given the post.

Patten's arrival heralded the most tense period in relations between Britain and China. Championing the democratic rights of the Hong Kong people put him unerringly onto a collision course with Beijing. A low point was reached when the Chinese government declared that all contracts, leases and agreements signed or ratified by the British Hong Kong administration without the approval of China would not be honoured after 30 June 1997, the last day of Britain's rule. Beijing also pointed its accusing finger at the private sector, including the British company Jardines, which it accused of supporting Patten's political agenda and damaging the international community's confidence in Hong Kong's future. For more on Patten and the handover, see page 44.

A loophole in the Right of Abode section of the Basic Law led to many mainland relatives of

Hong Kong citizens trying to be in Hong Kong by 1 July to claim residency. Migration became blurred as Hong Kong companies sought out talented professionals from the mainland, and Hong Kongers moved to China, or travelled there frequently, to take advantage of business opportunities in the new booming China.

Several opinion polls taken shortly before the handover showed that most Hong Kong people would have preferred to remain under British rule if they could control their own destiny, although it was deemed politically correct to say they loved the motherland. And although many were sceptical that Beijing would keep its promise to let Hong Kong's political system continue for another 50 years, most people had decided to accept the reality and adapt, aware that their future economic success was inextricably tied to China.

Finally, the day arrived: journalists from all over the world flew in to cover the events, while there was fevered last-minute activity to complete the Convention Centre in time for the ceremony. A slightly surreal party atmosphere, building over the preceding weeks, took over.

*The Hong Kong flag is lowered during the handover of Hong Kong to Chinese control after years of British colonial rule.*

## Post-handover

The SAR's first chief executive was selected by a Beijing-appointed committee at the beginning of 1997 from a choice of three candidates. Tung Chee-hwa, a Shanghai-born shipping tycoon who had received financial help from China in his earlier business days, was the obvious candidate from early on. Tung – along with his Chief Secretary Anson Chan and Financial Secretary Donald Tsang – had previously been a member of the colonial government appointed by Patten.

Legco was dismantled on 1 July 1997, and replaced with a Beijing-appointed provisional legislature. After taking office, Tung announced a new voting system for Hong Kong's first legislative election, set for May 1998, that gave the biggest say to business groups, a move believed to have been designed to sideline the most popular party, the Democrats.

## Hong Kong into the 21st century

Before the handover, a popular view was that Hong Kong under communist China would undergo political changes, while remaining stable and prosperous economically. What happened in the months after the handover was just the opposite. There were few political confrontations, apart from some dissent concerning the make-up of the SAR's first legislative body, and the PLA kept a low profile in its barracks. However, in late 1997 and through 1998 Hong Kong experienced a major economic crisis, as did many Asian countries. The Hang Seng Index dropped 6,000 points – about 40 percent.

A slow recovery began in 1999, but even by 2003 the economy was still in the doldrums, unemployment had soared and, in an ironic reversal of history, many locals began seeking work on the mainland. From March to May 2003 the SARS virus epidemic caused panic across the region – the Hong Kong public wore surgical masks and plastic gloves outdoors, and tourist numbers dried to a trickle.

As the city recovered, a growing frustration with the government's handling of the SARS outbreak and in particular its proposal to introduce controversial anti-subversion laws brought more than 500,000 peaceful demonstrators onto the streets to protest against the plans on 1 July 2003.

*Demonstrators protesting against perceived pro-Chinese changes to the school curriculum in 2012.*

The plans were shelved and the minister responsible, Regina Ip, resigned within the month. The following year 200,000 marched and established the tradition of annual July 1 marches, calling for more democracy and voting reforms.

Hong Kong's improving economic fortunes are largely thanks to the double-digit growth in China's economy, and increased Chinese tourist arrivals. Yet this success did little to help the chief executive. Unable to regain the public's confidence, Tung Chee-hwa stepped down in early 2005.

His replacement, appointed by Beijing, was Donald Tsang, a devout Catholic and career civil servant. Born in Hong Kong, Tsang was more comfortable dealing with press and public than his predecessor. While his popularity remained relatively high throughout his tenure, Tsang didn't dodge controversy entirely. His political reform package attracted vociferous pro-democracy demonstrations, which demanded that a date was set for electing Legco by universal suffrage. Tsang himself was re-elected as chief executive in 2007 by a 800-strong committee largely loyal to Beijing. In a reversal of fortunes, Tsang has since been embroiled in a number of high-profile corruption charges; he was found guilty of misconduct in public office in 2017 and sentenced to 20 months in prison.

In September 2012, Leung Chun-ying, or C.Y Leung, became the third chief executive of the

## END OF EMPIRE

The handover of Hong Kong to China saw more celebrations than at any other time in the territory's history. Most Hong Kongers forgot the politics and revelled in the occasion. As midnight approached on June 30, 1997, most major figures who had, or were to have, a hand in Hong Kong's future gathered in the Hong Kong Convention and Exhibition Centre.

Just before midnight, the Union Jack descended as the British military band played "God Save the Queen". Chris Patten shook hands with the crowds before boarding the royal yacht. Inside the convention centre, civil servants swore allegiance to the People's Republic of China in Mandarin.

The next morning, People's Liberation Army troops crossed over the border, welcomed by villagers lining the roads.

## The last governor

**Chris Patten bought the savvy of a Westminster politician to London's last major colonial outpost. His governorship was perhaps his greatest political achievement.**

Chris Patten, Hong Kong's last governor for the five turbulent years leading up to the handover, took over from David Wilson in 1992 with the avowed aim of protecting the interests of the Hong Kong people. Unlike his predecessors, who had arrived decked out in full ceremonial dress (plumed helmet and all), Patten wore a dark business suit – discreetly modernising the image of the office of governor in Hong Kong in the process. Despite, or perhaps because of some of his unorthodox ways, Patten soon proved to be a popular leader. Instead of sitting in his office, he went out into the streets to meet ordinary people, listened to their opinions and held question-and-answer sessions in public during which he addressed politically sensitive issues with a candid, sometimes controversial attitude.

*Farewell speech at the British Handover Ceremony; Prince Charles looks on.*

Patten announced various proposals for increased spending on welfare, health, housing and the environment. The most controversial move, however, was his proposal to reform the political system. China wanted no such shift towards greater democracy, and openly attacked Patten's political reforms. As a result, the Hang Seng Index dropped about 5 percent in October 1992, and brokers warned that unless Patten made a U-turn on his push for greater democracy, the stock market could suffer further.

### Electoral reforms

In 1994, Legco passed Patten's proposed electoral reforms by a narrow margin, inviting strong condemnation from China. The reforms were a halfway point between full direct elections for all members of the legislature and a more muted electoral plan. Legco remained far from being a directly elected legislature, but the change was still enough to draw more criticism from China.

The electoral reform was Patten's last major act in office. As China began to play an increasingly important role in Hong Kong society and the business sectors competed with each other to get on Beijing's good side, Patten was sidelined. Beijing simply refused to talk to him, making it difficult for him to take any further action.

Despite the many humiliating insults the Chinese leaders threw his way during his five years in office, Patten's political reforms and personal charisma won him the respect of Hong Kong's residents. At the British farewell ceremony on the night of 30 June 1997, Patten's forceful farewell speech received long applause from the crowd, and people shouted "We will miss you" as he and Prince Charles boarded the royal yacht *Britannia* for England.

With every passing year, the handover feels more and more like ancient history. The shift of sovereignty was followed, coincidentally, by an economic downtown, but prosperity has since returned and Hong Kong has rarely looked back as it moves forward. Patten would be proud that political awareness and civic pride have heightened over recent years. He'd also understand the basic law of Hong Kong life: the economy remains king.

SAR, elected from an expanded 1,200-strong voting committee. In contrast to previous elections, the contest was marked by tabloid-style scandal and mud-slinging. Leung was the second-choice candidate for long periods before a series of blunders and corruption allegations scuppered the chances of his rival, Tang Ying-yen. Leung faced some tough early decisions, opting to back down on plans to make all Hong Kong schoolchildren take China "patriotism" classes, and taking a hard-line on the increasing trend of pregnant mainland mothers crossing the border to give birth – both issues which had sparked protests in the preceding months.

## Pro-democracy protests

Further protests, the largest seen in a decade, ensued in 2013–14. Benny Tai Yiu-ting, Associate Professor of Law at the University of Hong Kong, launched a civil disobedience campaign and started the Occupy Central with Love and Peace movement to pressure Beijing and the SAR administration to introduce universal suffrage. Protests (Umbrella Revolution) continued in September–December 2014, resulting in the SAR promising to submit a "New Occupancy report" to the Chinese Central Government. In January 2015 a proposal for electoral reform was announced, but it was never implemented. In a later move that angered Beijing, US lawmakers put forward student protest leaders (Joshua Wong, Nathan Law and Alex Chow) and their pro-democracy Umbrella Movement as nominees for the 2018 Nobel Peace Prize.

The people of Hong Kong remained unable to select their own candidate in the 2017 elections – Beijing-supported Carrie Lam was appointed as the chief executive by the Election Committee and not by public vote. Meanwhile, in a worrying development, the Hong Kong National Party was banned in 2018 – the first restriction of its kind to take effect since Hong Kong was returned to China.

## One country, two systems?

In 2017 Hong Kong marked the twentieth anniversary of the establishment of the SAR with both fireworks and a protest. Even today, despite the "one country two systems", the Chinese national anthem plays at the start of the day's television broadcast, the PRC flag flies alongside the Hong Kong Bauhinia, and the school curriculum has changed to include the Basic Law and Putonghua. Cantonese has replaced English as the language of instruction in most schools, and speaking good Mandarin is now at least as important as having good English for those looking to get on. Mandarin is heard more on the streets of Hong Kong now, in part because 45.8 million Chinese tourists visit each year.

Analysts say "three flows from China" are now driving Hong Kong's economy – goods, visitors and capital. In 2010 the move back to Hong Kong from London of HSBC's CEO was seen as highly symbolic of the shift in the world's economic centre of gravity to China.

A generation that cannot remember Hong Kong as anything but part of China is coming of age, as a growing sense of civic identity is expressed through issues such as heritage conservation and the preservation of street markets. There is also increased concern about the environment, in particular what can be done to reduce pollution in a city whose haze obscures its iconic views all too often, and where roadside pollution reaches dangerously high levels.

The new generation are also sufficiently confident, and savvy in their use of the internet and social media, to co-ordinate large-scale political protests. The July 1 marches are seen as an established annual event. Only the targets change.

*Carrie Lam and her cabinet are sworn in on 1 July 2017.*

*Hong Kong is a food lover's paradise.*

鷄隻
35元

# CULTURE AND SOCIETY

**Hong Kongers are proud of their Chinese culture, one which emphasises hard work, the role of the family and – not least – the pursuit of financial success. As a thoroughly international city, Hong Kong is also open to influences which have produced some unique cultural quirks.**

*Affluent young Hong Kongers.*

For all its modernity and dynamism, Hong Kong's culture and society are underpinned by a strong foundation of traditional Chinese values and beliefs. The Confucian concepts of humility, perseverance, reverence for ancestors and respect for elders have been adapted to its modern, capitalist society. Confucius said that a person should always examine motives carefully before acting, since all individuals are directly responsible for their fate. As the teachings of the great sage permeated into Chinese society over the centuries, this has led to a belief that anything can be achieved through sheer will and hard work. The attitude is, "If you don't have any money, then go out and earn some!" rather than relying on government support or charity to provide financial assistance.

With this work ethic in mind, many parents work at least nine or ten hours a day, six days a week to provide for their children who will, one day, look after them in old age. Most of the family budget goes towards children's clothing, healthcare and education, so that they may enjoy what their parents never had in their youth. Children are expected to support their elderly parents and to honour the memory of deceased parents by regularly visiting their graves and making offerings.

Family values are very strong, and parents dote on their children by spending time and money on them. On Sundays and holidays, parents take the whole family, with grandparents in tow, for Western-style buffets or dim sum. After lunch, families wander around the streets and shopping malls, buying new toys and clothes for the children.

## Money and status

Successive famines, wars and political upheaval in China have taught the Hong Kong Chinese not to be complacent about financial security. They are eagle-eyed at spotting opportunities for making money; here "filthy lucre" really does seem to buy happiness, since material security is vital to one's sense of well-being. There is no other place in the world where people, rich or poor, are as business-minded and clued-up about property, stocks and horse-racing. It's no coincidence that *kung hei fat choi* – literally

*Laying offerings at Wong Tai Sin Temple.*

"congratulations on your wealth" – is a common greeting at Lunar New Year. As in most places in the world, of course, the quest for wealth is also motivated by self-respect or "face". Wearing designer labels and buying expensive dishes in a restaurant, such as lobster, abalone and shark's fin, are all ways of showing you have wealth. At the end of a meal, diners will fight to pay the bill, since generosity also gains face. Face and *guanxi* – lifelong obligations of mutual assistance – are crucial to relationships. That's why the Chinese prefer to give business to family and friends rather than deal with strangers, who might prove to be unreliable. In friends there is certainty.

*Hong Kong has one of the world's highest population densities and most people live in public housing.*

## WHAT'S IN A NAME?

One of Hong Kong's odder cultural quirks is the range of eccentric English nicknames chosen by the Hong Kong Chinese: Biscuit, Photosynthesis, Frandie, Wealthy, Xerox, Tweetie... This is in part the result of a desire to embrace the English-speaking world, and in part a way of identifying with a particular respected figure, a hobby or interest.

Emulation of the famous and successful accounts for the plethora of Jackie Chans in the territory, and may also explain some of the Wilsons – after the colony's penultimate British governor. Seemingly gauche names such as Lucky or Wealthy or the no-nonsense Money represent the aspirations of a people who have only enjoyed prosperity for a couple of generations.

Humour is apparent with names that echo the individual's Chinese name, such as Winky Wong (a version of Wong Wing-kee that has been used by more than one Hong Konger). Sometimes the name puns on the family name, as in Gypsy Lee or Ivan Ho. Hobbies or interests can play a role, scientific processes clearly being of fascination to Photosynthesis Wong. Fandie, Ankie and Banda represent a desire to be the only person in the entire world to have a certain name. And then there are the downright peculiar but memorable, such as Onions, Squash or Catherine (a man).

## The public persona

Many foreigners visiting Hong Kong have complained that the people are sometimes brusque to the point of rudeness. This has often been a result of cultural misunderstandings, but not always. Hong Kong does not have the "have a nice day" culture, and chit-chat about the weather seems unnecessary when there's business to be done. Even so, there has been a campaign to improve politeness to meet tourists' expectations. The customer service in many of Hong Kong's hotels and restaurants is second to none.

## Property and the cost of living

For financial reasons, Hong Kongers often marry later than mainland Chinese – for women, 29 is a typical age, for men, 31. Because of high property prices, most people, even married couples, have no choice but to live with their parents until they have saved enough money. Cramped living conditions, however, make life difficult for would-be lovers. Moments alone are rare, and the prying eyes of relatives are not conducive to romance. People often socialise in large mixed groups; parks are few and far between, so busy anonymous places such as malls or large theme parks offer a chance to be alone.

This is a capitalist society where Darwin's theory of the "survival of the fittest" predominates. Local tax laws give residents incentive to be among those that not only survive, but thrive. Residents keep most of what they earn – the highest income-tax rate is 17 percent, and only around 2 percent of the working population pays this, with over half paying no income tax at all.

However, Hong Kong has a high cost of living due to limited land, the expense of importing raw materials and food and high duties imposed on petrol and cars. On the other hand, there is no sales tax, and public transport is cheap. Luxury goods score high points in the "face" game, and some people will gladly blow all their disposable income on a Louis Vuitton bag even if they can't then afford much else.

Land prices have always been high, a result of the shortage of suitable terrain for construction. The government makes huge profits on land sales – a situation which fuels the desire for more and more land to be reclaimed from the sea. The largest and most successful Hong Kong companies, such as Cheung Kong and Sun Hung Kai, have built their fortunes upon this system.

*Hong Kongers love to shop.*

### LACK OF SPACE

Hong Kong is one of the world's most crowded environments, with correspondingly expensive property and often cramped living conditions. Over half of Hong Kong's population lives in public housing, where families benefit from low rents (the average monthly rent for public housing is HK$1,540) as well as shared income from family members, and are thus relatively well-off compared to low-income families in other parts of the world. However, lower-middle-class families are often caught: they do not qualify for public housing, and most property prices are way beyond their budget. The average apartment is just 500 sq ft (48 sq metres), enough for a living area, small kitchen and one, sometimes two, small bedrooms.

## Social welfare and health

Hong Kong may be one of the world's wealthiest cities, but not all share in its prosperity. An estimated 150,000, mostly elderly people, live in inadequate housing, with the worst-off in shacks or so-called "cages" (with room for a bed and nothing else, and usually packed several to a room), or out on the streets.

There is a welfare system for the elderly, with payments of HK$2,495–5,450 per month. The Mandatory Provident Fund, introduced in 1999, forces employees to invest up to 5 percent of their salary for retirement when the fund can be withdrawn as a lump sum.

Primary medical care is largely taken care of by private GPs in Hong Kong, while 90 percent of hospital admissions are at government-subsidised hospitals. The problem of overcrowded public wards and long waiting lists has drawn a great deal of criticism, however, and this has led to substantial growth in private medical insurance funded by both companies and individuals. Many employers offer health insurance to subsidise private healthcare.

*Hong Kong has steadily expanded in area as a total of 70 sq km (27 sq miles) has been reclaimed from the sea. Around 70 percent of this has taken place since 1980.*

Affordable government medical care is currently assured for the entire population through public funds and private donations, but the administration is considering making private health insurance mandatory.

## Crime

Hong Kong's over-the-top action movies often give the impression of a crime-ridden city which is a perpetual hunting ground for chopper-wielding tattooed thugs and armed robbers. In reality, one of the pleasures of Hong Kong is its lack of crime – the streets are safe at any time, and the chances of being mugged

*People queuing on Gough Street.*

or pickpocketed are significantly lower than almost anywhere in Europe or America. This is often mentioned as a major quality of life benefit, one that encourages expats to live in Hong Kong.

Organised crime does exist, though. The triad crime syndicates rely on a hierarchical structure, with ranks denoted by numbers that begin with four, representing the four elements, compass points and seas. The highest-profile gangs are "14K" and "San Yee On", whose illegal activities include loan-sharking, gambling, narcotics, prostitution, smuggling and extortion.

In 2016, Hong Kong had an estimated 8,000 drug abusers: 50.3 percent of them are heroin addicts, 29.4 percent use methamphetamine and 16.1 percent ketamine. The government takes a tough stance on narcotics. Possession of marijuana carries the same penalties as hard drugs: a criminal record and possible imprisonment. Still, Hong Kong's "work hard, play hard" culture, coupled with its affluence, has meant that recreational drugs are readily available.

*Hustle and bustle is daily life in Hong Kong, but even the busiest people stop for a shoe shine.*

## Education

Hong Kong's educational system is every bit as competitive as its business community. Children suffer great pressure to get into prestigious schools. The most sought-after are English or bilingual schools – English is widely used in business, medicine and law. As elsewhere in the world, some students commit suicide each year if they fail an important exam. Parental pressure often proves too much for children, who spend much of their time cramming for exams and studying foreign languages for overseas study. Tutors are hired to prepare toddlers for kindergarten entrance exams, an ordeal that sometimes requires two hours of testing to determine a child's Chinese, English and arithmetic skills.

The government regularly carries out studies to ascertain the standard of English spoken by teachers, to ensure that students get every opportunity to become confidently bilingual. The core competency remains Chinese, English and maths, but an overseas education is seen as a passport to a higher salary.

## Political awareness

Now that Hong Kong is in its third decade of "one country two systems", its residents seem to be developing a clearer identity. They are proud of what the city has achieved, and nostalgic about the tough years when they or their parents helped create the economic miracle. There is also an inner conflict between pride in being Chinese and lingering unease at Beijing's rule.

### HOU Q: CUTE OBSESSION

In tandem with much of the rest of Asia, Hong Kong is in thrall to Japanese pop culture and its obsession with all things cute – what is termed in Japan as *kawaii*, in Hong Kong as *hou Q*. The epitome of this is "Hello Kitty", the ubiquitous cat created by the Japanese company Sanrio which adorns over 20,000 products, from clothing to stationery. Sociologists say the fascination with Japanese style is fuelled by Asians' need to find a modern image of themselves, to form their own popular culture rather than borrow from the West. Or, as an 18-year-old Hong Konger expressed it: "Japanese society is very fast-paced and always changing. Everything is very cute and stylish."

*Relaxing on the beach at Shek O.*

Censorship in some sections of the media is a concern, but locals do voice freely their criticism of the Hong Kong government. There is some frustration amongst ordinary people that certain groups within society wield more influence than others, in particular the tycoons who control the property sector and monopolies. The mess of urban planning, and the issues of harbour reclamation, pollution and a lack of public spaces only adds to public vexation. Yet at the same time these very same tycoons, who have the ear of Beijing, are widely admired for their business acumen and sheer volume of wealth.

In the last couple of decades, political awareness has developed, and street protests have become a regular feature as local people have grown increasingly frustrated with the SAR government's decisions; there is a keen sense of injustice.

## The future

Hong Kong's economic success can be credited above all to one thing: its industrious people. As Beijing is well aware, any attempts

*Performance at the Avenue of Stars, which is modelled on the Hollywood Walk of Fame.*

*Catching up with the news at Lin Heung Teahouse on Wellington Street.*

to restrict freedoms could result in an exodus of a talented, highly educated workforce, with disastrous consequences for China. Most China-watchers believe that for Hong Kong to continue to thrive, it is here that China's economic reforms must coincide with the advance of democracy rather than its suppression. The concern that Shanghai could take over Hong Kong's privileged position as the gateway to China is voiced less often now, and some influential groups look to a future where Hong Kong forms a giant megalopolis with Shenzhen.

## POLLUTION AND THE ENVIRONMENT

Most visitors to Hong Kong are likely to notice the appalling quality of the air. Hazing out the views from The Peak, on bad days even making it difficult to see across the harbour, the pollution is frequently cited by residents as the worst single aspect of the SAR. Some of the smog is home-grown, but a good proportion is imported – a photo-chemical cloud drifting down on the northeast winds from the industrial zones of Guangdong. These winds are at their most persistent during the October–April period; pollution levels are usually lower between May and September as the wind blows in from the south and east, and heavy rain washes out the dust. Meanwhile, the waters are also filthy, and this and over-fishing has reduced local fish stocks by 80 percent.

In the past few years, these environmental problems have become a hot topic in Hong Kong, and some progress is being made on local emissions – some taxis and buses running on LPG gas, for example. Yet despite a great deal of debate (and protest), there is a lack of willpower from the authorities to do anything about it – partly as a result of a powerful business lobby reluctant to sanction anything likely to cut profit margins.

## Chinese arts and crafts

**Untainted by the communist dogma that justified ransacking cultural treasures during Mao's mainland rule, Hong Kong is regarded – alongside Taiwan – as one of the purest repositories of traditional Chinese culture and art.**

Chinese arts and crafts have a long history. Traditional forms include porcelain, embroidery, brocade, carpets, jade products, carvings (wood, bamboo and ivory) and paper decorations called "scissors-cuts" all with different styles and regional influences as well as brush painting and calligraphy. In Hong Kong, the most reliable places to buy these items are the China Arts and Crafts shops and the Chinese Products department stores on Hong Kong Island and Kowloon. For antiques, look no further than Hollywood Road and neighbouring Upper Lascar Row (more commonly known as Cat Street; see page 110).

### Fine products

Chinese **embroidery and brocade** have had a reputation for excellent quality since the days of trade on the Silk Road. The best silk products come from eastern regions where the climate is suitable for raising silkworms, while the dry north-western regions of the country produce fine-quality cashmere.

**Silk embroidery** from Suzhou, near Shanghai in eastern China, is especially well known for its fine workmanship and venerable history stretching back over 2,000 years. **Drawn work** from Shantou in eastern Guangdong also enjoys a good reputation overseas.

**Scissors-cut** is traditionally a product of rural China, where various kinds of colourful designs are created to decorate windows before Chinese New Year. Patterns include animals, fruit, flowers and characters from ancient Chinese folk tales or operas, often with themes of good harvests, prosperity and happiness.

**Carvings** of jade, ivory, wood, bone, rock and bamboo are a familiar sight in China. The best-known are jade carvings from Beijing, an art form that dates back to the Ming dynasty (1368–1644); ivory balls featuring legendary Chinese figures from Guangzhou; stone carvings from Shoushan in Fujian province; bamboo carvings from Huangyan in Zhejiang province; and high-quality ink-slabs made in Duanxi and Zhaoqing in Guangdong.

The Chinese invented **porcelain** in the 7th century AD, a good 1,000 years before Europeans managed to unlock the secret. The best variety comes from Jingdezhen County in Jiangxi province – fine, smooth and reminiscent of the ceramics made during the Yuan dynasty. Closer to Hong Kong, the ceramics produced at Shiwan (see page 219) are renowned for their quality.

*Crafts and statuettes for sale near Hollywood Road.*

**Chinese landscape painting** and **calligraphy** are generally mounted on a hanging scroll. In days gone by, the scroll was rolled up, stored away, and brought out on special occasions to be slowly unfurled, revealing only parts of a scene, subtly drawing the observer into the picture. **Miniature paintings** on shells, feathers, tree bark, deer horns and even thin strands of wheat straw are also popular souvenirs and gifts.

*A wide array of dim sum.*

# WHERE FOOD IS AN ART

**Cantonese cuisine has been exported around the world for decades and passed off as generic "Chinese food". Much of what makes it unique, however, is particular to this corner of southern China.**

It has been said that when the Chinese are confronted with something they have never seen before or do not understand, their first impulse is to try eating it. This folk philosophy has helped inspire one of the greatest cuisines the world has known.

Each region of China naturally evolved a distinctive cooking style that reflected its topography, climate, flora and fauna, the temperament of its people and their contact with outsiders. Foods of northern and western China developed separately from those of the southern and eastern coastal "rice bowl". Southern Chinese (mainly the Cantonese, but also sub-groups such as the Hunanese, Chiu Chow and Hakka people) like to complain that Beijing-based food lacks smoothness and subtlety. Beijing folks, meanwhile, argue that southerners grind, chop and dilute the flavour out of their food.

Whatever their regional biases, Chinese everywhere talk about their food the way foreigners might talk about art. This is probably because Chinese cuisine is regarded as an art form. And even if they aren't conscious of their food as a major cultural accomplishment, no Chinese can ever avoid talking about it. The most common Cantonese greeting, for example, is *sik tzo fan mei* meaning "Have you eaten?" Every dialect is rich in food symbolism. "You are breaking my rice bowl", wails the Chinese whose livelihood is threatened.

Even to learn simply how to say rice in Chinese requires an annotated dictionary. Consider the linguistic variables of Cantonese:

*Fresh meal.*

plain rice is *mai*; cooked rice is *faan;* rice porridge (commonly called congee) is *juk*; and harvested but unhusked rice is *guk*.

The traditional Chinese concept of a meal is very much a communal affair and one that provides strong sensory impact. Dishes are chosen with both taste and texture in mind, a stomach-pleasing succession of sweet-sour, sharp-bland, hot-cool and crunchy-smooth.

In a land that has experienced recurrent famine and natural disasters, wastage is not acceptable. Children are warned by their parents that if they leave any rice in their bowls, they will marry a pock-marked spouse and the more grains left in the bowl, the more pock-marked the partner will be.

Even during recent periods of poverty and privation, the Chinese have nearly always insisted on fresh food. Many Chinese still shop every day for fresh meat and vegetables. Cooks do not start with a particular dish in mind, but rather go to the market to buy what's fresh and in season, then create the meal.

To many outsiders, some Chinese foods seem bizarre, if not downright repulsive. The search for rare delicacies is common to all Chinese, but the Cantonese have pushed it to the extreme. Among them are monkey's brain, bear's paw, snake, dog, frog, sparrow, shark's fin, bird's nest, jelly fish and lizard. Unfortunately for the average Hong Kong Chinese who savours such outlandish fare, many of these delicacies are either illegal or virtually impossible to obtain. Hence, many are rare and expensive.

## Cantonese cuisine

The Cantonese live to eat and, at its most refined level, their gastronomy achieves a finicky discrimination that borders on cultism. In the Cantonese method of preparation, food is

*An abundance of leafy greens can be found in the markets.*

*Integral to Chinese cooking is the yin-yang philosophy of the correct balance of "hot" and "cold" ingredients. A hot (yang) item such as snake or chicken requires a compensating cool (yin) "partner" such as cabbage or tofu.*

cooked quickly and lightly, usually stir-fried in shallow water or an oil base in a wok. The flavour of the foods is thus preserved, not cooked away in preparation. Many dishes, particularly vegetables or fish, are steamed. This discourages overcooking and preserves a food's delicate and natural flavours (as well as its vitamins). Sauces are used to enhance and usually contain contrasting ingredients such as vinegar and sugar, or ginger and onion.

The Cantonese are very fond of seafood, as anyone who has visited one of Hong Kong's outlying islands will attest. Fish is typically steamed whole with fresh ginger and spring onions and sprinkled with a little soy sauce and sesame oil; fish eyes and lips are considered delicacies. Prawns and crabs steamed or in a black-bean sauce are very popular. The term "jumping prawns" signifies that they are alive, but it doesn't mean you are expected to eat them that way. Other seafood favourites include squid, in various forms including a delectable deep-fried version, octopus and crab. Shark's fin soup – golden threads of gelatinous shark's fin in a broth – is the centrepiece of Cantonese banquets, despite mounting ecological concerns (see page 70).

### FAUX CHINESE

Overseas visitors who are familiar with Chinese food in Western countries soon learn the authentic cuisine often has little to do with what they have been served in Chinese restaurants abroad. Take, for example, two supposed Cantonese dishes: sweet-and-sour pork is said to have been invented by the ever-resourceful inhabitants of Guangzhou solely for sweet-toothed foreigners. And chop suey was reportedly invented in San Francisco when a customer entered a restaurant at closing time, and the cooks threw their leftovers into a pot, served it up and in quiet jest called this oriental goulash "chop suey". Also, despite the Chinese preoccupation with luck and superstitions, American-style fortune cookies do not exist here.

*An assortment of fresh seafood.*

Vegetable dishes are ubiquitous, featuring leafy greens such as boc choi and choi sum, gently steamed and often liberally flavoured with garlic. Tofu, a versatile ingredient made from pressed soya bean curd, is another staple either steamed or deep-fried.

Chicken is commonplace and, in keeping with the Chinese sense of economy and variety, a single bird is often used to prepare several dishes. Chicken blood, for example, is cooked and solidified for soup, and the liver is used in a marvellous speciality called Gold Coin Chicken. The livers are skewered between pieces of pork fat and red-roasted until the fat becomes crisp and the liver soft and succulent. The delicacy is then eaten with wafers of orange-flavoured bread. Cantonese chicken dishes can be awkwardly bony for chopstick novices, although lemon chicken is prepared boneless with the skin coated in a crisp batter and served in a lemon sauce flavoured with onions, ginger and sugar.

For starters, choose something from the display of barbecued meats in the restaurant's display window. Cantonese barbecuing methods

*Pork is highly prized in Chinese cuisine.*

*Dried food is for sale at many markets.*

are unrivalled. Try goose, duck or, best of all, tender slices of pork with a golden and honeyed skin served on a bed of anise-flavoured preserved beans.

Also experience the taste sensation of double-boiled soups with duck, mushroom and tangerine peel, and a winter speciality called Monk Jumping over the Wall. This is a blend of abalone, chicken, ham, mushrooms and herbs so irresistible that monks are said to break their vows of vegetarianism once they smell it.

Snake is a traditional winter dish, often served as an energy-enhancing soup. Dog meat is also a winter dish but is illegal in Hong Kong: there are special tours across the border specifically to eat dog meat. Another Cantonese winter warmer to sample is a casserole of chicken and Chinese smoked pork sausage. These

## TOOLS AND TECHNIQUES

Many foreigners struggle with chopsticks (*faai jee* in Cantonese), with rice grains a particular menace. Thankfully, it's perfectly acceptable to raise the rice bowl to your lips and shovel the elusive morsels into your mouth. Scraping and slurping is not considered rude.

Chopsticks are thought to have been adopted because of a traditional Confucian distaste for knives – potentially dangerous weapons – on the dining table. If they prove impossible to handle, it is fine to use the porcelain spoon provided for soups as a scoop for other courses. And no one minds if you make a mess – it is even permissible to wipe your hands on the edge of the tablecloth.

A typical meal starts with a cold dish, which is followed by several main courses. Soup – usually clear, light broth – may be eaten after the heavier entrées to aid digestion. However, a thick and full-bodied soup may be served as a main dish, and a sweet soup often serves as a dessert at the end. There are no rules when it comes to ordering your meal. The main thing is to enjoy the food.

One mistake some foreigners make is swamping their rice with soy sauce, a crude act that robs it of its character and function. A Chinese meal should include enough spicy and savoury dishes to make the relative blandness of steamed rice an essential balancing agent.

*The Chinese penchant for bizarre culinary innovation reaches its apogee with bird's nest soup, for which the dried saliva lining a swiftlet's nest provides the base.*

sausages are sold in pairs and are usually served steamed on a bed of rice. In autumn, restaurants serve rice birds culled from paddy fields at harvest time. These are quite often eaten together with succulent Shanghai hairy crabs. Frogs are also found in the rice paddies, and these "field chickens" are often served at banquets in southern China. In Hong Kong markets they are sold live in plastic bags, and restaurants prepare them in many delicious ways, including deep-fried frog's legs cooked in a crunchy batter mixed with crushed almonds and served with sweet-and-sour sauce.

Probably the single most famous Cantonese culinary phenomenon is dim sum, a superbly tasty treat and a must on every Hong Kong tourist's itinerary (see page 64).

## Other Chinese cooking styles

Cantonese restaurants dominate in Hong Kong, but other distinctive forms of Chinese cooking – the subtle flavours of Chiu Chow and Shanghai, the spicy dishes of Sichuan and Hunan, northern specialities such as Peking Duck and Mongolian hotpot – are also well represented.

Chiu Chow cuisine is also known as Swatow (Shantou) food because this type of cooking originated around the city of Shantou in eastern Guangdong province. Seafood addicts enjoy such dishes as oysters fried in egg batter and clams served in a spicy sauce of black beans and chillies. Grey mullet is a favourite cold dish, and pomfret smoked over tea leaves and freshwater eel stewed in brown sauce are other highly recommended seafood wonders.

A Chiu Chow restaurant is also an appropriate place to try banquet-style food such as shark's fin soup and bird's nest soup. The owner of one restaurant in Hong Kong reputedly rents a mountain in Thailand that is said to harbour the finest collection of swiftlet nests in Southeast Asia. The nest itself is virtually tasteless, but its nourishing saliva linings are believed to rejuvenate the old. This delicacy is also eaten as a dessert flavoured with coconut milk or almonds. Another unusual avian meal is minced quail, cooked with water chestnuts and eaten wrapped in crisp lettuce leaves spiked with a dollop of plum sauce.

After Cantonese, the emphatically flavoured cuisine of the central province of Sichuan is perhaps the most familiar Chinese food to foreigners. Hunanese food is similar but arguably even spicier. Much of the emphasis comes from chillies, which appear in many guises: dried and fried in chunks, together with other ingredients; ground into a paste with a touch of added oil; as chilli oil; and crushed to a powder. Other ingredients important to Sichuanese cuisine are Sichuan "pepper" (the dried berry of the prickly ash or fagara), garlic, ginger and fermented soybean. Popular dishes include *mala doufu* (spicy tofu) and *gongbao* chicken (with chilli and peanuts).

A typical Sichuan eating experience is hotpot, or *huo guo*. Diners sit around a table with a pot of seasoned broth heated by a gas fire (charcoal was used in the past). Each diner adds

*Meals are an important communal affair in Hong Kong.*

bits and pieces of prepared vegetable, meat, fish and beancurd. The food cooks very quickly and can be fished out of the broth using chopsticks or a special strainer, then dipped in sesame oil, peanut sauce or a beaten egg.

The cuisine of the lower reaches of the Yangzi River, especially around Huaian and Yangzhou, gave rise to the term *huaiyang* to describe the food of China's eastern seaboard. This fertile area, known as the land of fish and rice, produces a wide range of crops as well as abundant fish, prawns, crab and eel. Huaiyang cooks often steam or gently simmer their food, rather than using the faster deep-frying style. Signature dishes include pork steamed in lotus leaves, Duck with Eight Ingredients, and Lion's Head Meatballs. For the most part, the cooking of Shanghai, Jiangsu and Zhejiang is usually regarded as being part of Huaiyang cuisine.

Over the centuries, culinary elements from all over eastern Asia have been liberally adapted and absorbed into Chinese cuisine, and it's difficult to trace the origins of some dishes. Peking Duck, prepared by roasting the duck over an open charcoal fire and slowly basting it with syrup until the skin is a deep, crispy brown, was originally Mongolian. Mongolian hotpot, called "steamboat" in Singapore and Malaysia, is in fact of central Chinese Muslim origins. It is probably the second best-known of the northern dishes, and as a winter food, is served between November and March in northern-style restaurants.

*Modern take on traditional cuisine at Little Bao.*

*Fiery chilli peppers.*

## HONG KONG'S BAKERIES

Bakeries occupy a special place in Hong Kong hearts, dispensing breakfast and snacks from the ubiquitous egg-custard tarts *(daan taht)*, doughnuts and doughy sausage buns to a wide range of colourful celebratory cakes and pastries. Young parents take their offspring to the same bakery they patronised when they were children, and after a spell overseas, Hong Kongers drop by their friendly neighbourhood cake shop, a reflex reaction that confirms their homecoming. And when a rent hike forced the closure of the famed Tai Cheung Bakery on Lyndhurst Terrace (Central) after 51 years of business, people took to the streets in (futile) protest.

*Egg-custard tarts, a Hong Kong bakery staple.*

A surprise for many at their first northern Chinese meal is that rice is not served unless specially requested. Wheat is the common grain staple in the north, so northerners traditionally eat steamed bread *(pao)* or tasty onion cakes instead of rice. One of the spectacular treats at a northern Chinese meal is handmade noodles called *lie mien*, often deftly made at the table by the chef, who turns dough into strands of noodles within seconds.

## A cosmopolitan culinary scene

Nowadays, while Cantonese and other Chinese cuisine predominates in Hong Kong, there is a vast array of other fare on offer. Stand beneath the escalator in Cochrane Street in Central, and within spitting distance you'll find a modern British gastropub, Russian, Indian and Thai restaurants, and a scarlet-hued sushi joint with platters humming round the bar on a conveyor belt.

Food hawkers still ply their trade on street corners although officialdom is seeking to eradicate them and a browse round a 7-Eleven or Circle K convenience store leads past microwaveable dim sum and pot noodles, packets of dried fish and fruit, as well as boxed drinks that might be mistaken for medicine.

The budget-minded can feast for a few dollars on seafood noodles at a seaside restaurant on one of the outer islands, or you can splurge in a five-star hotel, diving in and out of cosmopolitan buffets or settling down to a lengthy repast with maître d' and sommelier shimmering discreetly in the shadows.

Hong Kong's long-established Indian community has resulted in a good supply of curry houses all over the main urban areas, notably in Tsim Sha Tsui's Chungking Mansions (see page 146). Also very easy to find and usually excellent are the numerous Thai restaurants, as well as plenty of other Southeast Asian cuisine not just Malaysian and Singaporean but Vietnamese and Burmese, too. Japanese food is also very well represented. As in any large cosmopolitan city, there is no shortage of European (mainly French and Italian) and American restaurants (McDonald's outlets are everywhere, and extremely cheap), as well as other cuisines ranging from Egyptian to Argentinean.

*Dim sum soup dumplings.*

# DIM SUM

**Perhaps the most famous Cantonese culinary phenomenon, dim sum is one of Hong Kong's traditional delicacies and goes down a treat with visitors.**

From sunrise through to lunchtime people all over Hong Kong enjoy *yum cha* ("drink tea"), catching up with friends and eating dim sum ("little hearts"), small portions of Cantonese dishes and dumplings often served in bamboo baskets. To share the experience, head to a dim sum restaurant and join in the noise and enjoyment of this tasty Hong Kong tradition.

In Hong Kong (and neighbouring Guangdong province) people eat dim sum for breakfast or brunch, congregating in bustling, informal eateries that often open at the crack of dawn. In those traditional establishments where menus have not yet taken over, self-service trolleys stacked with small plates and steamer baskets are wheeled past. Steamed, pan-fried, deep-fried or congee (a rice-based, soupy dish) are the traditional categories for dim sum, although a few varieties are baked. Most common are the delicate steamed dumplings, which come with a range of fillings. Dessert dim sum is also available.

Novices often start with *siu mai* (shrimp and pork dumplings), *ha gow* (shrimp dumplings) and *cha siu bau* (steamed barbecue pork buns) – these three are probably the most popular dishes.

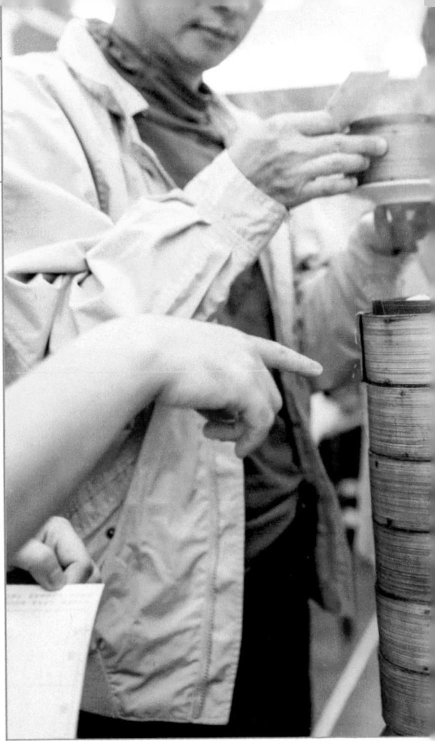

*In a traditional dim sum restaurant, diners replenish from the ever-circulating trolley rather than ordering everything in one go.*

*Siu mai come in several varieties, usually filled with pork and shrimp.*

*Dim sum is served in wicker baskets along with an ordering card.*

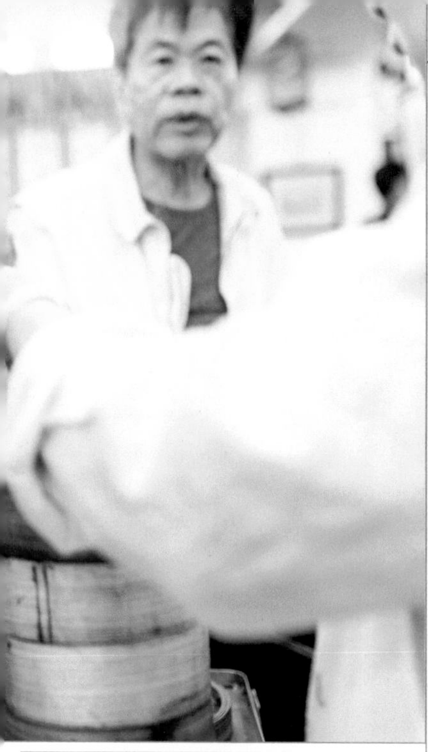

*Pai gwut are steamed ribs.*

*Chicken's feet (foong jao), chewy and not popular with Westerners, are usually marinated in a black bean sauce.*

## INFORMATION FOR NOVICES

*Preparing dim sum at Ling Heung Teahouse.*

**A dim sum restaurant can be daunting for foreigners with no experience of Chinese etiquette, so here are some pointers to follow.**

**At the table you will be presented with a bowl, plate, chopsticks and a small teacup. Tea is the first thing to order, after which you will be presented with the all-important "card", which resembles a large lottery ticket. Each time you order something the item will be ticked by the waiting staff. A few restaurants have English menus, but on the whole be prepared simply to look and point and try new things. Older establishments still have vendors wheeling trolleys around, each carrying a different speciality. If you can't see what it is they are selling, stop the trolley, with a polite but loud *ng goi* (excuse me). Sometimes there's a counter, so walk up with your card, open the baskets and point at what you want. When your teapot is empty, simply flip the lid over and someone will appear and top it up with hot water. When your bowl is empty it's time to sample another bamboo basket.**

*Jian dui is a fried pastry coated with sesame seeds.*

*A traditional Chinese medicine shop on Queen's Road West.*

# CHINESE MEDICINE

**Chinese remedies have been practised for 4,000 years and, aided by the international popularity of acupuncture, have been gaining recognition around the world.**

Traditional Chinese medicine is based on an array of theories and practices from both foreign and native sources. It was during the Zhou period (11th century–221 BC) that many of these theories first emerged. This stage of Chinese history, marked by near continuous fighting and misery, lasted several centuries. Against the background of this constant state of turmoil, many ideas took root that were to colour all aspects of life in China for the next 2,000 years including medicine, which itself was influenced by the teachings of Confucianism and Daoism.

Holism, the idea that parts of a human body form an integral, connected and inseparable whole, is one of the distinguishing features of Chinese medicine. Whereas Western medicine tends to treat symptoms in a direct fashion, Chinese medicine examines illnesses in the context of the whole person.

*Yin-yang* philosophy and the theory of five elements form a system of categories that explain the complex relationships between parts of the body and the environment. *Yin* and *yang* represent two opposite sides in nature such as hot and cold or light and dark. Each of the different organs is said to have *yin* or *yang* characteristics, and balance between the two is vital for maintaining health. Likewise, each organ is linked directly to a particular element: fire for the heart, earth for the spleen, water for the kidneys, metal for the lungs and wood for the liver. The way in which they interact affects a person's health, so, for example, the kidneys (water) nourish the liver (wood).

*A pharmacist weighs ingredients for a prescription.*

## Traditional versus modern

The mention of traditional Chinese medicine often conjures up images of acupuncture needles, aromatic herbs and strange animal parts. Yet, despite the exotic stereotype, it is increasingly gaining respect from both scientists and the general public in Europe and the US, particularly with regard to the alleviation of pain.

In China, scepticism and debate arose as to the value of traditional medicine during the first half of the 20th century, with progressive intellectual and political groups particularly hostile. After the founding of the People's Republic of China, competition between

Western and Chinese medicine was eradicated for practical as well as ideological reasons, with an attempt to integrate the two systems.

This integrated approach has persisted, and today medical care in China often consists of a mixture of both Western and traditional Chinese medicine, although the former, or *xiyi*, tends to be dominant. Large public hospitals *(renmin yiyuan)* in cities across the country offer both the traditional Chinese and Western approaches to medical treatment. Hospitals dealing exclusively with traditional Chinese medicine (TCM), or *zhongyi*, tend to be smaller, less well equipped and harder to find. In Hong Kong, the Chinese Medicine Council of Hong Kong (www.cmchk.org.hk) has been regulating the industry since 1999, and while there are no full-scale TCM hospitals, there are several places in Central and Sheung Wan that offer a basic consultation (an example is the Good Spring Company on the corner of Stanley Street, beside the Mid-Levels escalator).

The Chinese will usually visit a doctor trained in Western medicine if they feel that they are seriously ill and need to be treated quickly. If the problem is not too serious or

*Ingredients come from all kinds of animals.*

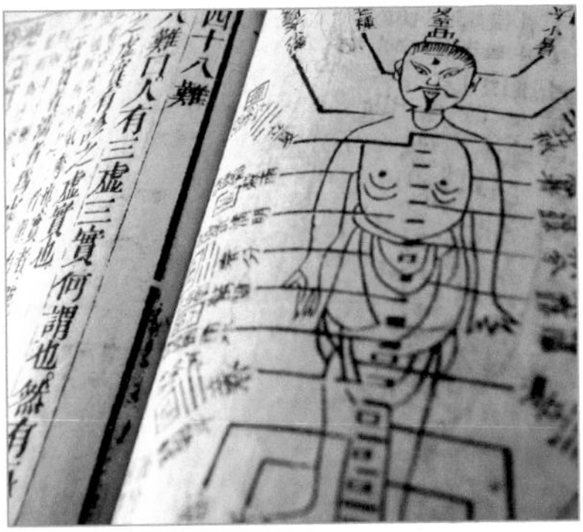

*Ancient Chinese medicine book from the Qing dynasty, recording the use of acupuncture and herbal medicine.*

urgent, the patient may seek out a traditional doctor to restore harmony to the body and thus provide a long-term cure.

## The pharmacy

Chinese pharmacies tend to have a unique odour. There are all sorts of exotic animals, insects and vegetables, all of which appear in the pages of the *Encyclopaedia of the Traditional Chinese Pharmacopoeia*, a weighty tome published in 1977, running to 2,700 pages and listing some 5,767 substances with medicinal or preventative properties. Have a look around the pharmacies in Western District and you will see birds' eggs, snakes wound up in spirals, toads, tortoises, centipedes, grasshoppers, dried fish, deer antlers and the genitalia of various unfortunate and often endangered animals (see page 70). And then there are the myriad herbs, blossoms, roots, berries, mushrooms and fruits dried and preserved. All traditional Chinese pharmacies are well stocked with ginseng roots, often shaped like a human figure.

Traditional cures are not only available from pharmacies. Wandering around a Hong Kong market, one may see herbs and produce for sale that are used as remedies rather than food.

*Increasingly accepted by many physicians, acupuncture was in 1997 approved as a legitimate and insurable treatment for pain by medical authorities in the United States.*

## Acupuncture

One effect of acupuncture that is undisputed and valued by a billion Chinese is the relief of pain. While others rely on drugs to moderate physical pain, the Chinese go to the acupuncturist. Cases of acute back pain, for example, can be cured by sticking just one needle in the *renzhong* point between the top lip and nose.

A new form of painless acupuncture, which does not use needles, is administered by ear. Small, round seed kernels are stuck onto certain points of the ear and massaged by the patient from time to time. This method is not only very successful in treating pain, but is also said to relieve such allergies as hay fever.

When entering an acupuncture clinic, you will notice one of the dominant aromas of the Chinese pharmacy that of the *moxa* herb, which is the same thing as Artemisia, or mugwort. It is considered especially helpful in treating illnesses that, in Chinese medical terminology, are classified as "cold"; for example, stomach and digestive complaints without fever, certain rheumatic illnesses, chronic pains in the back and cramped neck and shoulders. The mugwort is placed onto the acupuncture point or on the end of the acupuncture needle, or moulded into the shape of a cigar and rolled back and forth over the skin.

## Exercise

At some stage while in Hong Kong, visit a public park at dawn to witness the Chinese exercise arts of *taijiquan* and *qigong*. *Taijiquan* is the most common type of exercise, so-called shadow-boxing. *Qigong* is often translated in the West as breathing therapy.

Both exercises are based on the belief that the human body is endowed with the life energy, *qi*. If this can be harnessed and controlled, a person can influence the course of certain ailments that afflict the body. Body and breathing exercises are thus preventative forms of "medicine".

During the Cultural Revolution in China, *qigong* was banned because it was said to be too close to superstition. But in 1980, new *qigong* groups sprang up, and soon gained a large following. Some forms involve hardly any movement: breathing and "sinking into oneself" are of prime importance. Other forms, like the "wild goose" variety, entail a great deal of movement and are aesthetically appealing.

*For much of China's history, herbalists have attributed medicinal value to various foods. At times, the distinction between food and treatment can blur.*

*Chinese Herbal Tea has many medicinal properties.*

### FINDING THE RIGHT BALANCE

Traditional Chinese Medicine (TCM) entails more than just acupuncture: the knowledge of remedies *(zhongyao)* is an important factor. Patients are treated with different kinds of massage and chiropractics *(tuina)*, as well as breathing and movement therapies, such as *taijiquan* (shadow-boxing) and *qigong* (breathing therapy). While Hong Kong's main hotels offer extensive Western-style health treatments, it's worth re-establishing your inner harmony the local way. Start off with the familiar: a relaxing toe rub to boost circulation and free the flow of *qi*, or a full body massage: the Sunny Paradise Sauna (341 Lockhart Road, Wan Chai; tel: 2831 0123) is one of a number of venues around Hong Kong.

# The animal parts trade

**In addition to natural herbs, animal body parts are integral to many traditional medicine recipes. Globalisation, industrial processing and an expanding Chinese middle class mean some of the planet's most precarious species are under pressure.**

The Chinese have been using animal parts for medicinal purposes for well over 1,000 years. Yet for all its growing appeal across the world as people look for alternatives to Western drugs, there is a darker side. Wildlife, under pressure from intensive industrial and economic development in recent decades, is now being pushed to the brink of extinction by the increased demand for body parts.

The demand for tigers, for example, is forcing these magnificent creatures ever closer to extinction (recent studies estimate that there are only 30 to 80 South China tigers, 480 to 540 Siberian tigers and 400 to 500 Sumatran tigers left in the wild). Various tiger parts are used in Chinese medicine: eyeballs to treat epilepsy, the tail for various skin diseases, bile for convulsions in children, whiskers for toothaches, the penis for male impotence and the brain to combat laziness and pimples. Yet of all tiger parts, it is the bones that are most valued, used to treat rheumatism, weakness, stiffness and even paralysis.

*Endangered animals such as tigers and sharks are threatened by the Chinese medicine industry.*

Rhinoceros, bear and shark populations are also rapidly shrinking. Rhinoceros horn is reputed to be an aphrodisiac. Only about 30,000 rhinos remain in the wild, with another 1,000 in captivity. About two thirds of these are white rhinos and the remaining half consists of four other species. Without assistance, these could soon be extinct. Also greatly threatened by Chinese demand, bears from as far away as North America are cruelly farmed for their bile, used to treat a variety of ailments, and paws, which are used in soup.

## From celluloid predator to culinary victim

Like bear's paw, shark's fin, though not used exclusively for medicine, is a delicacy. Served most commonly as shark's fin soup, this broth is believed to benefit the internal organs. Sharks are caught and their top fin sliced off. They are then tossed back into the ocean, alive, to drown. In some areas, the shark population – essential to the ecosystem, as the shark is the top predator – is declining.

In recent years, human populations and expendable incomes have increased dramatically in Asia, along with a resurgence of interest in traditional cures. Use of traditional medicines is seen as a status symbol and also as a way to hold on to local customs amidst rapid social and economic changes.

While the effectiveness of these endangered animal products in medicine is still disputed, researchers confirm the benefits of the active ingredients present in a considerable number of Chinese prescriptions.

As endangered animal populations plummet, the use of their parts to feed an evergrowing demand is no longer sustainable. Hong Kong's government demonstrated its awareness of the fact in 2013 when it belatedly banned shark's fin from menus at official functions. One way or another, the trade in endangered animal parts for medicine must stop. This means finding an alternative to alternative medicine.

*The ancient Chinese martial art of t'ai chi has many health benefits.*

In both *taijiquan* and *qigong*, changes in mental and emotional states follow a certain pattern of movement. The most extreme of these is the "crane *qigong*", which involves violent, sometimes cathartic emotional outbursts. Practitioners may scream, cry, laugh, dance or jump around as they experience *fagong*, abandoning oneself to spontaneous movements.

## It's in the diet

The Chinese have little doubt of the efficacy of different foods for treating ailments and healing certain parts of the body. Consider three traditional delicacies: shark's fin, abalone and bird's nest. These are exquisite parts of an extensive cuisine, eaten for their sensory delights. Yet each is claimed to have medicinal value. Shark's fin and abalone are said to benefit internal organs, including the heart and kidneys. Abalone also regulates the liver and reduces dizziness and high blood pressure. Bird's nest, usually taken as a soup, allegedly cleanses the blood and the complexion.

Verifying such claims is difficult. The scientific method, which involves controlled experiments using known values and quantities, doesn't lend itself well to the analysis of claims that a food item can help cure physical illnesses. Moreover, to be valid, a result must be independently verifiable. Consideration must also be given to the placebo effect, where a valid result occurs because one believes in something's efficacy. Many say the success of Chinese cures is simply a question of mind over matter. However, recent research on the health effects of soybeans and green tea, for example, suggests that components in these two items have substantive medicinal value, possibly against some forms of cancer.

Herbal remedies have gradually gained respect around the world. Western nutritionists have always stressed that certain foods provide necessary vitamins and minerals that are good for the body; carrots for good eyesight, calcium for strong bones. Traditional Chinese medicinal foods simply take these scientific remedies one level further.

# BELIEFS AND SUPERSTITIONS

**Ancient beliefs such as fortune-telling and feng shui, as well as more traditional religious principles, continue to colour daily life in Hong Kong.**

*Lighting incense sticks at Man Mo Temple.*

Few modern-day city residents take their traditional beliefs more seriously than the Hong Kong Chinese. A constant undercurrent, counterpoint to the brash, modern metropolis, these values have been formed over the centuries through an interaction of the three primary Chinese religions or philosophies – Buddhism, Daoism and Confucianism – overlaid with elements of animism, superstition and folk tradition. Adding further to this esoteric mix is the Chinese tradition of ancestor worship. Some aspects of the core beliefs overlap with each other (for example, many temples are both Buddhist and Daoist).

These religions are complemented by the more overtly superstitious beliefs so important in Hong Kong. Feng shui (see page 74) is based around the central Chinese concept of qi (the energy, life force or spirit that is believed to exist in nature and all living creatures), an underlying principle in Chinese medicine (see page 69). Numerology (see page 75) is a more straightforward superstition. Throughout, two themes are universal: the desire for prosperity and longevity.

Yet it is often said that Hong Kongers worship one thing and one thing only: money. And it is true that the almost evangelical pursuit of

*A typical Chinese temple entrance features a spirit wall inside the main doorway to block the path of evil spirits. The red lanterns also offer protection, as well as symbolising well-being and happiness.*

*Temples in Hong Kong are dedicated to a particular deity, generally from the Daoist pantheon. Mo, the god of war (also known as Kuan Ti or Kuan Kung) is pictured here at Man Mo Temple (the temple is co-dedicated to Man, the god of literature). One of the most popular deities is Tin Hau, goddess of the sea and worshipped throughout coastal China, where she is variously known as Tianhou (in Mandarin Chinese), A-Ma (in Macau) or Matsu (in Taiwan).*

*Busy Wong Tai Sin Temple, dedicated to the Daoist god of healing and good fortune, is famous for its fortune-tellers.*

*Fish represent harmony and prosperity to the Chinese.*

*Ancestors' ashes are stored at Man Mo Temple. Ancestor worship is an ancient Chinese tradition. When someone dies, his or her soul is thought to enter the underworld and come under the threat of evil spirits. Offerings are made and "spirit money" burnt to protect the ancestor, who will in return offer protection to his or her descendants. It is also considered important to keep the grave clean. Eventually the remains are dug up and cremated.*

*Daoism is China's only true native religion, founded in the sixth century by Laozi (pictured), a semi-mythical philosopher. Chinese "popular" religions are often a blend of elements taken from Daoism, Buddhism and Confucianism.*

personal wealth seems to be hard-wired into much of the population. Deity worship is often used in the pursuit of worldly gains including advice on stock-market and horse-racing tips (witness the large number of offerings to the god of good fortune, Wong Tai Sin, at his temple).

## Feng shui

Most people agree that I.M. Pei's iconic Bank of China Tower is an impressive and attractive structure, but there is one negative aspect: its strikingly sharp angles channel bad feng shui onto its neighbours. Feng shui ("wind and water") is an ancient Chinese form of geomancy, and an important consideration when a new tower block is being planned. A feng shui master will advise on which direction it should face and where desks, beds or even a vase should be placed to attract the best luck and prevent bad fortune. A sheltered position, facing the water and away from a hillside, is considered auspicious, but although the Bank of China was built with these principles in mind, the fact that its aggressive angles arrowed hostile energy towards, amongst others, Government House and the HSBC Building, was not considered. The construction of the Cheung Kong Centre, at an angle askew to the bank and between it and the HSBC Building and a strategically placed willow tree at Government House have improved neighbourly relations.

*A Feng Shui compass.*

*Chim bamboo slips are used for drawing lots or divination.*

*Paper money is burnt so that ancestors can benefit in the other world, in which they need money and consumer goods (cars, flats, TVs, etc. are all made in paper form for this purpose). Offerings of incense and food are also considered to be important.*

*Fortune telling on Rua Do Cunha.*

*Fortune-telling can be a lucrative business in Hong Kong. Clairvoyants, usually in residence at a temple, read palms or the feet or face to predict the future. Other methods include using chim sticks (at temples such as Wong Tai Sin), or game-like activities such as throwing coins or other objects at a target, an example being the Wishing Tree near Tai Po. Following a fortune-teller's advice to the letter can impinge on daily life. In order to appease the fortune god, it may be deemed necessary to shave off all one's hair skinhead-style, or to wear a bright-red belt at all times.*

## LUCKY NUMBERS

*A Rolls Royce outside the Peninsula Hotel.*

**Hong Kong may be the only place in the world where someone would pay US$1.7 million for a vehicle licence plate. In 1994, local tycoon Albert Yeung did just that, investing in a licence plate bearing the single digit nine, considered lucky because the Cantonese word for "nine" sounds like the word for "eternity", "longevity" or "perpetuity".**

**Other lucky numbers include two, which stands for "easy", three for "living or giving birth", six for "longevity" and eight for "prosperity". But it is the combinations that are in most demand. For example, 163 means "live for ever" or "give birth non-stop", 168 equals "prosperity all the way", and 162 "easy all the way". Lucky licence-plate numbers became so much in demand that, in 1973, the government's transport department began auctioning them off to the highest bidders. The number eight has consistently drawn the highest bid. Today, all licence-plate numbers considered lucky in Cantonese are reserved and available only through auctions where they attract high prices.**

**The superstition over numbers also applies to street, apartment and telephone numbers. For example, the price for an apartment on the 14th floor can be 20 percent cheaper than that for the same flat on the 18th floor, because 14 in Cantonese means "definitely dies", while 18 means "definitely prospers". Some buildings get around this problem by simply omitting a 14th floor, going straight from the 13th to the 15th.**

*Villain hitting in Wan Chai; villain hitting or demon exorcising aims to curse one's enemies.*

*West Kowloon Bamboo Theatre.*

# THE PERFORMING ARTS

**Spend any time in Hong Kong and one will encounter a diverse catalogue of performing arts, including traditional opera, lion dances and Cantopop.**

Although Chinese opera is no longer the most popular performance art in Hong Kong and China, it remains an integral part of Chinese entertainment and culture. Originating from China's earliest folk music and dances, modern-day Chinese opera – a story put to music and dance – emerged during the Song dynasty (960–1279). Although Chinese opera came to be associated with festivals and state occasions at the 18th-century imperial court in Beijing, it was also popular among the common people.

In Hong Kong, a performance of Chinese opera is customary during important festivals in the Chinese calendar. Performances are usually held in bamboo-and-mat theatres temporarily erected in public areas. Chinese opera has many cultural and regional variations. Cantonese operas, which are naturally the most popular in Hong Kong, are quite different from Chiu Chow operas. Beijing operas are performed in the court's official dialect, Mandarin.

The repertoire is drawn from folklore, legends and historical events. The backbone of the performance is the actor-singer. In the same way as their Western counterparts, Chinese operatic singers undergo many years of intensive training to achieve a properly pitched falsetto. Singing artists are often accompanied by a traditional Chinese orchestra. Percussionists occupy one side of the stage, while the wind-and-string section sits opposite, leaving the main area of the stage clear for the primary performers. To foreign ears, the sounds of a Chinese opera seem bizarre and discordant, with the high-pitched dialogue, deafening gongs and drums echoing from the music pit.

*The painted mask is critical in Chinese opera.*

There were no actresses during Chinese opera's early development, because women were not allowed to make public appearances, so male actors took the female roles. As in Western opera, however, that tradition has died.

Make-up, movements, props and specific costume colours identify an actor's age, sex and personality the moment he or she appears on stage. Actors in Beijing operas wear extremely heavy make-up, a cosmetic style derived from the use of painted masks in older operatic forms. A white patch on the nose indicates a comic character of low rank; a completely white face suggests evil and treachery; a red face identifies a courageous but dim-witted man; and a black-faced actor is an ordinary person. There are 18 types of opera beards, each symbolising a different personality.

Headdresses are also a vital part of Chinese opera costume; the more important the character, the more elaborate the headdress. Costumes are exaggerated in style to achieve as great a theatrical effect as possible. Each colour identifies the rank, status and personality of the different operatic roles: purple for barbarians, yellow for emperors. Props are usually minimal, the idea being to leave as much as possible to the audience's imagination.

Though there are formal exceptions, it is acceptable for audiences to arrive late for a performance, leave early, walk around and chat, or

*Resplendent costumes embellish the operatic performance.*

*Chinese operas also incorporate mime, dance, swordplay and acrobatics. For the principal artists, gesture, movement and attitude are all as important as their spoken lines.*

even eat during a show, which may run from three hours to a whole day. When an actor sings especially well, the audience is expected to respond by shouting out praise and applauding.

Most of the traditional opera performances in Hong Kong are called *sumkung* (god's eulogy), as they are performed to celebrate special festivals or the birthdays of different gods. Many of these performances are related to Daoism and Buddhism. For example, during the Ghost Festival, operas are staged together with other activities to expiate the sins of the dead. On each occasion, performances can last up to five days.

To revive the popularity of Chinese operas, some artists have taken measures to rejuvenate both form and content. The most active reformer in Hong Kong is veteran Leung Hon-wai, who has formed his own operatic group and employed writers to produce new scripts, while a symphony orchestra was introduced to bring a more modern tempo.

Ironically, the first major reform of Chinese opera was started on the mainland by the late Chinese leader Mao Zedong's wife, who persecuted intellectuals during the Cultural Revolution. Under her instructions, traditional opera troupes put on "revolutionary model plays". They sang the praises of the Communist Party and condemned the evils of capitalism. Delicate young girls yearning for love were replaced by iron ladies sweating away in the fields. Symphonic music was introduced to add a stronger mood, while Western opera-singing techniques were applied to make revolutionary leaders stand out.

Rigid political propaganda aside, these revolutionary plays introduced modern elements to traditional Chinese operas and convinced veteran artists that new stories could work.

## Lion and dragon dances

A lion dance, in which two performers wear and manipulate a lion costume, is also an

*New Year dragon dances.*

integral part of festive occasions. This *qongfu*-related entertainment form is usually performed at festivals, or on special occasions such as the opening of a new business or a corporate anniversary.

Since the lion is considered a holy animal and seen as a spirit that has its own importance in Chinese mythology, lion dances are believed to bring good luck. Sometimes performances are accompanied by firecrackers to scare away evil spirits. There may also be a dragon dance to accompany the lion. The difference between the two dances is simple: the dragon is held aloft by a group of performers, who move the giant puppet from outside. They walk in set patterns to make the dragon look like it is flying. But the lion dance has a crew of only two, who move the large cloth or paper puppet from within. Also, in the lion dance performers can move the head in various ways, as well as the eyes, mouth and ears.

There are generally two types of Chinese lions: northern and southern. The differences are in their appearance and the way they move. While the northern lion has a furry yellow coat

*Chinese New Year parade.*

*A Cantopop singer.*

and a semi-rigid mouth, the southern version has a movable mouth and a more colourful body, but no long hair for fur.

## Music and film

Despite efforts to adapt to modern times, interest in traditional arts has been replaced by pop music and films. Mainland Chinese immigrants in the 1950s and 1960s brought to Hong Kong not only money and entrepreneurial skills, but also arts, culture and the Mandarin language. During the 1950s and 1960s, most of the well-known artists in Hong Kong were from Shanghai. In the 1970s, when contact between Hong Kong and Taiwan increased, Hong Kong's music scene was dominated by Taiwanese songs, mostly written by college students on the island ruled by the Guomintang (Nationalist) Party.

In the mid-1970s, some Hong Kong-born singers with a clear local identity started a movement to promote Cantonese pop songs, and by the early 1980s the first generation of Cantonese pop stars dubbed "Cantopop" by the local press appeared. Since the late 1980s, this local scene has been dominated by teen idols – young male and female singers in their late teens or early twenties whose popularity depends more on their looks than their voices. In the 1990s, the biggest local pop stars were described as "emperors" and "empresses", with the most famous performers called the "four

### WHERE TO SEE PERFORMING ARTS

Hong Kong's flagship venue is the Cultural Centre in Tsim Sha Tsui. Home to the Hong Kong Philharmonic Orchestra, the centre also plays host to many visiting artists and touring productions of hit musicals. The Hong Kong Arts Centre in Wan Chai is the place to go for theatre and the occasional concert, while City Hall (Central) is synonymous with dance and Chinese opera. The Academy for Performing Arts, close to the Arts Centre in Wan Chai, contains the Lyric Theatre and organises concerts by its own students and international musicians. The annual Hong Kong Arts Festival (Feb–Mar) brings together local talent and leading international performers.

*Tony Leung Chiu-Wai, star of the 2004 Hong Kong film '2046'.*

heavenly emperors" singers: Leon Lai, Jackie Cheung, Andy Lau and Aaron Kwok. Each developed his own loyal legion of fans who zealously track their idol's every public appearance. When heart-throb singer/actor Leslie Cheung died in a suicide jump from the top floor of the Mandarin Oriental hotel in 2003 the city was practically paralysed by grief. Tribute websites continue on the Internet, and fans still parade wreaths in public.

Life for the more traditional professional artists has got tougher, since the local society is so commercially oriented that people do not have much time for serious art. However, as the city gets more affluent, the government and its citizens are beginning to appreciate the high-quality arts.

There are eight professional performance companies in Hong Kong and hundreds of amateur groups. The most prominent players include the Hong Kong Philharmonic Orchestra, Hong Kong Repertory Theatre, Hong Kong Chinese Orchestra and the Hong Kong Dance Company. Founded in 1985, the Academy for Performing Arts in Wan Chai is one of the top performing-arts schools in Asia. Major cultural events include the annual Hong Kong Arts Festival and the Fringe Festival.

The profile of Chinese cinema has risen considerably in recent years. Hong Kong films are gaining international attention, and local film talent has become more influential following the achievements in Hollywood of director John Woo, actor Chow Yun-fat and action-star Jackie Chan, as well as the highly acclaimed, idiosyncratic work of director Wong Kar-wai. Hong Kong remains one of only a handful of places in the world where locally made films (mainly action and romance) can still outsell Hollywood.

*The top 5 highest-grossing-ever films in HK are all Hollywood offerings: Avatar (HK$178,029,000); Avengers: Age of Ultron (HK$132,747,000); Titanic (HK$128,003,000); Iron Man 3 (HK$106,390,000); and Transformers: Age of Extinction (HK$98,197,000).*

# BUSINESS AND MONEY

**Making money is Hong Kong's *raison d'être*: the fast buck is revered and the tycoon's status stops just short of beatification.**

*Financial display boards in Mong Kok.*

Even with its limited resources and space, prosperity and affluence are among the first impressions a visitor gets after arriving in Hong Kong. At HK$333,645 (US$42,964), per capita GDP is one of the highest in the world, although this is bolstered by a small elite of super-rich residents. The median monthly household income was HK$23,500 (US$3,027) in 2014. According to a 2017 Forbes report, there were 75 US-dollar billionaires and the city is thought to have the second highest concentration of millionaires in the world. Li Ka Shing, known locally as "Superman", is the richest of all: in 2017 Forbes estimated his personal wealth at US$31.2 billion (his initial fortune was created by manufacturing plastic flowers in the 1950s). The post-2008 global recession affected Hong Kong far less than most developed economies.

Hong Kong is a city riddled with contradictions. It continues to top lists of the world's "freest economies", yet there is no competition law and the property-rich cartels dominate major sectors of the economy. Around half the working population earns less than HK$130,000 (US$16,700) per year, and the wealth gap has increased in recent years with 11.6 percent of households surviving on an annual income of less than HK$72,000 (US$9,285).

## An economic success story

An excellent deep-water harbour and a strategic location on China's doorstep – the factors which brought the British here in the first place – have long encouraged Hong Kong's shipping and trading business. Today it is the world's second-busiest air cargo hub and third-busiest container port.

For the first century of British rule, Hong Kong developed as a trading port through which China did business with the rest of the world, but this entrepôt role rapidly diminished after World War II, as communist China became increasingly isolated. In a short time, the economy switched its focus to manufacturing. A large number of mainland entrepreneurs fled here after the Communist Party came to power in 1949. Bringing capital and business skills, they re-established themselves by setting up factories making textiles and toys. A sizeable workforce was on hand to provide the labour.

*Hong Kong has the world's highest proportion of über-expensive cars.*

Manufacturing gradually diversified into electronics, printing, publishing, machinery, fabricated-metal products, plastic products (the famous "made in Hong Kong" cheap toys), watches and jewellery. But this proved to be a relatively short-lived stage in Hong Kong's economic history.

Since the late 1980s, most companies have moved their processing operations to China, where labour is considerably cheaper. Hong Kong companies own half of the 400,000 or so factories in the Pearl River Delta. By 2015 the manufacturing sector accounted for just 1.2 percent of GDP, down from 24 percent in 1984. Today many companies have an office in Hong Kong that coordinates with overseas clients looking to have goods manufactured in China or elsewhere in Asia. If they don't have a factory of their own, they source one in China or Asia. The Hong Kong offices coordinate payments and shipping, and may also provide design services, quality control and production services. For the moment, most buyers are more confident to deal with Hong Kong-based companies, governed as they are by Hong Kong law.

As well as local success stories, Hong Kong is maintaining its role as a major international commercial and financial centre (a position it has held since the mid-1980s). There are around 3,500 international companies with regional offices in the city. Tourism is important too; Hong Kong welcomed over 59.3 million visitors in 2015.

In February 2017, Hong Kong's foreign currency assets stood at US$390.5 billion, making it the world's sixth-largest holder of foreign currency reserves.

## Links with China

The single most important factor in Hong Kong's current prosperity has been the opening up of China to foreign trade.

Until the late 1970s, the Hong Kong business sector was dominated by British companies,

> *Hong Kong is rich with the stories of tycoons who have ascended to the summit, fallen into the financial abyss, then climbed to the top once more, attaining legendary status.*

known as *hongs* by the Cantonese. The four leading British *hongs* were Jardine Matheson, Wheelock Marden, Hutchison Whampoa and the Swire Group. But in the last few decades, energetic and ambitious Hong Kong Chinese groups, with investments in shipping, property and the textile industry, have built new empires and taken over some of the British-founded concerns. Considering mainland China to be the biggest market in the world, Hong Kong entrepreneurs – with their blood and emotional ties to the mainland and their knowledge of the Chinese way of doing business – naturally edged out their British rivals.

With the advent of Deng Xiaoping's economic reforms in the late 1970s, Hong Kong's strategic position as the international community's gateway to China, and China's trade window to the outside world, suddenly became far more important. Both China and HK benefited hugely from their fast-developing economic ties.

These days China accounts for nearly half of Hong Kong's total trade in goods, making the mainland its largest trading partner. In 2015 just over 56 percent of all Hong Kong exports went to China, and just under 47 percent of all imported goods came from China. Hong Kong remains the largest investor in China; its companies employ an estimated 12 million people there and about 240,000 HK residents work in China. Being part of a motherland with a market of over 1.3 billion people just across the border means HK businesses are ideally placed to target consumers in China and to help international companies tap into the vast opportunities there.

*The Landmark, a prestigious development.*

*Hong Kongers have a sharp eye for business. As soon as they have saved enough money by working for other people, many of them venture into their own businesses.*

## Currency control

To provide a stable currency, the government introduced a linked exchange-rate system in 1983 that pegged Hong Kong's currency to the US dollar. The system was designed to align interest rates with those in the USA's then stable economy. The exchange rate was fixed at HK$7.8 to US$1. However, during the 1997 financial crisis that spread through Asia, many people questioned the wisdom of linking Hong Kong's currency to the US dollar so rigidly, and there is still periodic doubt as to whether the "peg" should remain. The HK dollar is now worth considerably less than the Chinese renminbi, which floats against a basket of currencies and which has increased on an almost daily basis since 2008. The renminbi has already become Asia's regional currency and has aspirations to global reserve currency status.

The peg still exists, but is coming under increasing pressure as the US economy continues to battle with an almighty debt burden and other economic issues. On the other hand, the US dollar's relatively weakness over recent years has made Hong Kong's currency more competitive.

## Further reasons for economic success

The global economic crisis meant Hong Kong's economy shrank by 2.5 percent in 2009 but it has achieved modest growth every year since and, overall, has increased by more than two-thirds since 1997. The government is quick to point out it likes to keep business people happy,

*Casino gambling is only allowed offshore in Hong Kong, but is hugely important in Macau.*

with its low and simple tax regime: profits tax is capped at 16.5 percent, and salaries tax at 17 percent. There is no capital gains tax, estate duty, VAT and sales tax.

The government's long-standing policy of minimum interference and maximum support for business has been a key factor in its prosperity. A sound legal and financial framework, a convertible and secure currency, a highly efficient network of transport and communication, a skilled workforce, the enterprising spirit of locals, a high degree of internationalisation and cultural openness all help, too. Hong Kong's financial markets have a high degree of liquidity and transparent regulations; the founding of the Independent Commission Against Corruption (ICAC) in 1974 effectively stamped out a serious corruption problem that was stifling growth, and has been of enormous benefit to Hong Kong (though it is still kept busy). There are few places in the world where it is easier to set up and register a business. On the other hand, local companies are increasingly competing with mainland companies, as the pool of skilled labour begins to extend into China.

For the moment, Hong Kong's position as gateway to China seems assured, but financial commentators suggest it may be overtaken by Shanghai, which is tipped to become one of the world's top three centres of commerce within the next 20 years.

## STOCK MARKET GAMBLING

Hong Kong's Hang Seng Index, which tracks the value of stocks and shares on the Hong Kong stock market, was set up in 1969 and is considered the key indicator of the SAR's economic health. Unsurprisingly for a place so obsessed with money, it appears, prominently, everywhere in the city: on gigantic screens in Central, in taxi cabs and outer-island ferries, in elevators, hotel lobbies and shopping centres. The financial crisis hit the stock market hard and, by the end of 2016, is was still around 5,000 points below the high it hit in October 2007.

Hong Kong's other form of gambling involves horses (see page 126), the "Mark 6" lottery and, of course, those frequent trips to Macau.

# MODERN ARCHITECTURE

**Few of the world's cities confront the visitor with their architecture as dramatically as Hong Kong, with its constantly shifting skyline.**

Hong Kong is a city that likes to flaunt its wealth, and nowhere is this more apparent than in its architecture. The acute scarcity of land, particularly on the dense urban strip of Hong Kong Island, and consequent high prices, have pushed buildings ever higher into the polluted skies. In fact there are more tall structures (over 13 storeys) here than anywhere else on the planet. Showpiece buildings vie for the prime spot and the most eye-catching design, augmented by gaudy night-time light displays.

This being Hong Kong, nothing stays still for long. At one time St John's Cathedral was the tallest building. In the early 1960s, the Mandarin Oriental Hotel took over the mantle, to be usurped by Jardine House (1973), the Hopewell Centre (1980), the Bank of China (1990), Central Plaza (1992), IFC2 (2003), and, the current incumbent, Kowloon's ICC Tower (2010).

But height isn't everything. With money to play with, architects have been able to produce some truly exciting designs. Prime examples are Norman Foster's widely admired HSBC Hongkong Headquarters, the Convention and Exhibition Centre and I.M. Pei's elegant Bank of China Tower.

*Government headquarters in Hong Kong.*

*The Lippo Centre, modern architecture in Admiralty.*

*The Convention and Exhibition Centre was extended, at great expense, for the handover ceremony in 1997. The result is unusual and spectacular.*

Hong Kong Island's constantly evolving skyline never fails to captivate, with the glass and steel towers framed against the forested backdrop of Victoria Peak.

Crowded living in Sham Shui Po.

## HIGH DEMAND, HIGH PRICES

*Bamboo scaffolding is used by Hong Kong's building trade.*

**The construction industry is big business in Hong Kong, and the government draws much of its revenue from the sale of land (income taxes are low). With supply exhausted and demand as high as ever, land has to be reclaimed from the sea, with construction companies willing to fork out staggering sums for the right to build on the new plots.**

**In contrast to the high-tech buildings themselves, the giant webs of scaffolding used in their construction are made entirely of bamboo. Extremely strong and durable, bamboo goes up four times faster than steel – no nails or screws are used – and withstands typhoons better. There are around 250 experienced bamboo scaffolders in Hong Kong, who clamber about barefoot hundreds of feet above the streets. Few use proper safety equipment, however, and there are several deaths each year.**

**Hong Kong Island has long held a monopoly on super-tall glass-and-steel towers, but Kowloon is catching up. With the end of height restrictions following the closure of Kai Tak Airport, development is rapid – and the ICC Tower (on the West Kowloon reclamation; see page 149) took over from IFC2 in 2010 as the tallest building in town. The New Territories are also getting in on the act, with the 319-metre (1,046-ft) Nina Tower at Tsuen Wan.**

*The Cultural Centre on the Tsim Sha Tsui waterfront. Oddly, there are no windows through which to admire the view across the harbour.*

*Posing for a picture by Kowloon's Avenue of Stars.*

AVENUE OF STARS
PROD.
SCENE
TAKE
DIRECTOR
DATE

*Chi Lin Nunnery temple complex, New Kowloon.*

*Fruit and vegetable market in Yau Ma Tei.*

# PLACES

## A detailed guide to Hong Kong, Macau, Shenzhen and Guangzhou, with principal sights clearly cross-referenced by number to the maps.

Today's Hong Kong can be divided into four parts: Hong Kong Island, the Kowloon peninsula, the New Territories and the numerous outlying islands. Hong Kong Island is 75 sq km (29 sq miles) of topsy-turvy real estate. The earliest British settlements were established here; it is now dominated by great banks, enormous futuristic buildings, opulent hotels, splendid residences on the Peak, surprisingly restful beaches and the territory's oldest Chinese communities. Across the Harbour – by the Mass Transit Railway, Star Ferry or via one of three tunnels – is Kowloon, with its millions of people packed into just a few square kilometres. Tsim Sha Tsui, the site of many hotels, bars and shops, is changing as fast as anywhere in Hong Kong, with massive developments above and below ground.

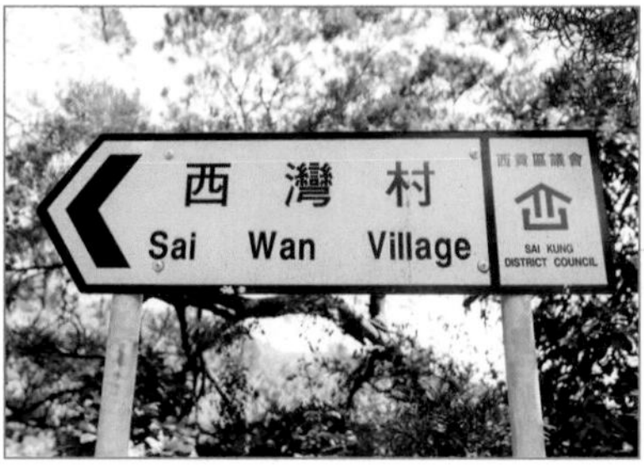


*Signpost to Sai Wan Village.*

Beyond the mountains which ring Kowloon to the north lie the anachronistically named New Territories, leased by the British for 99 years and handed back to China, together with the rest of Hong Kong, in 1997. A mix of empty hillsides, bucolic landscapes and bustling developments, it's a very different side of the SAR. Even more remote are the 230-plus outlying islands, some of which have remained uninhabited and unaltered since the day the Union flag was first planted and some, like Lantau, which have been radically redesigned to accommodate airports, theme parks and much else besides. To the west across the silt-laden waters of the Pearl River mouth is the former Portuguese enclave of Macau, now firmly established as the world's leading gambling destination. Across the border, the Pearl River Delta, anchored by the ever-expanding cities of Shenzhen and Guangzhou, is one of Asia's great economic powerhouses.

*Local signage.*

# Hong Kong

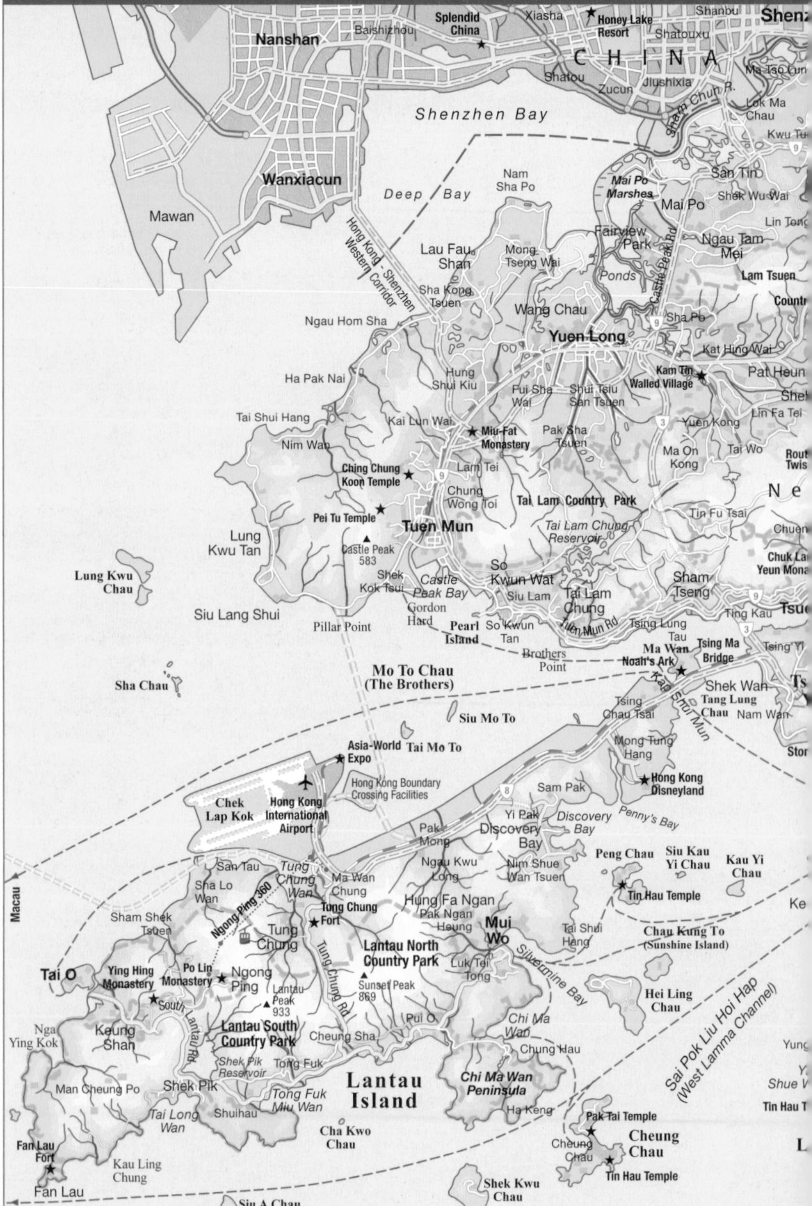

Splendid China
Xiasha
Honey Lake Resort
Shanbu
Nanshan
Baishizhou
Shatouxu
CHINA
Shatou
Zucun
Jiushixia
Shenzhen Bay
Sham Chun R.
Lok Ma Chau
San Tin
Wanxiacun
Deep Bay
Nam Sha Po
Mai Po Marshes
Mai Po
Shek Wu Wai
Mawan
Hong Kong - Shenzhen Western Corridor
Fairview Park
Ngau Tam Mei
Lin Tong
Lau Fau Shan
Mong Tseng Wai
Ponds
Castle Peak Rd
Lam Tsuen
Sha Kong Tsuen
Wang Chau
Sha Po
Ngau Hom Sha
Yuen Long
Kat Hing Wai
Ha Pak Nai
Hung Shui Kiu
Kam Tin Walled Village
Pat Heung
Fui Sha Wai
Shui Tsiu San Tsuen
Lin Fa Tei
Tai Shui Hang
Kai Lun Wai
Miu-Fat Monastery
Pak Sha Tsuen
Yuen Kong
Nim Wan
Ma On Kong
Tai Wo
Ching Chung Koon Temple
Lam Tei
Chung Wong Toi
Tai Lam Country Park
Pei Tu Temple
Tuen Mun
Tin Fu Tsai
Tai Lam Chung Reservoir
Lung Kwu Tan
Castle Peak 583
Lung Kwu Chau
Shek Kok Tsui
Castle Peak Bay
So Kwun Wat
Siu Lam
Tai Lam Chung
Sham Tseng
Siu Lang Shui
Gordon Hard
Pillar Point
Pearl Island
So Kwun Tan
Tuen Mun Rd
Tsing Lung Tau
Ting Kau
Brothers Point
Ma Wan
Noah's Ark
Tsing Ma Bridge
Mo To Chau (The Brothers)
Sha Chau
Kap Shui Mun
Shek Wan
Tang Lung Chau
Nam Wan
Tsing Chau Tsai
Siu Mo To
Asia-World Expo
Tai Mo To
Mong Tung Hang
Hong Kong Boundary Crossing Facilities
Sam Pak
Hong Kong Disneyland
Chek Lap Kok
Hong Kong International Airport
Yi Pak
Discovery Bay
Penny's Bay
Pak Mong
San Tau
Tung Chung Wan
Ngau Kwu Long
Nim Shue Wan Tsuen
Peng Chau
Siu Kau Yi Chau
Kau Yi Chau
Sha Lo Wan
Ma Wan Chung
Macau
Tin Hau Temple
Ngong Ping 360
Tung Chung Fort
Hung Fa Ngan
Pak Ngan Heung
Sham Shek Tsuen
Mui Wo
Tai Shui Hang
Chau Kung To (Sunshine Island)
Tung Chung
Lantau North Country Park
Tung Chung Rd
Tai O
Ying Hing Monastery
Po Lin Monastery
Ngong Ping
Luk Tei Tong
Silvermine Bay
Hei Ling Chau
Lantau Peak 933
Sunset Peak 869
South Lantau Rd
Pui O
Chi Ma Wan
Sai Pok Liu Hoi Hap (West Lamma Channel)
Nga Ying Kok
Keung Shan
Lantau South Country Park
Cheung Sha
Chung Hau
Shek Pik Reservoir
Tong Fuk
Lantau Island
Chi Ma Wan Peninsula
Man Cheung Po
Shek Pik
Tong Fuk Miu Wan
Tai Long Wan
Shuihau
Ha Keng
Pak Tai Temple
Cha Kwo Chau
Cheung Chau
Fan Lau Fort
Kau Ling Chung
Tin Hau Temple
Fan Lau
Shek Kwu Chau
Macau
Siu A Chau
Soko Islands
Tai A Chau

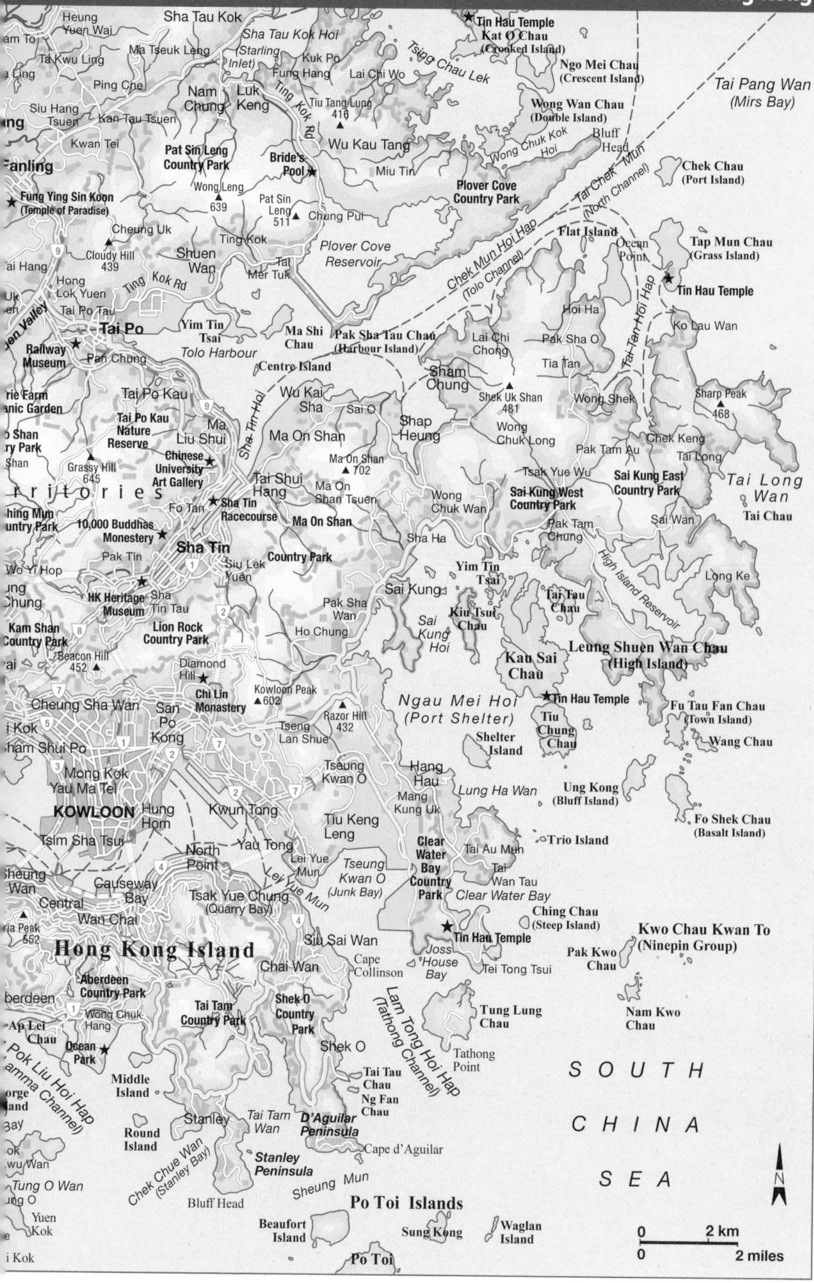
Sha Tau Kok
Heung Yuen Wai
Ta Kwu Ling
Ma Tseuk Leng
Sha Tau Kok Hoi (Starling Inlet)
Kuk Po
Fung Hang
Lai Chi Wo
Tsing Chau Lek
Tin Hau Temple
Kat O Chau (Crooked Island)
Ngo Mei Chau (Crescent Island)
Tai Pang Wan (Mirs Bay)
Ping Che
Nam Chung
Luk Keng
Ting Kok Rd
Tiu Tang Lung 416
Siu Hang Tsuen
Kan Tau Tsuen
Wong Wan Chau (Double Island)
Kwan Tei
Wu Kau Tang
Wong Chuk Kok Hoi
Bluff Head
Fanling
Pat Sin Leng Country Park
Bride's Pool
Miu Tin
Chek Chau (Port Island)
Tai Chek Mun (North Channel)
Fung Ying Sin Koon (Temple of Paradise)
Wong Leng 639
Pat Sin Leng 511
Chung Pui
Plover Cove Country Park
Cheung Uk
Ting Kok
Plover Cove Reservoir
Flat Island
Ocean Point
Tap Mun Chau (Grass Island)
Cloudy Hill 439
Shuen Wan
Tai Mei Tuk
Chek Mun Hoi Hap (Tolo Channel)
Tin Hau Temple
Hong Lok Yuen
Ting Kok Rd
Tai Po Tau
Tai Po
Yim Tin Tsai
Ma Shi Chau
Pak Sha Tau Chau (Harbour Island)
Lai Chi Chong
Hoi Ha
Tai Tan Hoi Hap
Ko Lau Wan
Railway Museum
Pan Chung
Tolo Harbour
Centre Island
Pak Sha O
Sham Chung
Tia Tan
Tai Po Kau
Wu Kai Sha
Sai O
Shek Uk Shan 481
Wong Shek
Sharp Peak 468
Tai Po Kau Nature Reserve
Ma Liu Shui
Sha Tin Hoi
Ma On Shan
Shap Heung
Wong Chuk Long
Chek Keng
Pak Tam Au
Tai Long
Chinese University Art Gallery
Grassy Hill 645
Ma On Shan 702
Tsak Yue Wu
Sai Kung East Country Park
Tai Long Wan
Tai Chau
Tai Shui Hang
Ma On Shan Tsuen
Wong Chuk Wan
Sai Kung West Country Park
New Territories
Fo Tan
Sha Tin Racecourse
Ma On Shan
Sai Wan
10,000 Buddhas Monestery
Pak Tam Chung
Sha Tin
Sha Ha
High Island Reservoir
Pak Tin
Siu Lek Yuen
Country Park
Wo Yi Hop
Yim Tin Tsai
Long Ke
HK Heritage Museum
Sha Tin Tau
Sai Kung
Kiu Tsui Chau
Tai Tau Chau
Pak Sha Wan
Sai Kung Hoi
Kam Shan Country Park
Lion Rock Country Park
Ho Chung
Leung Shuen Wan Chau (High Island)
Kau Sai Chau
Beacon Hill 452
Diamond Hill
Chi Lin Monastery
Kowloon Peak 602
Razor Hill 432
Ngau Mei Hoi (Port Shelter)
Tin Hau Temple
Fu Tau Fan Chau (Town Island)
Cheung Sha Wan
San Po Kong
Tseng Lan Shue
Tiu Chung Chau
Shelter Island
Wang Chau
Sham Shui Po
Mong Kok
Yau Ma Tei
Tseung Kwan O
Hang Hau
Mang Kung Uk
Lung Ha Wan
Ung Kong (Bluff Island)
KOWLOON
Hung Hom
Kwun Tong
Tiu Keng Leng
Fo Shek Chau (Basalt Island)
Tsim Sha Tsui
Yau Tong
Clear Water Bay Country Park
Trio Island
North Point
Lei Yue Mun
Tai Au Mun
Sheung Wan
Causeway Bay
Tseung Kwan O (Junk Bay)
Tai Wan Tau
Central
Tsak Yue Chung (Quarry Bay)
Clear Water Bay
Ching Chau (Steep Island)
Wan Chai
Victoria Peak 552
Hong Kong Island
Siu Sai Wan
Tin Hau Temple
Kwo Chau Kwan To (Ninepin Group)
Pak Kwo Chau
Chai Wan
Cape Collinson
Joss House Bay
Tei Tong Tsui
Aberdeen Country Park
Aberdeen
Tai Tam Country Park
Shek O Country Park
Lam Tong Hoi Hap (Tathong Channel)
Wong Chuk Hang
Tung Lung Chau
Nam Kwo Chau
Ap Lei Chau
Ocean Park
Shek O
Tathong Point
Pok Liu Hoi Hap (Lamma Channel)
Middle Island
Tai Tau Chau
Ng Fan Chau
SOUTH CHINA SEA
Stanley
Tai Tam Wan
D'Aguilar Peninsula
Round Island
Cape d'Aguilar
Chek Chue Wan (Stanley Bay)
Stanley Peninsula
Tung O Wan
Sheung Mun
Bluff Head
Po Toi Islands
N
Yuen Kok
Beaufort Island
Sung Kong
Waglan Island
0 2 km
0 2 miles
Po Toi

*The Central-Mid-Levels escalator is an extensive system of outdoor covered escalators.*

# CENTRAL, WESTERN AND THE PEAK

**With its mass of skyscrapers, the world of business and finance dominates Central District. In contrast, the traditional Chinese way of life still thrives in neighbouring Western District. Gaze down at it all from the rarefied heights of Victoria Peak.**

Central District – Chung Wan in Cantonese – is Hong Kong's business and financial hub, at the heart of the incredible cliff-face of high-rise buildings that extends along the north shore of Hong Kong Island. Wedged between the harbour and the precipitous slopes of Victoria Peak, this is where the money is: the financial powerhouses and glamorous high-end shopping malls, overlooked by the multi-millionaires' mansions up on The Peak.

To the west, Sheung Wan and Western District retain more elements of Hong Kong's past; this was the area that the British established as Victoria City in the 1840s, and from here the city has expanded and grown in every direction, including upwards. It all adds up to one of the most fascinating areas of modern Hong Kong.

Yet, like the rest of Hong Kong, there are few conventional tourist sights here: despite the efforts of the tourist board to highlight the past with such innovations as the Sun Yat-sen Trail, most of the "landmarks" en route are simply plaques recording some building or other that has long since disappeared. Instead, the fascination is in the contemporary, the everyday life of the place, the drama of the architecture, the amazing contrasts of scale and the sheer energy that emanates from the crowded streets.

And although most of the pedestrians on Central's streets are attired for business, and giant video screens flash the latest news and financial figures from around the world to passers-by, there are still strong elements of former days, with wayside hawkers selling novelties and knock-offs,

**Main Attractions**

Star Ferries
HSBC Building
Bank of China Tower
Lan Kwai Fong
SoHo
Man Mo Temple
The Peak Tram
The Peak (walks and views)

**Map**

Pages 98, 114

*From left to right is the Bank of China, the HSBC Building and the Old Supreme Court Building.*

*The Star Ferry is a quick and cheap way to travel between Hong Kong Island and Kowloon and provides scenic views over the harbour.*

incense sticks smouldering by tiny shrines, and delivery boys serenely pedalling through red lights with a cargo of fresh meat balanced in their bike's cast-iron basket.

## THE FINANCIAL CENTRE

The **Central Ferry Pier ❶**, the terminal for the Star Ferry on Hong Kong Island, is as good a place as any to begin exploring Central. With reclamation continually narrowing the harbour, the Star Ferry now occupies a site next door to the outlying islands' ferry piers. It features Edwardian-style embellishments and is more user-friendly than its 1950s predecessor, Edinburgh Place, which sparked protests by conservationists when it was demolished in 2007. Having seen many such upheavals since its formation in the 19th century, the Star Ferry Company was more philosophical about the move. (For more on the Star Ferry, see page 116.)

The beautifully presented **Hong Kong Maritime Museum** (www.hkmaritimemuseum.org; Mon–Fri 9.30am–5.30pm, Sat–Sun 10am–7pm) traces Hong Kong's long connection with the sea. The museum is laid out over three floors of Central Ferry Pier 8, with the more than a dozen galleries including a look at historic trade and sea routes with both China and the West and an immersive sense of a sailor's life at sea. It makes for a great introduction to the role of shipping in Hong Kong's historic development and contemporary prosperity.

The prosaically named **International Finance Centre (ifc) ❷**, a combination of smart shopping mall and offices, sits atop the Airport Express Central terminal. Just to the north in front of the ferry piers, and part of the same complex, is the **International Finance Centre Two (Two ifc) ❸**. It stands at 415 metres (1,362ft),

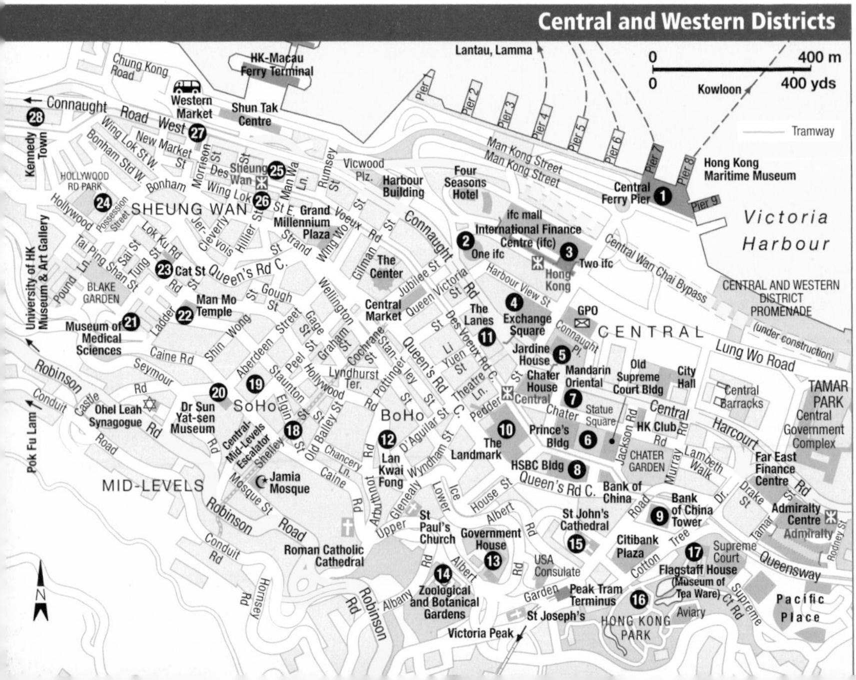

which makes it currently the 26th-tallest building in the world (fully 34 metres/112ft higher than the Empire State Building), and is capped by a mass of curving spires. When it was finished in 2003, IFC2 became the tallest of Hong Kong's 7,500-odd high-rise buildings, but in 2010 that title passed to the International Commerce Centre (ICC) across the harbour in West Kowloon (see page 140). Unfortunately there is no public access to the upper floors as they are leased by the Hong Kong Monetary Authority. The authority does open up to the public on the 55th floor with the HKMA Information Centre (Mon–Fri 10am–6pm, Sat 10am–1pm; free) where there are several interesting exhibits on Hong Kong's financial history as well as outstanding views over Central. Lower down, on the fifth floor, there is a pleasant outside terrace with bars and restaurants above the Lane Crawford department store. The tower block on the west side of the IFC houses the super-luxury **Four Seasons Hotel**.

Walkways connect the IFC to the rest of Central via **Exchange Square ❹**, home of the Hong Kong Stock Exchange.

Head east along the walkway to **Jardine House ❺**, whose distinctive 1,700-plus round windows have inspired the nickname "House of a Thousand Orifices". Opened in 1973 (when it was known as the Connaught Centre), it was for many years the tallest building in Hong Kong. Just behind is the **General Post Office** (GPO), and beyond that City Hall, which lost its waterfront position in 2008 when the (supposed) final part of the Central Wan Chai reclamation was built.

It's possible to get a good overview of all the current reclamation and proposals at the **City Gallery** (www.citygallery.gov.hk; daily 10am–6pm; English guided tour on Sun and public holidays at 4.30pm)

*The General Post Office in Central.*

*Taxis surrounded by pedestrian walkways.*

**TIP**

To get the most out of a walking tour of Central, visit on a weekday during working hours, as (Lan Kwai Fong/SoHo apart) this is not one of Hong Kong's after-hours locations – unlike Tsim Sha Tsui and Causeway Bay, many shops close by 7pm. Shops are open on Saturdays, but the energised atmosphere of the working week is lacking. Sundays are quiet, with shops shut, although the weekly Filipina get-together is in full swing.

on Edinburgh Place. This four-floor exhibition has a number of creatively designed and highly interactive exhibitions on major engineering projects of the past, present and future. The adjacent **City Hall** not only houses administrative offices, but a concert hall, theatre, marriage registry and three restaurants, including the popular Maxim's Palace (for dim sum).

## East to Statue Square

Between City Hall and the GPO, an underpass will take you to **Statue Square** 6 and Chater Road. On Sundays, throngs of Filipina maids gather here on their day off in a festive outdoor party. The 184,000 Philippine nationals, most of whom work here as maids, are the joint-largest foreign community living in Hong Kong – nearly double the number of British and American passport-holders, who total around 93,000 in all. The 2016 census revealed just over 150,000 Indonesian residents, who have a similar Sunday habit but tend to meet up in Causeway Bay's Victoria Park.

Statue Square was once graced with a statue of Queen Victoria, long transplanted to Causeway Bay, and replaced by a statue of Sir Thomas Jackson, an Irishman who managed the Hongkong and Shanghai Banking Corporation for 30 years around the end of the 19th century. Chinese and expatriate victims of World Wars I and II are commemorated at the Cenotaph, and Hong Kong's war veterans gather here on Remembrance Day every November.

The **Mandarin Oriental** 7 is one of the oldest and grandest hotels in Hong Kong. It's unusual to mention the Mandarin without the accompanying adjective "venerable", and at four decades old it's something of a treasure. Hong Kong's tallest building when it opened in 1963, the hotel had a US$140 million facelift in 2006 to keep up with the new wave of rivals.

This part of Central District is the financial hub of Hong Kong, home to the HQ of several major banks. Facing Statue Square is Norman Foster's striking US$1 billion **HSBC Building** 8, once the most

*Hong Kong Island's skyline including the Mandarin Oriental Hotel.*

expensive building in the world. It was completed in 1985, shortly after it was agreed that Hong Kong would be handed back to China in 1997, and built in such a way that it could have been dismantled and shipped to Singapore had things gone awry. A short way along Des Voeux Road, is the Cheung Kong Center, its dull 1999 design prompting the nickname the "box the Bank of China came in". With feng shui concerns to the fore, the height of 283 metres (927ft) is said to have been determined by drawing a line between the Bank of China and the HSBC Building. Asia's richest man, Li Ka-Shing is Cheung Kong's CEO and has offices on the top floor between the financial giants.

The dramatic 368-metre (1,209ft) **Bank of China Tower** ❾, designed by the American-Chinese architect I.M. Pei, is one of Hong Kong's most famous buildings. Opened in 1990, its bold design and sharp angles make "cutting-edge" an unusually apt description – and these angles, pointing directly at other financial institutions, are blamed for channelling bad feng shui to them (see page 74). Behind it is Citibank Plaza, another ultra-modern tower.

## Old Supreme Court Building

East of Statue Square is the colonial-style former Supreme Court Building and one-time home of Hong Kong's governing body, the Legislative Council (Legco). Built in 1912, it is topped by a statue of the Greek goddess Themis, and its Edwardian dome shows up brilliantly against the Bank of China Tower. The building was used as a torture chamber by Japanese police during World War II, and wartime shrapnel damage can still be seen on the eastern wall. History came full circle in 2015 when the building – closed since Legco moved out in 2011 – re-opened as the Court of Final Appeal. Across Jackson Road, **Chater Garden** is a rare open space that may host demonstrators, dancing off-duty maids or munching office workers on their lunch break. Until the 1970s, the site was occupied by the Hong Kong Cricket Club. The

*Designer stores on Des Voeux Road.*

verandah at the northern edge of the garden is a great place to view some of Central's iconic skyscrapers.

## Inland to Des Voeux and Queen's roads

Heading inland from the GPO, pedestrian thoroughfares take you over Connaught Road Central to **Des Voeux Road**, named after Sir George William Des Voeux, governor from 1887 to 1891. The tram stop here, at the junction with Pedder Street, is a blur of traffic on weekdays. Parallel to Des Voeux, **Queen's Road Central** was the area's original "Main Street" – until a little footpath was turned into Des Voeux Road, which eventually upstaged it. These days both are very busy, although Queen's Road has more in the way of shops.

## Shopping lanes and malls

Some of the side streets connecting Queen's and Des Voeux roads are well worth exploring. On **Pedder Street**, Shanghai Tang is one of Hong Kong's most successful homegrown fashion stores. British-Chinese entrepreneur David Tang, who first brought the territory the exclusive China Club, then Cuban cigars, turned his attention to making Chinese fashion chic. Across the street **The Landmark** ⓾ is a prestigious shopping mall with enormous stand-alone shops dedicated to luxury brands, a four-floor Harvey Nichols department store and The Landmark Mandarin Oriental hotel. Five floors surround a vast 6,000-sq metre (20,000-sq ft) atrium. Walkways connect the floors around the atrium with neighbouring buildings: **Chater House**, which has more than half a dozen Georgio Armani shops and an Armani bar; and **Prince's Building**, with a further abundance of marble and upmarket shops.

By way of contrast, **Li Yuen Street East** and **Li Yuen Street West**, generally known collectively as **The Lanes** ⑪, are narrow alleyways lined with stalls and shops that sell clothing, fabrics and counterfeit designer fashion accessories. Bargaining is still expected, and the atmosphere is completely different from that of the surrounding shops and malls.

*The Landmark shopping mall.*

## Party central

Behind Queen's Road Central, which was the waterfront road before land reclamation began in the 1850s, the terrain rises steeply. D'Aguilar Street leads up to the nightlife centre of **Lan Kwai Fong ⓬**, which together with nearby Wyndham Street and SoHo (see page 106), is the prime partying area for Hong Kong's young and trendy. Modern cuisine, funky bars, clubs, English pubs and tiny snack shops generate dollars and hangovers in equal measure, and late-night revellers can get everything from pizza to sushi in the wee hours. At weekends many bars stay open until 5am.

## Colonial relics

At the top of Lan Kwai Fong, **Wyndham Street** marks a boundary of the commercial and residential areas. Uphill from here are the tower blocks of the Mid-Levels, with desirable and expensive apartments.

Glenealy (one of the few streets in Hong Kong without a suffix) snakes steeply uphill and eastward onto Upper Albert Road and **Government House ⓭**, the grand home of the former colonial leaders of Hong Kong. After a spell as a state guesthouse during the Tung Chee-hwa administration, it is now the official residence of the Chief Executive of the HKSAR. The mansion dates from the 1850s but was remodelled by the Japanese during World War II, who added a tower with a vague Shinto look. There is a clear view of the building through the wrought-iron gates, which are opened to the public only a couple of times a year, usually in spring and autumn (no set dates).

The surrounding area is one of the few remaining parts of Hong Kong that retains a genuinely colonial feel. If you go any further up, the pocket of exotic greenery is quickly invaded by the high-rises of the Mid-Levels; lower down, the area is engulfed by banks and office towers.

Opposite Government House are the **Zoological and Botanical Gardens ⓮** (www.lcsd.gov.hk/en/parks/hkzbg; open daily 6am–7pm; free), a lush tropical retreat worthy of exploration. The small zoo

*St John's Cathedral, the city's oldest Anglican church.*

houses a variety of exotic wildlife, including an impressive collection of red-cheeked gibbons. It opened in 1864 and still retains elements of its original Victorian gentility, with added Eastern spirituality courtesy of the elderly Chinese who practice t'ai chi here.

### St John's Cathedral

Tucked away opposite the Citibank Plaza on Battery Path Road, and just below Government House, the Victorian Gothic **St John's Cathedral** ⓯ was consecrated in 1849 and is the city's oldest Anglican church. Note that Battery Path itself is a pleasant walk, beginning at the HSBC Building and leading past the cathedral to Hong Kong Park. The attractive red-brick **French Mission Building**, behind the Cheung Kong Center, is also more than 150 years old.

## Hong Kong Park

Follow Battery Path to the east of the cathedral along the footbridge to Citibank Plaza to reach the lush, green expanse of **Hong Kong Park** ⓰ (www.lcsd.gov.hk/en/parks/hkp; daily 6am–11pm; free). As Central's only large open space, it is busy all day long, with t'ai chi practitioners first thing in the morning, joggers and office workers, and bridal parties posing against a backdrop of waterfalls and shrubs. The aviary (daily 9am–5pm) is home to over 90

*Shoppers at Graham Street market.*

*SoHo has many boutique stores including art galleries, jewellery stores and clothes shops.*

### WALKING IN CENTRAL

Central's streets are clogged with pedestrians and traffic year round and are more easily navigated via the network of elevated walkways. These run from the GPO (first floor) past Exchange Square and the IFC to the Macau Ferry Terminal, and via Chater House and adjacent buildings as far as the bottom of Lan Kwai Fong. Numerous security guards en route are very obliging with directions. It the hottest months, it is quite an experience to use these walkways – moving between wilting heat and humidity and icy air-conditioning as the passage passes through malls and office blocks. The contrast is heightened by the decibel level, which oscillates between piped music in the malls and a piledriver din on the streets.

different species of birds from the rainforests of Southeast Asia, including various barbets, shamas, fairy bluebirds and bulbuls. Walk through a giant mesh up to 30 metres (100ft) high on a one-way elevated wooden walkway (enter near the Kennedy Road entrance).

The park is also home to one of Hong Kong's best examples of bespoke architecture – **Flagstaff House**, home to the **Museum of Tea Ware** ⓱ (tel: 2869 0690; Wed–Mon 10am–6pm; free). The building – of more interest than the museum – was completed in 1846 and is reputedly the SAR's oldest surviving colonial structure. It once functioned as the residence of the commander-in-chief of the British forces, when the area was Victoria Barracks.

## AROUND THE ESCALATOR AND SOHO

The character of Central begins to change as one walks westwards along Queen's Road Central away from the banks, shiny malls and shops and into an older, Chinese neighbourhood. The unique **Mid-Levels Escalator** ⓲ runs through the heart of this transitional zone between Central and Western District, which in recent years has become a lively nightlife centre.

The remarkable escalator itself was completed in 1993, at a cost of HK$245 million. Comprising 20 separate sections and running to 800 metres (2,625ft), it is the world's longest outdoor escalator system. It was built partly to ease traffic congestion in the narrow streets below, but the most significant effect has been to revive the areas alongside it. Around 54,000 pedestrians use it each day, double the original estimate.

The escalator starts at 100 Queen's Road Central, emerging from the largely vacant Central Market building to ascend the steep hillside, passing above Cochrane Street, across Hollywood Road to Shelley Street and then on to Conduit Road, up in the Mid-Levels. From early morning to sunset, canny shoppers pack Gage Street where stalls selling fresh meat, live fish and more line the street in front of noodle shops,

*Friends gather by the entrance of Hollywood Road Park.*

*The Central–Mid-Levels escalator.*

roast meat shops and hardware emporiums. It's worth descending to ground level on Graham Street to witness the market stalls displaying an astounding array of fresh fruit, vegetables and herbs.

Walk back up the hill to rejoin the escalator at Hollywood Road, famous for its antiques shops (see page 108).

## SoHo ⓳

Before the escalator was built, the area to the southwest of this part of Hollywood Road – Staunton, Shelley and Elgin streets – was rather run-down and seldom visited by outsiders. Now, as the hub of a nightlife area that has become known as SoHo (SOuth of HOllywood Road), these narrow streets are home to over 100 cafés, restaurants and bars, offering an ever-changing mix of venues with cuisines from all over the world, plus boutiques selling young designers' clothes, jewellery and trendy gifts.

With the escalator providing easy access for people from the financial and business district, and the upmarket Mid-Levels residential area, SoHo is busy every night of the week and an easy place for the out-of-town visitor to feel comfortable and not be tagged as a tourist. Its cosmopolitan vibe and eateries have now spread in all directions in the streets near the escalator. Restaurateurs are also setting up shop in Gough Street as well as along Peel, Cochrane and Aberdeen streets. This area is sometimes called NoHo, because it lies to the north of Hollywood Road.

**Old Bailey Street** has a typically SoHo eclectic mix of outlets that includes Hong Kong's New Age Shop and overlooks the now closed Victoria Prison. The prison is part of a complex that includes **Central Police Station** and Hong Kong Magistracy, built in stages between 1841 and 1925. The attractive old complex has been redeveloped to restore the 16 original heritage buildings and to add two new ones. It now houses the **Tai Kwun Centre for Heritage and Arts** (www.taikwun.hk; daily 11am–11pm), opened in 2018, a space dedicated to excellent contemporary art exhibitions, performing arts shows and community history.

*Colourful Man Mo Temple.*

*Cat Street market.*

Below the former Central Police Station, **Wyndham Street**, which connects with Hollywood Road, is also lined with restaurants, with a few art galleries interspersed. It connects neatly with the bijou SoHo bistros with the boisterous Lan Kwai Fong nightlife area.

## Above SoHo

Uphill from SoHo, between Caine Road and Conduit Road, the only site of note among the apartment towers is the Jamia Masjid, which was first built in 1890 and is Hong Kong's oldest mosque.

If you exit the escalator at Caine Road and walk for five minutes you will discover the Dr Sun Yat-sen Museum and – a few minutes' walk further along – the Museum of Medical Sciences.

## Dr Sun Yat-sen Museum

**Address:** 7 Castle Road, Central
**Tel:** 2367 6373
**Opening Hrs:** Mon–Wed & Fri 10am–6pm, Sat–Sun 10am–7pm
**Entrance fee:** charge, but free on Wed
**Transport:** MTR Central

Housed in a beautifully preserved mansion built in 1914, the **Dr Sun Yat-sen Museum** ⓴ tells the story of the Father of Modern China, and his time as a medical student in Hong Kong, exploring the colony's role in shaping his ideas about the modernisation of China – which led to

*Dining al fresco on Hollywood Road.*

revolution. While Sun never set foot in the hall, it is a useful starting point for painting a picture of the places along the **Sun Yat-sen Historical Trail**, which guides visitors through 12 significant sites in the Central and Western districts.

## Museum of Medical Sciences

The Old Pathological Institute, built in 1906 to step up the fight against the plague and infectious diseases in Hong Kong, is today home to the **Museum of Medical Sciences** ㉑ (www.hkmms.org.hk; Tue–Sat 10am–5pm, Sun 1–5pm). The small galleries include a reconstruction of an early 20th-century pharmacy, an autopsy room, and the contrasts between Western and Chinese medicine. A chance to take a break in its small Chinese herbal medicine garden warrants a detour on the way down Caine Road or up from Hollywood Road.

## Hollywood Road to Western

West of the escalator, Hollywood Road itself is well known for its abundance of shops selling all manner of Chinese (and other Asian) antiques, notably furniture, art and ornaments. Prices can be quite high, and – as always – it's best to shop around and look out for the logo of the HKTB's Quality Tourism Services Scheme (QTS; see page 153).

*Lan Kwai Fong, a popular nightlife area where many bars stay open until the not-so-early hours of the morning.*

## Man Mo Temple

**Address:** 124–126 Hollywood Road, Central
**Tel:** 2540 0350
**Opening Hrs:** daily 8am–6pm

*Dried food on sale at Queen's Road West.*

*Street vendors sell their wares on Hollywood Road.*

**Entrance fee:** free
**Transport:** MTR Sheung Wan
Follow Hollywood Road west to the corner of Ladder Street and the wonderfully dark and atmospheric **Man Mo Temple** ㉒, built around 1842 on what must have been a little dirt track at that time. Tourists regularly throng through Man Mo, but this doesn't inhibit the temple's regular worshippers from visiting to fill the temple with thick clouds of smoke from their joss sticks. The immense incense spirals hanging from the ceiling can burn for weeks.

Man is the god of civil servants and of literature. For most of imperial China's history, civil servants – or Mandarins – formed the best-educated and most high-status social group. Mo is the god of martial arts and war, and is more popularly known by his worshippers as Kuan Ti or Kuan Kung. Statues of the legendary Eight Immortals stand guard outside the temple; inside, two solid-brass deer (representing longevity) adorn the main chamber. Near the altar, there are two sedan chairs encased in glass. Years ago, when the icons of Man and Mo were paraded through Western on festival days, they were transported on these chairs.

## Ladder Street and Cat Street

These small streets are two of the most quirky of all local

**FACT**

People usually assume that the dark-green forested backdrop to the famous view across Victoria Harbour is "natural". In fact, the hillsides were stripped of their original forest cover over the centuries, and it wasn't until the 1940s and '50s that replanting took place. Early photographs clearly show the absence of trees, altering the scene almost as dramatically as the lack of buildings.

*Shopping at Cat Street market.*

**FACT**

On Hong Kong Island, the higher the altitude, the more desirable the property and the higher the rents – a pattern established in the early colonial years, when the upper slopes were considered less prone to malarial mosquitoes than those closer to sea level. How high up the hill one lives has long been seen as a straightforward measure of status.

thoroughfares. Named for its steepness, **Ladder Street** retains its 19th-century stone steps and zigzags down from Caine Road, past the Museum of Medical Sciences, to Hollywood Road and onto Queen's Road.

Just off this last stretch of Ladder Street, below Hollywood Road, is the street officially called Upper Lascar Row but much more commonly known as **Cat Street** ㉓, so-named because this was once where sellers offloaded stolen goods, or "rat" goods in Cantonese. Customers who chased the rats were known as the "cats". Sellers now trade in legitimate tourist trinkets such as communist memorabilia and jade, though the "antiques" may not always be quite as old as they look. Bargaining is the rule here – whether for a safety pin, a shoelace, or, if you should be so lucky, a Tang-dynasty porcelain horse. The area was once famous for seamen's lodging houses and brothels, and it was a hangout for criminals and low-life characters of all kinds. In nearby Lok Ku Road are the **Cat Street Galleries**, which are devoted to

*The aviary, Hong Kong Park.*

artwork and antique reproductions from all over Asia.

Continue west to **Possession Street** ㉔, so called because it was here that Captain Sir Edward Belcher landed in January 1841 to plant the Union flag and take possession of Hong Kong for Britain. No monument marks the exact spot where the British flag was planted, though a Hong Kong Tourist Board bollard at the junction of Possession Street and Hollywood Road gives a rough approximation. Belcher Street, west of Possession Street, is named after the feted captain of the HMS *Sulphur*.

*Buying traditional Chinese medicine on Queen's Road West.*

## WESTERN DISTRICT

Western District is located just to the west of Central, but is worlds away from the ultra-modern financial district. Ironically, considering its name, this is one of the least Westernised areas of Hong Kong, and provides a rare hint of the old city. The area begins officially at Possession Street and sprawls west to Kennedy Town.

One of Western's charms is that it is packed with shops and merchants trading in traditional goods, tea, rice and ingredients for herbal medicine. Find a Chinese herbalist, with his aromatic concoctions of snake musk, herbs, ginseng and powdered lizards, and you discover part of a pharmacopoeial tradition dating back 4,000 years.

### Sheung Wan

A buffer zone between the steel-and-glass skyscrapers of the financial district, Sheung Wan is the gateway to the more traditional, and residential, districts of Sai Ying Pun and Kennedy Town. Until recently, development here was on a building-by-building basis, so it is not unusual to find modern edifices poking up between older tenement buildings.

Heading inland from the urban expressway of Connaught Road, **Man Wa Lane** ㉕ is lined with the chop-makers who carve elaborate name stamps from blocks of stone. These chops are not only practical instruments (formal documents in both Hong Kong and China require a "chop", used as a signature), but works of ancient Chinese craftsmanship. Watching a Man Wa chop-carver sculpt a customer's name out of a small block of stone, ivory, jade or wood is an interesting experience. There are male and female chop styles: when background material is carved out, the chop is male; when the characters are carved out, it's female. The chop is also important in other Asian countries, particularly Japan.

### The heart of Western

As Queen's Road Central becomes **Queen's Road West**, the architecture becomes more traditional. Look out for the few open-fronted "shophouses", traditional wholesale trading houses and shops that overflow onto the pavements with a unique Hong Kong mix of everything from daily necessities to traditional Chinese medicine, money from the "Bank of Hell" and funerary items to burn at graves and handmade cake moulds and dim sum baskets.

West from Ma Wa Lane are some of the most aromatic streets in Hong Kong. **Wing Lok Street** ㉖, **Bonham Street** and **Des Voeux Road West** are the centre of the Chinese medicine trade in Hong Kong. Shops here specialise in selling herbs, ancient remedies, dried extracts of plants and animal parts. Specialists in delicacies such as bird's nest abound, as do stores selling a pungent range of dried seafood, including abalone, sea cucumber and – more controversially

*Taking a break on the Peak Trail.*

– shark's fin. Hong Kong is a major centre for the world's trade in shark's fin. Once a regional delicacy, eaten occasionally by wealthy Chinese families in a few areas of southern China, shark's fin soup has become extremely popular throughout Greater China as a prestigious treat at banquets. With increasing wealth in the region, many species of shark are facing extinction.

One block inland on **Hillier Street** and **Jervois Street** is a mix of small teashops, cafés, print shops and merchants selling wholesale goods. It is a great neighbourhood to explore on foot, for poking into little alleys and for getting lost in the web of side streets. Look for the tea merchants, noodle specialists, Chinese sweets and preserved nuts, as well as shops selling traditional Chinese pots, pans and bamboo steamers. On the cross-streets, minuscule stalls and workshops can often occupy less than 6 sq metres (20 sq ft) of space.

On Morrison Street, close to the harbour, stands **Western Market** ㉗, a red-brick Edwardian-style structure. It was opened in 1906 and served for more than 80 years as a food market. Recognised as a historical landmark, its elegant architectural features were preserved and restored, and in 1991 it was converted into a shopping complex. It offers a diversity of handicrafts, fabric and souvenir stalls, as well as a Chinese restaurant on the top floor, enlivened by afternoon "tea dances".

From Western Market you can take a walkway across Connaught Road West to the Shun Tak Centre, which houses the Macau Ferry Terminal. Now you are in Western proper: the name of this neighbourhood, **Sai Ying Pun**, means "Western military camp" and is so-named for the British camps which were established here in the 1840s. The steep steps of Centre Street connect Bonham Road with Queen's Road West, and the architecture betrays the historical boundaries. The Chinese were not allowed to live above High Street in the 19th century and the area retains a flavour of an

*A couple on the popular Peak Trail, which offers spectacular views across the harbour.*

## THE PEAK TRAM

Of Hong Kong's many and impressive engineering marvels, the Peak Tram remains one of the most impressive. Rising 396 metres (1,299ft) in just seven minutes, up gradients as steep as 27 degrees (1 in 2), the tram has been hauling human cargo up and down Victoria Peak since 1888, and hasn't had a single accident to date. There are only two cars, a clue that this is not a tram in the conventional sense, but rather a funicular, with the two carriages counter-weighting each other. Each holds 72 passengers and one driver and is pulled on 1,500-metre (5,000ft) steel cables wound on drums. The lower Garden Road terminus can be accessed by free open-top double-decker bus from Central Pier, while the upper terminus empties out into the Peak Tower mall. Trains run from 7am to midnight daily.

The Peak Tram is also occasionally used by those who live in one of Hong Kong Island's most gentrified neighbourhoods. In pre-tram days, long-suffering "coolies" used sedan chairs to transport the gentry up the mountainside. Such transportation disappeared long ago, but palanquins – large, covered sedan chairs – are still sometimes used during charity races.

older Hong Kong, with small earth-god shrines outside each shop. Above High Street, European architecture reappears, especially around Hong Kong University, which was founded in 1911.

### Further west

From Western it is possible to walk up towards the residential district of Pok Fu Lam. The hilly upper part of Western (which is actually part of the Mid-Levels) is quite different. Here the architecture is more Portuguese colonial than traditional Chinese – with tiled pitch roofs, stucco walls and projecting balconies. The **University of Hong Kong** has its campus here. The **University Museum and Art Gallery** (www.umag.hku.hk/en/; Mon–Sat 9.30am–6pm, Sun 1–6pm; free; bus 3B, 23, 40, 40M or 103) at 94 Bonham Road is worth a look. Housed in the 1930s Fung Ping Shan Building, it contains an interesting collection of pottery and porcelain dating back to the 7th century, although the most prized possession is the world's largest collection of bronzeware from the Yuan; contemporary art is exhibited in the adjoining T.T. Tsui Building. It also has a welcoming Tea Gallery where you can pause over a cup of Chinese tea.

Beyond the university is the residential district of Pok Fu Lam, while down by the harbour, **Kennedy Town** ㉘ is one of Hong Kong's oldest Chinese settlements, and one of the cheapest places to live on Hong Kong Island. Also here is the result of another huge land-reclamation project – the Western Harbour Crossing, Hong Kong's third cross-harbour tunnel to Kowloon.

## THE PEAK

The Peak, properly though rarely called **Victoria Peak** ㉙ (Shan Teng in Cantonese), is Hong Kong's most notable natural landmark, the residential aspiration of the upwardly mobile population and destination to more than 7 million visitors a year.

Yet it wasn't always regarded with such awe. A travel writer once described it as "beautiful in the distance, but sterile and unpromising upon more close examination"

*The magnificent view of Hong Kong from the Peak, across Victoria Harbour to Kowloon.*

**TIP**

The streets of SoHo are known for their bars and restaurants, but there are also a lot of good shops, mostly clustered on Staunton Street. If you're looking for non-mainstream fashion or accessories, this is one of the best places in Hong Kong.

(although that this was before reforestation took place – see page 109), and during the first six years of Hong Kong's history, hardly anybody travelled to its inhospitable heights. But as Hong Kong developed as a colony, the British sought out a hill resort away from the hot, malaria-infested lower elevations. Once the **Peak Tramway** was opened in 1888, the area quickly developed into one of the most sought-after places to live in Hong Kong – and has remained so ever since.

The upper terminus of the Peak Tram is the **Peak Tower** ㉚. Shaped like a wok, this is for many people one of the ugliest buildings in Hong Kong. Of course, the main reason for coming up to The Peak is to marvel at one of the world's finest vistas, which on Hong Kong's increasingly rare clear days should include a view all the way to mainland China. Many find the night-time views even more incredible, a vast glittering swathe of electric light, most spectacular immediately below in Central and Wan Chai as the buildings attempt to outdo each other in

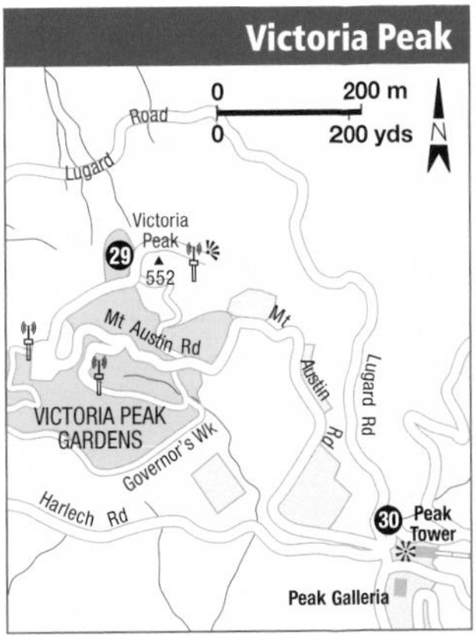


their eye-catching displays. The Peak Tower boasts shops and restaurants plus a viewing platform at the top of the "wok". From the Sky Terrace (www.thepeak.com.hk; Mon–Fri 10am–11pm, Sat–Sun 8am–11pm) you can enjoy a superb 360-degree panorama. There is also a Sky Gallery with regular outdoor exhibitions.

For indoor entertainment, the Peak Tower has its very own **Madame Tussauds** (www.madametussauds.com/

*Passengers on the Peak Tram.*

hong-kong/en/; daily 10am–10pm), with over 100 waxworks of Asian and international celebrities that delight photo-op-crazed visitors.

## Peak walks

There are a variety of superb walks from the Peak Tower. **The Peak Trail** follows Lugard and Harlech roads to complete a circuit of Victoria Peak, affording magnificent views across the harbour and Kowloon to the north, Cheung Chau and Lantau to the west, and the great masses of junks and sampans at Aberdeen to the south, with Lamma Island beyond. This gentle 3-km (2-mile) walk, well signposted and shaded from the sun, takes about 50–60 minutes round-trip from the Peak Tower.

The area around the Peak Tower is in fact **Victoria Gap**, whereas the summit of Victoria Peak itself (552 metres/1,811ft) lies to the west. Follow the Peak Trail until you reach Mount Austin Road, which winds up to the attractive **Victoria Peak Gardens**. The summit itself, with its pair of radio towers, is out of bounds.

It is possible to walk back down to Central and indulge in some of the finer views and footpaths through The Peak's wooded slopes. The **Central Green Trail** – marked by 14 bilingual signboards highlighting points of interest – winds its way down from Barker Road, across May Road and then via paths named Clovelly, Brewin and Tramway back to the Garden Road terminus. Another short, steep route through the forest, signposted to the Mid-Levels, descends northwards from Findlay Road (just below the Peak Tower) to the beginning of the Old Peak Road. A popular longer walk descends westwards through Pokfulam Country Park, and constitutes Stage 1 of the Hong Kong Trail. For more ambitious hikers, the rest of the trail heads east for some 50km (30 miles) all the way to Tai Tam and on to Shek O (see page 137). Nature-lovers can wander through forests of bamboo and fern, stunted Chinese pines, hibiscus and vines of wonderful, writhing beauty. Ornithologists log sightings of birds such as blue magpies and crested goshawks.

*The Peak Tower.*

# THE STAR FERRY

**Costing just a handful of Hong Kong dollars, the crossing of Victoria Harbour aboard one of the Star Ferries is an eight-minute visual feast.**

From ancient to modern, from Rolls-Royce to rickshaw, Hong Kong offers every mode of conveyance for rich and poor. But the territory's quintessential transport is the Star Ferry. Shunting back and forth across Victoria Harbour, these green-and-white ferries link the community together in a way that is both symbolic and endlessly practical.

The fleet would win few prizes for glamorous design. Even the grandly named *Celestial Star* (other names include *Morning Star*, *Meridian Star*, *Shining Star* and *Twinkling Star*) is just one of a dozen juddering, smoke-belching people-movers. Yet the clanking gangways, weather-beaten coxswains and solid wooden decks have a timeless character.

The first of the current "Star" fleet made their maiden voyages in 1898, although earlier ferries began operating a quarter of a century before that. Until Hong Kong Island was connected to Kowloon by road tunnel in 1972 and the Mass Transit Railway (MTR) in 1979, the Star Ferry was the prime way to cross the harbour – these days it is generally quicker to use the MTR unless you are travelling between points close to the piers.

*Aboard the Star Ferry.*

*As reclamation continues to narrow the harbour, the Star Ferry Pier in Central moved northwards in 2006. The location is now next to the Outlying Islands ferry piers in front of the ifc2 tower. The distance across to Kowloon is now shorter than ever, but journey times remain the same, as choppier waters prolong docking manoeuvres.*

*Star Ferries only ply between Hong Kong Island and Kowloon, but ferries to Lantau and elsewhere offer deck-top views and longer cruises. If you want a view, avoid the fast ferries, or – best of all – take a harbour cruise (these can be arranged via the HKTB).*

Not all Star Ferries are green and white – some feature (temporary) custom paint-jobs. The main route is between Central and Tsim Sha Tsui, but there are also Wan Chai to Tsim Sha Tsui and Hung Hom to Central and Wan Chai services.

*Central District's Star Ferry Pier has an Edwardian-style clock tower and overall retro appearance, replacing the functional 1950s design of its predecessor.*

## HONG KONG'S TRAMS

*Hong Kong's electric trams are an affordable way to see the city.*

A kind of double act with the Star Ferry, Hong Kong's fleet of electric trams was introduced in 1904, and has remained virtually unchanged since 1925, when the familiar double-decker cars came into service. Some of the 163-strong fleet now have comfy seating and air-conditioning. More are due to be upgraded over coming years but managers have promised the tinkering will not overwhelm the trams' antiquated charm, enjoyed by 230,000 people daily.

As with the Star Ferry, riding the tram is not only one of the city's best bargains (a flat fare of HK$2.50 on weekdays and HK$3.40 on weekends, however far you go) but also a great way to sightsee – as long as you can get a seat on the top deck, preferably at the front where the views are accompanied by a refreshing breeze. It's a great vantage point from which to observe the city go about its business. A seat at the rear of the top deck is also good, and gives wonderful photo opportunities.

Redecorated annually according to advertising-agency whim, the trams – known locally as the "ding-ding" for the bells that announce their arrival – run daily from 6am until midnight. The line runs right along the north coast of Hong Kong Island: from Kennedy Town in the west to the heart of the city at Des Voeux Road Central, from where the route proceeds along Queensway and through the middle of Wan Chai and Causeway Bay before continuing past Victoria Park to North Point or Shau Kei Wan in the east. A branch leads off to Happy Valley and the terminus south of the famous racecourse. Vintage-style trams can also be hired out for private parties.

*Tram stops are clearly signposted.*

*Hysan Place, a 36-storey shopping mall and office.*

# WAN CHAI AND CAUSEWAY BAY

**Wan Chai and Causeway Bay offer a taste of modern Hong Kong and have some of the SAR's best shopping and nightlife.**

**Main Attractions**

Hong Kong Convention and Exhibition Centre
Nightlife around Lockhart Road
Happy Valley horse racing
Causeway Bay shopping

**Map**

Page 120

East of Central lie two crowded, vibrant districts that wholeheartedly embrace the local passion for eating, drinking and shopping. Home to almost 200,000 people, Wan Chai and Causeway Bay have a great deal to offer anyone wishing to sample the authentic flavour of modern Hong Kong. The tramline (which was on the waterfront when it was built at the beginning of the 20th century) runs right the way through these districts, and provides cheap and convenient transportation as well as numerous photo opportunities from the top deck.

## Admiralty

**Admiralty ❶**, bridging Central and Wan Chai, used to be the site of a British naval station. These days it is an agglomeration of gleaming office towers and smart shopping malls.

When the British first came to Hong Kong, they were unable to find a suitable site for a naval garrison, so HMS *Tamar* was moored offshore just east of Central (or "Victoria" as it was then known). Many years later, after the Japanese occupation in World War II, the compound was moved ashore. After the handover, Tamar – as the compound became known – was turned over to the Chinese People's Liberation Army, which continues to occupy the eye-catching Prince of Wales Building. Beside it is the Hong Kong Central Government Complex, which houses meetings of the Legislative Council (Legco) as well as the offices of the Chief Executive. After years as a dusty sliver of undeveloped waterfront, Tamar now has a waterside promenade and a brand new public park, and makes for a pleasant stroll.

*Fishmongers sell fresh fish at Wan Chai Wet Market.*

*The Hong Kong Convention and Exhibition Centre is used for events from trade fairs to pop concerts.*

The epicentre of Admiralty is **Pacific Place**, one of Hong Kong's ritziest malls, showcasing the top names in fashion and housing three of Hong Kong's best hotels: the Conrad, Marriott and Island Shangri-La.

## WAN CHAI

From Admiralty, it is just a few minutes' walk to Wan Chai, which has long elicited knowing nudges from residents because of its reputation as a red-light district – although over the past years most of the girlie bars have been replaced by a lively mix of bars and pubs. By day, it is a regular business district where locals head for less expensive shopping and dining.

Wan Chai's multi-faceted character builds up in layers, starting with the older area between the hillside and the tramline, which segues into the lively nightlife district around Hennessy and Lockhart roads, and finally the smart waterfront area.

Close to the waterfront (north of multi-lane Gloucester Road), in an area sometimes known as Wan Chai North, are the **Academy for Performing Arts** ❷ and the **Hong Kong Arts Centre** ❸, two popular venues for theatrical and cultural performances. The Arts Centre also has galleries, rehearsal rooms and a café with views of the harbour.

Jutting out into the harbour is the futuristic **Hong Kong Convention and Exhibition Centre** ❹, which underwent a HK$4.8 billion extension in order to serve as the venue for the formal handover ceremony in 1997 – the building work was completed days (some say hours) before the ceremony. Over a decade on, the Convention Centre attracts over 3.3 million visitors a year to its exhibitions, conferences, trade shows and concerts.

The complex is adjacent to the svelte Grand Hyatt and the Renaissance Harbour View Hotel,

**Wan Chai and Causeway Bay**

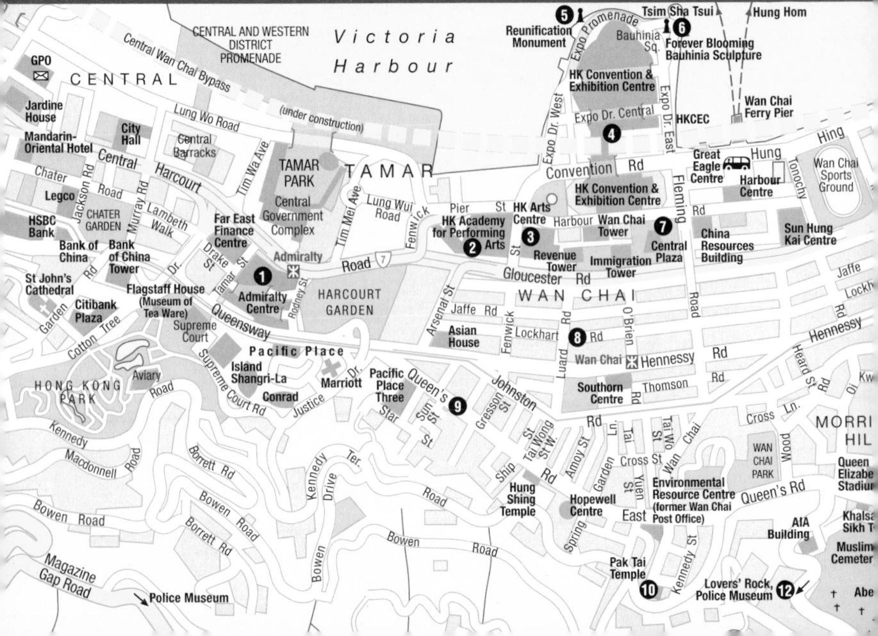

and fringed on the harbourside by a waterfront promenade. At its northernmost point are two rather odd-looking statues. The tall black obelisk is the **Reunification Monument** ❺, which was erected to commemorate the handover and signed in gold by former Chinese President Jiang Zemin. It remains a hugely popular spot for tour groups from mainland China. Close by is the gaudy, golden **Forever Blooming Bauhinia Sculpture** ❻. The bauhinia flower is indigenous to Hong Kong and, as the SAR's emblem, its five petals are printed on the Hong Kong flag. Further on past the tourist cruise operators is Wan Chai's own Star Ferry pier, with ferries to Tsim Sha Tsui.

## The heart of Wan Chai

Elevated walkways lead south from the Convention Centre to the 78-storey **Central Plaza** ❼ office tower, Hong Kong's third highest building at 374 metres (1,227ft), and on into the heart of Wan Chai around the MTR station and **Lockhart Road** ❽.

From here westwards is a lively neighbourhood with numerous bars and restaurants housed beneath ageing office buildings. During the 1960s, Wan Chai was a favourite rest-and-recreation destination for tens of thousands of troops fighting in the Vietnam War. It was during this period that the area earned its reputation as a tawdry but thriving red-light district, captured in the famous film *The World of Suzie Wong (1960)*. Five decades on, a few die-hard girlie bars on Lockhart Road remain and can be easily identified by their black-curtained doors. Today's Wan Chai is a mix of bars and all-night establishments that pull in a varied mix of expats, locals and out-of-towners, who start off in more expensive areas like Lan Kwai Fong and SoHo, then gravitate to Wan Chai to let rip.

*The Bauhinia Sculpture, and neighbouring Reunification Monument, are a favourite photo-stop for patriotic tourists from mainland China. There is a flag-raising ceremony here at 7.50am every day.*

**Wan Chai and Causeway Bay**

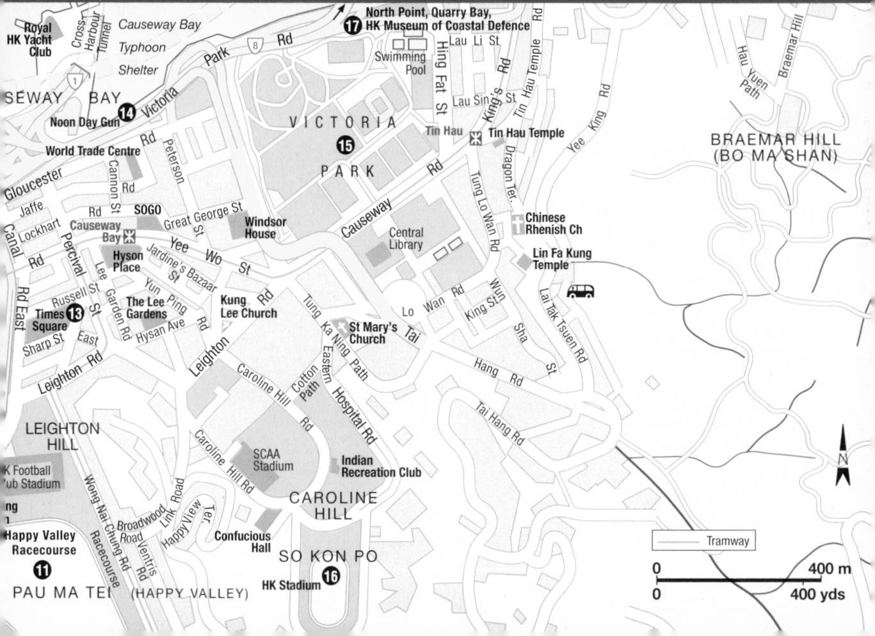

There are a few rather anachronistic British-style pubs in the area, but international-style bars – with sports and music on plasma screens and a young clientele – are the more typical after-hours offering.

## Queen's Road East

Two blocks inland from Lockhart Road, cross the tram tracks on Johnston Road and take a walk through Wan Chai Street Market. Wan Chai's huge urban regeneration project has seen some shophouses *(tong lau)* torn down in favour of offices – but others have been preserved, for instance the four elegantly restored tenement buildings at 60–66 Johnston Road.

Beyond the market, **Queen's Road East** ❾ is the place to track down home furnishings of all kinds, from cool, modern designer shops to Chinese traditional rosewood furniture.

This neighbourhood also has two traditional Chinese temples that provide a glimpse of the old way of life in stark contrast to their modern surroundings. On Queen's Road East next to a narrow lane of steps leading up towards the Mid-Levels is the tiny, dark **Hung Shing Temple**.

*A Hung Shing Temple in Wan Chai.*

Legend has it that this temple, built on top of huge boulders, was named after a Tang-dynasty official who was renowned for his extreme virtue and his ability to make predictions that proved to be of great value to traders. Perhaps by coincidence, several small banks in the neighbourhood are filled with groups of elderly "traders" who stare at computer screens to follow the share-price movements of the stock market.

Much more impressive is the **Pak Tai Temple** ❿ at the top of Stone Nullah Lane, a triple-halled temple noted for its 400-year-old, 3-metre (10ft) statue of the deity Pak Tai, who assures harmony on earth. The temple itself was not built until 1863. There are usually old men and women pottering around in the dark recesses of the temple, lighting incense sticks or laying out offerings.

Back on Queen's Road East, the former Wan Chai Post Office (1912), on the corner of Wan Chai Gap Road, now houses the **Environmental Resource Centre** (Wed–Mon 10am–5pm). Take a look inside at the original wooden

*The Hong Kong Racing Museum is dedicated to horse racing in Hong Kong and the Hong Kong Jockey Club.*

counter and red postboxes; nature-lovers can pick up a leaflet on the 1.5-km (1-mile) **Wan Chai Green Trail**, which starts beside the octogenarian mango tree and giant candlenut tree just outside.

Take a turn up 19th-century Ship Street to discover the shiny new Wan Chai on Star Street with lounge bars, teashops, restaurants and Pacific Place Three office tower.

## Happy Valley

At the eastern end of Queen's Road East is one of the oldest settlements on Hong Kong Island, developed after early colonial settlers abandoned Western District due to malaria. This second settlement was named Happy Valley, reportedly because a cartographer's girlfriend accepted his proposal of marriage there. It was far enough from the sea, somewhat deserted and, importantly, didn't have malaria-ridden rice farms in its vicinity.

Shortly after settling in Happy Valley, the colony's residents created the greensward and edifice that has made the area world-famous amongst horse racing fans: the Hong Kong Jockey Club's **Happy Valley Racecourse** ⓫. During the September to July season, races are held here most Wednesday nights – as well as at Sha Tin Racecourse at the weekend. A night out at the Happy Valley track is a quintessential Hong Kong experience and less expensive than most (see page 126).

If you can't make it to the actual races, visit the **Hong Kong Racing Museum** (daily noon–7pm, and till 9pm on race nights; free), at the Happy Valley Stand inside the racecourse. The museum has eight galleries and a video presentation that tell the history of horse racing in Hong Kong, and the locals' all-consuming obsession with it.

## Above the valley

For panoramic views, head up to leafy Bowen Road and Lovers' Rock. For more good views of the harbour, branch off uphill to the left at Wan Chai Gap Road for the **Police Museum** ⓬ (Tue 2–5pm, Wed–Sun 9am–5pm; free). The museum traces the history of the Hong Kong police

### TIP

On the hillside above Happy Valley, the 4km (2.5-mile) Bowen Road walk (accessed via Stubbs Road) is one of Hong Kong's best urban strolls. Along the route you'll come to Lovers' Rock, where locals flock on the 6th, 12th and 26th days of each lunar month to light joss sticks, hang wine bottles on the tree opposite the rock, and pray for harmonious marriages.

*Neon signs light up Lockhart Road by night.*

*Night time shopping on Jardine's Bazaar.*

force, packed with information on illegal narcotics, triads and occasional oddities such as the stuffed head of a tiger shot in 1915 after it killed a policeman.

## CAUSEWAY BAY

Beyond Canal Road to the east of Wan Chai is **Causeway Bay** (Tung Lo Wan), one of Hong Kong's premier shopping areas and a hive of activity from early morning until late at night.

Causeway Bay's modern history began in 1972 when the first Cross-Harbour Tunnel opened to link Hong Kong Island and Kowloon by road for the first time. There are now three cross-harbour tunnels, but this one is still the busiest. It transformed the neighbourhood into a thriving urban area, which these days is best known as a place where you can shop and dine late into the night and where retail space is some of the most expensive on the planet. The streets are often crowded to the point of being uncomfortable, even by Hong Kong standards, and pollution levels are notoriously bad, exacerbated at times by the "canyon effect" of its narrow streets and tall buildings, which trap exhaust fumes.

*Every year tens of thousands gather in Victoria Park to mourn those who died in the Tiananmen Square protests of 1989.*

**Times Square** ⓭, a few blocks south of the crossroads near Sogo Department Store in Causeway Bay, is the area's biggest mall, with 14 floors of shops and restaurants, plus a cinema. The streets around include an exhaustive mix of factory outlets, designer boutiques and high-end fashion. There are also two other major malls nearby, the elegant Lee Gardens on tree-lined Hysan Avenue, and Hysan Place, off Lee Garden Road.

### On the waterfront

The bay here was spanned by a causeway before it disappeared into a great land-reclamation project in the 1950s; the former coastline is traced by Tung Lo Wan Road, while the present-day "bay" is occupied by the **Royal Hong Kong Yacht Club** (nostalgic members voted to keep the club's royal title, although the Chinese translation makes no allusion to the House of Windsor) and the Typhoon Shelter.

This part of Hong Kong's waterfront features the **Noon Day Gun** ⓮, a peculiar colonial relic that was referenced in Noël Coward's *Mad Dogs and Englishmen*. Nobody knows for sure why the gun is fired at noon every day, but the story goes that the ritual dates back to the mid-19th century (although the present cannon was installed in 1982), when one of the Jardine's opium ships sailed into the harbour and an over-excited minion gave the vessel a 21-gun salute. The egotistical governor was incensed that a mere trader should receive the same greeting as himself, so he ordered that the gun be fired at noon every day in perpetuity. Despite the demise of the colonial era, the (Jardine-owned) tradition looks likely to continue just as long as Jardine keeps trading.

### Victoria Park

Causeway Bay is bounded on the east by **Victoria Park** ⓯, named after Queen Victoria, whose statue (moved here from Statue Square in Central after World War II) can be seen surveying the activities of her former subjects. One of the less loyal daubed her with red paint, and traces are still visible despite the efforts of cleaning staff. This welcome swathe of parkland has a swimming pool, jogging tracks and tennis courts and is popular with t'ai chi devotees in the early morning. Tens of thousands of people gather here on special occasions, such as Chinese New Year (when flower markets dominate) and, notably, during the Mid-Autumn Festival, when the park is illuminated with lanterns.

At the southernmost reach of Causeway Bay, the striking form of the 40,000-seat **Hong Kong Stadium** ⓰ is the SAR's largest outdoor venue, and host to the annual Rugby Sevens.

## North Point and beyond

Beyond Victoria Park, the urban strip continues more or less unbroken all the way to Shau Kei Wan. If you have the time, it is interesting to take a tram through these residential areas (you can then return westwards more rapidly by MTR). You'll pass through the old Shanghainese residential neighbourhood of North Point to the newly emerging bars and restaurants of **Quarry Bay**, and the shopping extravaganza of **Tai Koo Shing**.

Further east at Shau Kei Wan, the **Hong Kong Museum of Coastal Defence** ⓱ (http://hk.coastaldefence.museum; Fri–Wed 10am–6pm, Oct–Feb until 5pm; free on Wed), details HK maritime military history. The museum is housed in a 19th-century fort, 15 minutes' walk from Shau Kei Wan MTR station. The **Hong Kong Film Archive** (www.filmarchive.gov.hk; Fri–Wed 10am–8pm, or 15 minutes after last screening) near Sai Wan Ho MTR is also well worth a look, while the up-and-coming strip of bars and restaurants at **Lei King Wan** (aka SoHo East) is just around the corner.

*298 Computer Centre in Causeway Bay.*

### THE RUGBY SEVENS

The Hong Kong Rugby Sevens is one of the biggest parties in the city. Twenty-four national teams take part at the Hong Kong Stadium in Causeway Bay, and the atmosphere and festivities make for a riotous event. The South Stand is infamous as the place where elaborate fancy dress and heavy drinking are the order of the day.

Held on the third weekend in March, tickets sell out quickly (www.hksevens.com). If you miss out, it's possible to share some of the atmosphere in the marquees at the Sevens Village, next door in the grounds of the Indian Recreation Club. Matches are shown live on a huge plasma screen with handy bar access, and the party goes on into the night.

*The busy crossing by Sogo department store.*

# HORSE-RACING

**The Wednesday evening races under floodlights at Happy Valley are one of the most enjoyable nights out in Hong Kong, with a great atmosphere and excitement.**

From September to July, there's a buzz in the air most Wednesdays on Hong Kong Island, as form guides and newspaper pundits are carefully studied ahead of the floodlit night races on turf at Happy Valley race track. Most visitors who attend say that this is one of the most enjoyable experiences of their time in Hong Kong.

Catch a tram to Happy Valley or take a taxi (ask your driver for a racing tip – you can then of course tip him to return the favour), pay HK$10 at the public entrance and then wander between the trackside beer garden, open-air or air-conditioned stands. Dress code is casual and refreshments are cheap, with good-quality pizza slices and meat skewers costing just HK$40, and jugs of beer starting at HK$125. There are up to eight races between 7.15pm and 11pm.

The HKTB operates a Come Horseracing Tour that will pick you up from your hotel and provide seats in the Visitors' Box, with a buffet and open bar for HK$1,090 per person.

*Bring your passport, pay HK$150 for a Tourist Badge, and you can enter the members' enclosure (no shorts or flip-flops!).*

*The weekend races at Sha Tin see even larger crowds (with far fewer tourists). The track hosted the equestrian events at the 2008 Olympics.*

*Racing at Happy Valley dates back to 1846, and typically attracts over 50,000 punters each Wednesday evening – the amount of money gambled is extraordinary, and contributes around 12 percent of Hong Kong's tax revenue.*

The quality of the horses and racing is high. Annual cup races attract international racing fans and thoroughbreds from all over the world.

*Jockeys and their horses are led out onto the Happy Valley racetrack.*

## HOW TO BET

*It is easy for anyone to bet at Happy Valley.*

Even if you are a complete beginner at the horses, it is very easy to join in. The Jockey Club produces a guide in English for the Wednesday night races that clearly details the form, trainer, owner, jockey, etc, of each horse, and lets you at least pretend you are making an informed choice. Most counter staff speak good English and are patient with non-gambling foreigners having a flutter.

The simplest punt is for a Win. Opt for a Place and your horse has to come first or second if less than seven horses start, or in the top three if seven or more start. For a Quinella you choose three horses, and if any two of them finish in the top three you're a winner. For a Trio you bet on which horses will come in the first three places, but in any order, while a Tierce is the same but must be in the correct order. Minimum bet is HK$10. There are leaflets available to explain all bets.

*Horse-racing is entrenched in local culture, as seen in this float at the Cheung Chau Bun Festival.*

## Hong Kong Island

## Hong Kong Island

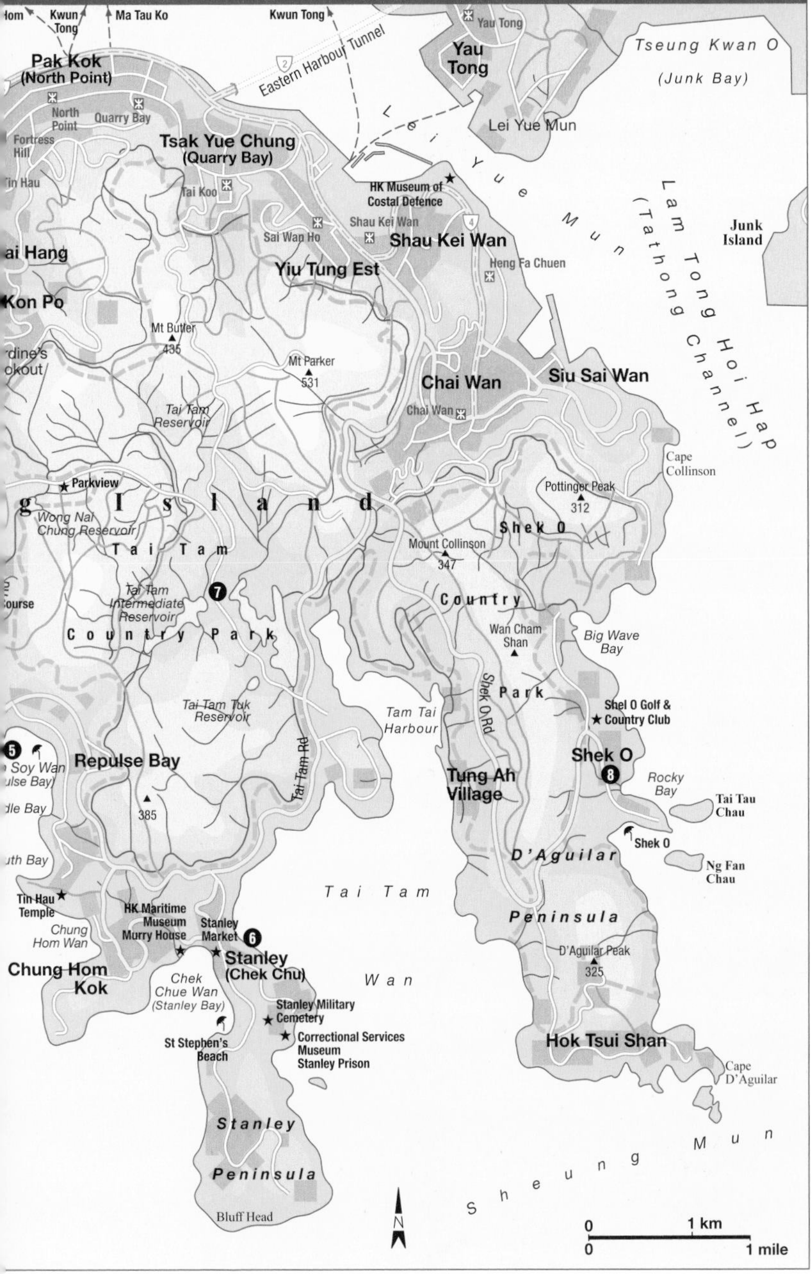

*Fun for the whole family at Ocean Park.*

# THE SOUTH SIDE

**The southern part of Hong Kong Island acts as alter ego to the commercial north. Except for the busy spots of Aberdeen and Stanley, much of the coast here is relatively unspoiled and uncrowded.**

**Main Attractions**

- Aberdeen
- Ocean Park
- Repulse Bay Beach
- Stanley Market
- Big Wave Bay and Shek O

**Map**

Page 128

In contrast to the northern coast of Hong Kong Island, which has changed almost beyond recognition in recent times with successive land-reclamation projects, the rocky southern shoreline remains more or less as nature intended. There are four country parks here, along with 290,000 or so residents, some of whom live in the most sought-after real estate in the SAR. With its lush vegetation and sweeping views of the South China Sea and outlying islands, this is the easiest place to escape the heavily urbanised strip on the other side of the mountains. Ocean Park's pandas, dolphins and hair-raising rides are a major draw, while elsewhere there are some good beaches, challenging walks and pleasant villages to discover.

## ABERDEEN

The harbour town of **Aberdeen** (Heung Gong Tsai) ❶ is the only place on the south coast with an urban feel. It can be reached by road from Kennedy Town through the residential district of Pok Fu Lam and past the Cyberport development, although most visitors take a more direct route south from Wan Chai through the Aberdeen Tunnel along Stubbs Road and Magazine Gap Road.

Named after the earl who was Secretary of State for the Colonies in 1848, Aberdeen is chiefly notable for the huge numbers of vessels bobbing in the water along its shoreline, and the over-the-top Jumbo Kingdom's floating restaurants (see page 132). No longer a fishing village, the main town is now all high-rises and concrete, but the natural typhoon shelter is packed with boats of all kinds, from wooden fishing boats

*Watching the sun set at Shek O.*

and *kaidos* (small cargo boats) to ferries, junks, sampans and yachts. A floating population of around 20,000 people once lived in boats in Aberdeen harbour, but today most of their descendants have opted for re-settlement in high-rise accommodation on dry land. With fish stocks down 80 percent since the 1950s, Hong Kong's fishing industry is in decline, hard hit by overfishing and pollution. While a few people are living in relative luxury on modern junks in the harbour, most of Hong Kong's "boat people" are from two main ethnic groups: the Tanka (literally, the egg people, so called because they used to pay taxes with eggs rather than cash) and the Hoklo, originally from Fujian province.

A ride through the harbour is an interesting experience. Eager sampan drivers, often persistent elderly women, are usually on the lookout for tourists and will offer rides (you will probably have to bargain for a price: HK$60–80 for 20 minutes is about right). Alternatively, look out for the Jumbo signs on the harbourfront, and you can hop on the free shuttle boat for a five-minute ride to the flamboyant floating restaurants. Opposite the Jumbo, the sleek white yachts are owned by members of the Aberdeen Marina Club, which is one of the most exclusive and expensive private clubs in the SAR. This area is also home to some of Hong Kong's last boat-builders and repairers.

### Tin Hau Temple

Back on dry land, the **Tin Hau Temple** on Aberdeen Main Road is rather shabby for most of the year, but comes alive during the Tin Hau Festival in April or May, when thousands of boats converge on Aberdeen's shores and the temple is decorated with paper shrines and lanterns. Lion dances are performed outside – an event that's charged with atmosphere and highly photogenic.

### Along the promenade

The Aberdeen promenade has been brightened up in recent years and now features plaques telling the story of the town and the boat-dwellers. At its western end, the **Aberdeen Wholesale Fish Market** is at its busiest in the morning, when customers turn up to select and collect the best produce for seafood-loving Hong Kong diners.

*Aberdeen Chinese Permanent Cemetery.*

## JUMBO DINING

Opened in 1976, the irresistibly kitsch Jumbo Floating Restaurant has been part of the Aberdeen scenery for decades. The Jumbo seats more than 4,000 diners and is one of the world's largest floating restaurants. Gaudy dragons greet you at the entrance and fairy lights mark out every curve and line of the vessel. Amalgamated with the smaller and slightly less palatial Tai Pak Floating Restaurant, "Jumbo Kingdom" is self-declared "theme park on the sea" and a magnet for selfie-taking tourists.

There is a free shuttle from two clearly marked piers on the Aberdeen waterfront. Hop on and take a look around the well-stocked fish tanks and the tea shop. The food in the indoor restaurants has improved in recent years, but isn't the best in Hong Kong. That said, the former rooftop storage area has been converted to a bar restaurant, The Top Deck at the Jumbo, and is a great place for a drink or a light meal, with outdoor seating and panoramic views across the harbour sampans and luxury cruisers in the typhoon shelter.

Up on the steep hillside above the fish market is the quaintly named **Chinese Permanent Cemetery**, entered through a pagoda-style gate. From the cemetery there is an excellent view across Aberdeen; higher still is the starting point for various hikes in the Aberdeen Country Park.

The shoreline around the Aberdeen Typhoon Shelter that connects the town's waterfront with nearby Ocean Park includes a promenade in the western section. In 2016 the South Island MTR line extension reached this area.

Further west along the coast is the controversial **Cyberport development**, which has struggled in meeting its original ambition to become Hong Kong's hi-tech centre.

## Ap Lei Chau

Across the harbour from the bumper-to-bumper fishing boats, the high-rise towers of **Ap Lei Chau** (Duck's Tongue Island) ❷ pack in almost 90,000 people. The main reason to detour here is to visit Horizon Plaza, on Lee Wing Street, a former warehouse now packed with 28 floors of shops. As well as floor after floor of contemporary, antique and reproduction furniture stores, carpet stores, and gourmet food and wine outlets, Horizon Plaza also has designer fashion discount "warehouses".

## Ocean Park ❸

**Address:** Wong Chuk Hang; www.oceanpark.com.hk
**Tel:** 3923 2323
**Opening Hrs:** daily 10am–6pm
**Entrance fee:** charge
**Transport:** 629 Ocean Park Citybus from Central piers and Ocean Park MTR, 973 from Tsim Sha Tsui (Star Ferry)

From Aberdeen, go east past the Police Training School at Wong Chuk Hang to one of Hong Kong's biggest homegrown attractions. Opened in 1977 at a cost of HK$150 million, Ocean Park is a combination of theme park and oceanarium. The complex is divided into two sections, a lowland site and a headland site,

**TIP**

Buses from Exchange Square, Central, to the southern parts of Hong Kong Island include: no. 70, the main route to Aberdeen, and nos. 66 and 260, which run to Stanley and Repulse Bay. For Ocean Park, take nos. 629 or 629A (express service) from the Admiralty MTR station; Shek O is best accessed by taking no. 9 from the Shau Kei Wan MTR.

*Sparkling lights on the Jumbo Floating Restaurant.*

**TIP**

If you are travelling direct to Stanley from Central, take the no. 6 bus from Exchange Square, which bypasses the Aberdeen Tunnel. You'll have the best views from the top deck going over the top along Wong Nai Chung Gap Road. Pass spindly skyscrapers appearing precariously balanced on the hillside, and enjoy the inexpensive white-knuckle ride down to Repulse Bay and Stanley.

linked by a 1.4-km (1-mile) cable-car. For more on Ocean Park see page 192.

## East to Repulse Bay

Beyond Ocean Park to the east is a region of rocky coasts and smooth white sands – home to 12 of Hong Kong's 40 gazetted beaches. On summer weekends it can seem as if half the population of Hong Kong have made their way here. A few locations, such as Rocky Bay on the road to Shek O, have virtually no public facilities, but offer unparalleled views and uncrowded stretches of sand and sea. Others, like Repulse Bay, attract bus-loads of tourists, fast-food restaurants and, at weekends, about as much peace and quiet as a carnival. Repulse Bay, Stanley, Tai Tam and Shek O are also home to several residential developments that command some of the highest real-estate prices and rents in the world.

**Deep Water Bay** ❹, the first beach beyond Aberdeen and Ocean Park, has some beautiful mansions, and is reputed to enjoy some of the best feng shui in Hong Kong. It also has a nine-hole golf course managed by the Hong Kong Golf Club (open weekdays to the public). Further along the road is the exclusive Hong Kong Country Club. The long stretch of beach here offers a quiet place to soak in the sun or go for a swim.

## REPULSE BAY

**Repulse Bay** (Cheen Soy Wan) ❺ is easily identified when you see the apartment block with a square hole in the middle. The bay was named after the battleship HMS *Repulse*, which took an active part in thwarting pirates who plundered here in the mid-19th century. Now widened to several times its original size and developed into a playground for tourists as well as urban Hong Kongers, Repulse Bay Beach has everything except peace and quiet.

The hills that rise steeply from the shoreline have a sombre history. It was here that invading Japanese troops came pouring down at the end of 1941 during World War II. The Repulse Bay Hotel, once one of the finest hotels in the East, was a military target because British and

*Ocean Park is one of Hong Kong's biggest attractions.*

Canadian troops used it as a base to keep open the road between Stanley and Aberdeen. After three days of fighting, the hotel was taken, and Commonwealth prisoners were marched to Eucliffe Mansion (this folly has also been demolished and replaced by villas), about half a kilometre (1⁄3 mile) from the hotel. Most of the prisoners were executed, and survivors were incarcerated at the Stanley Internment Camp.

The hotel was also demolished in the 1980s, and on the site today is The Repulse Bay, a luxury apartment complex; it has captured some of the old-world style in its renowned restaurants with verandas overlooking the lawn and beach. The complex includes the famous blue apartment building with the hole in its midst.

## STANLEY

Fifteen minutes' drive further southeast is **Stanley** (Chek Chu) ❻, popular with Hong Kong residents for its restaurants and seaside ambience. Named after Lord Stanley, a 19th-century Secretary of State for the Colonies, Stanley was the largest indigenous settlement in Hong Kong when the British first set foot here in 1841. In fact, the local Tin Hau Temple documents that the town was founded in 1770 by the pirate Cheung Po Tsai, who had taken control of the island.

### What to see in Stanley

**Stanley Market** (www.hk-stanley-market.com; daily 10am–7pm), the principal attraction on Stanley peninsula, draws thousands of visitors at weekends – locals in search of a bargain as well as tourists looking for souvenirs to take home. A few steps from New Street, where the buses stop, is an extensive covered market packed with shops and stalls selling clothes (factory over-runs or seconds), rattan, fresh food, ceramics, budget art, hardware, brass objects, Chinese crafts – in fact, almost anything.

At the end of the open-fronted restaurants and bars along Main Street, which skirts Stanley Main Beach, there is a modern shopping mall, directly opposite one of the SAR's most impressive architectural projects. **Murray House**, a former

*The Ocean Park cable car connects the two sections of the site.*

*Shops and cafés line Stanley's waterfront promenade.*

*Murray House, one of the oldest buildings in Hong Kong, was relocated stone by stone from Central to Stanley.*

British Army barracks dating from 1848, was moved stone by stone from Central (it was located on the site now occupied by the Bank of China tower) and rebuilt on the waterfront. It houses a number of suave restaurants, many of which have sea views.

### The Old Police Station

East of the bus terminus is the **Old Stanley Police Station**, one of 94 declared monuments in Hong Kong. The early British settlers regarded a posting to Stanley Police Station (built in 1859) as highly dangerous. Only a dirt track connected the town to the city of Victoria (now Central), and pirates frequently attacked and robbed the garrison. Stanley was all but abandoned in the 1850s, until the original police station was replaced by the building which stands today. The station is also thought to have been the last point of resistance to the advancing Japanese forces in the Battle of Hong Kong during World War II. On Christmas Day 1941, the town's commanding officer refused to believe the British had surrendered, and so the town fought on for a day after troops elsewhere had laid down their arms. That this historic building is currently occupied by a supermarket says a great deal about the parlous state of Hong Kong's heritage.

### Other sights

Down the road is **Stanley Prison**, which is still in use, while the two-storey building topped with a mock guard tower next to its parade ground houses the quirky **Correctional Services Museum** (www.csd.gov.hk; Tue–Sun 10am–5pm; free). Its nine galleries chart the history of Hong Kong's penal system, with creepy exhibits like a mock gallows and fake cells. It was also in Stanley Prison and at nearby St Stephen's College that the Japanese interned 2,800 non-Chinese civilian men, women and children.

To the right of the prison is the **Stanley Military Cemetery**, where tombstones commemorate early colonial military families, as well as those who died during World War II at the Battle of Hong Kong or at Stanley Internment Camp. Near the cemetery is **St Stephen's Beach**, with a watersports centre that hires out

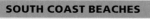

## SOUTH COAST BEACHES

If the weather's good and the water's clear, Hong Kong's beaches are great places to hang out. A total of 40 of them are gazetted (10 on the south coast of Hong Kong Island), which means there are facilities including toilets, showers, changing rooms, barbecue pits – and lifeguards from March to November. The sands are kept clean, but water quality varies dramatically – ratings are posted at lifeguard stations (along with a long list of things you are not allowed to do).

The nearest beach to Central is at Deep Water Bay, while along the coast is the larger, but more crowded, Repulse Bay beach. South Bay (Nam Wan), just below Repulse Bay, has a relaxed beach scene and the best view of the sunset. At weekends DJs at the open-air South Bay Beach Club provide a soundtrack. St Stephen's is the nicer of Stanley's two beaches and has a watersports hire centre. The east side of Cape D'Aguilar has the best surf: Big Wave Bay is the place for surfers and has a surf hire shop, while Shek O attracts a mixed group – beach-goers and surfers jostle with boogie boarders, swimmers and inflatables.

sailing dinghies, windsurfing boards and kayaks if you can produce the appropriate certificate.

## Beyond Stanley

From Stanley you can reach two country parks with access to more remote beaches, or take on a stage or two of the Wilson, Hong Kong or Tai Tam trails and hike to some of the least visited spots on the island.

To reach **Tai Tam Country Park**, head north along Tai Tam Road towards the **Tai Tam Reservoirs ❼**, which feature Victorian aqueducts and dams. Made up of four reservoirs, Tai Tam can only meet Hong Kong's needs for three days (most of Hong Kong's water supply is piped in from China). The park covers fully one-fifth of Hong Kong Island, and the reservoirs are a popular picnic spot. The well-marked walk up along the Hong Kong Trail to the north leads past pretty woodland and waterfalls; during the week it's most likely to be deserted. At the top, a trail around Wong Nai Chung Gap traces the events of the Battle of Hong Kong in 1941.

### Big Wave Bay and Shek O

Following Tai Tam Road, then Shek O Road, around Tai Tam Bay will take you to the east coast of Hong Kong Island, where **Big Wave Bay's** consistent surf and easily accessible location is a big draw for the Hong Kong surfing community. Boards and suits can be rented from the Surf 360 shop, just off the beach.

Just to the south, **Shek O ❽** is a pleasant village whose market place has a collection of shops selling beach paraphernalia. There are also some laid-back restaurants well known for both Chinese and Thai cuisine. Stroll out to Shek O Headland, facing the islands of Tai Tau Chau and Ng Fan Chau, and to the right is the most easterly point of the island, Cape D'Aguilar.

Alternatively, take it all in by walking along the **Dragon's Back** from the trail marker above To Tei Wan to Shek O (stage 8 of the Hong Kong Trail), which takes hikers along ridges around these peaks for two or three hours before dropping down to Big Wave Bay.

**TIP**

The large blue apartment building with the big square hole in the middle is the best-known sight in Repulse Bay. Some say the hole is a passageway for the heavenly dragon to come down from the mountains; others say it was put there to generate good feng shui; still others say it was just the architect's attempt at being funky. A replica of the old Repulse Bay Hotel stands in front of the apartment block, preserving a soupcon of grace from days gone by.

*Shopping for bargains at Stanley Market.*

*Kowloon is one of the world's most crowded areas.*

# KOWLOON

**Always regarded as playing second fiddle to Hong Kong Island, the districts of Tsim Sha Tsui, Yau Ma Tei and Mong Kok in Kowloon nevertheless define the chaos and bustle of the SAR.**

Named after the nine dragons *(gau lung)* of legend that live in the hills that mark its northern edge, the Kowloon peninsula is one of the world's most crowded areas, with more than 2.2 million people squeezed into its 47 sq km (18 sq miles).

At the southern end is Tsim Sha Tsui (pronounced "chimsachoi"), an irrepressible shopping district studded with several important cultural centres. Further north are the more traditional areas of Yau Ma Tei and Mong Kok, where, despite the addition of a few new malls and high-rises, life is still very much lived on the streets and in the many street markets.

Kowloon is quite different from the glittering island across the harbour – it's a little rougher round the edges, and on the go later into the night. Away from the main tourist areas along and beside Nathan Road, where the broadest mix of nationalities and cultures can be seen any time of the day or night, Kowloon is "more Chinese", or perhaps some might say, more Hong Kong.

By day, save for the views from the waterfront and a few idiosyncratic sights, it is not an especially attractive place. A lack of planning cohesion over the years has led to a sometimes bizarre mishmash of designs and styles, from the ritzy to the ramshackle. However, Kowloon sparkles in the neon glow of night time. The physical charge that runs through countless signs and light-fittings is reflected in the electric atmosphere at street level.

Yet things are changing, the transformation kickstarted in part by the closure of Kai Tak Airport in 1998, after which buildings were allowed to soar beyond the former flightpath limits.

**Main Attractions**

- Views from waterfront promenade
- Hong Kong Space Museum
- Hong Kong Museum of Art
- Nathan Road
- Kowloon Park
- Hong Kong Science Museum
- Hong Kong Museum of History
- Temple Street Night Market

**Map**

Page 144

*Nathan Road, Kowloon's main thoroughfare.*

Property developers dashed in to begin creating a new skyline for Hong Kong Island to look at, and look up to.

These days Kowloon has the tallest building in Hong Kong, and the fourth tallest in the world: the 484-metre (1,588-ft) **International Commerce Centre** (ICC). Located on top of the Kowloon MTR station and surrounded by luxury highrise apartment towers, the 118-storey ICC has a viewing platform on the 100th floor and one of the highest hotels in the world, the Ritz Carlton Hong Kong, perched above (see page 150).

## AROUND THE STAR FERRY PIER

The obvious place to start exploring Tsim Sha Tsui is at the **Star Ferry Pier** ❶, where the ferries land from Central and Wan Chai. The functional concourse is the location of Hong Kong's most accessible **tourist information office** (run by the HKTB and open daily 8am–8pm), on the immediate right of the disembarkation point.

Just east of the Star Ferry Terminal is Tsim Sha Tsui's most obvious landmark, the former Kowloon–Canton **Railway Clock Tower**. Dating from 1921, the tower is the final vestige of the historic Kowloon–Canton Railway (KCR) Station, once the Asian terminus of a system that ran all the way (with a few changes en route) back to Europe. In the mid-1970s it was replaced by a new station to the east, at Hung Hom.

*The venerable Clock Tower.*

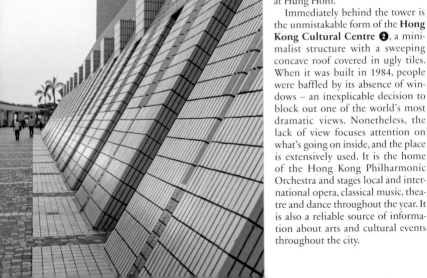

*The Hong Kong Cultural Centre.*

Immediately behind the tower is the unmistakable form of the **Hong Kong Cultural Centre** ❷, a minimalist structure with a sweeping concave roof covered in ugly tiles. When it was built in 1984, people were baffled by its absence of windows – an inexplicable decision to block out one of the world's most dramatic views. Nonetheless, the lack of view focuses attention on what's going on inside, and the place is extensively used. It is the home of the Hong Kong Philharmonic Orchestra and stages local and international opera, classical music, theatre and dance throughout the year. It is also a reliable source of information about arts and cultural events throughout the city.

*View of Kowloon from the Hong Kong Convention and Exhibition Centre.*

## Along the promenade

From the Star Ferry Pier eastward along the harbour, a **waterfront promenade** extends past the Cultural Centre and InterContinental Hotel towards **Tsim Sha Tsui East** and **Hung Hom Bay**, a stretch of reclaimed land packed with hotels, offices and shops. This provides a great vantage point for viewing the north shore of Hong Kong Island, one of the most spectacular cityscapes in the world. At 8pm each night, anywhere along the promenade is good for watching the Symphony of Lights, the world's largest sound and light show that illuminates the glittering skyline more than ever.

Beyond the Cultural Centre the promenade skirts the InterContinental Hotel and the New World Centre and becomes the **Avenue of Stars** ❸ – decorated with tributes to the famous and less so of Hong Kong and Chinese cinema, with Hollywood-style stars set in the pavement. Some of the monikers – Fung Bo Bo, Ivy Ling Po, Tso Tat Wah – will be familiar only to film buffs, but many other characters are honoured here, including San Francisco-born Bruce Lee, John Woo from Guangzhou, Beijing native Jet Li and Malaysian Michelle Yeoh, the first Asian Bond girl.

## Hong Kong Space Museum ❹

**Address:** 10 Salisbury Road; www.lcsd.gov.hk/CE/Museum/Space
**Tel:** 2721 0226
**Opening Hrs:** Mon, Wed–Fri 1–9pm, Sat–Sun & public holidays 10am–9pm
**Entrance Fee:** charge, but free on Wed
**Transport:** MTR Tsim Sha Tsui

Just behind the Cultural Centre, the igloo-like **Hong Kong Space Museum** is a favourite with kids. Its unmissable planetarium dome screens astronomical and natural-history documentaries, some in OMNIMAX Sensaround format. Its displays include interactive scale-model rockets and genuine astronaut suits.

*The Avenue of Stars.*

## Hong Kong Museum of Art ❺

**Address:** 10 Salisbury Road; hk.art.museum
**Tel:** 2721 0116
**Opening Hrs:** Mon–Wed, Fri 10am–6pm, Sat–Sun 10am–7pm
**Entrance fee:** charge, but free on Wed
**Transport:** MTR Tsim Sha Tsui

Hong Kong's largest public art gallery is currently undergoing a thorough, modernising renovation and is scheduled to reopen in 2019. It is the main venue for major visiting art exhibitions. The Museum of Art also displays traditional and contemporary calligraphy and painting, along with historic photographs, prints and artefacts of Hong Kong, Macau and Guangzhou. Other galleries exhibit Chinese antiquities and modern Chinese art.

### Salisbury Road

Across the road from this swathe of unattractive architecture, various stretches of Salisbury Road have been under renovation since the 1990s, and are most easily accessed by subway via the underground Sogo department store.

Across the road from the Cultural Centre is a petite 19th-century building that functioned as the **Marine Police Headquarters** ❻ until 1996. In a plan that squeaked through before the government began to get serious about heritage conservation, it's been restored and reopened as a 10-suite boutique hotel (Hullett House; www.hulletthouse.com), which has a series of bars and restaurants crafted from restored stables and holding cells. The adjacent area, once home to a lofty promontory with sweeping sea views, has been re-landscaped and converted into a new faux-Victorian mall called 1881 Heritage. Typhoon signals were once hoisted from a lighthouse here.

On the right side of the YMCA is the magnificent **Peninsula Hotel** ❼, which celebrated its 90th birthday in 2018.

A short distance east is Signal Hill Garden, which houses the **Blackhead Signal Tower** ❽ (daily 9–11am, 4–6pm; free). The tower was built in 1907 to house the time ball by which ships in the harbour adjusted their chronometers.

*The Harbour City complex.*

## Maritime gateway

Immediately north of the Star Ferry Pier is **Star House** ❾, where *cheongsams*, porcelain, and almost every kind of Chinese handicraft, are on sale at the Chinese Arts and Crafts store.

Adjoining Star House on Canton Road is the mammoth **Harbour City** complex ❿, encompassing **Ocean Terminal**, **Ocean Centre** and Gateway Arcade. Inside there are over 700 shops and boutiques, plus three Marco Polo hotels and dozens of restaurants. More than 20 luxury cruise lines include Hong Kong as a port of call and regularly moor at the two berths here, although ships as large as the *Queen Mary II* are forced to moor at the deeper, but semi-industrial, Kwai Chung Container Terminal rather than disgorging their passengers directly into the malls and other entertainments of downtown Tsim Sha Tsui.

Running parallel with today's cruise ship and ferry terminals is **Canton Road**, which marked the waterfront until the 1950s. Today it is the "front door" of Harbour City and home to an increasing number of designer-brand megastores. It also borders the western edge of Kowloon Park.

## The heart of Tsim Sha Tsui

The "Golden Mile" was a nickname given to **Nathan Road** ⓫ in the 1960s after it had been transformed from a sleepy, tree-lined residential boulevard into a gaudy, neon-lit street lined with electronics shops, tailors, boutiques and other shops targeting tourists more than locals. Shops have changed, signs have multiplied, but Nathan Road still remains the core of the Tsim Sha Tsui shopping and entertainment district. This has now spread out along the various cross streets, where rundown mansion blocks packed with shabby guest-houses and trading offices are oddly wedged between the shops, luxury hotels and the occasional skyscraper.

From the west side of Nathan Road, Peking and Haiphong roads connect with increasingly upmarket Canton Road. To the east there's plenty of shopping along Carnarvon, Cameron and

*The Hong Kong Museum of Art is the city's main art museum, and regularly changes its exhibitions.*

*Afternoon tea at The Peninsula.*

### THE PEN

Back in the early 1920s, the newly formed Hong Kong and Shanghai Hotels Company commissioned architects to design "the finest hotel east of Suez". The Peninsula, as the property was named, opened in 1928 and almost instantly moved Hong Kong's social centre of gravity several hundred metres/yds north. In those early days of long-haul travel, guests arrived at the Kowloon Canton Railway terminus on Tsim Sha Tsui promenade after a first-class train journey from Europe via Moscow, Beijing and Shanghai, or disembarked from luxury liners moored on what is now Canton Road. Early guests included George Bernard Shaw, Noël Coward and philanthropist Cornelius Vanderbilt Jr.

Traditions have been assiduously maintained, and one can still enjoy an afternoon tea in the sumptuous gilt corniced lobby, accompanied by a string quartet on the balcony. One of the few concessions to progress has been the addition of a new tower block in 1994, which soars upwards from the original U-shaped building and is topped off with a twin helipad. The Pen's fleet of Rolls Royce limousines, its swish restaurants, luxurious spa and sophisticated bars, ensure that it remains the consummate Hong Kong hotel.

## Kowloon

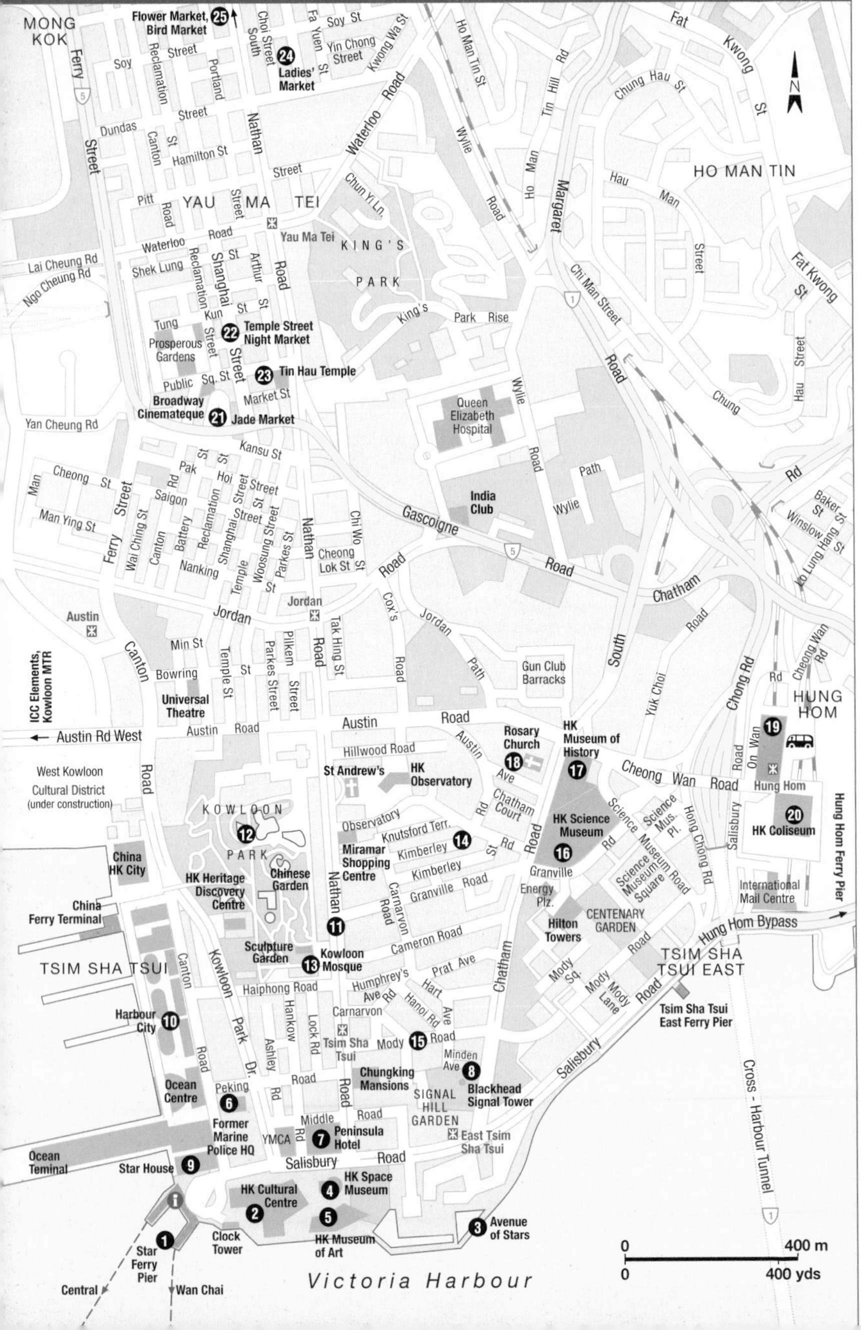
MONG KOK
Flower Market, Bird Market 25
Ladies' Market 24
YAU MA TEI
Yau Ma Tei
KING'S PARK
HO MAN TIN
Temple Street Night Market 22
Tin Hau Temple 23
Broadway Cinemateque 21 Jade Market
Tung Prosperous Gardens
Queen Elizabeth Hospital
India Club
Jordan
Austin
Gun Club Barracks
ICC Elements, Kowloon MTR
Austin Rd West
Universal Theatre
West Kowloon Cultural District (under construction)
HUNG HOM
Rosary Church 18
HK Museum of History 17
St Andrew's
HK Observatory
19
Hung Hom
20 HK Coliseum
Hung Hom Ferry Pier
KOWLOON PARK 12
HK Heritage Discovery Centre
Chinese Garden
Miramar Shopping Centre
14
HK Science Museum 16
China HK City
China Ferry Terminal
International Mail Centre
Hung Hom Bypass
11
Energy Plz.
Hilton Towers
CENTENARY GARDEN
Sculpture Garden
13 Kowloon Mosque
TSIM SHA TSUI
TSIM SHA TSUI EAST
Tsim Sha Tsui East Ferry Pier
Harbour City 10
Tsim Sha Tsui
15
Minden Ave 8 Blackhead Signal Tower
Chungking Mansions
SIGNAL HILL GARDEN
Ocean Centre
6 Former Marine Police HQ
YMCA
7 Peninsula Hotel
East Tsim Sha Tsui
Ocean Terminal
Star House 9
HK Cultural Centre 2
4 HK Space Museum
5 HK Museum of Art
3 Avenue of Stars
1 Star Ferry Pier
Clock Tower
Central
Wan Chai
Victoria Harbour
Cross - Harbour Tunnel
0 400 m
0 400 yds
N

Granville roads: here you will find factory outlets, inexpensive accessory shops, fashion boutiques and numerous bargains.

Nathan Road itself now boasts the very upmarket Lane Crawford department store, as well as larger mid-priced fashion shops, cut-price cosmetics stores and plenty of jewellery and electronic shops, where "buyer beware" is the order of the day. There are also the less salubrious looking arcades that overflow with a fascinating mix of booths and shops, including the ground floor of Chungking Mansions.

## Kowloon Park ⓬

**Address:** Haiphong Road
**Opening Hrs:** 5am–midnight
**Entrance fee:** free
**Transport:** MTR Tsim Sha Tsui

The shady old banyan trees of **Kowloon Park** date back to when the British Army's Whitfield Barracks were established here in the 1890s. The 13.5-hectare (34-acre) park includes a Chinese garden with lotus ponds, children's playground, maze and an aviary park (access often restricted due to avian flu concerns). A **Sculpture Walk** displays work by local artists and is the venue for kung fu demonstrations every Sunday afternoon (2.30–4.30pm). At the northern end there's a large sports complex and indoor and outdoor swimming pool (daily 6.30am–noon, 1–5pm and 6–10pm). Two blocks of former Whitfield Barracks, which were built in 1910 to house British and Indian troops, have been cleverly restored to create the **Hong Kong Heritage Discovery Centre** (www.amo.gov.hk; Mon–Wed, Fri 10am–6pm, Sun 10am–7pm). Galleries host temporary exhibitions and a permanent display that attempts to define Hong Kong's cultural heritage.

### East of the park

At the southeastern corner of the park, on Nathan Road, is the **Kowloon Mosque ⓭**, with its four minarets and large, white marble dome gracefully standing out from the clutter of shops and restaurants opposite. Built in 1984, it serves Hong Kong's 300,000 Muslim

*Kowloon Mosque.*

*Haiphong Road, packed with evening shoppers.*

## WHERE

Nathan Road is the central trunk of Kowloon running north from Tsim Sha Tsui through Yau Ma Tei to Mong Kok's Boundary Street, which marks the line drawn in 1856 when the land to the south was ceded to the British "in perpetuity". In 1898 the districts immediately surrounding colonial Kowloon were, along with the New Territories, leased to the British until 1997.

residents, of whom about 50,000 are Chinese. The original mosque building, built in 1894, served the British Army's Muslim Indian troops.

Across the road are three colonial buildings, each over 100 years old, fronted by equally gracious banyan trees. At no. 138 the Victorian Gothic-style **St Andrew's Church** (1904) is the oldest Anglican church in Kowloon. Next door, set back from the road is the former Kowloon British School, which opened in 1902 and now houses the **Antiquities and Monuments Office** (not open to the public). Up the hill behind Nathan Road, the **Hong Kong Observatory** has been monitoring the weather here since 1883.

Alongside the entrance to Observatory Road is the refreshingly mid-market Miramar Shopping Centre, while just south are the trendy restaurant and entertainment areas of **Knutsford Steps**, **Knutsford Terrace** and **Kimberley Road** ⓮. This area also has a remarkable number of bridal shops, where young couples flock to hire or buy all manner of bridalware and to sit for pre-wedding photographs of the happy couple in full wedding gear that will be on display at their wedding celebration.

*Temple Street Night Market gets into full swing in the early evening.*

*Haiphong Road marks the southern limit of Kowloon Park.*

## CHUNGKING MANSIONS

Built in 1961 in a prime Nathan Road location, Chungking Mansions (36–44 Nathan Road) is one of Hong Kong's most unlikely – and ugliest – tourist draws. This hulking tenement provides shelter to frugal backpackers and newly arrived migrants in scores of clean but ludicrously cramped guesthouses, accessed by unreliable lifts and eerie stairwells. Among the moneychangers and wholesalers on the ground floor are various stalls where you can buy anything from Bollywood DVDs, saris or samosas to electronics and alarm clocks. Head up to the mezzanine floor and tuck into some Nepali snack food and take in the quintessential Kowloon scene. For the Chinese movie fan it's a chance to experience the twilight world portrayed in Wong Kar Wai's brilliant *Chungking Express*.

## Mody Road

Linking Nathan Road to Chatham Road is **Mody Road** ⓯ which, together with neighbouring Hanoi Road, is going from grubby to groovy at a lively pace. The makeover of this slightly rundown area was kick-started in 2007 by the completion of K11, a 64-floor skyscraper. The tower has brought upmarket office space, what it claims is Hong Kong's first "art mall", and the Hyatt Regency Tsim Sha Tsui.

## TSIM SHA TSUI EAST

Chatham Road runs parallel to Nathan Road and is home to two good museums and Hong Kong's largest university.

### Hong Kong Science Museum ⓰

**Address:** 2 Science Museum Road; hk.science.museum
**Tel:** 2732 3232
**Opening Hrs:** Mon–Wed, Fri 10am–7pm, Sat–Sun & public holidays 10am–9pm
**Entrance Fee:** charge, but free on Wed
**Transport:** MTR Tsim Sha Tsui East

The Science Museum has over 500 exhibits on permanent display in 18 galleries covering topics from telecommunications to food science. Highlights include the flight simulator and a 22-metre (72ft) twin-tower energy machine, which is the largest of its kind in the world. The majority of exhibits are interactive and aimed at making the wide range of technology and science topics accessible for its primary audience of school students and young children.

### Hong Kong Museum of History ⓱

**Address:** 100 Chatham Road South; hk.history.museum
**Tel:** 2724 9042
**Opening Hrs:** Mon, Wed–Fri 10am–6pm, Sat–Sun & public holidays 10am–7pm
**Entrance fee:** charge but free on Wed
**Transport:** MTR Tsim Sha Tsui East

Just opposite the Science Museum, the **Hong Kong Museum of History** documents the story of Hong Kong from neolithic times right up to the end of colonial rule. The Hong Kong Story is the core exhibition, taking

*The ground floor arcade at Chungking Mansions is as close as Hong Kong gets to a "Little India".*

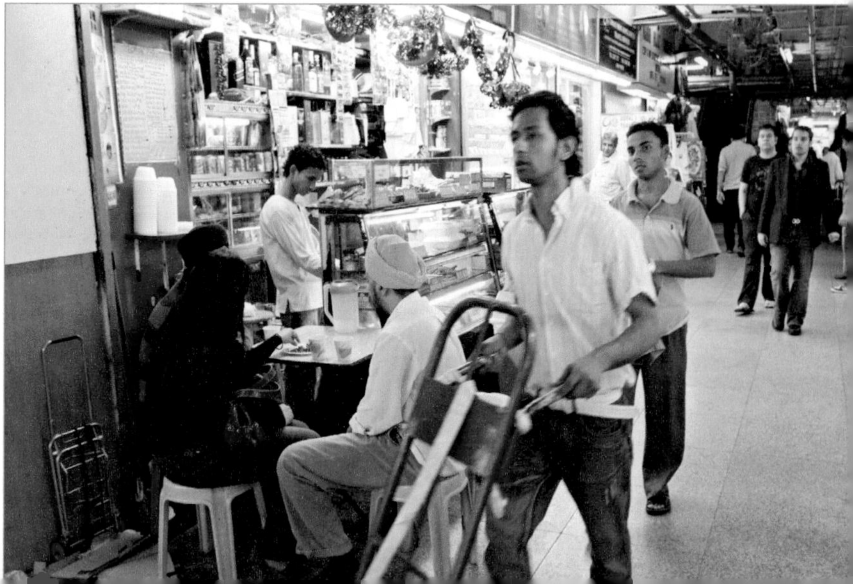

in developments from the Devonian period 400 million years ago to the 1997 handover, spreading over two floors and across eight galleries. Most exhibits focus on more recent history, with imaginative mockups of traditional teahouses and various street scenes. There are 53 interactive displays and scores of fascinating old photographs.

Across Chatham Road, the **Rosary Church** ⓲ was completed in 1905 to meet the needs of the growing Catholic community, as a result of a donation from a Portuguese expatriate, Dr Anthony Gomes.

From the Tsim Sha Tsui East area it is easy to return to the bright lights and shops of Tsim Sha Tsui. A network of underground walkways links the new Tsim Sha Tsui East station with various points around Tsim Sha Tsui and the MTR.

## Hung Hom

Further east beyond the History Museum is **Hung Hom Railway Station** ⓳, built in 1975 to replace the old Kowloon station (by the Tsim Sha Tsui Clock Tower) as the terminus for trains from China. There are departures every two or three days to Beijing and Shanghai, and several daily to Guangzhou. Ten minutes' walk away is Hung Hom Ferry Pier, with services to Central, Wan Chai and North Point.

The unusual-looking inverted pyramid situated on the harbour side of the station is the 12,000-seat **Hong Kong Coliseum** ⓴, one of the SAR's largest music venues. The indoor stadium hosts sell-out shows by Cantopop idols and international stars.

*Jade Market.*

*Yau Ma Tei Jade Market.*

## YAU MA TEI

Jordan MTR station at the northeast corner of Kowloon Park marks the transition from Tsim Sha Tsui to the more traditional Yau Ma Tei.

At the junction of Jordan and Canton roads there are several jade and ivory shops selling mahjong sets. Shanghai Street still has shops selling red Chinese wedding dresses, embroidered pillowcases and other items for a Chinese bride's trousseau, as well as fascinating shops making pots and pans to order.

Ning Po Street and Reclamation Street are well known for their shops selling paper models of houses, cars and notes from "Hell Bank" that are burnt at funerals, which assure that the deceased will be well-off in the afterlife. At the junction of Kansu and Battery streets the **Jade Market** ㉑ (daily 11am–6pm) is packed with stalls. Dealers offer jade in every sculptable form, from large blocks of the raw material to tiny, ornately carved chips (see page 150).

### Temple Street Night Market

Shanghai Street continues north to Public Square Street, where you'll find an area once famous for its temples, but now renowned for the **Temple Street Night Market** ㉒ (www.temple-street-night-market.hk; daily 4pm–11pm). Running parallel to Shanghai Street, stalls start setting up in the late afternoon, but the market comes to life after dusk. Best known for its fake designer goods, this is the perfect place to hunt down that tacky memento, with stalls selling souvenir T-shirts, lighters, watches, bags, jeans, old coins, crafts, small electrical gadgets, mobile phones and toys. It's also good for bargain price clothes. Palmists and physiognomists vie to reveal your destiny, and there are numerous *dai pai dongs* – basic Hong Kong-style diners serving up tasty seafood and hotpots to eat at functional fold-up tables and stools perched on the edges of the street.

One of the temples that gave the market its name is the **Tin Hau Temple** ㉓ (complex open daily 7am–5.30pm) on Public Square Street, which was originally built closer to the harbour, and locals still visit it regularly to worship Tin Hau, the protector of fisherfolk, whose image is draped in intricately embroidered scarlet robes. To the right of the altar are 60 identical deities that represent every year of the 60-year lunar calendar. Worshippers place "Hell Bank" notes under the god dedicated to the years of their birth.

Hong Kong's only arts cinema, **Broadway Cinematheque**, is two blocks along from Temple Street, past Reclamation Street, opposite the elegant 1920s-built former Yau Ma Tei Police Station on Public Square Street. As well as four screens showing a broad mix of films, there is the laid-back Kubrick Bookshop Café to relax in and mull over your movie options.

### West Kowloon reclamation

Further west lies a 40-hectare (100-acre) parcel of reclaimed land

*Shoppers can sit and eat at one of the many basic diners along the edges of Temple Street Night Market.*

which is being developed to create the long-awaited **West Kowloon Cultural District** (WKCD). More than two decades in the making, the complex has been held up by several public consultations and controversies, although construction is finally underway, and parts of the development are already open to the public. The space will feature commercial development as well as cultural facilities (sleek art centres and gleaming museums), green space, retail, dining and nightlight options. Museums will include the M+ Museum for visual culture; the M+ Pavilion, currently open to the public and holding exhibitions until the M+ Museum is completed; the Xiqu Centre, dedicated to the heritage of Xiqu; the Hong Kong Palace Museum, dedicated to bronze and jade items, paintings, ceramics and life in the Imperial Court; and the Lyric Theatre Complex, staging international dance and theatre performances. For updates on construction, visit www.westkowloon.hk.

At the time of writing, the M+ Pavilion, Nursery Park and waterfront promenade were already open to visitors. Spectacular views of the harbour and the Hong Kong skyline can be had from the promenade. Nearby, the very-much completed **Union Square** development provides a stark contrast, and includes Hong Kong's tallest residential block at 75 storeys, the Elements shopping mall and the city's tallest building – the **International Commerce Centre** (ICC; see page 140) – which towers above the Kowloon MTR station at 484 metres (1,588ft). The Sky 100 (www.sky100.com.hk) observation deck on the 100th floor gives exceptional 360-degree views of the city while the floors above are home to the seriously-swish Ritz Carlton Hong Kong.

## MONG KOK

Mong Kok (properly Wong Kok in Cantonese: a long-dead sign writer got his letters mixed up) was for many years associated with sleaze. The area got a shock in 2004, when Langham Place, a glitzy combined office block, shopping mall and five-star hotel, opened next to the

*Tropical fish on sale at the Goldfish Market.*

### CHINA'S FAVOURITE STONE

Jade was formerly the preserve of China's elite. Belief in its powerful essence is nearly as old as Chinese civilisation itself, and its prominence in Chinese art and literature attests to its longstanding value. Jade was prized for the aesthetic beauty of the stone, the skill needed to carve it and the magical properties it was believed to possess.

Most jewellery was made from jade, favoured over gems and precious metals, and some people held that the stone glowed with the vitality of the owner or became tarnished if the wearer fell ill. The Chinese have long believed that wearing jade ornaments imparts good health, good luck and protection from evil spirits.

There are two types of jade: jadeite and nephrite. Early jade objects were carved from nephrite, a softer form of the stone that can be worked with primitive tools.

The best-known single piece of jade is Jade Mountain of the Great Yu Taming the Flood. According to records, the uncut stone was discovered in Xinjiang province and weighed more than 5 tonnes, requiring more than three years to transport to Beijing and six years for a team of artisans to carve.

*Ladies' Market in Mong Kok is one of the most popular markets in Hong Kong.*

MTR station right in the heart of what used to be the seediest part of town. The shoddy bars and one-room bordellos continue to operate in nearby side streets, but the writing is on the wall. **Langham Place** – whose developer spent a dozen years buying up the tenements from different owners – is the future, soaring 255 metres (840ft) to the heavens.

A glimpse of an older Mong Kok can be seen at Lui Seng Chun, 119 Lai Chi Kok Road. A typical mid-20th century *tong lau* (shophouse), its ground floor was occupied by a bonesetting medicine shop, while an extended family lived upstairs.

Many well-known Mong Kok streets, like Fa Yuen Street – known locally as "Sneaker Street" because of the preponderance of sports shops – have been earmarked for redevelopment by the government's Urban Renewal Authority. However, residents and traders have tended to put up stiff resistance to the intermittent plans that come along and most retain a wonderfully ungentrified commercial air.

On the east side of Nathan Road, on Tung Choi Street, the so-called **Ladies' Market** ㉔ (www.ladies-market.hk; daily midday–11.30pm) sells everything from fake designer accessories and clothing to cheap cosmetics and toys. It is also a popular area for late-night shopping and dining. At the northern end of Tung Choi Street, Goldfish Market is a group of shops specialising in tropical fish and unusual goldfish.

Ten minutes' walk to the north, approaching Boundary Street, the colourful **Flower Market** ㉕ (www.flower-market.hk; 8am–dusk) has a fascinating selection of cut flowers, house plants and feng shui flora. Nearby is the photogenic **Yuen Po Street Bird Market** (daily 7am–8pm) precinct, accessible through a traditional gateway and containing a string of melodious songbird stalls.

*Yuen Po Street Bird Market.*

# SHOPPING

**Trading, buying and selling, shopping – it's why Hong Kong was founded and what it still does best.**

*Upper Lascar Row, more commonly known as Cat Street, is filled with stalls selling real and fake antiques, bric-a-brac and memorabilia.*

Hong Kong prides itself on being a shopper's paradise, and most locals are insatiable shoppers. If you love to shop, you will love Hong Kong. Whether it's in a mall – Hong Kong has some of the largest and most glamorous in the world, packed with designer names – or down on street level in one of the lively street markets or dusty "antique" stores, there is no shortage of finds.

These days, Hong Kong may not be the bargain basement it once was, but there is no sales, value-added- or luxury tax, which gives it the edge over some other Asian destinations. Best of all, Hong Kong's compact size means that it's easy to cover a lot of shopping ground in a remarkably short time.

## Hong Kong's markets

There's plenty of fun to be had at Hong Kong's street markets. Ladies' Market and Temple Street Night Market in Kowloon are overflowing with a mix of tacky souvenirs, cheap clothes and the odd "real find", with a unique urban Kowloon backdrop. By day the Flower Market near Prince Edward MTR is packed with unusual flowers and plants. To see, and smell, an authentic Hong Kong wet market, visit the

*It is easy to find clothing in all price brackets. Home-grown mid-priced brands include Giordano, Bossini and Esprit. For funkier finds and factory outlets, head to Causeway Bay and explore the side streets of Kowloon.*

*The SOGO shopping centre in Tsim Sha Tsui.*

## SECURE SHOPPING

*Consumers at Fortress, an electronic equipment retail outlet.*

Shopping in Hong Kong can sometimes be a fraught business for the amateur. Consumers can trust shops showing a Quality Tourism Services (QTS) sign, identifiable by the logo of a red junk with the Chinese character for quality written in black inside, which will provide genuine products, display prices clearly, provide product information and offer good customer service.

When buying electrical goods, consider whether you need an international guarantee and not just a local Hong Kong version. Goods that seem suspiciously cheap may only be guaranteed for the local area, and repairs or replacements will have to be carried out in Hong Kong.

Beware "bait-and-switch" tactics, where retailers showcase a product at an ambiguous price, accept a deposit and then claim the item is out of stock before pressuring the buyer to accept an inferior product. Finally, always ask for a proper receipt which clearly states purchase details, and avoid street touts.

The problem of retailers cheating tourists is no longer rife, but if you do have a problem you should contact the HKTB or the Consumer Council (www.consumer.org.hk/ws_en; tel: 2929 2222).

*Hong Kong is well known for its electronics shops, although real bargains are hard to find.*

*Mao Memorabilia on Hollywood Road.*

*Shanghai Tang, an international clothing company founded by Hong Kong businessman David Tang.*

*Attractively decorated chops (Chinese name stamps) make good souvenirs. Man Wa Lane in Western District is the best place to find them.*

Sheung Wan Municipal Services Building, or Graham Street in Central. Also in Central, The Lanes sell souvenirs, sportswear, pashminas, linen, knitwear and chinoiserie. Stanley Market sells similar goods plus factory over-runs, but its popularity is due to the number of stalls, and the chance to relax in a seaside café-bar to recharge your batteries.

*Colourful flowers on display at the Flower Market in Kowloon.*

*A stall at Ladies' Market on Tung Choi Street.*

*Hong Kong's street markets are as much about the atmosphere as the shopping. Check every item thoroughly, and don't be afraid to bargain via the stallholder's calculator. "Ho gwai" – very expensive! – is the only phrase you need to know.*

*Hong Kong merchants have traditionally grouped together according to what they sell. Antique-lovers, collectors and art fans will find a whole street of stores selling antiques and bric-a-brac along Hollywood Road and neighbouring Cat Street. The Jade Market on the corner of Kansu and Battery streets has 450 stalls selling jade items.*

## SHOPPING IN SHENZHEN

*Luohu Commercial City, a major mall complex in Shenzhen, just across the border from Hong Kong.*

**Shenzhen appeals to bargain hunters, but be warned that anything overly cheap is likely to be knock-off tat, and genuine brand goods will likely cost more than they do back home. Some beautiful new malls have sprung up over the last decade or so, though many Hong Kong shoppers still see no need to venture beyond Lo Wu Commercial City, right on the border. This vast shopping arcade sells cheap clothes and shoes, factory over-runs, outrageous fake-designer goods, pens, cufflinks, toys and all manner of home furnishings, electronics, and a phenomenal number of handbags, wallets and purses.**

**There are over 2,000 booths spread over five floors. Clothes can be tailor-made, or they will copy a favourite garment for a fraction of the price in Europe or North America. The whole of the fifth floor is devoted to a fabric market surrounded by tailors. Jewellery rules on the second floor, with plenty of pearls, semi-precious stones and costume jewellery. With inflation and the rising value of the renminbi, prices are considerably less cheap than they were a few years back, but there are still bargains to be had.**

*Stanley Market is the closest Hong Kong gets to a Western-style market. It is best-known for its clothing (mostly casual wear), including silk and leather items, but there is a lot more for sale besides – everything from surfwear and designer kids clothes to art and antiques.*

# NEW KOWLOON

**In addition to being home to Hong Kong's most famous temple and the region's largest Buddhist nunnery, these urban districts at the upper end of Kowloon peninsula merit exploration for those interested in the grittier side of the SAR.**

**Main Attractions**

Kowloon Walled City Park
Wong Tai Sin Temple
Chi Lin Nunnery
Lei Cheng Uk Tomb

**Map**

Page 157

Kowloon proper ends at Boundary Street in Mong Kok, which between 1860 and 1898 defined the frontier between Hong Kong and China. Although officially part of the New Territories, the districts immediately north of this street are more commonly known as New Kowloon. The densely populated neighbourhoods of Kwun Tong, Kowloon City, Wong Tai Sin and Sham Shui Po, wedged up against the mountains to the north, are occupied by housing estates, shopping malls and decaying factories and warehouses – this was the location of most of Hong Kong's light industry until it shifted over the border to China in the 1980s. Many of the older buildings are being torn down and replaced with more upmarket residential towers and mega malls.

*Kowloon Walled City Park, where the Kowloon Walled City once stood.*

## Kowloon City

**Kowloon City ❶** is best seen on foot, starting at Lok Fu MTR Station. Walk up Wang Tau Hom East Road as far as Junction Road, then turn left and continue west. Along Junction Road, the **Chinese Christian Cemetery** on the left is a stark reminder of the lack of space in Hong Kong, with graves stacked up like sardines on concrete terraces.

Next door to the cemetery is the tiny Hau Wong Temple, with traditional roof tiles and incense spirals hanging from the rafters. Built in 1730, the temple is dedicated to Yang Liang Jie, a loyal and courageous general of the exiled Song dynasty's boy-emperor Ping. The general's birthday is celebrated on the 16th day of the sixth month of the lunar calendar. The temple-keeper acts as a medium interpreting the advice of Hau Wong

*The Chi Lin Nunnery is the largest Buddhist nunnery in East Asia.*

by means of *kay fook* – praying for the god's blessing.

### Remembering the Walled City

Continue past the temple for 10 minutes until the junction with Carpenter Road, then turn left and head past Kowloon City Plaza on the left to reach **Kowloon Walled City Park** ❷ (www.lcsd.gov.hk/en/parks/kwcp; daily 6.30am–11pm; MTR Lok Fu). The park marks the area where the notorious Walled City stood until it was finally demolished in 1992.

Opened in 1995 by then Governor Chris Patten, it is an attractive space in the middle of dowdy swathes of grey urban decline. Modelled on the Jiangnan garden style of the early Qing dynasty, it features a chess garden as well as the Mountain View Pavilion, from which Lion Rock looms large to the north. The southern gate of the old Walled City has been preserved, along with two old

**New Kowloon**

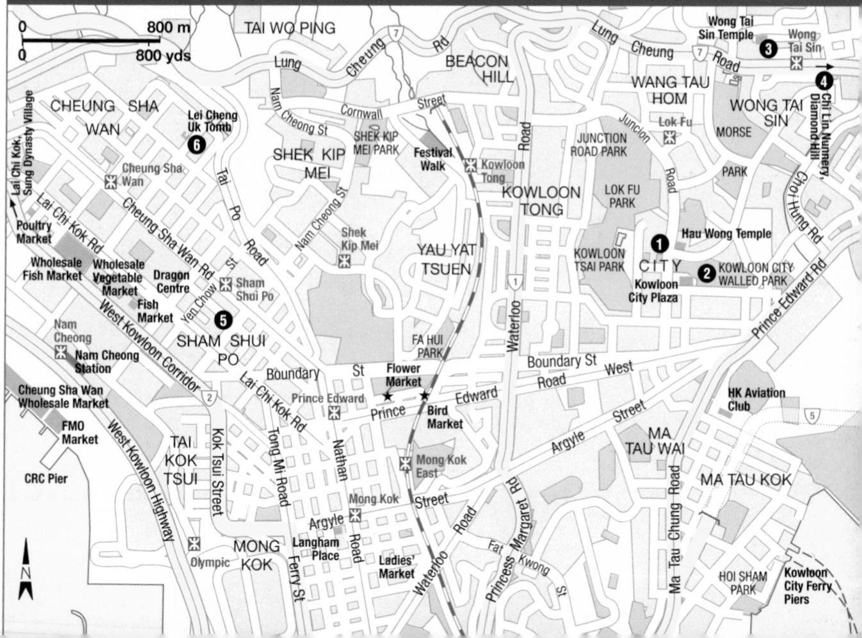

cannons, while an information centre contains a photographic exhibition detailing the peculiar history of the city, its demise and the subsequent construction of the park, as well as displaying relics found within the walls.

### Wong Tai Sin Temple ❸

**Address:** 2 Chuk Yuen Village, Wong Tai Sin; www.siksikyuen.org.hk
**Tel:** 2327 8141
**Opening Hrs:** daily 7am–5pm
**Entrance fee:** free
**Transport:** MTR Wong Tai Sin

Probably the liveliest and most colourful place of worship in Hong Kong, and the most rewarding for outsiders to visit, is **Wong Tai Sin Temple**, which sits opposite the eponymous MTR station.

Wong Tai Sin, the Daoist god of healing, is said to have discovered the secret of transforming cinnabar (vermilion, a red mercuric sulphide) into an elixir for immortality. A painting of the god was brought to Hong Kong from China in 1915, and was first placed in a small temple in Wan Chai, before being moved to Wong Tai Sin to benefit, it was said, from the feng shui between formidable Lion Rock and the sea. Since Wong Tai Sin is also the god of good fortune, the Chinese, who are too cautious to rely solely on luck, flock to the temple to ask him for advice on all matters, including such worldly concerns as horse-racing and stock-market tips. The sound of rattling *chim* – a container holding dozens of fortune sticks – resounds all day long. English-speaking fortune-tellers will also provide chapter and verse on the future using a number of other methods. They are especially good (from a parental point of view) with children.

The optimum times to visit are during Chinese New Year or at Wong Tai Sin's birthday on the 23rd day of the eighth lunar month (between mid-September and mid-October), when thousands of worshippers crowd into the temple to light incense, burn paper money and rattle *chim* sticks.

*Young woman at Wong Tai Sin Temple with a bamboo chim stick, used for fortune telling.*

### THE WALLED CITY

In pre-colonial times, the site that was to become the notorious Walled City was occupied by a fortress. It continued to be used by the Chinese after 1841 (partly to monitor British activities), and when Britain leased the New Territories (which included this part of Kowloon) in 1898, the site was excluded. At first, the Qing-dynasty officials remained, but British troops were soon dispatched, and they were expelled.

Yet British law was never fully implemented within the walled compound, and it soon deteriorated into a semi-lawless enclave that was left to its own devices. After World War II, illegal low-rise blocks began to appear, resulting in a multi-storey squatter area with unauthorised electricity and water supplies. By the 1950s, the dank alleyways had become a real-life vice city – a squalid haven for drug addicts, triad gangs, illegal immigrants and brothels, as well as unlicensed doctors and dentists.

In true imperial style, the British simply turned a blind eye, but through the 1970s pressure mounted for them to act. Beijing vehemently opposed demolition plans, regarding it as Chinese territory, but eventually 35,000 residents were resettled in housing estates, and the entire block was razed to the ground, a process completed in 1992.

## Chi Lin Nunnery ❹

**Address:** 5 Chi Lin Drive, Diamond Hill; www.chilin.org
**Tel:** 2354 1888
**Opening Hrs:** daily 9am–4.30pm, garden 6.30am–7pm
**Entrance fee:** free
**Transport:** MTR Diamond Hill

One MTR stop to the east of Wong Tai Sin, the **Chi Lin Nunnery** is the largest Buddhist nunnery in East Asia. Nuns have lived here since 1937, but today's structure dates only from 1998, having been rebuilt in wood without the use of a single metal nail. The complex comprises a number of Buddhist halls and the tranquil garden with lotus ponds in front of the main entrance.

*Wong Tai Sin Temple.*

The Hall of Celestial Kings houses a statue of the Maitreya Buddha (Milefo), the Buddha of the Future and a heavenly being who will descend to Earth to save humanity. Guardians of the Four Directions surround him. On the left is a hall commemorating the goddess of mercy, Guanyin, who sits inside a grotto. On the right is Baishiyaja Guru (Medicine Master), accompanied by the Sun and Moon Bodhisattvas, Buddhist redemption deities. The most impressive statue is the golden Sakyamuni Buddha, resting on a lotus altar in the Main Hall. Across the road, the Nian Lin Garden (daily 7am–9pm; free) is one of the most beautiful Chinese gardens in Hong Kong.

*Nian Lin Garden.*

Also following Tang aesthetics, the garden features ornamental rocks, pavilions, water features and beautifully shaped rare trees. A Buddhist vegetarian restaurant is hidden behind a waterfall.

## Below Lion Rock

The relentless sea of high-rises starts thinning to the north of New Kowloon, around Kowloon Tong MTR station. This area, wedged between Kowloon City and Sham Shui Po, is the wealthiest in Kowloon and is full of luxury low-rise housing, plus the highest concentration of nurseries, schools and universities in the city – amounting to over 200 institutions. In a typically odd Hong Kong style, the area is also famous for its "love hotels", discreetly situated behind high walls, with gates manned by security guards. Rooms at 41 Cumberland Avenue, Bruce Lee's former home, were also once rented by the hour. It's no longer a brothel, but calls for the property to be converted into a permanent tribute to the kung fu star have so far been unheeded.

For visitors there's more of interest at **Festival Walk**, a massive mall above Kowloon Tong MTR station, which has restaurants, an 11-screen cinema and an ice rink.

## Sham Shui Po

**Sham Shui Po** ❺ is situated to the west of Kowloon Tong, well off the tourist trail but nonetheless easily accessed by MTR. The area is as good a place as any to get an idea of the development of Hong Kong's architecture, from grim H-block resettlement estates hastily constructed in the 1950s to clean, modern apartment blocks erected in the 1980s. Sham Shui Po Police Station, at Lai Chi Kok Road and Yen Chow Street, is one of Kowloon's remaining colonial pre-war buildings. During World War II, the station was occupied and used by the Japanese to interrogate prisoners of

*A street in Sham Shui Po.*

war, and nowadays residents report a ghostly British soldier wandering around at night.

If you're in search of electronic goods, Sham Shui Po is high-tech heaven – even though much of it looks like a flea market. Arcades and stalls selling computers and related merchandise can be found on Yen Chow Street and Ap Liu Street, where there are also street stalls selling cheap goods – from old stereos and vinyl records to broken computers, TVs and household appliances. Many of the latest gismos are parallel imports – *sui foh* – goods imported directly from other countries available at lower prices, but without guarantees or instructions. Rip-offs do occur, and it's advisable to check items before buying. The Dragon Centre on Yen Chow Street is a 10-storey mall with ice rink on the eighth floor, and a children's entertainment arcade.

## Lei Cheng Uk Tomb 6

**Address:** 41 Tonkin Street, Sham Shui Po
**Tel:** 2386 2863
**Opening Hrs:** Mon–Wed, Fri–Sun 10am–6pm
**Entrance Fee:** free
**Transport:** no. 2 from Kowloon Star Ferry Pier, MTR Cheung Sha Wan

The Lei Cheng Uk Housing Estate is home to one of Hong Kong's archaeological treasures, discoveries made in 1955 by workers excavating the hillside. The tomb here is a Han-dynasty burial vault dating back to between AD 100 and 200, when Kowloon was under the administrative control of the Wu Empire, which took control of southern China in the period following the collapse of the Han Empire. Four barrel-vaulted chambers form a cross under a domed vault, and there are a few funerary exhibits on show. A 3-D animation helps you to visualise the tomb.

*Stall selling electronic merchandise in Sham Shui Po.*

# HONG KONG'S FESTIVALS

Performing the Fire Dragon Dance at the Heritage Mid-Autumn Festival.

## The city is at its most colourful and exuberant during the many traditional Chinese festivals.

Despite the brash modernity, Hong Kong is a city whose population remains close to its roots, where temple deities and ancestors are honoured with equal fervour. These traditions are at their most vibrant and visible during the colourful Chinese festivals.

**Lunar New Year**, in January or February, is the major annual event, a time for being with family, when most businesses shut down for at least a week. Children and the unmarried receive *lai see*, lucky red packets containing newly minted money. Employees get a bonus. Shops are decorated in fine style, and there are noisy dragon dances and processions. On the 15th day of the Lunar New Year the **Spring Lantern Festival** involves the hanging of colourful traditional lanterns in homes, restaurants and temples. Fishermen decorate their boats in bright colours and flock to Tin Hau temples around the territory on the **Birthday of Tin Hau**, the goddess of the sea, in April or May. At various Tin Hau temples – notably at Sai Kung in the New Territories – there are parades with lion dances and floats. The **Cheung Chau Bun Festival** (see page 189) in May is one of the most exciting local festivals; figures in historical costumes parade on stilts or ride on floats across the island. During the **Dragon Boat Festival** in June, elaborately decorated dragon boats race to the beat of loud drums. Many people's favourite is the **Mid-Autumn Festival** (Moon Festival) in September: paper lanterns of all shapes and sizes are illuminated and taken out to public parks – notably Victoria Park in Causeway Bay. People also eat special sweet cakes known as mooncakes.

*The Spring Lantern Festival takes place in the grounds of the Lantern Exhibition at the Hong Kong Cultural Centre Piazza. This exhibition is part of the Chinese New Year Celebrations.*

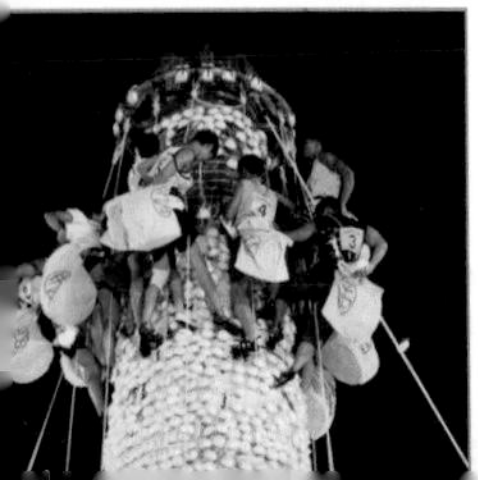

*The Cheung Chau Bun Festival originated as a peace offering to the ghosts of pirates.*

*Lion dances are performed to bring good luck and usher in the Lunar New Year, accompanied by firecrackers to scare off evil spirits. Sometimes there will be a dragon dance as well: this involves a larger group who hold the dragon aloft, whereas the lion dance is performed by just two people.*

*The climax of the Chinese New Year celebrations is the awesome fireworks display over the harbour. Most of the city's skyscrapers are lit up with stunning displays throughout the festive period.*

## THE CHINESE ZODIAC

**Chinese festivals operate using the lunar calendar. Beginning with Chinese New Year in late January or early to mid-February, the year is divided into 12 months of 29 days, with an extra month added every two and a half years.**

**The calendar operates in 60-year cycles, divided up into five smaller cycles of 12 years. Each year is represented by an animal, and each of the five cycles by an element (wood, water, metal, earth and fire). As with Western astrology, the year of a person's birth is thought to provide clues into his or her character. The 12 animals are:**

**Rat: (1948, 1960, 1972, 1984, 1996, 2008, 2020) charming, imaginative but quick-tempered.**

**Ox: (1949, 1961, 1973, 1985, 1997, 2009, 2021) a leader, conservative and patient.**

**Tiger: (1950, 1962, 1974, 1986, 1998, 2010, 2022) sensitive, emotional, stubborn.**

**Rabbit: (1951, 1963, 1975, 1987, 1999, 2011) popular, sentimental, cautious.**

**Dragon: (1952, 1964, 1976, 1988, 2000, 2012) charismatic, clever, prone to indiscretion.**

**Snake: (1953, 1965, 1977, 1989, 2001, 2013) wise, thoughtful, charming, intuitive.**

**Horse: (1954, 1966, 1978, 1990, 2002, 2014) hard-working, intelligent but egotistical.**

**Ram: (1955, 1967, 1979, 1991, 2003, 2015) artistic, pessimistic, generous.**

**Monkey: (1956, 1968, 1980, 1992, 2004, 2016) intelligent, witty, popular but distrustful.**

**Rooster: (1957, 1969, 1981, 1993, 2005, 2017) extravagant, brave, hard-working.**

**Dog: (1958, 1970, 1982, 1994, 2006, 2018) honest, faithful, dependable but a worrier.**

**Pig: (1959, 1971, 1983, 1995, 2007, 2019) clever, sincere, honest but prone to set difficult goals.**

*Hong Kong's Dragon Boat Festival (June) owes its existence to an event around 200 BC. Chu Yuan, a poet who had fallen out of political favour with the king, jumped into a river in protest and drowned. The frantic paddlers of today recreate the desperate actions of Yuan's friends as they tried to save him.*

*Incense burner at the foot of the Big Buddha on Lantau Island.*

公司敬送

*Tai Long Wan beach, a beautiful part of Hong Kong.*

# THE NEW TERRITORIES

**Hong Kong's northern hinterland is well off the tourist trail, which is surprising given its magnificent scenery. Some splendid beaches and ancient walled villages add to the appeal.**

**Main Attractions**

Ten Thousand Buddhas Monastery
Hong Kong Heritage Museum
Tai Po Kau Nature Reserve
Sai Kung
Hiking in Sai Kung Country Park
Hong Kong Wetland Park
Kam Tin Walled Villages
Kadoorie Farm and Botanic Garden

**Map**

Pages 168, 179

The buffer between the dense urban area of Kowloon and the boundary with mainland China, the New Territories are an odd mixture. Nobody is ploughing with water buffalo any longer, but there are corners where time seems to have not so much stood still as gone into reverse. Conversely, other areas are as modern as anywhere else in the SAR, notably the New Towns such as Sha Tin and Yuen Long – and this is where more than half of Hong Kong's population live. Transport links are good, with the MTR's East Rail running straight up the middle to the border with mainland China, supplemented by the MTR West Rail, Tseung Kawn O and Ma On Shan lines, as well as the Light Rail. Away from the electrified rails, there are calm beaches to seek out, remote villages and lofty mountains to hike – after all, some two-fifths of the SAR is designated as country park.

## SHA TIN AND SURROUNDINGS

**Sha Tin** ❶ is one of Hong Kong's largest new towns, but it also offers plenty of recreation. Massive housing projects occupy what were once lush rice paddies whose produce was reserved for the emperor, while the New Town Plaza, an extensive shopping and entertainment complex, offers cinemas, designer boutiques and a musical fountain that never fails to draw appreciative crowds.

### Ten Thousand Buddhas Monastery

**Address:** Po Fook Hill, Pai Tau Village, Sha Tin; www.10kbuddhas.org
**Tel:** 2691 1067
**Opening Hrs:** daily 9am–5.30pm
**Entrance fee:** free

*The walk up to the Ten Thousand Buddhas Monastery.*

**Transport:** Citybus 170 (from Aberdeen), MTR Sha Tin

The Sha Tin Valley has several places of worship including the remarkable **Ten Thousand Buddhas Monastery** ❷. Follow the signposts from Grand Central Plaza and IKEA, then climb the 431 steps flanked by gold-painted effigies of enlightened beings up the hillside above Sha Tin station. Founded in 1949, the monastery has five temples. The name is, in fact, over-modest – the main altar room alone accommodates close to 13,000 Buddha statues along its walls. The temple is guarded by huge, fierce-looking statues of various gods, and by similarly ferocious watchdogs that are chained up in the daytime. The complex also contains an impressive nine-storey pagoda of Indian architectural design, commemorating a Buddha who was believed to be the ninth reincarnation of Prince Vishnu.

A further 69 steps up the hill is the **Temple of Man Fat**, containing the preserved remains of the man who created this temple-and-pagoda complex: Yuet Kai, a monk who spent a lifetime studying Buddhism and living a meditative life. His greatest

**New Territories East**

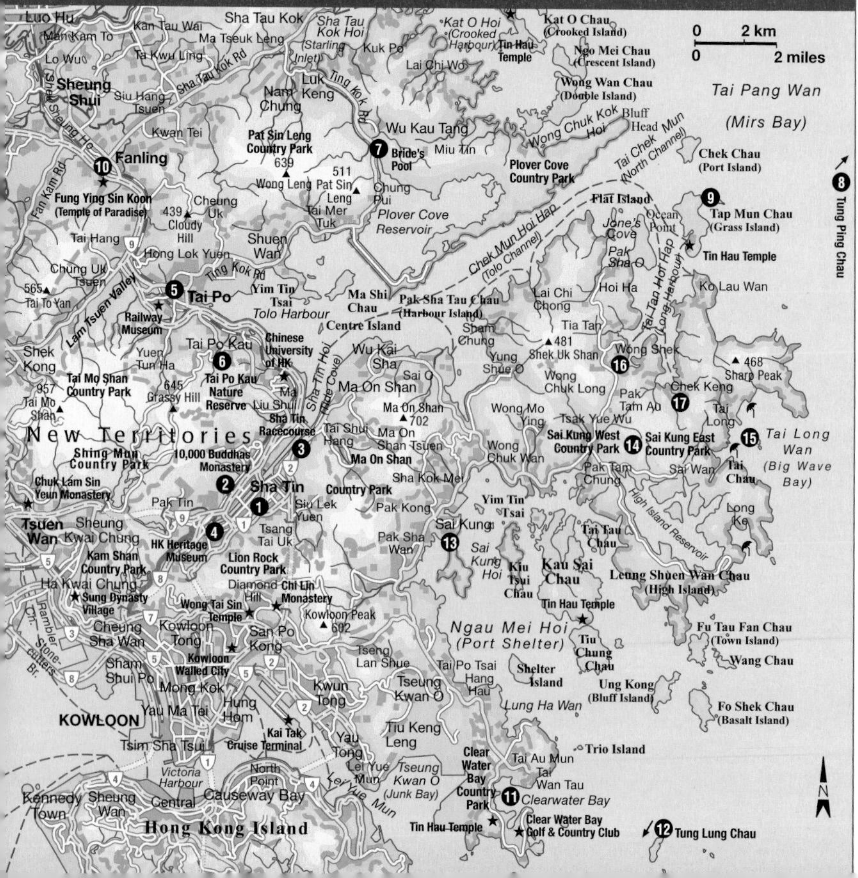

concern was to achieve immortality – an objective which seemed to have failed when he died and was buried. Yet when his body was exhumed (to be moved to its final resting place, according to Chinese custom), it was perfectly preserved and radiated a ghostly yellow glow. Since there was obviously something supernatural about Yuet Kai, it was decided to preserve his body in gold leaf for posterity.

From the Ten Thousand Buddhas Monastery you can look across the valley at **Amah Rock**, which looks like an *aa maa*, or mother, with a baby on her back. Legend has it that a local fisherman went to sea and did not return. His wife waited patiently for his return but he did not appear. After a year the gods took pity on her and turned her into stone. Today the rock is a place of worship for Chinese women, and stands as a symbol of women's loyalty and fidelity.

A major destination in the valley is the Hong Kong Jockey Club's **Sha Tin Racecourse** ❸, which has its own MTR station. Around 30,000 punters flock here for the weekend race days, but the crowd can triple on cup days such as the Hong Kong Derby, the Queen Elizabeth II Cup and the Hong Kong International Races. Tourists can buy special tourist badges at the track or at off-site betting offices, which grant them access to the members' enclosure and a front seat on Hong Kong's racing world. For more on horse-racing, see page 126.

## Hong Kong Heritage Museum

**Address:** 1 Man Lam Road, Sha Tin; www.heritagemuseum.gov.hk
**Tel:** 2180 8188
**Opening Hrs:** Mon, Wed–Fri 10am–6pm, Sat–Sun 10am–7pm
**Entrance fee:** charge, but free on Wed
**Transport:** KMB routes 72A, 80M, 86, 89, 282, MTR Che Kung Temple

If you are in Sha Tin already, it is easy to take a five-minute taxi ride from the main station to the superb and spacious **Hong Kong Heritage Museum** ❹. This is Hong Kong's largest museum, with 12 exhibition halls including Hong Kong's

*Sha Tin Racecourse is popular with both locals and tourists.*

**FACT**

Punters at the Hong Kong Jockey Club's Sha Tin Racecourse check the racing statistics and watch the thoroughbreds going through their paces on the world's longest television screen. Measuring 70.4 metres (231ft), the LED screen is as long as a Boeing 747. An average of 40,000 people bet on every race, giving the Jockey Club a race-day turnover in excess of HK$1 billion.

only formal tribute to one its most famous (albeit US-born) sons, Bruce Lee. Other highlights include the T.T. Tsui Gallery of Chinese Art, an exhibition devoted to the development of the New Territories, one on the history of Cantonese opera and another detailing the evolution of local toys.

Two stops along from Sha Tin is the Chinese University of Hong Kong, with its highly respected **Art Museum** (www.cuhk.edu.hk/ics/amm; tel: 3943 7416; Mon–Sat 10am–5pm, Sun 1–5pm; free) showcasing a collection of over 7,000 pieces from its extensive collections of Chinese art from ancient to pre-modern times.

## TAI PO AND THE NORTHEAST

Further north (back on the main MTR East Rail line) is the market town of **Tai Po** ❺, which means "buying place". The Old Town is at the northeastern end of Tolo Harbour, where the highway crosses the Lower Lam Tsuen River. The **Hong Kong Railway Museum** (www.heritagemuseum.gov.hk; Wed–Mon 10am–6pm; tel: 2653 3455; free), complete with vintage train carriages, is housed in the former train station between today's Tai Wo and Tai Po Market MTR stations – a 10-minute walk: follow the map and signs in MTR stations. Alternatively, take a taxi.

Catch bus 64K or hop in a taxi from Tai Wo station to visit the **Wishing Trees**, a pair of banyans which have become popular with locals for their alleged properties. The idea is to make a wish, write it down on the streamer provided and then hurl this into the tree. Unfortunately, the two elderly banyans started collapsing under the strain, and for now wishes are placed nearby on a wooden rack.

One of the best places to escape from urban Hong Kong is the **Tai Po Kau Nature Reserve** ❻.

### Tolo Harbour

To the northeast, the coast around **Tolo Harbour** has become more built up in recent years, but once past Shuen Wan, Ting Kok Road must rank among the most picturesque routes in Hong Kong, leading round to the Plover Cove Reservoir,

*Bride's Pool.*

Bride's Pool and Starling Inlet. A ride on KMB bus 75K from Tai Po Market to Tai Mei Tuk lets you enjoy the panoramas. At weekends and on public holidays, the roadside barbecue areas teem with noisy groups, but even then, a five-minute walk into the hills brings peace and solitude. The area around **Bride's Pool** ❼, with waterfalls and woodland glades, is especially beautiful, while the village of Luk Keng to the north still has several fine old inhabited houses. Like many semi-abandoned villages, Luk Keng was once home to a few thousand people. Its decline began in the 1950s and 60s, when rice farming became unprofitable. The nearby village of Nam Chung marks the northern end of the **Wilson Trail**, a 78km (49-mile) walking route that runs from Stanley on Hong Kong Island to the northern end of the New Territories.

## Mirs Bay Islands

Out at Mirs Bay (Tai Pang Wan) in the far northeast of the SAR, **Tung Ping Chau** ❽ (not to be confused with Peng Chau near Lantau) is one of Hong Kong's remotest islands, just 3km (2 miles) off the Guangdong coast. From its hilltops, you can get a panoramic view of the mainland's Bao An area. Once supporting a population of close to 3,000, there are no residents now, though the remaining deserted hamlets have become part of the tourist attraction. Ping Chau has a fascinating landscape, made up of what are known as 'thousand layer rocks' – colourful and unusually shaped sedimentary rock. The island is now one of the eight areas making up the Hong Kong Geopark (www.geopark.gov.hk).

At the northwestern end of Mirs Bay close to the Sai Kung peninsula is **Tap Mun Chau** ❾ (also called Grass Island), a 30-minute boat ride from Wong Shek Pier. A dramatic decline in fish stocks has caused a collapse of the fishing industry, and of communities like Tap Mun: today many of the houses stand empty, although the village retains a single seafood restaurant, Loi Lam's, that makes the journey worthwhile (and is packed out at weekends). A path winds through the village, up past the fortress-like police

*The Hong Kong Heritage Museum is one of the New Territories' main attractions.*

*Statues at the Ten Thousand Buddhas Monastery.*

### TAI PO KAU NATURE RESERVE

A short taxi ride from Tai Po Market MTR station, or a 20-minute walk from the car park near the 14-milestone on Tai Po Road, Tai Po Kau is the oldest of Hong Kong's reserves. Planting began here in 1926 as part of the government's attempt to reforest the New Territories (much of the original forest cover had long since disappeared, and what was left was destroyed during the Japanese Occupation).

Today, the 460 hectares (1,136 acres) of forest shelter a good proportion of Hong Kong's flora and fauna. Native tree species include litsea, giant bean, sweet gum, camphor, acacia, paperbark and the joss-stick tree (*Aquilania sinensis*) – used for making fans and joss sticks. A colourful variety of birds – including such exotica as rufous-capped babblers, scarlet-backed flowerpeckers and greater necklaced laughing thrushes, amongst an assortment of bulbuls and minivets – make the reserve their home. March, April and September are the best "birding" months. Mammals are also well represented, although mostly difficult to observe – the exception being the rhesus macaque monkeys, which can be quite aggressive, particularly if there is food around (avoid feeding them). Barking deer, civet cat, pangolin and porcupine are far more elusive.

*Temple door god on a temple in Tap Mun. Temple door gods protect the temple.*

station, and onto a grassy plateau whose brisk winds make it extremely popular with local kite-flyers.

There are terrific views from the northern point of the island, particularly from the top of the hills next to the 100-year-old **Tin Hau Temple**. While there are dozens of Tin Hau temples all over Hong Kong, this one is special because it is the last before the open sea. When the east winds roar, their sounds can be heard in a crevice under the altar – this eerie howling is seen as a warning of storms to come. Former island residents who may have emigrated to all parts of the globe will make a special effort to come back to the temple for major festivals.

Parts of Tap Mun are covered with thick, impenetrable scrub, but in the upper reaches much of it is abandoned agricultural land, and the cows that once pulled ploughs are now feral and roam freely.

## Fanling

**Fanling** ❿ and its neighbour Sheung Shui are new towns with over a quarter of a million residents. Fanling is also home to the largest Daoist institute in Hong Kong – **Fung Ying Sin Koon** (www.fysk.org; Temple of Paradise; daily 9am–5pm), close to Fanling MTR station. There is an intricate system of pathways around this rebuilt temple, and plenty of shady benches suitable for meditation.

From Fanling station, it's a short ride on the 64K minibus to the **Leung Yuk Tau Heritage Trail**, starting at **Shung Him Tong** – a village founded in 1901 by Hakka Lutherans fleeing persecution across the border. The trail wends its way around several walled villages before reaching the venerable **Tang Chung Ling Ancestral Hall** (Wed–Mon 9am–1pm, 2–5pm; free). Originally built in 1570, the hall remains a focal point of the Tang clan.

On a more earthly level, the well-known **Hong Kong Golf Club** (www.hkgolfclub.org) just outside Fanling has three exceptionally good 18-holers, known as the Old, the New and the Eden. It is the site of the Hong Kong Open Tournament every February, and is open to non-members on

*Sunrise over Fanling.*

### THE TIN HAU FESTIVAL

Tin Hau, the Daoist sea goddess, is revered by fishermen all along the China coast. Also known as Matsu and A-Ma, her deification is based on the legend of Lin Moniang, a Fujianese girl who lived in the 10th century. Asleep during a storm, she dreamt that her two fisherman brothers were drowning, and that she managed to save them. When the brothers miraculously survived the real storm, the story spread, and Lin became the object of fishermen's prayers for protection from the dangers of the sea.

The festival of her birth on the 23rd day of the third lunar month (mid-April – mid-May), is a noisy celebration at its liveliest around the Tin Hau Temple in Joss House Bay.

*Fresh seafood in Sai Kung.*

weekdays, though visitors will require a handicap certificate.

## CLEARWATER BAY TO SAI KUNG

These eastern areas of the New Territories are some of the most attractive parts of Hong Kong. The Sai Kung peninsula is the most scenic area, with rolling hills, mountains, reservoirs, craggy coves and over 70 islands. It is at its most rewarding if you can hike into the hills or take to the water on a ferry, speedboat or junk.

### Clearwater Bay

The **Clearwater Bay peninsula** ⓫ is a sought-after residential area that is blessed with some great beaches and possibly the freshest air in Hong Kong. The single access road leads past the former **Shaw Brothers Movie Studio** to reach the exclusive **Clearwater Bay Golf & Country Club**, easily recognised by its landmark pyramid-shaped clubhouse. Non-members can play here, but green fees are high.

An indentation in the shoreline forms **Joss House Bay**, which comes to life once a year on the birthday of the sea goddess Tin Hau. Hundreds of fishing junks and sampans head for the **Tin Hau Temple** here to pay their respects to the Queen of Heaven and Goddess of the Sea. This temple was built by two brothers allegedly

### SHAW BROTHERS

Clearwater Bay Road runs past the former Shaw Brothers Movie Studio, once a cornerstone of the local film industry. Founded by six brothers from Shanghai in 1958, for three decades the studio often churned out over 30 films a year. Best known for their martial arts movies, the brothers also produced romance, opera and dramas; many of their 1,000-plus films are now considered classic Hong Kong movies. Shaw Brothers has one of the world's most advanced film production and digital post-production facilities in a US$180 million building on the hill above Tseung Kwan O. The patriarch of the empire, Sir Run Run Shaw, was awarded a BAFTA Special Award in 2013, at the age of 106, shortly before he passed away in January 2014.

*Scene from a Shaw Brothers martial arts film.*

**TIP**

There are some good beaches around Clearwater Bay, and compared with the wilder stretches of sand further north in Sai Kung, they are easily accessible on the no. 91 bus from Diamond Hill MTR station.

saved by Tin Hau after their junk was destroyed by a typhoon in the 10th century. To cope with up to 10,000 visitors during the annual Tin Hau festival, ferries run for one day only from North Point on Hong Kong Island.

## Tung Lung Chau

Also known as Nam Tong Island, **Tung Lung Chau** ⓬ is located off the southern tip of the Clearwater Bay peninsula. The island's biggest attraction is **Tung Lung Fort** (Information Centre Wed–Mon 9am–5pm; open access to the fort) built about 300 years ago. To find the fort, follow the path from the hamlet at the ferry pier over the rolling, open landscape of northern Tung Lung. The fort is perched on a low headland in the northeast. It was abandoned in 1810, but its interior is reasonably well preserved, with the bases of the partitions between the rooms visible.

On the north shore of Tung Lung Chau are some rock carvings on the cliffs depicting the daily lives of people who lived in this area several hundred years ago. It is a perfect place to enjoy the beautiful sea view, with waves rushing to the shore and hiking trails lead along the cliffs and hills. As with most of the outlying islands, there is no regular ferry to Tung Lung, but kaido boats from Sai Wan Ho on Hong Kong Island operate on most weekends (tel: 2513 1103).

## Sai Kung

Hiram's Highway branches off Clearwater Bay Road just before the University of Science and Technology, and leads down to the town of **Sai Kung** ⓭. The road is named after a brand of sausage made by Hiram K. Potts that the highway's builder, John Wynne-Potts, devoured by the tin. While the fringes of Sai Kung have fallen prey to development, this town and its neighbouring villages retain a strong seaside flavour. Along the seafront, sea creatures in tanks are a sure sign that seafood is on the quayside restaurants' menus, and Sai Kung Town also has good pubs and alfresco international restaurants. Further east along the seafront you can catch the

*View of Clearwater Bay, towards the golf club.*

ferry to Kau Sai Chau, the only public golf course in Hong Kong.

The road from town runs out to **Sai Kung Country Park** ⓮, the starting point of the **MacLehose Trail**. The trail stretches for 100km (60 miles) through mostly open country, from one side of the New Territories to the other, across the high grassy hills as far as Tuen Mun. The trail is well marked, and there are places to camp along the way. Some parts are extremely steep and hard-going, but anyone who is used to hiking should have no problems tackling the shorter sections or any of the other walks in this area. At the very end of the road into the country park, **Hoi Ha** provides a small stretch of sand on the edge of the eponymous marine reserve.

The jewel in Sai Kung's crown is **Tai Long Wan** (Big Wave Bay) Beach ⓯. The usual way of getting there involves a two-hour trek, either around the High Island Reservoir or by cutting across the hills along the MacLehose Trail Stage 2 from the road at Pak Tam Au. Others opt to take a bus or taxi to Wong Shek (see page 175) and hop on a speedboat (around HK$60 for small groups) for a thrilling 15-minute ride round to Chek Keng, then join the MacLehose Trail and hike for an hour over the ridge to the bay. Whichever way you arrive, the effort is more than worth it. There are two long swathes of very pale and powdery sand, and usually enough surf to make it worth lugging a surfboard over the hill. There is also a café-cum-shop selling cold beer and hot noodles, and enough open space to romp far and wide. The one downside of Tai Long Wan is that there is a strong undertow, so don't swim out too far. A day of rest and relaxation here makes it difficult to believe that this is part of Hong Kong.

Beyond the crest at Pak Tam Au, the road swoops down through woods and little villages to Wong Shek pier, but from just below the top it's worth pausing to admire the pristine views.

At **Wong Shek** ⓰ (Bus 94 from Sai Kung) the Jockey Club watersports centre hires out dinghies and windsurfing boards (tel. 2328 2311; closed Tue). This is also a popular picnic and barbecue site – perhaps

*MacLehose Trail sign.*

*On the Lung Yeuk Tau Heritage Trail.*

## ISLAND-HOPPING FROM SAI KUNG

Offshore from Sai Kung village, some of the most easily accessible outlying islands sit in the Inner Port Shelter (Ngau Mei Hoi), a former British military firing range that makes a very photogenic start to the trip. Sampan owners will either make a one-hour tour for about HK$100 (bargain hard!), dropping you off for a short stroll at whichever island you desire, or charge around HK$300 to take you to your destination and then pick you up later. One of the nicest beaches is at Hap Mun Bay on Kiu Tsui Chau (Sharp Island), with fine sand and water that is usually clear. You can also camp overnight here, and there are barbecue pits for a cook-out. If recent visitors or perhaps a recent storm have left the beach in a mess, don't hesitate to move on round the harbour: there are other strands on Pak Sha Chau (White Sand Island) and tiny Cham Tau Chau (Pillow Island). Yim Tin Tsai (Little Salt Field) Island is remarkable for its Catholic chapel, which sees little use now, as many of the islanders have moved away. Remember that whichever island you pick, you should take enough food and drink to keep you going; sunscreen and mosquito repellent are also advisable.

*The male fiddler crab has one large claw, used for defending its territory and attracting females.*

because it's seen as the "end of the line", just about as far away from the city as it's possible to get by road.

**Chek Keng** ⓱ is nearly deserted nowadays, but it's fascinating to wander round the old buildings and paddy fields and imagine the time when the New Territories were a land apart, with people living on what they could earn from soil and sea. This remains a gloriously empty part of Hong Kong that even locals know little about.

*Hikers in Sai Wan.*

## THE WESTERN NEW TERRITORIES

Looking to the northwest from Hong Kong Island, the view across the harbour to the shore of the western New Territories is dominated by container ships, cranes and a network of bridges crossing from Lantau to Tsing Yi Island and on to Kowloon. Kwai Chung container port is one of the three busiest ports in the world, transporting goods from factories in Guangdong to ports worldwide.

The busy port and the need for road and rail links to the airport on Lantau prompted the investment of public funds into huge infrastructure projects, including some dramatic new bridges. Opened in 1997, the **Tsing Ma Bridge** ⓲ is some 2.2km (1.5 miles) long, with majestic 200-metre (650ft) twin towers. It links Lantau (and the airport) with Tsing Yi Island. The entrance

*The white sand beach at Tai Long Wan.*

to the Rambler Channel between Container Terminal 9 on Tsing Yi and the eight other container terminals at Kwai Chung, is spanned by Stonecutters' Bridge, 1.6km (1 mile) long, with cables radiating from its 295-metre (970ft) towers. The Lantau Link Visitor Centre (Mon–Fri 10am–5pm, Sat–Sun 10am–6.30pm, closed Wed), on the North West Tsing Yi Interchange, explains how the bridge was built, and how it continues to work, while the adjacent viewing platform has spectacular views of the bridge and surrounding countryside.

## Tsuen Wan

Behind the industrial area at Kwai Chung is the urban sprawl of the new town of **Tsuen Wan** ⓳. The Chinese presence here seems to have begun in about the 2nd century AD. In the 13th century, the Chinese Empire extended to this area because the emperor was being driven south by invading Mongols. In 1277, the emperor and his entourage arrived in Tsuen Wan. Later, in the mid-17th century, when the Formosan pirate Koxinga was building his empire, the Manchu government ordered a mass evacuation of coastal areas to save the populace from the marauding buccaneer. Koxinga's forces demolished the vacated settlement of Tsuen Wan, and it was not repopulated until the end of the 17th century.

The main reason to make the long MTR journey out here is to poke around the **Sam Tung Uk Museum** (Wed–Mon 9am–6pm; free), a beautifully restored Hakka walled village. The narrow alleyways trace a path past a central ancestral hall, an exhibition room and rows of tiny cubicles stocked with period furniture and farming tools.

Tsuen Wan's most modern building is also the sixth tallest in Hong Kong. The top 40 storeys of the 319-metre (1,046ft) Nina Tower is L'Hotel Nina, named like the tower after the late Nina Wang, who was Hong Kong's richest woman when she died in 2007, leaving her fortune to her feng shui master.

## Beyond Tsuen Wan

West of Tsuen Wan, the Tuen Mun Highway passes another impressive

**TIP**

The Yuen Yuen Institute (daily 9am–5pm; free) near Tsuen Wan is popular on organised tourist itineraries. It was set up in 1950 and is the only temple in Hong Kong dedicated to all three major Chinese religions: Daoism, Buddhism and Confucianism, and actively promotes the integration of the three religions' philosophies. There is a good vegetarian restaurant on site.

*The Tsing Ma Bridge, Hong Kong's 'Golden Gate'.*

**FACT**

With land always at a premium in Hong Kong, the issue of the 7 million population's final resting places occasionally comes to the fore. With niches in well-known temples and columbaria commanding such high prices, a number of illegal facilities were discovered in 2010 on remote islands and areas in the New Territories – and, in a few cases, inside apartments within residential housing blocks.

airport-related bridge – **Tsing Long** – before reaching the sprawling New Town of **Tuen Mun**.

Near **Castle Peak**, the large mountain west of Tuen Mun that is mostly occupied by army firing ranges, and adjacent to the Ching Chung Light Rail Transit (LRT) station, is the huge temple of **Ching Chung Koon** ⑳ (daily 9am–5.30pm). Dedicated to Lui Bun, one of the so-called Daoist immortals, the temple houses numerous valuable Chinese art treasures (not on show). Despite a starring role in the opening scene of Bruce Lee's *Enter the Dragon*, in Hong Kong it is best known as a columbarium, where the ashes of the deceased are stored. Niches containing ashes, often featuring photographs of the deceased, are looked after by temple attendants. Ching Chung Koon is also home to a few elderly residents, for whom it provides medical services. There is a vegetarian canteen selling basic, filling fare for visitors.

On the slopes of Castle Peak stands a temple that is smaller but no less intriguing for that – **Pei Tu Temple** ㉑, dedicated to the eponymous monk, a famous figure in Chinese mythology.

*Tsuen Wan skyline, with the L'Hotel Nina on the left.*

## Yuen Long

In 1898, when the British took a census of their newly leased New Territories, **Yuen Long** ㉒ was a traditional market town set among 50 or so villages in the middle of the largest flood plain in the New Territories. The census logged 23,000 people in the Yuen Long district. Now the population is almost 615,000, most of whom live in the high-rise blocks of Tin Shui Wai and Yuen Long new towns. A few remarkable remnants of the past remain, however, and the area can be explored via the overland Light Rail, buses and the MTR. It is also the starting point for exploring the mangroves and mudflats of Hong Kong's wetlands.

From Tin Shui Wai MTR it's a short walk to the **Ping Shan Heritage Trail**, a short 1km (0.6-mile) stroll through more than half a dozen historical Chinese buildings of which the highlight is the only surviving intact pagoda in Hong Kong – the **Tsui Sing Lau** (Pagoda of Gathering Stars), built in 1486 to improve the village's feng shui.

## Hong Kong Wetland Park

**Address:** Wetland Park Road, Tin Shui Wai; www.wetlandpark.gov.hk
**Tel:** 3152 2666
**Opening Hrs:** Wed–Mon 10am–5pm
**Entrance Fee:** charge
**Transport:** KMB & Citybus nos. 967, 264M, 276B, LRT Wetland Park

The Hong Kong Wetland Park allows visitors to explore the diversity of Hong Kong's wetland ecosystem by following wooden decking paths that meander through an area of coastal marshland.

Within the 61-hectare (151-acre) area there are several hides with good-quality telescopes for bird-watching. So far 241 bird species have been recorded here, including

*Sunrise in Tai Mo Shan.*

numerous varieties of egrets and herons, and the rare black-faced spoonbill. An indoor visitor centre houses educational interactive exhibitions on conservation issues.

## The Mai Po Marshes

For the dedicated birdwatcher or naturalist, a visit to the **Mai Po Marshes** ㉓ is a must. Managed by the World Wide Fund for Nature (WWF), this expanse of mangroves and mudflats is a stopping point on the migratory routes of more than 400 different species of birds. The WWF runs scheduled tours, but visits must always be booked in advance (tel: 2471 3480; www.wwf.org.hk; charge).

## Kam Tin walled villages

East of Yuen Long, the walled villages of **Kam Tin** ㉔ can be reached easily by MTR (Kam Sheung Road station) or the 64K bus. The most popular for visitors is the Kat Hing Wai village, which stands incongruously surrounded by modern housing as heavy vehicle traffic trundles past (to get there, take the MTR West Rail to Kam Sheung Road Station). Some 400 people live there, and most of them still share the same surname, Tang.

**FACT**

The five Great Clans in the New Territories first moved into Guangdong during the Han dynasty, then to Hong Kong during the Song and Yuan dynasties. The five clans were the Tang, Hau, Pang, Liu and Man. The Tangs settled in the Yuen Long area and were the architects of the buildings along the Lung Yeuk Tau and Ping Shan Heritage Trails and the Kam Tin walled villages.

**New Territories West**

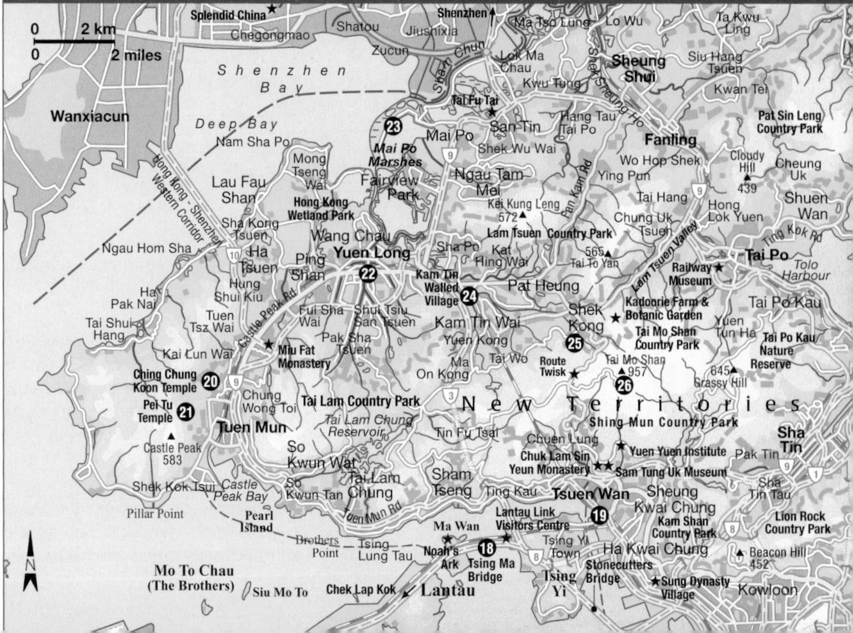

# Hiking in the hills

**One of Hong Kong's greatest assets is its mountainous countryside, and the open grassy hills of the New Territories offer superb hiking opportunities.**

In a rocky gully the air is dank. Far above, hidden by a wall of trees, are the upper slopes of Tai Mo Shan (957 metres/3,140ft), the great massif that encompasses the central New Territories, and Hong Kong's highest point. Cutting down through the mountain, water cascades beyond rocks green with slime. Lower down, gurgling amidst bamboo thickets, the stream descends into the sprawling bowl of the Shing Mun Valley.

Further to the east, on the beautiful Sai Kung peninsula, the steep grassy slopes of Sharp Peak (468 metres/1,535ft) plunge down to Tai Long Wan – a bay ringed by crescent beaches. Ranges stretch into the distance, looming above seldom-visited valleys.

*Girl hiking in High Junk Peak, one of the three treacherous peaks in Hong Kong.*

In the far northeast is Pat Sin Leng (639 metres/2,096ft) – grand, challenging and the northern limit of the Hong Kong uplands. Jagged ridges rise up above sheer escarpments. Valleys with rich biodiversity occupy land where, just 40 years ago, rice farmers tilled the land. Old homes, empty and forlorn, stand amidst the fields.

The New Territories' countryside remains largely empty. With its steep peaks, deep valleys and ocean views, it epitomises the Chinese term for "landscape" – **shan shui,** literally "mountains and water", which defines a particular style of traditional Chinese painting.

## Local hikes

The landscape is criss-crossed with numerous hiking trails, varying from family walks to signposted nature trails to rugged upland and coastal hikes leading into areas where one rarely sees another soul. Excellent public transport makes access quite easy.

From the Shing Mun Valley, a 14km (9-mile) hike takes you up and across impressive boulder slopes, past the massive summit of Tai Mo Shan, and down through the lush and beautiful Pak Nga Shan Valley – site of Kadoorie Farm and Botanic Garden (see page 181).

The ideal hike on the Sai Kung peninsula is the route that connects Sharp Peak with Tai Long Wan, a circular route of about 15km (9.5 miles). Noodle shops in a few places offer welcome refreshment, and the clean beaches are great for swimming.

The hike up and over the Pat Sin Leng range is only about 10km (6 miles), but the distance can be misleading. Here a series of sharp up-and-down peaks mark a dramatic, airy ridgeline, with the views sweeping south towards Hong Kong and north into China proper.

For the ambitious, the MacLehose Trail (see page 175) crosses the entire width of the New Territories, extending east–west for some 100km (62 miles), while the Wilson Trail (70km/44 miles) runs north from Stanley on Hong Kong Island to the Pat Sin Leng range.

Built in the 1600s, the fortified village shelters behind walls 6 metres (20ft) thick, with guard-houses at each corner, arrow slits for fighting off attackers and a moat, although the authenticity may seem compromised by some modern buildings inside. Visitors can enter for a nominal charge, although the ladies in traditional Hakka dress are experienced models and will expect a fee for a photograph.

## Across the central mountains

From Kam Tin it is possible to take a scenic route via **Shek Kong** ㉕, once the British military garrison and airfield but now home to a skeleton force of the Chinese People's Liberation Army. The far end of the village marks the start of **Route Twisk** (an acronym for Tsuen Wan/Shek Kong), one of the most panoramic drives in Hong Kong.

An alternative route is to take the 64K bus that crosses the HKSAR from Yuen Long to Tai Po, and for just a few dollars enjoy the sights along the Lam Kan Road as it winds along through the contrasts of the 21st-century New Territories – scrap metal yards, abandoned cars, containers and creeper-covered heavy machinery among sprawling villages of Spanish villas, surrounded by majestic mountains and lush forests, with glimpses of the spires of Hong Kong and Shenzhen on either side.

From the top of Route Twisk near Hong Kong's highest peak, **Tai Mo Shan** ㉖ (957 metres/3,140ft), one can look over to China and down to Hong Kong Island. Continue on Lam Kam Road to Pak Ngau Shek in the Lam Tsuen valley to reach Kadoorie Farm.

## Kadoorie Farm and Botanic Garden

**Address:** Lam Kam Road, Tai Po district; www.kfbg.org.hk
**Tel:** 2483 7200
**Opening Hrs:** daily 9.30am–5pm
**Entrance Fee:** charge
**Transport:** MTR Kam Sheung Road, then 64K to Tai Po

Located at the foot of Tai Mo Shan in grounds of 1.5 sq km (0.5 sq mile), **Kadoorie Farm** is about as far from urban Hong Kong as it is possible to get. Set up in the 1950s, when it provided pigs and chickens to help newly arrived refugees become self-sufficient, Kadoorie has since evolved into a conservation centre and wild animal sanctuary and is a pioneer of organic farming in Hong Kong.

It's a fairly steep walk up the landscaped hillside to the peak, Kwun Yum Shan (552 metres/1,811ft), but the magnificent views across the New Territories to Shenzhen bring a fitting reward. Alternatively, you can call ahead to coordinate your visit with the twice-daily shuttle bus that runs from the farm to the peak.

### KIDS

Kadoorie Farm is a great place to take children. As well as the chance to experience the local flora up close, there's an amphibian and reptile house, insect house and various farm animals to see. Injured birds of prey are treated and released back into the wild from the Raptor Sanctuary, and there is also a wildlife rescue centre.

*Vivid greenery at Hong Kong Wetland Park.*

# HONG KONG'S WILD SIDE

## A series of country parks occupy over 40 percent of the SAR's land area, and offer easily accessible respite from this most stressful of cities.

One of the many unusual aspects of Hong Kong is the contrast between some of the world's most densely populated urban areas and the utterly empty countryside that surrounds them. In parts of the New Territories and Outlying Islands it is possible to walk for mile after mile in dramatic mountain scenery, enjoy superb natural views, and see no one for hours on end.

For its modest size, Hong Kong has some impressive mountains – at 957 metres (3,140ft) Tai Mo Shan is on a par with the highest mountain in England, and several others in the New Territories and Lantau are not far behind. A well-signposted network of hiking trails extends across all 24 country parks, with some longer distance routes such as the MacLehose, Wilson and Hong Kong Island trails.

Areas of woodland occur at lower and middle levels, sometimes as a result of reforestation, but most upland areas were deforested long ago by the agricultural needs of villagers. The higher areas are almost all grassland and shrubland, bright green in summer, brown in the dry winters.

*Grass fires are common in Hong Kong when the humidity drops during the dry months from October to January, sometimes ravaging entire hillsides. Warnings are displayed at country parks when the risk is high.*

*The coastline of the New Territories has some fine stretches of beach – nowhere more so than at Tai Long Wan on the eastern edge of Sai Kung Country Park.*

*A fiddler crab at Hong Kong Wetland Park.*

## HONG KONG'S FAUNA AND FLORA

*The odd-looking litchi lantern bug.*

Located on the eastern edge of the Eurasian landmass, Hong Kong lies in a transition zone between the cooler lands to the north and the tropical south. The cool winters brought by the northeast monsoon winds mean that the natural vegetation cover is not tropical "jungle", but rather broad-leaved forest with temperate oaks and laurels as well as tropical species such as lianas, banyans and fan palms. The original forest cover disappeared centuries ago to be replaced either by agriculture or grassland (on the hills), but some areas are now successfully reforested.

A wide variety of wildlife survives in Hong Kong. The Tai Po Kau Nature Reserve shelters rhesus macaques, pangolins, civet cats and barking deer as well as a large diversity of birds, amphibians and reptiles. The Mai Po Marshes are an important resting point for migratory birds. Marine life has been badly hit by pollution, but Chinese river dolphins can still be seen off the coast of Lantau.

*Waterfall at The Peak.*

*A rhesus macaque at Tai Po Kau Nature Reserve. Although this species and the closely related long-tailed macaque are indigenous to the region around Hong Kong, the present population of rhesus macaques are descendants of individuals released into the area in 1913.*

*The largest of Hong Kong's indigenous snakes, the Burmese python, continues to grow throughout its life and can reach over 9 metres (30ft) in length.*

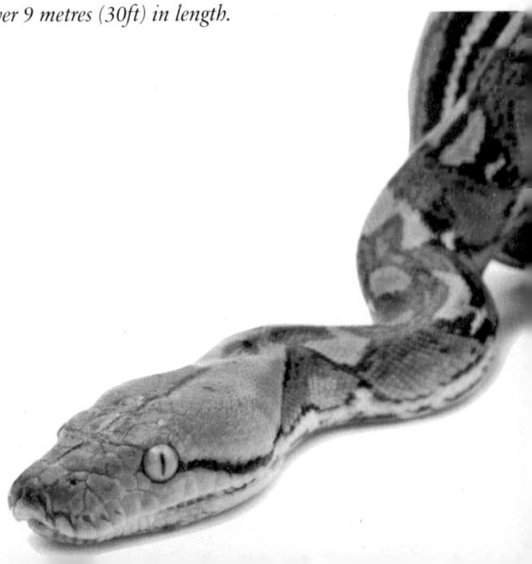

# THE OUTLYING ISLANDS

**Each of the three principal outlying islands, Lantau, Cheung Chau and Lamma, make a rewarding day trip from the city. Attractions include sandy beaches, seafood restaurants, appealing villages, beautiful scenery and – on a different note – Lantau's Disneyland theme park.**

**Main Attractions**

- Po Lin Monastery and the Big Buddha
- Ngong Ping Cable Car
- Tai O
- Cheung Sha Beach
- Disneyland
- Cheung Chau village
- Pak Tai Temple
- Yung Shue Wan to Sok Kwu Wan Walk

**Map**

Page 187

A substantial majority of Hong Kong's visitors arrive at the state-of-the-art international airport on what used to be an "outlying island", but one which is now joined by road-and-rail suspension bridge to Kowloon. Within a short space of time they are being whisked into the city aboard the smooth Airport Express train, passing not towering skyscrapers but lofty mountains which are part of Lantau's country parks. Such are the contrasts on Hong Kong's islands.

Lantau's peaceful countryside has suffered from the dual onslaught of the airport and the construction of the Disneyland theme park, but Hong Kong's other large outlying islands, Lamma and Cheung Chau, are far less developed. Here there are no proper roads (just narrow concrete paths), and few structures are higher than three storeys. The remainder of the islands – more than 230 of them – are either uninhabited or support small rural communities.

This scattered archipelago provides a glimpse of Hong Kong through the looking-glass, a portion of the South China coast that reflects both rapid change and timeless cohesion. Naturally, many young islanders have moved away into the city and left their homes to ageing parents. Until recently, fishing was the main source of income for the remaining islanders, but times have changed, and the most profitable businesses are now property, restaurants and tourism.

## LANTAU

**Lantau** ("broken head" in Cantonese) is by far the largest of Hong Kong's islands. Its north and east are dominated by the new airport, a four-lane highway, and double

*The 'boat people' of Tai O village have built their homes on stilts over Tai O Creek.*

*A couple holds sticks of burning incense at Po Lin Monastry.*

railway lines which thunder along the shore to the apartment blocks of Tung Chung, Tsing Ma Bridge and the Disneyland theme park. The rest of the island is predominantly rural. In the south are long beaches and small townships such as Mui Wo (Silvermine Bay), linked by ferries and packet boats *(kaido)* to Peng Chau (pleasant, though hardly a must-see) and Cheung Chau. In the far west of Lantau, Tai O and Fan Lau are favourite destinations for day-trippers, and there are good coastal and hill walks.

The centre of Lantau is dominated by lofty mountains, notably Lantau Peak (934 metres/3,064ft) and Sunset Peak (869 metres/2,851ft), criss-crossed with wandering pathways and dusty trails linking a number of Buddhist monasteries. The 70km (43-mile) Lantau Trail and other intersecting side routes are good for a short stroll, a day trip or overnight trek. A particularly good hike circles the vast (20,900-million-litre/5,500-million-gallon) **Shek Pik Reservoir**, on the western slopes of Lantau Peak. Alternatively, a coastal path runs from Shek Pik round to Tai O.

## Po Lin Monastery ❶

**Address:** Ngong Ping, Lantau; www.plm.org.hk
**Tel:** 2985 5248
**Opening Hrs:** daily 8am–6pm
**Entrance Fee:** free

**TIP**

Ferries operate from Pier no. 6 in the Outlying Islands' ferry piers in Central to Mui Wo (Silvermine Bay) on Lantau approximately every 30–50 minutes throughout the day on weekdays, and every 40–60 minutes at weekends. Journey time is either 30 minutes on a "fast ferry" or 50 minutes on an "ordinary ferry". For information, tel: 2131 8181. It is a very scenic 45-minute bus ride from Mui Wo to either Ngong Ping or Tai O.

*The Big Buddha, officially the 'Tian Tan Buddha', on Lantau Island.*

**TIP**

Much of the central part of Lantau is dotted with small Buddhist monasteries. West of Po Lin in the direction of Tai O on Lantau's northern coast is an excellent walking path that traverses mountain ridges, canyons and streams en route to Lantau's Ying Hing Monastery, a haven rich with traditional Buddhist paintings and statues. The monastery sits on a slope and commands a fine view of the surrounding mountains, farmland and the South China Sea.

*At the base of the Big Buddha.*

**Transport:** no. 2 bus from Mui Wo Ferry Pier, no. 23 from Tung Chung (or by taxi or cable car), MTR Tung Chung, then taxi or cable car

Up on the mountainous central spine is one of Hong Kong's best-known attractions, the red, orange and gold **Po Lin Monastery** (Precious Lotus Monastery). The large complex, which dates back to the 1920s, is busier and noisier than the average Buddhist retreat. Its canteen serves good vegetarian meals between 11.30am and 4.30pm. The real crowd-puller, however, is the 26.4 metre (87ft) tall **Tian Tan Buddha,** known colloquially as the "Big Buddha". The three-storey base on which Buddha sits is modelled on the support structure for the Hall of Prayer For Good Harvests at Beijing's famous Tian Tan temple and explains the statue's name. A long flight of steps leads up to the statue and there are fantastic views from the top when the weather is clear, while an exhibition in the base of the statue explains how it was built.

The monastery has managed to retain a semblance of serenity despite the proximity of the airport and the number of tourists who come here to see the Big Buddha – their access eased by the Ngong Ping 360 cable car (see page 186).

## Ngong Ping Village

A recent arrival on the Po Lin tourist trail, the **Ngong Ping Village** is a slightly tacky Buddhist-themed attraction (Mon–Fri 10am–6pm, Sat 10am–6.30pm; free) complete with gardens, teahouses and theatre shows about Buddhism for adults and children – rather quixotically offering a "Journey of Enlightenment".

An alternative way to reach the central Lantau heights is by taking the **Ngong Ping 360 Cable Car** (www.np360.com.hk; Mon–Fri 10am–6pm; Sat–Sun 9am–6.30pm; charge) from Tung Chung (a short walk from the MTR station), which gives views across Lantau and the airport – although haze can spoil this. Glass-floored cabins add extra excitement to the journey. Once at the top, stroll through Ngong Ping's gardens to the Big Buddha.

*Ngong Ping Village, a Buddhist-themed tourist attraction on Lantau Island.*

## Tung Chung Fort

Best accessed by hiking from Ngong Ping or Lantau Peak, **Tung Chung Fort** overlooks the eponymous new town. A fort has existed on the site since the 12th century, protecting the area from pirates and other "outer barbarians". The thick ramparts, including six old cannons, date back to the 19th century, when the Qing Army established a garrison here; this remained until the New Territories (of which the Outlying Islands form a part) was leased to Britain in 1898.

## Tai O

One of Lantau's older communities, remote **Tai O** ❷ is located on the northwest coast, closer – as the crow flies – to Macau than to Central. Here, the Tanka "boat people", who traditionally lived on their boats near shore, have become semi-land dwellers. Along **Tai O Creek**, they have also built rickety homes on stilts over parts of the creek.

The old rope-ferry that was once a feature of Tai O has been replaced by a bridge. Beneath its arch, boatmen offer trips out to see Hong Kong's

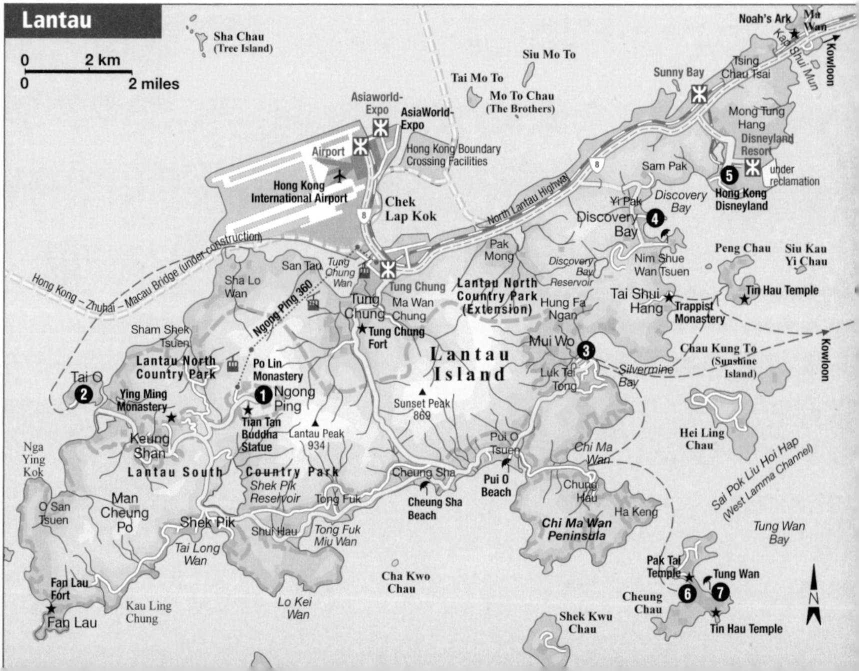

pink dolphins, who somehow manage to exist in the polluted waters offshore. However, a better option is to take a trip with the environmentally sensitive **Hong Kong Dolphinwatch** (www.hkdolphinwatch.com).

## Mui Wo and the southern beaches

Lantau is famed for the long, smooth and often empty beaches that line much of its southern coastline. The most popular and crowded beach is at **Mui Wo** (Silvermine Bay) ❸. A clutch of bars and restaurants has opened in the village, roistering affairs that become very busy at weekends.

A 15-minute bus ride will take you to the stunning, sweeping bay that is Cheung Sha Beach. Stretching for 3.2km (2 miles), it is one of Hong Kong's longest beaches and offers watersports and other activities. Kite-surfing, skim-boarding, alfresco dining and a small village of teepee-style accommodation make the stretch of Cheung Sha known as **Palm Beach** a real getaway.

Largely cut off from the rest of the island is a major real-estate development called **Discovery Bay** ❹, a well-planned but rather soulless complex that includes a golf course. "DB" is a magnet for expats with a hankering for suburbia, and has elicited comparison with *The Truman Show*.

*Shoppers in Tai O Village, Lantau Island.*

*Tai O Village viewed from across Tai O Creek.*

## Hong Kong Disneyland ❺

**Address:** Sunny Bay, Lantau. park.hongkongdisneyland.com
**Tel:** 1 830 830
**Opening Hrs:** daily 10am–8.15pm
**Entrance fee:** charge
**Transport:** R11, R21, R22, R32, R44, KMTR Disneyland

Hong Kong's long-awaited theme park opened its doors to the public in 2005, complete with its own MTR station, two hotels, shops, restaurants and the sort of amusements that thrill at more-or-less similar (if larger) venues in Paris, Tokyo and the US. There are seven themed areas. For more details see page 192.

## CHEUNG CHAU

Cheung Chau ("long island" in Cantonese) is the most densely populated of the outlying islands. The curving waterfront promenade, the *praya*, is one of the most pleasant places in Hong Kong, especially after sunset when its alfresco restaurants burst into life only yards from the fishing vessels bobbing at anchor. Home to Hong Kong's first and so far only Olympic gold medallist (from Atlanta 1996), Lee Lai-shan, Cheung Chau has a strong windsurfing tradition, centred on Afternoon Beach (Kwun Yan Wan).

## Cheung Chau village ❻

The village of **Cheung Chau**, near the ferry dock, is a tangle of alleyways. There are no vehicles on the island apart from small, motorised carts and an amusing bonsai-sized police car, fire engine and ambulance, a phenomenon that grants an automatic serenity. Head off in any direction from the ferry terminal and you will pass a variety of modern and traditional shops and numerous seafood restaurants.

A short distance to the left of the ferry dock, up the main road, is **Pak Tai Temple**, built in 1783 and dedicated to the god Pak Tai, protector of fishermen and the island's saviour from plague during the late 1700s. Inside, in front of the altar, are statues of two generals, Thousand-Li Eye and Favourable Wind Ear, who were said to be able to see or hear anything at any distance.

### The Bun Festival

Each year the island hosts the four-day **Bun Festival**, usually in May. Known as *Ching Chiu* in Cantonese, it originated many years ago after the discovery of a nest of skeletons, believed to be the remains of people killed by pirates. The island was subsequently plagued by a series of misfortunes; to placate the restless spirits of the victims, offerings were made once a year. How pastry buns came into this story is anybody's guess.

During the festivities, giant bamboo towers covered with edible buns are erected in the courtyard of Pak Tai Temple. In the past, the local men would climb up the towers to pluck their lucky buns – the higher the bun was, the more luck it would bring. After one of the towers collapsed in 1978, bringing broken bones and bruises rather than luck, the free-for-all was stopped. The ritual was

*Disneyland on Lantau Island.*

**TIP**

Ferries operate from the Outlying Islands Ferry Piers in Central to Cheung Chau every 30 minutes daily. For information call First Ferry, tel: 2131 8181. Lamma ferries are run by Hong Kong and Kowloon Ferry Ltd (hkkf), tel: 2815 6063. Services run at 20–60- minute intervals to Yung Shue Wan, less frequently to Sok Kwu Wan.

revived in 2005 in a more controlled environment; now only pre-qualified competitors can risk their necks.

Another attraction during the festival are the colourfully clad "floating children", who are hoisted up on stilts and paraded through the crowds. Other festive events include performances of Chinese opera and dramatic lion dances.

## Around Cheung Chau

Scattered about the island are several temples dedicated to Tin Hau, goddess of the sea. Cheung Chau was once the haunt of pirates, including the notorious Cheung Po Tsai. As on the other outlying islands, "Family Trail" walks are well-marked and lead to **Cheung Po Tsai Cave** as well as other scenic spots.

There are also some excellent beaches. The main strand is **Tung Wan** ❼, on the other, eastern, side of the narrow isthmus from the harbour. Below the Warwick Hotel at the southern end of the sands is a 3,000-year-old Bronze Age rock carving. Other good beaches are Afternoon Beach (Kwun Yam Wan), just past the rock carving, and Pak Tso at the island's southwestern tip.

*Fishing boats dot the sea around Lamma Island.*

*The Birthday of the Lord Buddha is celebrated at Po Lin on the eighth day of the fourth lunar month (almost always in May).*

## LAMMA

The second-largest of the outlying islands is **Lamma**. Rich in grassy hills and picturesque bays, the rugged terrain means that there is only a very small area of farmland. Archaeologists have associated Lamma with some of the earliest settlements in the region.

Lamma has a population of around 6,000, mostly concentrated in and around the village of Yung Shue Wan. Among them are a sizeable number of expatriates (over 60

**LAMMA POWER**

Identifying Lamma from a distance is easy thanks to the three chimney-stacks near the island's northwest tip. This coal-burning power station provides all the electricity for Hong Kong Island.

In a nod to environmental concerns, Hong Kong Electric built one 46-metre (151ft) wind turbine on the hillside above Yung Shue Wan. Given its breezy open location, Lamma Winds – as it is officially called – is a pleasant spot to stroll up to and take in the views, particularly if you don't have time to do the Sok Kwu Wan hike. From Yung Shue Wan, walk towards Hung Shing Ye for five minutes until you reach a crossing with a wider "road". Turn left and follow this uphill for 15 minutes.

nationalities live here), who value the green surroundings, peace and quiet (and the low rents). Despite the frequent ferry service to Central, only 30 minutes away, this roadless island remains distinctly slow-paced – although it can get crowded with day-trippers at weekends.

## Yung Shue Wan

**Yung Shue Wan** (Banyan Bay), at the northern end of Lamma, is one of two ferry gateways to the island. The village has a good supply of restaurants serving Japanese, Thai, Mediterranean and Indian cuisine, as well as several Chinese seafood establishments on the waterfront.

On a side street just past the town's main intersection is Yung Shue Wan's 100-year old **Tin Hau Temple**, guarded by a pair of stone lions. Inside, behind a red spirit stand (to deflect evil spirits), is the main shrine with images of the beaded and veiled Tin Hau.

### The walk to Sok Kwu Wan

It is only a short stroll from Yung Shue Wan out into the countryside. The main path, signposted to **Hung Shing Ye Beach**, passes neat vegetable plots and three-storey buildings (nothing higher is permitted, with the exception of the power station chimneys that loom behind the hill to the right). The beach itself is a pleasantly clean stretch of sand.

The path then rises steeply into the hills as it heads south to Sok Kwu Wan, Lamma's other main village. This popular walk, which can be completed in an unhurried hour and a half, treats hikers to views out across the sea, while on the other (left) side the vista extends across the Lamma Channel to the scattered tower blocks of Hong Kong Island's southern shore.

**Sok Kwu Wan** lies on the eastern shore of a long fjord-like inlet known as Picnic Bay, and is a popular weekend pleasure-junk mooring. The bay brims with floating fish farms, all tended by a fleet of boats of various shapes and sizes, and is one of the main suppliers of Hong Kong's seafood restaurants. Not surprisingly, the village has a long string of seafood restaurants, beguiling in the evening with bright lighting displays and marvellous aromas. Entrepreneurial villagers have set up the **Lamma Fisherfolk's Village** (www.fisherfolks.com.hk; daily 10.15am–6pm; charge includes shuttle) in a red-sailed junk in the bay, to teach visitors about traditional fishing communities and their crafts.

## Po Toi

**Po Toi** is a group of islands located in the southernmost area of the SAR, southeast of Stanley, and inhabited by only a handful of people. Reached by *kaido* from Aberdeen or Stanley, the main island, Po Toi, is home to a large rock resembling a snail. Under the rock is a cave with carvings shaped by wind and rain. The open-air restaurants near the pier in the south serve excellent seafood. For details on the islands in Mirs Bay and the eastern New Territories, see page 171.

*From the 7th century until the 1960s, Tai O was a centre of the salt industry. These days, however, the dried salted fish sold to tourists in the narrow village streets is largely imported from the Philippines.*

*Residents of Cheung Chau Island go about their day.*

# THEME PARKS

**Hong Kong's Disneyland and long-running local competitor Ocean Park make the SAR a good bet for a family holiday.**

When Hong Kong Disneyland opened in 2005, it seemed that the writing was on the wall for its local counterpart, Ocean Park. A major renovation and expansion soon put paid to that idea, and now both parks attract a similar number of thrill-seeking locals and tourists. In fact, each offers a quite different day out – as the name suggests, an aquarium forms a big part of Ocean Park's draw, while Disneyland has its own unique appeal for small children. Both have rollercoasters and other rides for thrill-seekers – although Ocean Park has more for older kids.

**Disneyland** (see page 188 for opening times and other details) is divided into seven themed areas (Main Street USA, Fantasyland, Adventureland, Tomorrowland, Grizzly Gulch, Mystic Point and Toy Story Land). Tickets give access to all. As with other Disneyland parks, be prepared to queue – it's best to avoid weekends and the hottest months: waiting in line with bored, over-heated children is no fun for anyone.

As well as its impressive aquariums, **Ocean Park** (see page 133), on Hong Kong Island's south coast, has a mile-long cable car, various thrilling rides, dolphin shows and pandas.

*Meeting the familiar Disney characters never fails to thrill the smaller children.*

*There is a nightly fireworks display over Disneyland's Sleeping Beauty Castle, at the centre of Fantasyland, one of the park's seven themed areas.*

*Entertainment for all at Ocean Park.*

*Children ride the carousal at Ocean Park.*

A hungry panda bear at Ocean Park.

## AN ALTERNATIVE THEME PARK

*Animals leaving 'Noah's Ark', Ma Wan Island.*

**Though unlikely to ever challenge its two big brothers on visitor numbers, Hong Kong's newest park (opened 2009) is probably the most coherently themed of the lot. The enormous wooden ark at the centre of Noah's Ark (www.noahsark.com.hk; daily 10am–6pm, charge) is claimed to be the first built to the exact measurements given in the Bible, so large that it seemingly props up Tsing Ma Bridge. Elsewhere there is a pleasant park with 67 pairs of full-sized animal sculptures, a Solar Tower, which explains the universe from the creationist's perspective, and an Ark Expo which spells out the dangers facing the environment. Though evangelical Christian education is at the heart of things, the Giant Swing, and various other climbing exhibits provide high-altitude kicks for the kids. It's located on Ma Wan Island, accessible by boat from Central or buses from Tsing Yi.**

*Ocean Park has many attractions including rollercoasters and other white-knuckle rides.*

*São Paulo church.*

*Grand Lisboa Hotel.*

# MACAU

**A major tourism drive has brought flashy casinos and rapid change to the tiny territory, but the unique Portuguese ambience still survives.**

**Main Attractions**

- Largo do Senado Square
- Ruins of São Paulo
- Monte Fort
- Macau Museum
- Santo Agostinho Church
- A-Ma Temple
- Macau Tower
- NAPE
- Guia Lighthouse
- Coloane Village

**Map**

Page 200

If ever the Pearl River Delta had "bling", it's now, and nowhere is this more obvious than in Macau. Established by the Portuguese in 1557 as the first European colony on China's shore, Macau was for much of recent history a sleepy outpost, playing second fiddle to its high-profile neighbour. Things have changed quickly since it returned to China in 1999 – becoming, like Hong Kong, a Special Administrative Region of the People's Republic.

These days Macau has a new lease of life as the "leisure capital of Asia". Cashing in on the new wealth in China, and the Chinese love of gambling, what was until recently a rather low-key casino scene has exploded into a brash, gaudy, full-scale celebration of greed which has usurped even the mighty Las Vegas. A huge reclamation project has merged the islands of Coloane and Taipa to form a new entertainment area of spectacular themed casinos and luxury hotels. Nowadays more than 2.4 million visitors a month pour in by ferry from Hong Kong or over the land border, the majority of them making a beeline for the Baccarat tables.

Yet amidst all the crowds and pizzazz, sizeable areas of old Macau survive – graceful old buildings redolent of southern Europe, overlooking cobbled streets shaded by ancient banyan trees. If it's a peaceful "Mediterranean in China" experience you are after, head over to the main square of either Taipa or Coloane village for lunch.

## MACAU'S HISTORIC CENTRE

In the years leading up to the 1999 handover, the Portuguese (who in 2014 still accounted for around 2 percent of the resident population)

*Signposts in Largo do Senado Square.*

*Southern European architecture, often with an unmistakable oriental element, gives much of old Macau a unique flavour. The central square, Largo do Senado, is lined with superb examples, both secular and ecclesiastical.*

set about ensuring that Macau's cultural heritage – and their influence – would be preserved. Buildings were renovated, squares re-cobbled, and pastel paints once more brightened up the grey streets.

The 25 sites that now comprise the Historic Centre of Macau were added to Unesco's World Heritage list in 2005, acknowledging their importance as the oldest and most intact example of European architecture on Chinese soil and as a symbol of cultural exchange between East and West. Sites include Chinese temples, Portuguese churches, scenic squares and the first lighthouse in China. Best explored on foot, there are two well-signposted main routes, which are fairly shady, and there are enough buildings open to the public to provide respite on a humid day.

## Largo do Senado Square ❶

The best place to start any foray into Old Macau is the **Largo do Senado** (Senate Square), the old city's main square, covering some 3,700 sq metres (4,425 sq yds), which has been repaved with a bold Portuguese wave-pattern mosaic. A handy tourist information centre is situated right on the square (daily 9am–6pm).

Across the main road (Almeida Ribeiro) is the **Leal Senado** ❷ (Loyal Senate; Tue–Sun 9am–9pm), regarded by most as the best example of Portuguese architecture in Macau. It now houses the Institute of Civil and Municipal Affairs. The Leal Senado was dedicated in 1784, and its façade completed in 1876. The title "Loyal" was bestowed on Macau's Senate in 1809 by Portuguese King John VI, who was Prince Regent at the time, as a reward for continuing to fly the Portuguese flag when the Spanish monarchy took over the Portuguese throne in the 17th century. An inscribed tablet here, dating from 1654, grants Macau its sacred title: "City of the Name of God, Macau, There is None More Loyal". Head up the staircase to the fine wrought-iron doors and beyond to a small courtyard with azulejos tiles. Up more stairs, the library (Mon–Fri 1–7pm) and council chamber show

*Largo do Senado Square is paved with distinctive Portuguese mosaics.*

fine examples of Old World woodwork. Half the offices on the ground floor have been converted into a gallery that is used for special exhibitions (Tue–Sun 9am–9pm).

### Ecclesiastical treasures

Back on Largo do Senado square, opposite the tourist office, is the white church of **Santa Casa da Misericórdia** ❸ (Holy House of Mercy), with its small museum of religious artefacts (Tue–Sun 10am–1pm, 2.30–5.30pm). At the northern end of the square is the butter-coloured **São Domingos** ❹ (St Dominic's), one of the oldest of Macau's churches. It dates from the 17th century, but the Spanish Dominicans built a chapel and convent on this site as early as 1588. At the back is the **Museum of Sacred Art** (daily 10am–6pm).

Take a short walk up a *travessa* to the **Sé** ❺ (Macau Cathedral; daily 7.30am–6.30pm), mother church of the Macau diocese after 1850, which at the time included all of China, Japan and Korea. The stained-glass windows are the main attraction of this rather plain building.

## São Paulo ❻

From São Domingos follow the pavement north along one of Macau's main shopping streets before turning uphill to the ruins of **São Paulo** (St Paul's; daily 9am–6pm). Its towering façade and impressive grand staircase are the most striking of all Macau's churches. Unfortunately, the site must have bad feng shui. The first church on the site was destroyed by fire in 1601. It was rebuilt, but in 1835 another inferno swept through the church, destroying the adjacent college and a library reputed to be the best east of Istanbul. The classical façade – crafted by Japanese Christians who had fled persecution in Nagasaki – survived. In 1904, efforts were made to rebuild the church, but little progress was made. Still, today the grand façade of São Paulo remains Macau's most enduring icon.

## Fortaleza do Monte ❼

**Address:** Praceta do Museu de Macau
**Tel:** (853) 2835 7911
**Opening Hrs:** daily 7am–7pm
**Entrance Fee:** free

**TIP**

Macau has several tourist information offices: the central office is at Largo do Senado, open daily 9am–6pm, tel: (853) 8397 1120. The office at the Macau Ferry Terminal is open daily 9am–10pm, tel: (853) 2872 6416. There are kiosks at the border gate (daily 9.15am–6pm) and the airport (daily 9am–1.30pm, 2.15–7.30pm, 8.15–10pm).

*Leal Senado building.*

## Macau

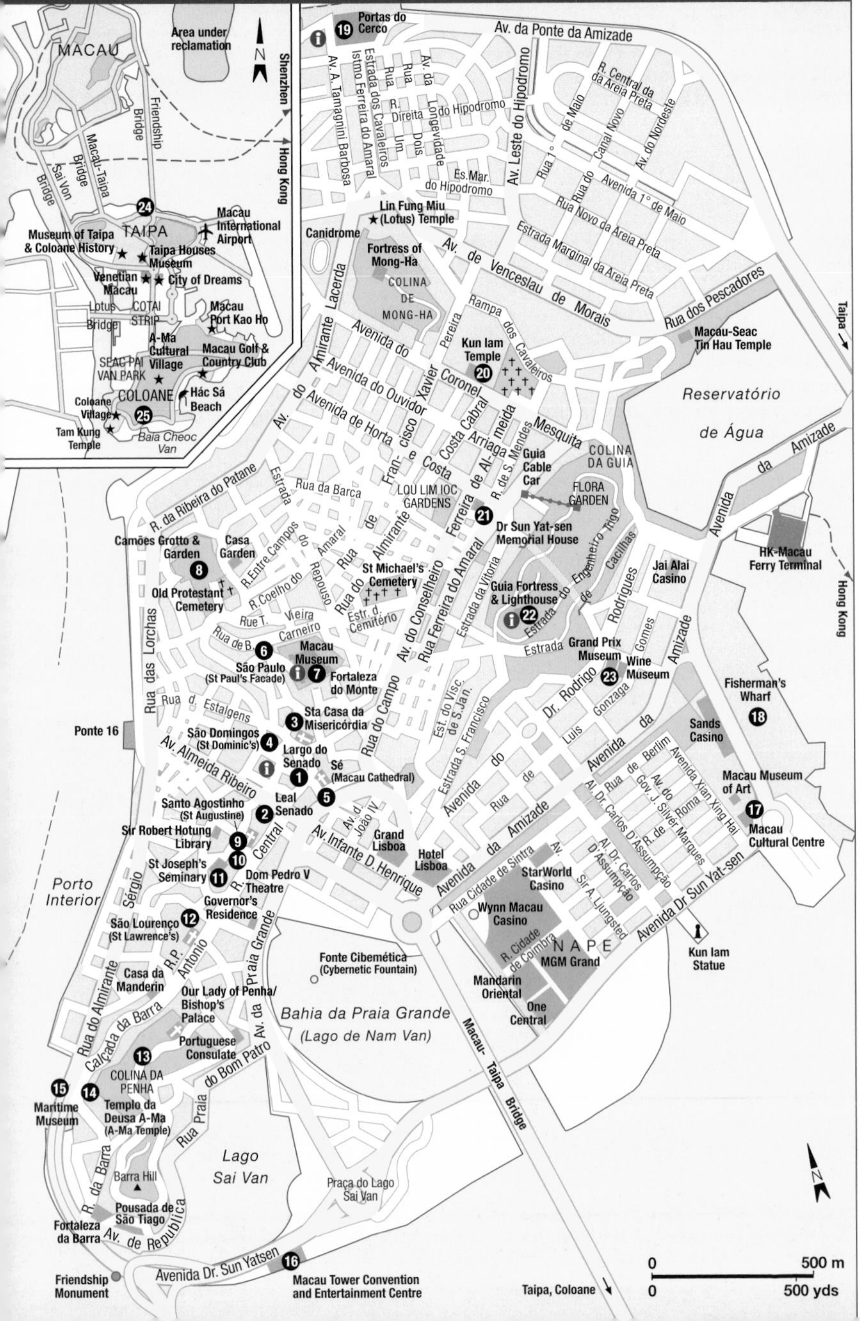

MACAU
Area under reclamation
Shenzhen
Hong Kong
Friendship Bridge
Macau-Taipa Bridge
Sai Von Bridge
TAIPA
Macau International Airport
Museum of Taipa & Coloane History
Taipa Houses Museum
Venetian Macau
City of Dreams
Lotus Bridge
COTAI STRIP
Macau Port Kao Ho
A-Ma Cultural Village
Macau Golf & Country Club
SEAC PAI VAN PARK
COLOANE
Hác Sá Beach
Coloane Village
Tam Kung Temple
Baia Cheoc Van
Portas do Cerco
Av. da Ponte da Amizade
Av. A. Tamagnini Barbosa
Istmo Ferreira do Amaral
Estrada dos Cavaleiros
Rua Um
Rua Dois
R. Direita
Av. da Longevidade
do Hipodromo
Av. Leste do Hipodromo
R. Central da da Areia Preta
Rua 1° de Maio
Rua do Canal Novo
Av. do Nordeste
Es.Mar. do Hipodromo
Avenida 1° de Maio
Rua Novo da Areia Preta
Estrada Marginal da Areia Preta
Lin Fung Miu (Lotus) Temple
Canidrome
Fortress of Mong-Ha
COLINA DE MONG-HA
Av. de Venceslau de Morais
Rua dos Pescadores
Taipa
Macau-Seac Tin Hau Temple
Reservatório de Água
Av. do Almirante Lacerda
Avenida do Coronel Mesquita
Rampa dos Cavaleiros
Pereira
Kun Iam Temple
Avenida do Ouvidor Arriaga
Avenida de Horta e Costa
Xavier
Francisco
Costa Cabral
Ferreira de Almeida
R. de S. Mendes
Guia Cable Car
COLINA DA GUIA
FLORA GARDEN
Avenida da Amizade
HK-Macau Ferry Terminal
Hong Kong
R. da Ribeira do Patane
Estrada
Rua da Barca
LOU LIM IOC GARDENS
Dr Sun Yat-sen Memorial House
Camões Grotto & Garden
Casa Garden
R.Entre Campos
do Amaral
Rua de Almirante
Repouso
St Michael's Cemetery
Estrada do Engenheiro Trigo
Cacilhas
Jai Alai Casino
Old Protestant Cemetery
R.Coelho do
Rua do Conselheiro
Rua Ferreira do Amaral
Estrada da Vitoria
Guia Fortress & Lighthouse
Estrada de Rodrigues
Rue T. Vieira
Carneiro
Estr. d. Cemitério
Rua de B.
Macau Museum
São Paulo (St Paul's Facade)
Fortaleza do Monte
Av. do Campo
Estrada
Grand Prix Museum
Wine Museum
Gomes
Rua das Lorchas
Rua d. Estalgens
Est. do Visc. de S.Jan.
Estrada S. Francisco
Dr. Rodrigo
Gonzaga
Fisherman's Wharf
Sta Casa da Misericórdia
Ponte 16
São Domingos (St Dominic's)
Largo do Senado
Luis
Avenida da
Sands Casino
Av. Almeida Ribeiro
Sé (Macau Cathedral)
Rua de Berlim
Avenida Xian Xing Hai
Macau Museum of Art
Santo Agostinho (St Augustine)
Leal Senado
Avenida do
Rua de
Al. Dr. Carlos D'Assumpção
Av. do Gov. J. Silver Marques
R. de Roma
Macau Cultural Centre
Sir Robert Hotung Library
R. Central
Av. d. João IV
Grand Lisboa
Av. Infante D. Henrique
Hotel Lisboa
Avenida da Amizade
St Joseph's Seminary
Dom Pedro V Theatre
Rua Cidade de Sintra
StarWorld Casino
Al. Dr. Carlos D'Assumpção
Sir A. Ljungsted
Avenida Dr Sun Yat-sen
Porto Interior
Sérgio
Governor's Residence
Wynn Macau Casino
São Lourenço (St Lawrence's)
R.P. Antonio
Praia Grande
R. Cidade de Coimbra
NAPE
MGM Grand
Kun Iam Statue
Fonte Cibemética (Cybernetic Fountain)
Casa da Manderin
Mandarin Oriental
Our Lady of Penha/ Bishop's Palace
One Central
Bahia da Praia Grande (Lago de Nam Van)
Rua do Almirante
Calçada da Barra
Av. da
Macau-Taipa Bridge
Portuguese Consulate
do Bom Patro
COLINA DA PENHA
Maritime Museum
Templo da Deusa A-Ma (A-Ma Temple)
Rua Praia
Lago Sai Van
Rua da Barra
Barra Hill
Praça do Lago Sai Van
Pousada de São Tiago
Fortaleza da Barra
Av. de Republica
Avenida Dr. Sun Yatsen
Friendship Monument
Macau Tower Convention and Entertainment Centre
Taipa, Coloane
0
500 m
500 yds
N

Overlooking the façade of São Paulo are the massive stone walls of the fort (usually called **Monte Fort**), built in the early 1600s. When Dutch ships attacked and invaded Macau in 1622, the half-completed fortress was defended by 150 clerics and African slaves. A lucky cannon shot by an Italian Jesuit, Geronimo Rhu, hit the powder magazine of the Dutch fleet's flagship and saved the city. Access is free, and there are great views over the city from the cannon-lined ramparts.

The **Macau Museum** (www.macau-museum.gov.mo; Tue–Sun 10am–6pm; free on 15th of every month) was opened on the site of the fortress in 1998. Three floors of lively and well-captioned exhibits chart the history of the enclave and its citizens, from its first settlement through to the handover to the Chinese.

## Camões Grotto & Garden ❽

A 15-minute stroll to the west of the fort will take you to the picturesque **Camões Garden** (daily 6am–10pm), where Luís de Camões, the celebrated Portuguese soldier-poet, is said to have composed part of the national epic, *Os Lusiadas* (The Lusiads). A bronze bust of Camões rests in the garden's grotto. Above the grotto is an observatory built by a French explorer, Count de La Pérouse. The garden features in many paintings by George Chinnery, the most famous 19th-century "China Coast" artist, who is buried in the nearby **Old Protestant Cemetery**, which is a fascinating historical snapshot of the early foreign community here.

Nearby **Casa Garden** (Mon–Fri 9.30am–6pm) is an 18th-century house and garden that was home to East India Company officials and is now a cultural institute.

## South of Largo do Senado

Most of Macau's Unesco-listed sites lie to the south of Largo do Senado, across Avenida de Almeida Ribeiro, in a string all the way to the southern tip of the peninsula. The first of these is **Santo Agostinho** ❾ (St Augustine; closed until further notice), an attractive baroque-style church that is the largest in the region. Spanish Augustinians founded a church here

*The magnificent façade of São Paulo (St Paul's) is probably Macau's best-known landmark.*

*By the walls of the fort.*

**SHOP**

Within two minutes' walk of the A-Ma Temple there are a handful of long-established Portuguese restaurants on Rua Almirante Sergio Porto Interior, including A Lorcha and Restaurant Littoral.

in 1586, but the present structure dates from 1814, and its ornate façade from 1875.

Across the square (Largo de Santo Agostinho) and also on the Unesco list is the **Sir Robert Hotung Library** (www.library.gov.mo; Mon–Sat 10am–7pm, Sun 11am–7pm), dating from 1894, and the beautifully restored **Dom Pedro V Theatre** ⑩. Built in 1860, this was the first western-style theatre in China, and often opens for concerts and performances during Macau's many arts festivals.

Another venerable building on the square (but accessed from Rua do Seminario around the corner) is **St Joseph's Seminary** ⑪ (church open daily 9am–6pm), dedicated in 1728 when its sole purpose was to establish Jesuit missions in China – a task it performed with gusto. Today its vast halls, classrooms and living quarters have mostly disappeared, but its architecture and sculptures are worth viewing, and the beautiful chapel is open to the public. The statues within were salvaged from São Paulo in 1835.

*Brightly coloured Portuguese-style house.*

A little further south, the imposing pale-yellow church of **São Lourenço** ⑫ (St Lawrence's; daily 7am–9pm) is raised up above street level and surrounded by a small garden. The church was originally built in the 1560s, and most families of Portuguese sailors used to gather on the front steps of the church to pray and wait for their return, so it was known in Cantonese as Feng Shun Tang (Hall of the Soothing Winds). The elegant church was most recently rebuilt in 1846. The grand double staircase leading up from the street, iron gates, towers and crystal chandeliers are European, but the roof is made of Chinese tiles.

## The southern tip

Take a detour up **Colina da Penha** ⑬ (Penha Hill) for sweeping views and to visit the **Chapel of Our Lady of Penha**, dating back to 1622 but largely rebuilt in 1837. While not listed as a Unesco site, the chapel and **Bishop's Palace** next door were once the centres of Roman Catholic missionary work in the region.

Continuing on the Unesco World Heritage route, there are more

*Worship at the A-Ma Temple.*

*Tin Hau Temple*

examples of the influence of different cultures on architectural styles. The peaceful piazza of Largo do Lilau marks one of the earliest Portuguese residential areas. Nearby, the **Casa da Mandarin** (Mandarin's House) on Antonio de Silva Lane is a traditional Chinese courtyard-style residence, dating back to 1881. Further south, the **Moorish Barracks** (daily 9am–6pm) were built in 1874 to house policemen recruited from another Portuguese enclave, Goa.

## A-Ma Temple and the Maritime Museum

The **A-Ma Temple** ⓮ (Templo da Deusa A-Ma; daily 7am–6pm) squats beneath Barra Hill, at the entrance to Macau's Inner Harbour. It is the oldest temple in the territory, said to date back 600 years to the Ming dynasty. It was certainly there in 1557, when Macau was ceded to Portugal. The original temple is believed to have been erected by fishermen from southeast China and dedicated to Tin Hau, the patron goddess of fishermen known as A-Ma in Macau. It was then called Ma Kok Miu (Ma Point Temple). The Chinese named the area A-Ma-Gao, or the Bay of A-Ma. The oldest surviving part of this temple is a lower pavilion to the right of its entrance. There is a coloured bas-relief stone carving here said to be a rendering of a Chinese junk that carried the goddess A-Ma from Fujian province through typhoon-ravaged seas to Macau, where she walked to the top of Barra Hill and ascended to heaven.

In front of the temple is the interesting **Maritime Museum** ⓯ (www.museumaritimo.gov.mo; Wed–Mon 10am–5.30pm; half-price on Sun), with displays tracing the history of shipping in the South China Sea.

North of the A-Ma Temple, Macau's run-down **O Porto Interior** (Inner Harbour Area) is hoping to share in the boomtown success of elsewhere in Macau, with its own Vegas-style casino. The 2.3-hectare (5.75-acre) Ponte 16 casino and entertainment resort includes a Sofitel hotel. Facing Zhuhai – and using a classic Chinese formulation – Ponte 16 boasts that it has "one river, two banks" scenery and European-Chinese architecture.

**FACT**

There is disagreement over the correct spelling: Macau or Macao? The latter form is making something of a comeback, and the burgeoning casino industry seems to prefer it. Most official sources, as well as locals and westerners, continue to use "Macau", however. To add to the confusion, it is known as Aomen in the pinyin spelling of Mandarin Chinese.

*São Lourenço church.*

**TIP**

You must be over 18 to enter a casino in Macau, and there is a dress code of sorts – men may not wear sleeveless T-shirts or shorts, while women are allowed to do so. Sandals are not normally allowed, and flip-flops are a definite no-no. Taking photographs inside the gaming area is strictly forbidden.

To the south, the impressive walls of the old **Fortaleza da Barra** (Fortress of Barra) rise far above the avenue guarding the entrance to the Inner Harbour.

## NEW MACAU

Much of what can be termed New Macau has been built on reclaimed land to the south and east of the natural peninsula, an area known as the NAPE, which forms a grid of casino- and hotel-lined streets close to the Hong Kong Ferry Terminal. Further south, beyond Nam Van Lake and its colourful, if erratic, "cybernetic fountain", lies Macau's most prominent tourist attraction – the 338-metre (1,110ft) **Macau Tower** ⓰. Take the lift to the observation deck (www.macautower.com.mo; Mon–Fri 10am–9pm, Sat–Sun from 9am) for 360-degree views of Macau, and look through its glass floors (not recommended for vertigo sufferers). Thrill-seekers can "skywalk" around the edge of the handrail-free platform, climb all the way to the top of the mast, or leap off in a controlled bungee jump.

*Portuguese mosaic floor tiling in Coloane.*

From the tower it's easy to see Macau's changing shape and other new landmarks. The orange-and-white **Hotel Lisboa** that was once the main landmark now looks quaintly retro and is dwarfed by new developments, including the garish 44-storey **Grand Lisboa** hotel and casino that is modelled on a lotus root but also resembles a giant mirror-covered turnip.

*Fisherman's Wharf.*

## The NAPE and Fisherman's Wharf

To the south of the Avenida da Amizade lies the **NAPE** (Novos Aterros do Porto Exterior), a rectangle of reclaimed land that is one of the most up-and-coming areas in Macau. The area is home to some typically opulent 21st-century Macau developments – the copper-coloured Wynn Macau, the gold-and-silver MGM Grand, the 34-storey StarWorld Casino and the golden Sands Macau, symbolising the new breed of Vegas-style gambling palaces for which Macau is becoming famous. There are also a large number of restaurants and bars in the immediate vicinity.

The state-of-the-art **Macau Cultural Centre** ⓱ (www.ccm.gov.mo) is located at the junction of Avenida Man Sing Hai and Avenida Dr Sun Yat-sen, and has two auditoria that host a regular programme of performances and shows. Next door, the spacious galleries of the **Macau Museum of Art** (www.mam.gov.mo; Tue–Sun 10am–6.30pm) are spread over five floors and host major international exhibitions. There is a permanent collection of over 3,000 works of Shiwan ceramics, calligraphy and art from Macau and China.

Towards the Hong Kong Ferry Terminal you'll find the entrance of the über-kitsch **Fisherman's Wharf** entertainment area ⓲ (www.fishermanswharf.com.mo; daily; 10am–10pm; free admission but charge for rides). The large complex contains theme-park rides, hotels, a casino, an exhibition centre, shops and dozens of restaurants dishing up food from all over the world.

## NORTHERN MACAU

Between Barra and the border with Guangdong, the northern end of Macau is predominantly nondescript residential and semi-industrial blocks. As in Hong Kong, most of the once-flourishing garment and textile businesses have moved over the border. By 2020, Macau's Light Rail network will loop around here, connecting the border gate with the downtown area, the airport and Cotai.

### Border gates

At the modern border gate between the Special Administrative Region and Zhuhai over the road in mainland China, a park has been created around the former gateway, **Portas do Cerco** ⓳, which was built in 1870 and is inscribed with a quote from Portuguese poet Camões: "Honour your country, for your country is watching you". The crossing is open from 7am to midnight, and the casino shuttle buses line up to meet the punters arriving from the mainland by land.

Around 500 metres/yds to the south is the **Fortress of Mong-Ha**, on the hill of Colina de Mong-Ha, constructed to provide a defence vantage to guard the Portas do Cerco. Built in 1849, the fort's barracks now hold the 24-room Pousada da Mong-Ha and

*The bronze Kun Iam statue on the NAPE waterfront, designed and crafted by Portuguese artist Christina Reiria.*

*Macau Tower and the Macau–Taipa Bridge at night.*

## Macau's casinos

**Macau's mega-casinos pack in the punters and pull in around six times more cash per year than the Las Vegas strip. As one Forbes writer put it, Macau is now officially "Vegas on steroids."**

Macau's premier entertainment rattles to the sound of a spinning roulette ball and moves at the speed of a croupier shuffle. Gambling – or gaming, as the industry would have it – seems to have become Macau's entire raison d'être, lightening the pockets of the Chinese and Hong Kong masses and making a lucky few – mainly corporate executives and shareholders – very rich indeed. At present, the 42 (and counting) casinos fall into two distinct groups. The first is epitomised by the original Lisboa, owned by gazillionaire Stanley Ho, who for many years grew (metaphorically) fat on a gaming monopoly. These older casinos are comparatively low-rent, with milling hordes crowding around the tables and snatching at the handles of the fruit machines, known as Hungry Tigers in these parts.

*The mass gaming floor in Starworld casino.*

The second group is very different. In 2002 it was finally agreed to open the industry up to other players from outside the region. Sheldson Adelson's Las Vegas Sands was the first to enter the fray, building the Sands Macau, a gilded edifice on the Macau peninsula. The Greek Mythology Casino gave a totally new face to the low-key island of Taipa, and American mogul Steve Wynn soon followed suit and opened his first Asian casino, Wynn Macau's, a stone's throw from Ho's new venture, the fantastically lurid Grand Lisboa, and daughter Patsy's joint venture with Vegas, the MGM Grand Macau.

### The strip

To the south, meanwhile, development continues on reclaimed land that links the islands of Taipa and Coloane. Cotai, as it has been named, is already home to the spectacularly vast Venetian Macau Resort which, with 3,400 slot machines and 800 gaming tables, has the largest casino. The "Cotai Strip" is now a trademark of the Venetian's owner, Las Vegas Sands, which also owns the three hotels of the Sands Cotai Central development, the Conrad, Holiday Inn and the 3,896-room Sheraton Cotai Central. However, "the strip" is only part of Cotai; other mega developments include The City of Dreams, a joint-venture between Australia's gaming giant Crown and Ho's son Lawrence, and the US$3 billion Galaxy World Resort, home to three hotels and, of course, another massive casino.

Even the financial crisis didn't stop China's newly flush punters streaming in; on the contrary, it's more than likely that some of Beijing's massive "stimulus" package was sloshed across the Baccarat table. The crises ended up marking a possibly permanent changing of the gambling guard. In 2009 the entire state of Nevada (248 casinos) took US$847.1 million, a drop on the previous year, while tiny Macau (34 casinos at the time) claimed US$1.42 billion, snatching the title of the world's No. 1 gambling destination. Revenues continue to surge at a dizzying rate, and as long as "gaming" remains illegal on the mainland, it's unlikely to lose that mantle.

Macau's Institute of Tourism Studies, whose students now staff the small hotel and restaurant.

## Temples and memorials

Near the southern foot of Colina de Mong-Ha sits **Kun Iam Temple** ⓴, dedicated to Guanyin, the Buddhist goddess of mercy, and dating back to 1627. The first Sino-American Treaty was signed here in 1844 by Ki Ying, China's viceroy in Guangzhou, and Caleb Cushing, who was the United States' "Commissioner and Envoy Extraordinary and Minister Plenipotentiary" to China.

Most organised tours make a quick visit to the **Dr Sun Yat-sen Memorial House** ㉑ (Wed–Mon 10am–5pm). The memorial is close to the Kiang Vu Hospital where Sun practised medicine as one of the first Western-trained Chinese doctors in this area, before he became known as the father of modern China.

Nearby are the Suzhou-style **Lou Lim Ioc Gardens** (daily 6am–9pm), with lotus ponds, bridges and ornamental mountains, resembling a classical landscape painting.

## Macau's highest point

The **Colina da Guia**, the highest point in Macau, rises to the east of the Sun Yat-sen House and is home to the **Guia Fortress and Lighthouse** ㉒ (daily 9am–6pm), one of Macau's classic landmarks – albeit one that is becoming harder to spot amid all the new skyscrapers. Part of the Historic Centre of Macau, this 17th-century Western-style lighthouse – the oldest on the Chinese coast – once guarded the coastal approaches. Besides the views, there is a small art gallery. A cable car links the hilltop with a small local park and aviary at **Flora Garden** below (6am–8.30pm).

Each November, the streets of Macau are taken over by the Macau Formula 3 Grand Prix and the Macau Motorcycle Grand Prix. Learn more about the "Guia Race" history of these exciting road races at the **Grand Prix Museum** ㉓ (Wed–Mon 10am– 6pm) at 431 Rua de Luis Gongazaga Gomes in the basement of the Tourism Activities Centre. Next door, the Wine Museum (Wed–Mon 10am–6pm; charge) tells the story of Portuguese wines.

**TIP**

If you are heading straight to the Cotai strip casinos (or Coloane or Taipa) from Hong Kong, consider taking Las Vegas Sands' CotaiJet Service (www.cotaijet.com.mo) to avoid tedious immigration queues and traffic jams. They run approximately every half hour between the Macau Ferry Terminal and the Taipa Ferry Terminal (near Macau airport). For more information see page 231.

*Rua Do Cunha, a narrow pedestrian street in Taipa.*

**KIDS**

With its fake sky, canals and gondalas, most children will enjoy exploring the Venetian. There are regular child-friendly exhibitions and events such as Ice World, where the attractions include Dreamworks characters rendered in ice. Across the road, City of Dreams has special effects at the immersive Bubble theatre and Franco Dragone's The House of Dancing Water show. There is also has an enormous indoor play area for the under-12s.

## TAIPA AND COLOANE

The "other" Macau is not on the peninsula that is generally regarded as Macau, but consists of the two outlying islands of Taipa and Coloane – which are now really one island, joined together by Cotai – 620 hectares (1,550 acres) of reclaimed land, home to The Venetian casino.

### Taipa

**Taipa** ㉔ was once the centre for junk-building and firecracker manufacture, and in the early 1700s became the busy centre for Western trade with China when an imperial edict banned English and French ships from Guangzhou, insisting they moor at Taipa instead.

Today it has its share of new casinos, including the hilarious Greek Mythology Casino complete with Roman centurions, and the more sophisticated Altira Macau. Bets can be placed on horses at the Macau Jockey Club Racecourse, which has weekly meetings throughout the year on either Friday nights or Saturday or Sunday afternoons, and occasionally both.

In **Taipa Village** local history and developments are explained in the three-storey mint-green **Museum of Taipa and Coloane History** (Tue–Sun 10am–6pm). Head east along Rua Correia da Silva and explore the narrow streets around the village square, where you will find many good restaurants.

Overlooking the main square is **Our Lady of Carmel**, a neoclassical church built in 1885. Nearby, on the Avenida da Praia, is the **Taipa Houses Museum** (Tue–Sun 10am–7pm), five beautifully restored houses, each of which now functions as a museum: the Macanese House, House of the Islands, House of the Portugal Regions, Exhibition Gallery and House for Reception. From this olde-worlde location you can gaze across the water to the amazing City of Dreams and the vast **Venetian Macao-Resort-Hotel**: nowhere is the contrast between new and old Macau more striking.

### Coloane

**Coloane** ㉕ is almost twice as big as Taipa, and what was once the

*The Venetian, vast in scale and ambition.*

last hiding place for pirates is now a green retreat from the SAR's bustle, casinos and construction with beaches, country parks and a charming village to explore.

Peaceful Coloane Village lies in the southwest of the island. The Chapel of St Francis Xavier, built in 1928, commemorates the successful recapture of a group of children kidnapped by pirates in 1910. The chapel looks onto Coloane's tiny Portuguese-style village square, which comes alive with restaurant tables and festivities at weekends and during holidays.

From the square you can explore the narrow lanes that hide a few small furniture shops and cafés. It all makes Coloane an easy place to spend half a day exploring – and an even easier place to sit with some Portuguese wine and Macanese food and watch the world go by while others lose and win fortunes at the gaming tables a few miles away.

Further south, by the pretty bay at Cheoc Van, there's an open-air pool next to the white sandy beach. The Pousada da Coloane overlooks the bay, and from this pleasant family-run hotel and restaurant you can follow a well-signposted trail for 45-minutes up to the island's peak and the **A-Ma Cultural Village** (www.a-ma.org.mo; daily 8am–6pm). On the last part of your climb, you will hear piped music coming from speakers hidden in the bushes shortly before being rewarded by the sight of a vast, Qing-dynasty-style complex complete with temples, a bell tower, drum tower, the Tian Hou Palace and a museum. The 170-metre (560ft) peak is marked by an impressive 20-metre (65ft) statue of the goddess A-Ma, which can be seen from the sea. Shuttle buses run between the complex and the Façade at Estrada de Seac Pai Van every 30 minutes.

Coloane's other hotel is the grander Westin Resort Macau, built into the hillside overlooking Hac Sa (black sands) Beach. The Macau Golf and Country Club's 18 holes begin on the hotel's "roof". Close to the beach is the ever-popular Fernando's restaurant where lunches rarely finish before dusk.

*Largos Dos Bombeiros.*

*Coloane's seafront promenade.*

*Louhu district's dazzling night skyline.*

## Pearl River Delta

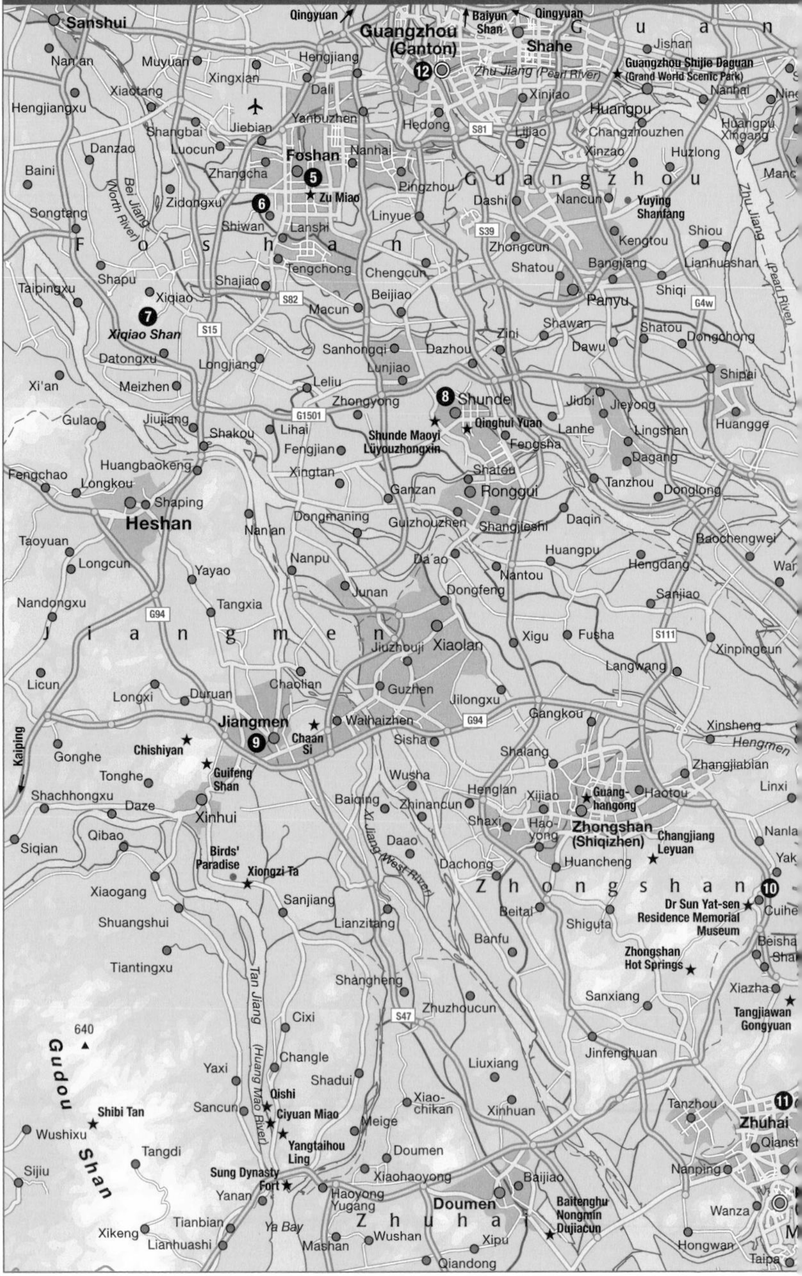

# Pearl River Delta

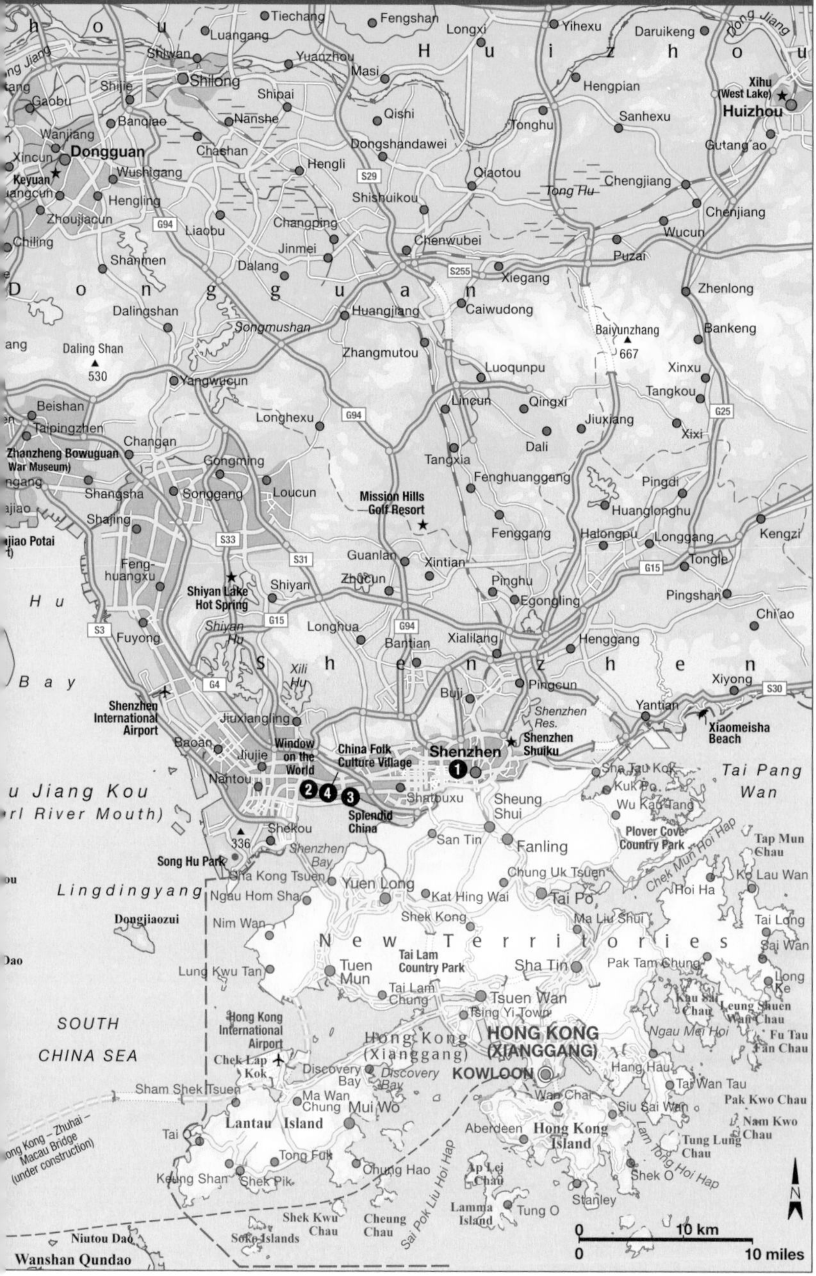

*Pedaloes in Lizhi Park, overlooked by the enormous KK100 skyscraper.*

# SHENZHEN AND THE PEARL RIVER DELTA

**Just across the China border, the swarming city of Shenzhen has graduated from being Hong Kong's sweatshop and is rapidly taking on its neighbour's air of glitz and sophistication. Some notable mainland characteristics remain though.**

The past three decades' stupendous growth in the Pearl River Delta (PRD) – with the Special Economic Zone (SEZ) of Shenzhen at the forefront – has been a key part of China's recent transformation. Occupying around 40,000 sq km (15,500 sq miles), the delta was once totally consumed by manufacturing, contributing around 30 percent of China's total exports. These numbers are now on the decline as factories relocate inland and to other parts of Southeast Asia. There are upsides in terms of pollution – while sometimes bad, the air tends to be better here than in Beijing or Shanghai – and the wealth generated during the boom years has made the region among the most modern and developed parts of China.

The Delta's transfiguration from paddy fields to stocks and shares deals, described by *The Economist* magazine as "so huge as to transform global trading patterns and investment flows", began in earnest in 1992. The then paramount leader Deng Xiaoping toured China's southern provinces, passing on the message that to get rich was glorious. SEZs with looser regulations and taxation started up in Shenzhen and Zhuhai shortly after. Investors from Taiwan and Hong Kong hurtled in, putting their international marketing savvy to prime use, to be swiftly imitated by their mainland counterparts.

The PRD still produces a large proportion of the world's electronics, motor parts, shoes, toys, furniture, textiles, clocks, watches, lighting and ceramics. There are around 200,000 factories here, approximately half of which are owned by Hong Kong companies whose workers largely originate from the less industrialised inland areas of China. These migrant

**Main Attractions**
**Lo Wu Commercial City**
**Window of the World**
**Splendid China**
**Opium War Museum, Humen**
**Zu Miao Temple, Foshan**
**Shiwan (ceramics)**

**Map**
**Pages 212, 219**

*The always bustling Donmeng Pedestrian Street.*

*Manicures and pedicures at Lo Wu Commercial City.*

workers typically live in dormitories on site at factories, and send money back to their families at home.

## SHENZHEN AND ENVIRONS

**Shenzhen ❶**, slap bang next to the Hong Kong border, was always going to do well. This is the new face of the PRC, where capitalism has been given pretty much a free hand after decades of communism. Nowadays its Mission Hills Golf Club, which embraces a dozen 18-hole championship courses (designed with help from the likes of Jack Nicklaus, Nick Faldo and Vijay Singh) stands in the *Guinness World Records* as the world's largest. Shun Hing Square, some 384 metres (1,260ft) tall, is the 21st-highest building in the world. Yet in the late 1970s, there was little here except for a farming community and a dingy border town.

Shenzhen Bao'an International Airport lies to the west of the city and has good ferry and coach links to Hong Kong. There has been talk of one day creating a "mega-metropolis" comprising Hong Kong and Shenzhen, but for now there are six land borders between the two; most visitors from Hong Kong take the MTR to either Lo Wu, the busiest border crossing point, or Lok Ma Chau, and walk across to enter mainland China. Both crossings link directly into the Shenzhen metro network.

Shenzhen offers a (rather unrepresentative) glimpse of the People's Republic to Westerners visiting Hong Kong, while Hong Kongers themselves visit in search of cheaper dining, nightlife and recreation, not to mention the shopping bargains at the emporia where the goods are "inspired by" major fashion companies like Prada and Chanel.

### What to do in Shenzhen

One of the most extensive retail romper rooms is the exhausting **Lo Wu Commercial City Ⓐ** (Luo Hu in pinyin), on the right after you exit the customs hall. Jewellery, clothes, leather goods, knick-knacks and a cornucopia of other merchandise are packed one atop the other here – although shops selling the same sort of items tend to cluster together. The

*Dongmen Pedestrian Street celebrates Chinese New Year.*

cardinal rule is to bargain fiercely. Offer less than a third of the asking price and settle for no more than half. Stallholders will calculate the price in Renminbi or HK dollars, but you will get a better deal if you use the former.

Shenzhen's other main shopping areas are **Dongmen** Ⓑ, with a wide range of shops and some good tailors, and at **Huaqiang Lu** Ⓒ, where electronics goods stores can be found. There is little difference in price compared to Hong Kong as far as mainstream electronics brands are concerned: the bargains lie in goods manufactured for the domestic market, although the price is a fair indication of the quality and life expectancy of any item.

Even half a day's shopping in Shenzhen is likely to take it out of you, so take time out to enjoy some inexpensive grooming. Lo Wu Commercial Centre has dozens of low-key nail bars and well-priced – if a tad spartan – massage parlours and beauty salons.

If Shenzhen has a Wild West vibe during the daytime, wait until the evenings. International hotels are a safe bet unless you are partying with locals. The main bar areas are International Bar Street in Futian and **Shekou** Ⓓ, a more expat-friendly residential area.

## The theme parks

It's tempting to regard Shenzhen as one enormous wacky theme park, and there's certainly no shortage of the real thing. The three main parks are clustered together in the Nanshan District, about 12km (8 miles) west of the downtown area. There are combination tickets available if you wish to see more than one park. **Window of the World** ❷ (daily 9am–10pm) showcases facsimiles of everything from Thai palaces and Japanese teahouses to European monuments – none more spectacular than the impressively large scale model of the Eiffel Tower.

In a rather similar vein, **Splendid China** ❸ (daily 10am–6pm) packs the whole country into one park, while the **China Folk Culture Village** ❹ (daily 9am–9pm) presents 56 different ethnic perspectives.

The **Shenzhen Museum**, on Fuzhong San Lu in Futian District (Tue–Sun 10am–6pm; free), is home to

*Chinese New Year Parade in the Folk Culture Village, Shenzhen.*

*Replica of the Eiffel Tower in the Window of the World Park.*

### THE RISE AND RISE OF SHENZHEN

The creation of Special Economic Zones (SEZs) during the 1980s, with their modern and relaxed business and tax regulations, kick-started the transformation of the Pearl River Delta, and nowhere was this more pronounced than in Shenzhen. Pell-mell, the factories and skyscrapers grew almost overnight, immigrants from all over China poured into the burgeoning city to make their fortunes, highways were rolled out, airports and railways constructed, and arable land smothered in concrete. The few hundred peasants who once eked out a living here dispersed in a phenomenon that was to become a byword for fast living, cheap shopping and a no-holds-barred race to the future.

Four decades later and Shenzhen is one of the richest cities in China. Per capita income is around eight times the national average, and the population has risen from 700,000 to 11 million in 25 years. Between 1992 and 2016, the city's GDP increased more than thirty-fold, from Rmb 32 billion to 1.95 trillion. Of course, the relentless growth has its downside. As inequality rises, so does crime: you are around nine times as likely to be mugged in Shenzhen as in Shanghai, and the air pollution can be choking.

*People hang wishes on the tree for good luck in the Foshan Ancestral Temple.*

more than 20,000 cultural relics, with permanent exhibitions on the history of the Pearl River Delta. Exhibitions on folk history include Hakka culture and Hakka roundhouses.

## AROUND THE DELTA

Away from Shenzhen, much of the Pearl River Delta is a mix of sprawling industrial parks, odd swathes of farmland and occasional golf courses interspersed with a few less developed hilly areas. The areas to the west of the river delta itself are, on the whole, more attractive than those to the east.

### Humen and the opium pits

While international trade is now all the rage in the Delta, early attempts by Western traders to introduce opium to China in the 19th century met with stiff official resistance, commemorated at both a park and a museum in the town of **Humen**, right on the river delta, around 25km (15 miles) northwest of Shenzhen Airport. It was at Humen that Commissioner Lin Zexu (see page 32) contaminated several thousand chests of opium with quicklime in 1839, then deposited the haul in the so-called opium pits on the shore to the south of town. The British retaliated, sparking the First Opium War, and Lin was exiled. In the **Opium War Museum** (Yapan Zhanzheng Bowuguan; www.ypzz.cn; daily 8.30am–5pm) in Zhixin Park, much is made (and rightly so) of the perfidiousness of foreign merchants who started the conflict that ended with the Chinese forces vanquished and the ceding of Hong Kong in 1841. On the coast some 5km (3 miles) south of Humen town, the original opium pits are worth a visit (8am–5pm).

### Foshan and Shiwan

The busy city of **Foshan** ❺ lies southwest of Guangzhou. It's a dusty centre of ceramics and textile production, but hidden away from the grids of factories is the 1,000-year old **Zu Miao Temple complex** (21 Zumiao Lu; daily 8.30am–6pm) The temple is well preserved, with many finely sculptured friezes made from limestone, ash of shells, paper,

## TRANSPORT TO/FROM SHENZHEN

**Hong Kong–Shenzhen**

**Trains:** Every 6–8 minutes from Kowloon to the border terminus of Lo Wu (5.30am–11.07pm) or, slightly less frequently, to Lok Ma Chau (5.35am–9.35pm). Journey takes around 45 minutes. Shenzhen station is located just over the border.

**Ferries:** 20+ daily ferries between Hong Kong/Kowloon and Shekou port (50 mins); 11–13 daily between Hong Kong Airport and Shekou (30 mins); 5–8 daily between Hong Kong Airport and the Fuyong Ferry Terminal (Shenzhen Airport; 45 mins).

**Buses:** Frequent shuttle buses (typically every 30 mins) run from several locations around Hong Kong, including Central, Tsim Sha Tsui and the airport, to downtown Shenzhen, Shekou and Shenzhen Airport.

**Shenzhen–Macau**

**Ferries:** 3 daily to/from Shekou port (80 mins). Also hourly Shekou–Zhuhai (1 hr).

**Shenzhen–Guangzhou**

**Trains:** 3–5 express per hour (55–70 mins), plus slower trains (1.5 hrs).

**Buses:** frequent departures (1.5 –2 hrs).

**The Shenzhen Metro**

Shenzhen's metro system opened in 2004 and has since developed at warp-speed. There are currently eight lines: the "green" Luobao line is probably the most important, running from Lo Wu , through the central Dongmen area, out past the theme parks, through the rapidly developing Nanshan district and on to the airport; the "red" Longhua line runs north–south from the Futian border crossing (beside Lok Ma Chau) to Qinghu; the "blue" Longgang line also begins in Futian and ventures northeast past the Universiade park; the "purple" Huanzhong line does a northerly loop around the city; while the "yellow" Shekou line runs east–west all the way out to the Shekou port and peninsular. Three new lines opened in 2016: the "navy" line, travelling west–east from Xili Lake to Tai'an; the "grey" line through Nanshan, Futian and Luohu; and the Airport Express, linking Bao'an International Airport and the city centre. Trains run every 6–8 minutes 6.30am–11pm.

rice, straw and sand. The once colourfully painted friezes depict fables and scenes of Foshan's history. Many of the friezes have faded to an antique tone, which adds to the temple's charm.

**Shiwan ❻**, just 2km (1.25 miles) southwest of downtown Foshan, has been making ceramics for centuries, and is home to many porcelain factories that these days welcome tour groups. The fires at the **Nanfeng Ancient Kiln** (daily 8am–5pm) are said to have been alight and firing pottery since the Ming era. The four-day firing process is explained by way of a series of English-language signs.

In the Nanhai district of Foshan, **Xiqiao Shan ❼** is a hilly area with villages that have retained some of their 19th-century flavour. Xiqiao is one of the more peaceful areas in Guangdong, one that still thrives on its local produce and river trade. From the town, it's possible to travel by cable car to visit the statue of Guanyin on the crest of the nearby hill and walk along stone paths that wind through even smaller villages, rocky plateaux and waterfalls, including Feiliutian Chi, which is reckoned to be the most picturesque.

## South to Macau

**Shunde ❽**, on the road from Guangzhou to Zhuhai, is renowned for its Qing garden, and has some photogenic back lanes and canals. Further south, the large town of **Jiangmen ❾** is eminently missable, although the Ming-era villages in the surrounding countryside – centred round a watchtower – are a pleasant reminder of architectural whim in former days. Closer to Zhuhai, and on the coast, the memorial garden at **Cuiheng ❿** pays tribute to its best-known son, Dr Sun Yat-sen, China's first republican president. **Zhuhai ⓫** is the last major city before Macau, and is steadily growing in importance as a Special Economic Zone.

*Pottery waiting to be glazed.*

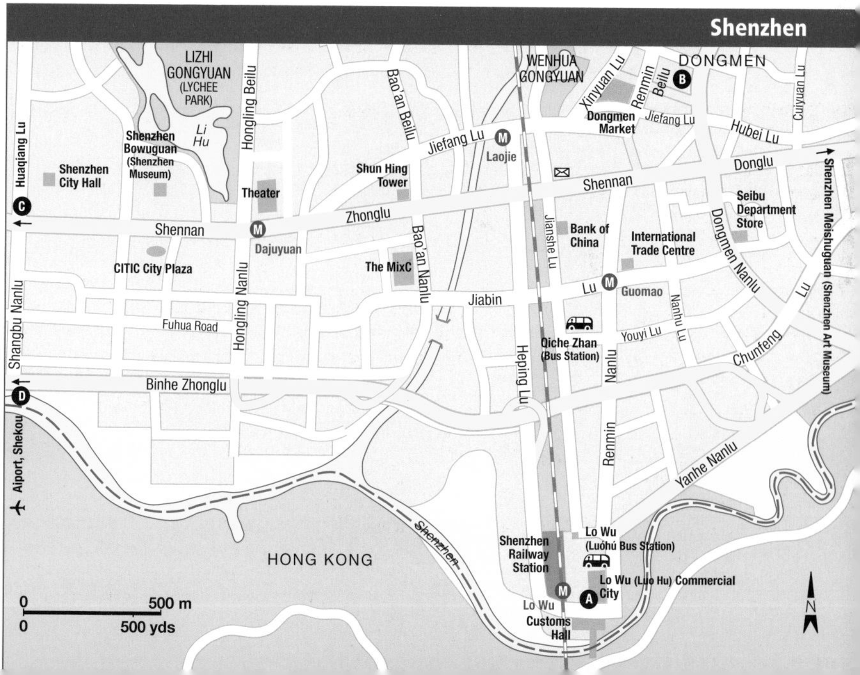

# GUANGZHOU

**One of the first Chinese cities open to the outside world, Guangzhou has long had economic modernisation as its goal. Still, despite the usual urban bustle, some of old Canton remains.**

**Main Attractions**

Pearl River Cruise
Shamian Island
Chenjia Si Temple
Sun Yat-sen Memorial Hall
Yuexiu Park
Baiyun Shan

**Map**

Pages 212, 222

In **Guangzhou** ⓬ – always one of China's more dynamic cities – there is a palpable sense of the energy fuelling the country's rapid transformation. This is a boisterous urban centre with all the blemishes one associates with modern cities, air pollution and traffic jams included. The greater metropolitan area – with countless factories and accompanying migrant workforce – is home to over 14 million. The city is highly accessible from Hong Kong thanks to frequent high-speed rail links (see page 232). Though most of the passengers who pack these carriages are business travellers, Guangzhou is an easy and popular trip for tourists, albeit one which requires a full China visa. In contrast to Shenzhen, the city retains a distinct identity and is relatively well endowed with traditional tourist sights. These have been added to in recent years with the development of a cultural zone in the eastern reaches of the city centre, where there is a dazzling opera house and a lavish museum dedicated to Cantonese culture.

Guangzhou is thought to have been founded in the third century BC as an encampment by the armies of the Qin emperor, Qin Shi Huangdi. During the Tang dynasty (618–906), the city was already an international port, although for centuries it remained second to Quanzhou (Marco Polo's Zaytun, up the coast in Fujian province). Trade with Europe began after the Portuguese established themselves in the region after 1514, and from 1757 to 1842, Guangzhou was the only Chinese port open to foreigners and was at the centre of the build-up to the First Opium War (see page 32). It later became one of China's four treaty ports.

Following the overthrow of the Qing dynasty in 1911, the city

*View across Zhujiang New Town.*

attracted reformers and revolutionaries. Sun Yat-sen established the headquarters of the Guomintang (Nationalist Party), the first modern political party in China. Later, Mao Zedong and Zhou Enlai worked and taught in Guangzhou during a brief period of cooperation between the two political groups. During the Mao era, while the rest of China was closed to foreign trade, Guangzhou resumed its role as China's trading window on the word, continuing to do business at the international Canton Fair. In recent years, even though it has lost ground to the economic miracle that is modern Shanghai, the city has consolidated its prosperity and is a magnet for migrant workers.

## AROUND THE CITY

Guangzhou is defined by the Pearl River (Zhu Jiang), which flows through the centre of the city from west to east. Places of interest are scattered around a wide area.

### Shamian Island A

The most attractive neighbourhood to explore is around **Shamian Island**, a preserved relic of colonial times in the southwest of the city. Originally a sandbar on the northern bank of the Zhu Jiang, the small island was reclaimed and expanded, then divided in 1859 into several foreign concessions, primarily French and British. A canal was dug, and after ten o'clock in the evening two iron gates and narrow bridges kept the Chinese off the island.

Shamian is compact and feels very much like a resort area, in sharp contrast to the hustle of the rest of the city. A programme of gentrification has renovated a number of old colonial buildings and nurtured open-air restaurants and riverside cafés, whilst former Catholic and Anglican churches have been reopened for worship.

### Qingping Market

To the north of Shamian Island, along Qingping Lu, is **Qingping Market B** (Qingping Shichang), long known for selling every imaginable animal for food. It has changed in recent years – in part because of SARS – and there are fewer exotic mammals on display. However the

*Bridge over the Pearl River lit up by a lightshow in central Guanzhou city.*

*Guangzhou Metro line 3.*

sight of live scorpions and turtles, or live fowl, cats and rabbits kept in small dirty cages still shocks. The nearby streets of pet shops offer some new conflicts to puzzle over. Stalls lining Dishipu Lu and Daihe Lu sell jade, jewellery, old timepieces and Mao paraphernalia.

Around 1km (0.6 mile) to the north, the parallel streets of Xiajiu Lu and Changshou Lu form the centre of a lively shopping and dining area. Behind the Guangdong Restaurant, a narrow side alley called Shangxia Jie leads to **Hualin Si** ❸, said to have been founded by an Indian monk in 526, although the existing buildings date from the Qing dynasty. There are 500 statues of luohan, pupils of the Buddha, in the main hall.

## The waterfront

The Bund (Yanjiang Lu) runs eastwards along the waterfront from Shamian to **Haizhu Qiao** ❹, built in 1933 and the oldest steel bridge across the Pearl River. Around 2km (1.5 miles) east of the bridge on Er-Sha Island is the **Guangdong Museum of Art** ❺ (Guangdong Meishuguan; 38 Yanyu Lu; www.gdmoa.org; Tue–Sun 9am–5pm; free). Its dozen exhibition halls display some of the more avant-garde examples of Chinese art, with exhibitions of work by local students and an outdoor sculpture area.

## A cathedral and a mosque

To the northwest of Haizhu, the 50-metre (160ft) double towers of the **Sacred Heart Catholic Cathedral** ❻ (Shishi Jiaotang) are plainly visible. Built in the early 1860s it holds services under the auspices of the Patriotic Catholic Church.

Further north is the onion-shaped dome of **Huaisheng Si** ❼, dating back to 627 and founded by a trader said to be an uncle of the Prophet Mohammed. The 25-metre (82ft) minaret, the **Guang Ta Pagoda** (Naked

**Guangzhou**

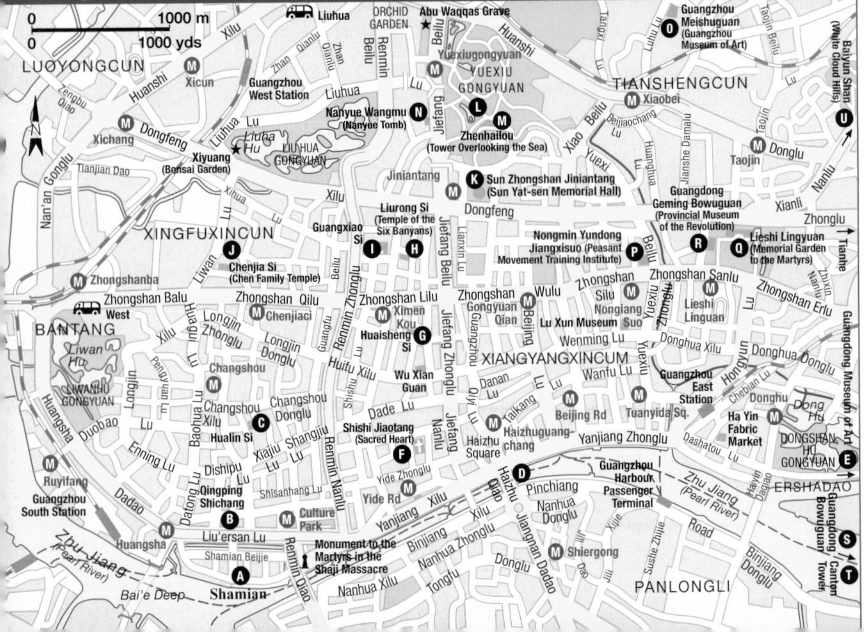

Pagoda), dominates an area where high-rises are competing to capture the skyline. The mosque functions as a cultural centre for Guangzhou's Hui Muslims, who comprise about 5 percent of the city's population.

## Liurong Si H

**Address:** 87 Liurong Lu
**Opening Hrs:** daily 9am–5pm
**Entrance Fee:** charge
**Transport:** Ximen Kou

North of Zhongshan Lu, one of the city's main east–west thoroughfares, a narrow street leads to the **Liurong Temple** (Temple of the Six Banyan Trees). It was built in 1097 together with the **Hua Ta Pagoda** (Flower Pagoda), although a temple has stood here since the sixth century. Each storey has doorways and an encircling balcony – climb to the top to be rewarded with a great view of Guangzhou's urban sprawl.

## Guangxiao Si I

**Address:** 109 Guangxiao Lu
**Opening Hrs:** daily 6.30am–5pm
**Entrance Fee:** charge
**Transport:** Ximen Kou

**Guangxiao Temple** (Temple of Bright Filial Piety) was preserved during the Cultural Revolution on orders from Premier Zhou Enlai. The temple is believed to date back to sometime around AD 400, although most buildings are of 19th-century vintage. The entrance is marked by a brightly painted laughing Buddha, and the main hall is notable for its ceiling of red-lacquered timber, while the rear courtyard has some of the oldest iron pagodas in China.

The **Dongtie** and **Xitie pagodas** (Western and Eastern Iron pagodas) date back to the city's earliest beginnings. There is a 10th-century stone pagoda behind the main hall with sculptures of the Buddha placed in eight niches.

## Chenjia Si J

**Address:** Zhongshan Lu
**Opening Hrs:** daily 8.30am–5pm
**Entrance Fee:** charge
**Transport:** Chenjia Si

**Chenjia Si** (Chen Family Temple), located on the western end of Zhongshan Lu close to the eponymous subway station, is one of

### TIP

A cruise on the Pearl River (Zhu Jiang) is a pleasant way of seeing Guangzhou, particularly in the evening when the city looks at its best – all the bridges, and many of the skyscrapers on either bank, are imaginatively festooned with lighting displays. Boats depart from Tianzi and Dasha piers on the north bank, and most cruises last for 90 minutes, with the option of dining aboard. Several companies compete for business, though the focus is on domestic tourism. Ticket booths at both piers display prices and packages.

### CITY TRANSPORT

Guangzhou's **metro system** is extensive, and the network connects most places of interest. Trains are clean and run every few minutes from 6am to midnight. Tickets (actually a disc which is inserted in the turnstile) cost from Rmb 2, and stored-value cards are an option. Stations are marked by red signs with a split Y symbol, and signage and ticket machines are bilingual. **Taxis** fill in the gaps that the metro has yet to reach; ask your concierge to write your destination in Chinese, as few drivers speak any English. All cabs have meters. The **bus** network is comprehensive, but slow and crowded. There are fewer **bicycles** these days, but this can still be a good way of getting about – bike hire is available on Shamian Island.

*Cars speed past a building on Shamian Island.*

*Guangzhou's ultra-modern Opera House, designed by Zaha Hadid.*

China's more whimsical temples. The temple, built in 1894, has six courtyards and a classical Chinese layout, and is decorated with friezes crafted in Shiwan, near Foshan (see page 218). The largest frieze depicts scenes from the epic *Romance of Three Kingdoms*, with thousands of intricate figures against a backdrop of ornate houses, grandiose gates and pagodas. There is a giant altar of gold-leaf plating and additional wood, brick and stone friezes along the rooftops.

The temple houses the **Guangdong Folk Arts Museum** with displays from all over China, including embroidery, ethnic minority costumes, porcelain figures and jade carvings.

## Around Jiefang Lu

The **Sun Yat-sen Memorial Hall** (Sun Zhongshan Jiniantang) **K**, set within a lush 6-hectare (15-acre) park, is easy to spot with its eye-catching blue roof tiles. The octagonal hall, built shortly after the death of Sun Yat-sen in 1925 and completed in 1931, now houses a large theatre and lecture hall.

*View of Guangzhou from the Baiyun Mountain.*

Guangzhou's largest park, **Yuexiu** **L**, is beautifully landscaped with three artificial lakes, rolling hills, rock sculptures and lush greenery. Its centrepiece is the **Tower Overlooking the Sea** (Zhenhailou) **M**, a memorial to the seven great sea journeys undertaken by the Muslim eunuch admiral Zheng He to East Africa, the Persian Gulf and Java between 1405 and 1433. Today, the tower houses a **municipal museum** showcasing the history of Guangzhou (www.guangzhoumuseum.cn; daily 9am–5pm).

Nearby is the marble and granite **Sun Yat-sen Monument**, which sits on a hill above the Sun Yat-sen Memorial Hall.

On the other side of Jiefang Beilu from Yuexiu Park is the **Nanyue Tomb** **N** (Xihan Nanyue Wangmu; daily 9am–5pm), the tomb of the Nanyu emperor. In 1983, bulldozers uncovered the tomb of the emperor Wen Di, who ruled southern China from 137 to 122 BC. Now an underground museum, the site houses the skeletons of the emperor and 15 courtiers, including concubines, guards, cooks and a musician, who were buried alive with the emperor. Thousands of funeral objects from jade armour to bronze music chimes are displayed in adjoining rooms.

## Eastern districts

East of Yuexiu Park, on the edge of Luhu Park, is the **Guangzhou Museum of Art** **O** (Guangzhou Meishu Bowuguan; www.gzam.com.cn; 13 Luhu Lu; Tue–Sun 9am–5pm), with an impressive collection of ancient and contemporary art and sculpture (including genuine terracotta warriors from Xi'an).

Close to the junction of Yuexiu and Zhongshan Lu is the former Kongzi Miao, or Confucius Temple, which lost its religious function during the "bourgeois revolution" of 1912. In 1924, the **Peasant Movement Training**

**Institute** **P** (Nongmin Yundong Jiangxisuo; daily 9am–5.30pm) was opened here as the first school of the Chinese Communist Party. The elite of the Party taught here: Mao Zedong (his work and bedroom are on show), Zhou Enlai, Guo Moruo and several others.

After the collapse of a workers' uprising in 1927, the communists were forced to retreat from the cities. A park and memorial, **Lieshi Lingyuan** **Q** (Memorial Garden to the Martyrs) situated just to the east of the Peasant Training Institute, was created in 1957 in memory of the uprising and its nearly 6,000 victims. Nearby is the **Guangdong Geming Bowuguan** **R** (Provincial Museum of the Revolution; daily 9am–5pm), a reminder of the role of the Guomintang (Nationalist Party) and its predecessors since the First Opium War.

## Zhujiang New Town

On the northern banks of the Pearl River, east of the historic city centre, lies Zhujiang New Town, a US-style gridded district that has been raised from the dust over the last decade. Studded with five-star hotels, mammoth towers such as the Guangzhou International Finance Center, and a beautiful opera house, it points the way to several tourist attractions. The mesmerizing exterior design of the **Guangdong Museum** **S** (Guangdong Bowuguan; hwww.gdmuseum.com; 2 Zhujiang Donglu; Tue–Sun 9am–5pm; free) is as impressive as its enormous collection, which excels on ceramics and painting, but also has items such as Duan inkstone which specifically reflect Guangdong's historic cultural industries.

On the opposite side of the river is the hard-to-miss 600-metre (1969ft) -high **Canton Tower** **T** (Guangdong Ta; www.cantontower.com; 222 Yuejiang Xilu; daily 9am–10pm) the tallest structure in China thanks to the enormous antennae. The tower sells a variety of packaged tourist experiences which include a theme park-style vertical drop ride on the outside of the tower and an outdoor observation deck 488 metres (1,600ft) above ground level.

## Baiyun Shan

An easy half-day trip to the north of the city leads to **Baiyun Shan** **U** (White Cloud Hills), a series of hills overlooking Guangzhou. To get there take a taxi or, if you feel up to it, bus no. 24 from the south side of Renmin Park – journey time is 30 minutes. A cable car ascends to the top, where you can walk to several other peaks. Souvenir stands and teahouses are found at various peaks and precipices in the area, ideal places to sit back and take in the surrounding hills. If you prefer to walk up to the peak, there is a paved road as well as stone paths that wind up through the trees.

**FACT**

In its earliest times, Guangzhou was called Panyu, and the name Guangzhou first appeared during the period of the Three Kingdoms (AD 222–280). The city was formerly known to Westerners as Canton: from the Cantonese pronunciation of the provincial name "Guangdong", the Portuguese derived the name of Cantão; from Cantão came Canton.

*Yuexiu Park.*

*Window shopping in Gough Street, Central District.*

# TRAVEL TIPS

# HONG KONG

## TRANSPORT

Getting there .................. 228
By air .......................... 228
By rail .......................... 229
By sea .......................... 229
Getting around ............... 229
Public transport ......... 229
Macau transport ....... 231
Regional Transport ........ 231
By boat ....................... 231
By helicopter ............ 232
By rail .......................... 232

## A-Z

Accommodation ............ 233
Addresses ...................... 234
Admission charges ........ 234
Age restrictions .............. 234
Budgeting for your trip ............................. 234
Climate .......................... 234
Crime and safety ........... 235
Customs regulations ..... 235
Disabled travellers ........ 235
Embassies & consulates ................. 236
Emergency numbers ..... 236
Etiquette ....................... 236
Health and medical care ........................... 236
Internet ......................... 237
Left luggage .................. 237
LGBTQ travellers ........... 237
Lost property .................. 237
Maps ............................ 237
Media ............................ 237
Money ........................... 237
Opening hours ............... 238
Postal services .............. 239
Shopping ....................... 239
Smoking ......................... 239
Student travellers .......... 239
Telephones .................... 239
Time zone ...................... 240
Toilets ............................ 240
Tourist information ........ 240
Visas and passports ...... 241
Weights and measures ................. 241

## Language

Tones ............................. 242
Pronunciation ................ 243
Numbers ........................ 243
Common words and phrases .............. 243
Nouns ............................ 243
Questions ....................... 243
People ........................... 243
Adjectives ...................... 243
Taxis .............................. 244
Health and emergencies ............. 244
Food and drink .............. 244
Glossary ......................... 244

## Further Reading

Fiction ........................... 246
History and current affairs ............................ 246
Nature/walking guides ........................ 246
Macau ............................ 246
China ............................. 246
Other Insight Guides ..... 246

# TRANSPORT

## GETTING THERE AND GETTING AROUND

### GETTING THERE

#### By air

##### *Hong Kong Airport*

Hong Kong is a major international air-traffic hub for the region, handling just over 70 million passengers in 2016. The impressive Hong Kong International Airport (HKIA) is located at Chek Lap Kok, on the northern shore of Lantau and about 34km (21 miles) from Central. The Y-shaped building is highly efficient. With two runways and two terminals, HKIA can handle 68 flights per hour at peak times. Aircraft are received at a plethora of gates; moving walkways and an Automated People Mover speed arrivals to Immigration, where queues are dealt with swiftly. Suitcases are usually circling the carousel when you reach the baggage hall, and there is a large shopping mall, left-luggage office, post office, plus plenty of food and beverage outlets. The 1,171-room Regal Airport Hotel is connected to Terminal 1, while a Marriott and 9-hole golf course are accessed via SkyPlaza, a giant entertainment and retail complex alongside Terminal 2. Enquiry hotline: 2181 8888; www.hkairport.com.

The **Airport Express** (tel: 2881 8888) railway, which runs from right inside the terminal building, is the easiest and quickest way to get into town – trains reach Hong Kong Island in just 23 minutes, with stops at Tsing Yi and Kowloon stations. Single fares cost HK$90–100, returns HK$160–180. Many hotels operate free shuttle buses to and from the Airport Express stations.

Numerous **buses** link the airport with the city. Airbus services (prefixed "A") run at regular intervals to Hong Kong Island, Kowloon and the New Territories, and most run from 6am to midnight. The fare to Central is around HK$35. Slower "commuter" buses (prefixed "E") run at similar times. There are night buses, and shuttle buses to Tung Chung MTR station.

The **taxi fare** to Kowloon should be around HK$250, and HK$300 to Hong Kong Island – slightly more if you're carrying heavy luggage. Only the red taxis are able to take passengers to these downtown areas. There are direct **ferry services** from the airport to Macau and Shenzhen, as well as a fleet of **buses to destinations in Guangdong**.

##### *Other airports*

**Macau International Airport** (tel: 2866 1111, or see www.macau-airport.com) provides a convenient gateway for travellers from many points in Asia. A number of **low-cost airlines** operate out of Macau, so it can be economical to fly to destinations in Southeast Asia and China from here. The airport is on the east side of Taipa Island, and is linked by bridges to the downtown area. Taxi fares are about 40 Patacas (written as MOP$40). The regular AP1 bus serves major hotels, the Ferry Terminal and the border gate – the fare is MOP$3.30.

**Shenzhen** Bao'an International Airport (eng.szairport.com) is not (yet) a major port of entry into China. If you are planning onward travel to other mainland cities, it is generally cheaper to fly from Shenzhen than from Hong Kong. The airport is linked to Hong Kong by a ferry and bus service, and is situated northwest of the city on the delta coast.

**Guangzhou's** gleaming Baiyun International Airport is 28km (18 miles) and a 45-minute drive from downtown. It has evolved into an increasingly important international hub. In addition to flights across the mainland and Asia, there are direct links to London, Paris, Los

Angeles, Melbourne and Sydney. For flight information, tel: 020-3606 6999, www.baiyunairport.com. Buses and taxis shuttle passengers to and from the airport. Expect to pay between RMB120–150 for a taxi.

### By rail

MTR operates direct intercity trains from Shanghai and Beijing to Kowloon's Hung Hom Station on alternate days, as well as daily services to the Guangdong cities of Changping, Guangzhou, Foshan and Zhaoqing (www.it3.mtr.com.hk). The high-speed network that covers much of the China mainland is not yet plugged into Hong Kong so journey times are relatively slow: just over 19 hours to/from Shanghai, and 23 hours to/from Beijing. Note that Hong Kong usually appears as "Jiulong" – putonghua for Kowloon – on Chinese pinyin timetables, noticeboards and tickets. If travelling by train from other destinations in China, Guangzhou is the main rail hub, and 12 direct intercity through trains run between Hung Hom and Guangzhou East daily. Alternatively you can head to Shenzhen and walk across the border at Lo Wu, then catch an MTR train south to Kowloon once you have cleared customs.

*Tram stops are frequent and clearly signposted.*

### By sea

Numerous cities in Guangdong province are connected by sea with Hong Kong, and it is also possible to take a ferry from Xiamen in Fujian province. See page 231 for details on regional transport.

## GETTING AROUND

Hong Kong is an easy city to get around, once you are armed with a bilingual map, and have worked out where Hong Kong Island, the harbour and the Kowloon peninsula are in relation to one another. Public transport is excellent, but be aware, however, that since this is such a densely populated city, trying to navigate your way around in the rush hour is challenging – even impossible at times – for the uninitiated. Travelling at this time of day may also make you feel less than charitable towards the local population. If you're waiting for a taxi on the street away from a taxi rank, it's every man for himself. Don't expect anyone to acknowledge whether you have been there 10 seconds or 10 minutes. If you think it's your turn, just take the taxi.

### Public transport

#### *Rail: the MTR*

Hong Kong has a fast and efficient rail system with clear signage in English and Chinese. All trains are air-conditioned and operate from around 6am until just after midnight.

All trains in Hong Kong are operated by the MTR (tel: 2881 8888, www.mtr.com.hk), in a network now comprising ten railway lines serving Hong Kong Island, Kowloon, North Lantau and the New Territories. An additional Light Rail line serves Tuen Mun and Yuen Long. The MTR also runs the Airport Express (see page 228).

Adult single fares vary according to the specific departure and destination stations. They range from HK$4.50–55, though a typical downtown fare will be HK$13 or less. There is a 10 percent discount if you use an Octopus card (see panel). There are also ticket deals for tourists: a HK$55 tourist pass (HK$25 for children aged 3–11) allows unlimited travel during any 24-hour period on the Island, Tsuen Wan, Kwun Tong, Tseung Kwan O, Tung Chung and Disneyland Resort lines. For HK$85/120 you can get a one or two day pass which includes rides to the mainland China border at Lo Wu and Lok Ma Chau. The Airport Express Travel Pass is the best bet for anyone arriving by air for a short stay in Hong Kong. It costs HK$220/300 for one or two Airport Express journeys and three consecutive days unlimited travel on the MTR.

#### *Buses*

Six different bus companies provide services in Hong Kong, covering all the major areas as well as speedy connections to and from the airport. Routes are reduced at night. Fares range from HK$1.90 for short journeys in the city to HK$45 for longer trips into the New Territories. Final destinations are marked in English and Chinese on the front top panel. Drivers rarely speak much English, but timetables and route maps are posted at bus stops. Exact change is needed, or use an Octopus Card.
**Enquiries:** Citybus (tel: 2873 0818) and New World First Bus (tel: 2136 8888), which run on Hong Kong Island, Kowloon and the New Territories, are owned by the same company (www.nwstbus.com.hk). Other operators are Kowloon Motor Bus (KMB; tel: 2745 4466; www.kmb.hk); Long Win Bus Co. (tel: 2261 2791), which serves the airport; Discovery Bay Transportation

*Hong Kong's efficient railway system, the MTR.*

Services (tel: 2987 0208); and the New Lantao Bus Co. (tel: 2984 9848; www.newlantaobus.com) on Lantau Island.

### Ferries

The nine-strong Star Ferry fleet crosses the harbour between Central and Wan Chai, on Hong Kong Island, and Tsim Sha Tsui on the Kowloon side from 6.30am–11.30pm every day (top deck HK$2.50, lower deck HK$2 Mon–Fri, top deck HK$3.40, lower deck HK$2.80 weekends and public holidays). There are also routes from Hung Hom to both Central and Wan Chai. Departures are every 6–12 minutes depending on the time of day, and the journey takes about eight minutes Central–Tsim Sha Tsui, and around 15 minutes Wan Chai–Tsim Sha Tsui.

Ferries to the Outlying Islands – Lamma, Lantau (including 24-hour service to Discovery Bay), Cheung Chau and Peng Chau – leave from the ferry piers to the north of the IFC tower on Hong Kong Island. Fares start from HK$11. Fast ferries cost more.

### Minibuses/maxicabs

These 16-seater passenger vans, coloured cream with either a red or green side-stripe, run on fixed routes but will stop anywhere except on double yellow lines. They are usually faster than regular buses, but not as cheap. Destinations are usually written in English at the front of the van. Call out clearly when you want the driver to stop. Fares vary from HK$2–25. Vans with a green stripe (maxicabs) take Octopus Cards or exact change only. Those with a red stripe do not take Octopus Cards but will give change.

### Taxis

It is usually easy to hail a taxi on the street, although at busy times you may need to join a queue at a taxi rank – best at a hotel. Taxis in Hong Kong and Kowloon are coloured red and, in theory, can take you anywhere in the territory apart from non-airport destinations on Lantau. However, sometimes you will come across taxis on Hong Kong Island which are so-called "Kowloon taxis": otherwise identical, these will only take passengers across to Kowloon – which can be frustrating. Green taxis operate in the New Territories, and blue cabs on Lantau Island. All taxis can carry passengers between the airport and the rest of Hong Kong.

The initial fare is HK$22 for red taxis, HK$18.50 for green, HK$17 for blue. There are additional charges for each item of luggage that's stored in the trunk, animals and travelling via tunnels, which are all posted inside the taxi. Passengers must wear a seatbelt (when available) whether sitting in the front or rear.

Many taxi drivers can speak some English and know the main hotels and tourist spots in Hong Kong, but to avoid problems, take your destination written down in Chinese. If you encounter difficulties, all cabs are equipped with a radio telephone, and somebody at the control centre should be able to translate.

Taking passengers for a ride by a circuitous route is not unknown, and drivers will sometimes refuse a fare, usually if the journey will take them out of their way as they are about to finish work. You may call a police

## OCTOPUS CARDS

Visitors staying more than a few days should buy an Octopus stored-value card, which permits travel on the rail systems, buses, some minibuses and ferries at reduced fares. It can also be used at many public phones, photo booths, vending machines and for purchases at a number of retail outlets such as 7-Eleven, Starbucks and local supermarkets. Octopus cards are sold at service counters at Airport xpress and Mass Transit Railway stations. The minimum price is HK$150, which includes a refundable HK$50 deposit. Children aged 3–11 and those over 65 pay reduced fares. For enquiries, tel: 2266 2222. www.octopuscards.com.

## TRAMS

Hong Kong Island's historic "ding-ding" trams are both an inexpensive way to get around and a tourist attraction in their own right. The tramlines run across the north of Hong Kong Island west and east. Stops are frequent, and you can simply hop on and off as you please. The flat fare is HK$2.30, or $1.20 for under-12s and $1.10 for over-65s (exact change required or use an Octopus Card), and the service operates between 6am and 1am. Sit on the top deck for the best views (see page 117).

The **Peak Tram** is a funicular railway and has been running since 1888. It takes eight minutes to reach the upper terminus from the terminus on Garden Road, Central, running every 15 minutes, between 7am and midnight daily.

The Peak tram adult return fare is HK$45, single $32, children $20 and $12.

officer or phone the complaint hotline, tel: 2527 7177, but to save time it is probably better to walk off and find another taxi. If you lose something in a taxi you can call 1872 920 to try and trace it. You will need to pay a charge for them to search for you whether or not you get your belongings back.

## Macau transport

The huge rise in visitor numbers to Macau has resulted in traffic problems, and taxis are often difficult to find away from hotels, casinos, the ferry pier or the border crossing. Many casinos operate free shuttle buses from the ferry terminal.

### *Buses*

Buses and minibuses are easy to use in Macau, with the English destination written on the front along with the Chinese. Bus stops have routes and numbers clearly marked. Exact change is needed. A battalion of buses wait at the ferry terminal and stop at most major hotels, casinos and tourist sites. Fares are cheap, ranging from MOP$3.20 for anywhere on Macau peninsula to MOP$6.40 for Hac Sa on Coloane.

### *Taxis*

The former Portuguese colony has a fleet of black or yellow taxis. The initial fare is MOP$17. Drivers here speak less English than those in Hong Kong, and many carry a list of tourist sites written in English and Chinese in their cab. There is a small surcharge for large items of luggage.

### *Pedicabs*

As an echo of the quieter colonial past, there are a small gaggle of pedicab drivers who wait for custom at the jetty terminal. You will need to bargain with the driver – a typical price is around MOP$150 per hour, but note that a lot of Macau is hilly, with the roads being congested and unsuitable for these two-seater bicycle cabs.

For information on public transportin Shenzhen and Guangzhou, see page 218.

## REGIONAL TRANSPORT

## By boat

### *Hong Kong–Macau*

There are numerous ways to travel from Hong Kong to Macau by sea. Fares for sea crossings vary between services and the class of ticket, the time of the day, and the day of the week you travel. First Ferry runs its high-speed catamarans from the China Ferry Terminal in Tsim Sha Tsui. Turbojet services are slightly more expensive and more frequent, and they leave from the Macau Ferry Terminal at the Shun Tak Centre in Sheung Wan, Hong Kong Island. Tickets range between HK$164 and HK$200 for economy class one way. For the most up-to-date information

*Taxi ranks are well sign posted.*

on fares, check with the company providing the service or the Hong Kong offices of the Macau Government Tourist Office, tel: 2831 5566; www.macautourism.gov.mo.

Shun Tak Holdings' Turbojets carry the largest percentage of passengers between Hong Kong and Macau, and take about an hour. Refreshments are provided on board, with complimentary newspapers, coffee and tea on the first-class top deck. Departures are every 15 minutes from 7am until 1am, and then roughly one an hour. Turbojets also operate a route direct from Hong Kong Airport to Macau, although there are only seven departures daily. Contact Turbojet on tel: 2859 3333, www.turbojet.com.hk.

The New World First Ferry "flying cats" are two-deck catamarans that carry 400 passengers. They leave every half-hour between 7am and midnight from China Ferry Terminal TST. Contact First Ferry on tel: 2131 8181, www.nwff.com.hk. You can also go straight from Hong Kong to Taipa on Cotai Jet Ferries (tel: 2359 9900; www.cotaijet.com.mo), which depart from the Macau Ferry Terminal every half an hour 7.30am–6pm and, approximately, every hour up from 6pm–midnight. From Taipa there are either hourly or half hourly ferries from 7am–3am. Tickets cost from HK$154 on weekdays and from HK$167 at weekends. This is a good option if you are heading straight for the Cotai casinos or for Taipa/Coloane.

It is wise to buy your return ticket in advance, especially if you are travelling at the weekend or during a public holiday, as tickets can sell out.

**Baggage**

Baggage is limited to 9kg (20lb), and there is not much space on board for large suitcases. The Left Luggage Service Centre, G/F Shop G02, Shun Tak Centre (6.30am–12.30am) charges HK$20 per piece per hour.

### *Hong Kong–Guangdong*

Ferries operate between Hong Kong and several Guangdong cities including Zhuhai and Shekou (for Shenzhen Airport). The ferry service which once served Guangzhou has long since ceased to operate, usurped by modern road and rail links. Most ferries leave from Hong Kong's China Ferry Terminal on Canton Road, Tsim Sha Tsui. Tickets can be bought from the terminal or CTS offices.

## By helicopter

SkyShuttle (in HK, tel: 2108 9898; www.skyshuttlehk.com) operate a **helicopter** service between Hong Kong and Macau. There are flights every 30 minutes from 9am until 10.59pm. The flights use helipads on the Macau Ferry Terminal in the Shun Tak Centre in Hong Kong and the Macau Ferry Terminal in Macau. One-way fares are HK$4,300, rising to HK$4,800 during holiday periods. Journey time is around 20 minutes. There is also a less frequent helicopter service between Macau and Shenzhen.

## By rail

### *Guangzhou–Hong Kong*

Twelve daily trains link Guangzhou's East Railway Station and Hunghom Station in Kowloon. Travelling time is just under two hours. There is also a daily train between Zhaoqing and Hong Kong, via Guangzhou and Foshan, with a travelling time of four hours.

In Guangzhou, away from the station itself, most hotels and the CTS (China Travel Service) office can help with train tickets. In Hong Kong, tickets can be purchased through travel agents, hotels, CTS offices and at Hunghom Station (tel: 2947 7888). If tickets to Guangzhou are sold out, take the MTR to the border terminus of Lo Wu (a 40-minute journey, with departures roughly every 10 minutes). Shenzhen Station is a few minutes' walk across the border.

There are dozens of trains daily between Shenzhen and Guangzhou. Travel times can be up to two hours if departing the central Guangzhou Railway Station (Guangzhou Huoche Zhan), though regular bullet trains make the trip from Guangzhou East (Guangzhou Dong Zhan) in around 50 minutes.

All trains are air-conditioned.

## STREET SIGNS

All street signs are in both English and Chinese. Hong Kong street maps usually have both English- and Chinese-language sections in the back to make it easier to find your destination. Problems may arise when using taxis or asking directions. Where the English name of a street or district is a transliteration of the Chinese, the complexities of Cantonese pronunciation may still make it unintelligible to the average driver. From the opposite perspective, many downtown roads are named after historic colonial figures or places, with the Chinese version an attempt at transliteration in Cantonese. Once again, the gulf in pronunciation between the two languages sometimes makes them mutually unintelligible. Other roads reference the same landmark, building, person or place but use the original word in the respective languages, making them sound very dissimilar. If in doubt, try to have your destination written in Chinese script.

# A – Z

## AN ALPHABETICAL SUMMARY OF PRACTICAL INFORMATION

## A

### Accommodation

#### *Hotel areas*

Hong Kong's relatively small size means that you are never much more than an hour from the city centre and harbour. The majority of tourists stay in Tsim Sha Tsui, on the Kowloon side of Victoria Harbour, although the most luxurious hotels tend to be located on Hong Kong Island, in the districts of Central, Wan Chai and Causeway Bay.

Business travellers' choice of hotel is determined by the purpose of their trip. There are plenty of top hotels close to the main financial and business districts on Hong Kong Island. If a Hong Kong Convention and Exhibition Centre event is the focus of the trip, then a hotel within walking distance in Wan Chai is useful. For business people using Hong Kong as a base for travel to southern China, hotels in the New Territories may be best.

The low level of personal crime in Hong Kong means that there are no districts to avoid. If you would like to escape the more dense urban areas it is perhaps worth investigating the handful of hotels located in the New Territories and the Outlying Islands; travel times into Central will be between 30 minutes and one hour.

In Macau, the choices range from goliath Las Vegas-style casino resorts on the Macau peninsula or Cotai to quiet escapes on Coloane. Business travellers to Guangzhou can enjoy the sumptuous new hotels around the rapidly developing Tianhe commercial district while Shamian Island is probably the most pleasant base for leisure travellers. Shenzhen, Shekou and Dameisha have well-equipped resorts, and any hotel within 15 minutes of Lo Wu is ideal for shopping.

#### *Prices and booking*

Hong Kong has some of the world's best hotels, but they are also among the most expensive, with budget options limited. Rooms at the best hotels start at more than US$400. Flexible travellers will find prices cheaper Monday to Thursdays, though prices remain high throughout Hong Kong's various trade fairs and public holidays. Check with the hotel's website, travel agents or hotel-booking websites for the best time to take advantage of cheaper rates – reliable websites include Asia Travel, www.asiatravel.com; Asia Hotels, www.asiahotels.com; C-Trip, www.ctrip.com; and Wotif, www.Wotif.com.

Visitors arriving at the airport without hotel bookings can make reservations at one of two booths operated by the Hong Kong Hotels Association (open 6am to midnight) in the arrivals area of Terminal 1. Travel agents at Macau Ferry Terminal display hotel rates clearly and offer ferry and room deals.

There is no sales tax in Hong Kong; however hotels add a 10 percent service charge to bills.

In Macau, prices are generally much cheaper than Hong Kong but tariffs increase sharply at weekends. Rooms are often fully booked on Saturdays and around major public holidays. Prices at top hotels in Shenzhen and Guangzhou are also markedly cheaper than Hong Kong but the price gap is narrowing. A double room in a five-star hotel will likely cost in excess of US$250, more during trade fairs or public holidays.

For more details about hotels, check with the Hong Kong Hotels Association (tel: 2375 3838), or try the Hong Kong Tourist Board at www.discoverhongkong.com.

Many Chinese tourists are chain smokers. If you are not a smoker, insist firmly on a non-smoking floor when booking, and double check your request has been met when you arrive.

## Addresses

Hong Kong continues to use the address system inherited from the British and addresses are easily understood by tourists. Roads all have corresponding Chinese and English names, though the way in which they correspond may not always be obvious. Some are Chinese names rendered in Romanized script; many roads on Hong Kong Island and Kowloon were originally named after historic British figures and the Chinese version is an attempt at transliteration in Cantonese; others still reference the same landmark or building, though the Chinese word may sound completely unlike the English. When using taxis, it often pays to have your address written down in Chinese script.

In mainland China, addresses are ordered in the opposite way, with the largest unit – the city, or district – appearing at the top of addresses. In contrast to Hong Kong, the ground-level of any given building is known as the first floor (1/F). English road names are always the pinyin (Romanized) version of the original Chinese name. Large roads are often divided into geographic sections, and it's common to see the words Dong, Xi, Bei, Nan and Zhong feature before the word Lu (road). These refer, respectively, to east, west, north, south and central sections.

## Admission charges

Government-owned museum and gallery admissions are good value in Hong Kong. Average charges are around HK$10 for adults and HK$5 for seniors and students. Children under three are free, and many museums are free to all on Wednesdays. To make your money go further, the HK$50 Museum Pass gives annual unlimited access to seven of the city's most popular museums and a discount to Disneyland Park.

Privately owned venues are more expensive. Adults pay HK$265 at Madame Tussauds, while children aged 3 to 11 years cost HK$215. A day of fun at Ocean Park is HK$219 for children and HK$438 for adults. Both offer small discounts for booking online. At cinemas, tickets average HK$80 for adults with a small reduction for children. Admission to all parks and beaches is free.

## Age restrictions

The legal age of consent for sexual activity in Hong Kong is 16. Licenced bars, restaurants and clubs cannot serve alcohol to anyone below the age of 18, though there is no age restriction on drinking outside these premises. Drivers must be over the age of 18.

# B

## Budgeting for your trip

Having stayed steady for most of the past decade or so, prices are slowly starting to rise. The Hong Kong dollar is pegged to the US dollar, so how far your money goes will always be relative to the strength and weakness of the greenback.

Hotel prices can vary throughout the year. The busiest times at Hong Kong hotels are during the main public holidays in China and the large trade fairs in April and October. Outside these times prices can drop considerably though room tariffs are always higher on weekends. Researching your options will pay off, as many hotels have regular promotions on their websites, and travel agents and online hotel-booking sites negotiate special rates.

Once in Hong Kong, transportation is a bargain. For HK$11 (US$1.50) you can travel up to 10 stops on the MTR or cross Hong Kong Island by public bus. It costs HK$2.30 to ride the length of the island by tram and on Hong Kong's other iconic transportation, the Star Ferry, you will spend next to nothing crossing the harbour.

Discovering the range of food in Hong Kong is part of the experience, and prices can vary dramatically. You can expect to pay US$15 or less per person at a very reasonable Chinese restaurant. A meal for two in a mid-range restaurant can cost upwards of US$100 with wine. At the best restaurants diners expect to pay US$250 plus for two.

To stretch the budget further, look out for special menus and budget set menus at cafés and restaurants. "Business lunch" set menus are great value.

There are bargains to be had at the best hotels. The hotel buffet is an institution and a great way to sample a huge variety of cuisine, or satisfy different tastes within a group for a reasonable price. It's an event in itself and a treat for gastronomes.

Standard drinks in Hong Kong cost around US$8 and can be double in luxury hotel bars and the trendiest venues. Look out for Happy Hours.

# C

## Climate

Hong Kong has a humid, subtropical climate. There are,

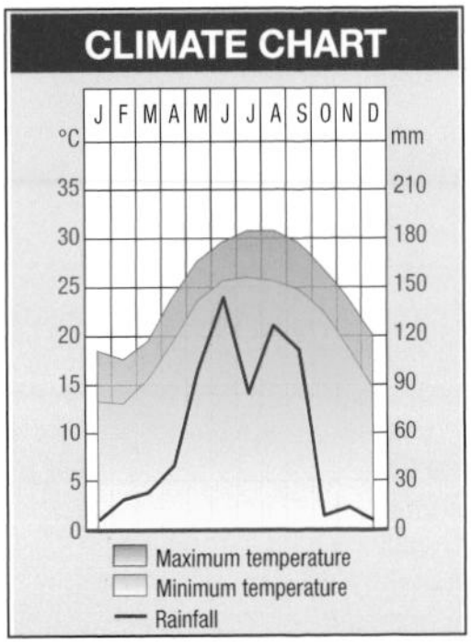

however, four distinct seasons. The ideal time for travelling to Hong Kong is from the end of September to early December, when the weather is warm, the air is relatively dry and it seldom rains. The average daytime temperature is around 24°C (75°F), with humidity around 70 percent.

### *What to wear*

Despite the latitude, winter (late December to early March) temperatures can be slightly chilly, especially in the rural areas, so it is advisable to bring light woollens and sometimes a coat. The average daytime temperature is 17°C (63°F), with humidity around 75 percent.

Temperatures and humidity rise abruptly in spring, when daytime temperatures shoot up from 20°C (68°F) in March to 28°C (82°F) in May. In summer, which lasts until early September, temperatures hover around 30°C (86°F) and humidity is consistently above 70 percent. Even at night it is rare for the temperature to dip below 26°C (79°F), and even when it doesn't rain you will quickly be dripping with sweat. Wear light clothes, but bring something with long sleeves for the summer – because many restaurants and shops have very effective air-conditioning.

Macau's climate is the same as Hong Kong's. Temperatures in Guangzhou are slightly higher in summer, slightly lower in winter, and there is rather more rain through the year.

## Crime and safety

One of the great joys of Hong Kong is the low level of crime and the resultant freedom from fear of crime. In the main commercial and entertainment areas you are safe to walk alone at any hour of the day, and most of the night. Tourists are more obvious targets for pickpockets in the busiest areas, but normal precautions should suffice.

## TYPHOONS

From June to early September, it is not uncommon for Hong Kong to experience tropical storms or typhoons (the name derives from *dai fung* – big wind). If you are in Hong Kong when a typhoon hits, you will find that virtually everything comes to a complete standstill.

The Hong Kong Observatory has standard typhoon warnings that vary according to how close a typhoon is to Hong Kong. Usually, this begins with a typhoon number one (T1) signal, which may shortly escalate to a number three. When the number eight signal is raised, it means Hong Kong may suffer a direct hit. Schools, offices and shops close immediately and everyone goes home. A rare typhoon number ten is almost certain to mean serious damage, as the storm sweeps through the territory causing floods and sometimes deaths. Watching typhoon news bulletins can be dramatic and exciting, but when everything closes you will be stuck for anything to do. Hotels, however, do continue to operate. In fact, locals often go to hotel restaurants as they are the only places likely to be open during a typhoon. Stay inside during a typhoon, as fatalities have been known to occur in both urban and rural areas, mainly due to objects and structures that fall in the strong winds.

The frequency of direct hits is erratic: of the fourteen since 1946, only two have occurred in the past 30 years (York and Mangkhut). In April 2008, typhoon Neoguri passed close to Hong Kong, the earliest storm for over 50 years.

Both Guangzhou and Macau are considered safe destinations for tourists. Avoid touts, and do not be tempted to pursue goods and services offered to you on the street.

More caution is required in Shenzhen. Hong Kong residents have reported muggings. Dress down for a visit to Shenzhen and leave your jewellery behind. Stick to busy public areas. When shopping, do not let the lure of a bargain make you forget your common sense.

## Customs regulations

Hong Kong is a free port, so you can bring as many gifts as you like in and out of the territory. Wine and beer are also duty-free, though passengers are restricted to 1 litre of liquor with an alcohol content of 30% or more. Firearms must be declared and handed into custody until departure. Duty-free tobacco allowances for visitors are 19 cigarettes, a single cigar or 25g tobacco.

### *Departure tax*

Hong Kong imposes a HK$120 Air Passenger Departure Tax on all passengers aged 12 years and above departing Hong Kong International Airport or by helicopter at the Hong Kong Macau Ferry Terminal. This will be included in the price of the airline ticket and no money is payable at the airport.

# D

## Disabled travellers

The Hong Kong Council of Social Services has compiled a useful accessibility guide for buildings and tourist attractions, www.hkcss.org.hk.

Taxis are often the best way to get about in Hong Kong, and reasonably priced. The train networks have a very inconsistent level of access. Station announcements are in Cantonese, Mandarin (Putonghua) and English.

*Travellers at Chek Lap Kok airport.*

Easy-Access Travel is a subsidiary of the Hong Kong Society for Rehabilitation, and has a fleet of specially adapted buses so it can cater for visitors with limited mobility. Day trips, full itineraries and advice are available. Email: eat@rehabsociety.org.hk, tel: 2772 7301, www.rehabsociety.org.hk/e.

# E

## Embassies & consulates

**Australia**, Harbour Centre, 23–4/F, 25 Harbour Rd, Wan Chai. Tel: 2827 8881.
**Canada**, 8–9th floor, Berkshire House, 25 Westlands Road Quarry Bay. Tel: 3719 4700.
**France**, Admiralty Centre, Tower II, 25–26/F, 18 Harcourt Rd, Admiralty. Tel: 3752 9900.
**Germany**, 21/F, United Centre, 95 Queensway, Admiralty. Tel: 2105 8788.
**Ireland**, 20/F, 33 Des Voeux Road, Central. Tel. 2535 0700
**Japan**, 46–47/F, One Exchange Square, 8 Connaught Place, Central. Tel: 2522 1184.
**New Zealand**, Rm 6501, Central Plaza, 18 Harbour Rd, Wan Chai. Tel: 3115 8944.
**Singapore**, Unit 901, 9/F, Tower 1, Admiralty Centre, 18 Harcourt Rd, Admiralty. Tel: 2527 2212.
**South Africa**, Rm 1906-08, 19/F, Central Plaza 18 Harbour Rd, Wan Chai. Tel: 3926 4300.
**United Kingdom**, 1 Supreme Court Rd, Admiralty. Tel: 2901 3000.
**United States**, 26 Garden Rd, Central. Tel: 2523 9011.

## Emergency numbers

For police, fire and ambulance services in Hong Kong and China, dial 999. In Macau call 999 for emergencies, or 919 for police.

## Etiquette

Hong Kong's incredible density means residents have learned to cope with minimal personal space. However, for such a crowded city, Hong Kong is relatively fastidious when it comes to public etiquette. Food and drink is forbidden on the orderly MTR, queues are well observed and jaywalking is frowned upon. Bad habits are pointed out in infomercials broadcast across the media landscape. It is the polar opposite on the other side of the mainland border where elbows fly on subway trains, queues rarely exist and jaywalking is often a necessity if you wish to cross the road.

# H

## Health and medical care

No vaccinations are required for Hong Kong, but it is advisable to consider inoculations against Hepatitis A. Tap water is safe in Hong Kong, but you may find bottled water more palatable. The most important thing is to keep well hydrated in the heat and humidity. Food from street stalls is usually just as safe as that served in licensed cafés and restaurants. Asia's most prominent pharmacy brand, Watson's, is headquartered in Hong Kong and there are stores across the territory, including many MTR stations and shopping malls.

## ELECTRICITY

The voltage in Hong Kong is 200/220 volts, 50 cycles. For a place of such international standing, it is surprising that Hong Kong still does not seem to have standardised plug fittings. However, hotels will certainly have adaptors to make any appliance work.

### *Medical services*

**Hong Kong**
**Adventist Hospital**, 40 Stubbs Rd, Happy Valley. Tel: 3651 8888, www.hkah.org.hk.
**Central Medical Practice**, 3/F, Baskerville House, 13 Duddell Street, Central. Tel: 2824 0822, www.centralhealth.com.hk.
**Prince of Wales Hospital**, 30–32 Ngan Shing St, Sha Tin, New Territories. Tel: 2632 2211, www3.ha.org.hk/pwh.
**Queen Elizabeth Hospital**, 30 Gascoigne Rd, Kowloon. Tel: 2958 8888, www3.ha.org.hk/qeh.
**Queen Mary Hospital**, 102 Pokfulam Rd, Hong Kong. Tel: 2255 3838, http://www3.ha.org.hk/qmh.

**Macau**
**Kiang Wu Hospital**, Estr. Coelho do Amaral. Tel: 2837 1333.
**S. Januário Hospital**, Estr. do Visconde de S. Januário. Tel: 2831 3731.

**Shenzhen**
**Shenzhen People's Hospital**, 1017 Dongmen Bei Lu. Tel: 2553 3018.

**Guangzhou**
**Guangzhou Can Am International Medical Centre**, 5/F, Garden Hotel, 368 Huanshi Dong Lu. Tel: 8386 6988, www.canamhealthcare.com.
**Guangzhou No. 1 People's Hospital**, 602 Renmin Bei Lu. Tel: 8399 2090.

# I

## Internet

Most hotels charge for in-room internet service. Free Wi-Fi access is becoming more widespread in hotels, and the government is building a citywide free GovWiFi network. You can also access the web for free with a Wi-Fi code in many coffee shops and some restaurants and bars.

# L

## Left luggage

Facilities are available at Hong Kong Airport, and in Kowloon at Hung Hom Station and the Hong Kong China City Building.

## LGBTQ travellers

Hong Kong is still fairly conservative, and gay marriage is not yet an option in the territory, but there's a cosmopolitan LGBTQ scene, scattered around Central and Soho. For more on gay nightlife in Hong Kong visit www.travelgayasia.com.

The annual Hong Kong Pride Parade (www.hkpride.net) and Gay Games – to be held in Hong Kong in 2022 (www.gaygameshk2022.com) – also highlight the city's laissez-faire attitude.

*Relaxing over lunch.*

## Lost property

To report lost or stolen property, contact the Hong Kong Police. Call 2860 2000 to find out the location of the nearest police station. If you think you left your property in a taxi, it may be worth contacting the taxi lost property line which will – in theory at least, and for a charge – inform all taxi drivers. Tel: 1872 920.

To report a lost credit card, call American Express on 2811 6122, MasterCard on 800-966-677 and Visa on 800-96-725.

# M

## Maps

There are numerous maps available in Hong Kong. The Hong Kong Tourist Board provides welcome packs (which include maps) at airport, seaport and border crossings from mainland China. The laminated Insight Fleximaps to Hong Kong, Macau, Shenzhen and Guangzhou are durable, detailed and easy to use, and each has a full street index. If you are travelling into China, maps with place names in both English and Chinese are useful. If you can point at a place name written in Chinese with a friendly smile, many a misunderstanding can be avoided.

## Media

### Newspapers and magazines

Hong Kong has a large number of newspapers and magazines, most of which are published in Chinese. Hong Kong continues to enjoy a free press despite being part of China, and the territory is noted as a media centre for the region.

By far the most influential newspaper in Hong Kong is the daily English-language *South China Morning Post*. A second English daily, *The Standard*, is handed out free on the streets, Monday to Friday. Two of the most popular Chinese-language dailies are the rather sensationalist *Oriental Daily News* and the *Apple Daily News*.

A listings magazine worth looking out for is *Time Out Hong Kong* (www.timeout.com/hong-kong), published every fortnight. Tourists who want an opinionated insider's view will find the restaurant, club and entertainment reviews worth a read. *Time Out* also includes reviews of events in Macau.

### Radio and television

Over a dozen radio stations are broadcast in Hong Kong, though there is now only one dedicated English-language channel, RTHK. Some other stations offer an element of programming in English. The BBC World Service is available 24 hours a day. For local news, Hong Kong's two TV stations, TVB and ATV, each broadcast one English-language channel and one Chinese-language channel. If you are staying in a hotel you should have access to a selection of regional and international broadcasters in English via cable and satellite.

## Money

The Hong Kong dollar is the standard unit of currency and comes in denominations of

## PUBLIC HOLIDAYS

The fact that many Hong Kong residents work a five-and-a-half-day week and have short periods of annual leave is compensated by a relatively large number of public holidays every year – 17 in total. These are as follows:

**1 January:** New Year's Day
**January/February:** Lunar New Year (three-day holiday)
**March/April:** Good Friday and Easter Monday; Ching Ming Festival (5 April)
**May/June:** Dragon Boat Festival; Buddha's Birthday (lunar); Labour Day (1 May)
**1 July:** SAR Establishment Day
**September/October:** The day following the Mid-Autumn Festival
**1 October:** National Day
**October:** Chung Yeung Festival
**25 December:** Christmas (two days).

### Macau

As for Hong Kong, but with some additional days: **National Day** (1 October) is a two-day holiday in Macau. There are public holidays for **All Souls' Day** in **November**, the **Feast of the Immaculate Conception on 8 December** and the **Winter Solstice on 22 December**. The Macau Special Administrative Region Establishment Day (**20 December**) replaces Hong Kong's 1 July holiday.

### China

There are seven official holidays in China. Two of these are three-day holidays for Lunar New Year and National Day, though these morph into a full week with staff and schoolchildren working over the prior weekend to give themselves a full seven day break. These periods are known as "Golden Weeks", though conditions are unpleasant for travellers as prices increase and transport networks heave. If possible, avoid travelling to the mainland at these times:

**1 January:** New Year's Day
**Lunar New Year:** officially three days (Jan/Feb), but nearly all offices, banks and government departments close for a full week.
**Qingming Festival**: April 4 or 5
**1 May:** Labour Day, plus two following days
**Dragon Boat Festival:** Fifth day of the fifth lunar month (usually June)
**Mid-Autumn Festival:** Mid-way through the eight lunar month (usually September)
**National Day:** officially three days from October 1, but nearly all offices, banks and government departments close for a full week.

HK$1,000, $500, $100, $50, $20 and $10 notes plus HK$10, $5, $2 and $1 coins. The dollar is divided into 100 cents, and there are coins of 50¢, 20¢ and 10¢ denominations. The dollar rate fluctuates against most major international currencies but it is pegged to the US dollar at approximately 7.8 Hong Kong dollars to the US dollar.

There are three note-issuing banks in Hong Kong: Hongkong and Shanghai Bank, Standard Chartered Bank and the Bank of China. Most banks will exchange foreign currency and generally display exchange rates on digital boards. They usually offer better rates than the money-changers in the major tourist areas, there's usually a HK$50 charge for a single transaction. Cash machines are plentiful in the urban areas, and allow the withdrawal of local currency with most major credit cards.

Macau's official currency, the pataca (MOP$), is divided into 100 avos. There are banknotes in denominations of 1,000, 500, 100, 50, 20 and 10 patacas and 10, 5, 2, and 1 pataca coins. The pataca is linked to the Hong Kong dollar, which is accepted as currency in Macau.

Hong Kong dollars are not widely accepted in Guangzhou and Shenzhen, though some shops may accept the currency, albeit at punitive rates. It's advisable to change your money into renminbi (RMB) before you enter the mainland. The basic unit is the yuan, often called kuai. One yuan is worth 10 jiao. Banknotes come in 100, 50, 10, 5 and 1 yuan denominations; plus 5, 2 and 1 jiao.

### Tipping

Tipping is customary in Hong Kong in bars, restaurants and hotels. A 10-percent service charge is added to the bill in many restaurants, but it is still customary to add a further 5 percent to go direct to the staff. Taxi drivers do not expect to be tipped, but rounding up the fare to the nearest dollar or two is appreciated.

In places frequented by tourists in Macau, Shenzhen and Guangzhou tipping is increasingly common practice; follow the same guidelines as Hong Kong.

## O

### Opening hours

Office hours in Hong Kong are 9am to 5.30pm or 6pm. Small shops, grocers and markets are open before 8am, but major stores and shopping centres generally open around 10am. Banks open between 8.30am and 4.30pm, but times may vary between branches and banks.

While shops in Central close by 7 or 8pm, elsewhere it's late-night shopping every night. In particular, many shops in Causeway Bay, Tsim Sha Tsui and Mong Kok stay open until 10 or 11pm seven days a week, including public holidays.

Bars and restaurants are free to choose their own opening times. Things start to quieten down in the main entertainment districts after 1am. If you want to drink and party all night you will find venues.

In Macau, restaurants and bars are open late, but after midnight most of the action is centred around the 24-hour casinos. In Shenzhen and Guangzhou shops and shopping centres are open in the evening, and although locals like to dine early, there are many places to eat and drink late at night.

# P

## Postal services

Airmail stamps are available from convenience stores and vending machines outside post offices. The General Post Office in Central, 2 Connaught Road, also sells a selection of cards and gifts.

Most post offices are open 9.30am to 5pm Monday to Friday and 9.30am to 1pm on Saturday. The General Post Office at 2 Connaught Place, Central, is also open from 9am to 5pm on Sunday while, on the Kowloon side, the Tsim Sha Tsui Post Office, located at 10 Middle Road, is open Sundays, 9am to 2pm.

If you choose to mail presents and purchases rather than carry them home, Hong Kong Post is cheap, efficient and can also courier documents and parcels. In Hong Kong, Macau, Shenzhen and Guangzhou hotels will assist guests with posting mail and packages.

In Macau, the main post office is located in picturesque Senado Square. If you are tempted by antique and reproduction furniture, shops can assist in arranging shipping. Shenzhen shoppers rely on the post office on the ground floor at the Lo Wu shopping centre to ease their burden after bargain hunting. In China it is probably much simpler to use the postal services at business and tourist hotels.

# S

## Shopping

Hong Kong has frequently been called a shopper's paradise, and it is certainly true that most Hong Kong citizens are insatiable shoppers. Options range from colourful night markets and glitzy shopping malls to multi-storey department stores and bustling narrow streets full of antiques and bric-a-brac. Hong Kong may not be the bargain basement it once was – indeed prices in the major malls are often higher than in equivalent shops in the West – but shopping may nonetheless prove one of the most compelling activities of any trip to the territory for many visitors. There is certainly no shortage of supply.

### *Shopping malls*

Hong Kong's malls are destinations in themselves, and are full of cafés and restaurants in which to take a break. Many also house cinemas and entertainment such as ice-skating rinks. Shopping hours vary, but generally continue until late every day of the week. Even during public holidays most shops are open, the exception being during the week of Chinese New Year. As a guide, shops in Central close around 7pm, but the other main areas tend to stay open until 10pm, sometimes even later. The sales start in mid- to late June and December. Malls are landmarks in Hong Kong. Taxi drivers will recognise their names rather than the street they are on, and most are part of an MTR station development.

## Smoking

Smoking remains an integral part of some aspects of Chinese culture, though its popularity seems to be on the decline in Hong Kong. Health infomercials regularly warn of the dangers of the practice, and a blanket ban on smoking in all indoor places – restaurants, bars and clubs included – has been in place since 2009. Some nightlife venues do turn a blind eye and tobacco control inspectors are kept busy issuing fines.

## Student travellers

Students over the age of 11 years do not benefit from many travel discounts in Hong Kong, Macau and the mainland. Some cultural events offer slightly reduced ticket prices for students with identification.

# T

## Telephones

Hong Kong is well known for having one of the most advanced telecommunications systems in the world. Virtually the entire network consists of fibre-optic cabling with digital switching, which means a whole host of advanced telecommunications services are available to local users.

### *International calls*

All hotels offer international direct-dial services at an inflated price.

**International dialling codes:**
**Hong Kong:** 852
**Macau:** 853
**Shenzhen:** 86-755
**Guangzhou:** 86-20
**In Hong Kong:**
**Directory Assistance:** 1081 (in English)
**Collect Calls:** 10010
**International directory enquiries/overseas numbers:** 10013
**International access codes:**
**AT&T:** 800 96 1111
**MCI:** 800 96 1121
**Sprint:** 800 96 1877.

### *Local calls*

Local telephone calls are free of charge, so it may be possible to use the telephone in shops,

*Electronics on sale at 298 Computer Centre.*

bars and restaurants that have a landline. Many shopping malls and convenience stores even have a complimentary phone for customers to use. Most hotels charge for local calls from guest rooms.

### Mobile phones

Hong Kong has one of the highest rates of mobile-phone ownership – at 235 percent there are over twice more phone subscribers than residents. Mobile phones can be rented at Hong Kong International Airport. To avoid roaming changes, you can buy pre-paid SIM cards with a Hong Kong number and a fixed number of minutes from convenience stores or the telephone companies' shops. These cards are compatible with tri-band and dual-band phones. Mobiles can be used on the MTR subway system.

### Public phones

Public phone booths are becoming increasingly rare. It generally costs HK$1 for five minutes, and calls can be paid by phone card or coins. Stored-value phone cards are available from retail stores of telephone companies and convenience stores.

## Time zone

Hong Kong, Macau, Shenzhen and Guangzhou all operate on the same time zone (Beijing time). This is GMT +8 hours (EST +13 hours). There is no daylight savings time, so from early April to late October, when Europe and America put their clocks forward by one hour, Hong Kong is seven hours ahead of London and twelve hours ahead of New York.

## Toilets

Toilet facilities at tourist attractions in Hong Kong are generally clean, well maintained and always free of charge to use. Public toilets in other locations are of a variable standard, and soap and paper may be absent. To be on the safe side, always carry a small pack of tissues. Shopping centres and restaurants usually have clean facilities.

There are few public toilets to be found in Macau, and clean public toilets are a rarity in Shenzhen. However, in recent years Guangzhou has opened some acceptable new public toilets, complete with star rating. Patrons must pay a small fee of one or two yuan.

## Tourist information

The Hong Kong Tourism Board (HKTB) is the official government-sponsored body representing the tourism industry of Hong Kong, and offers many useful services and helpful publications. HKTB also provides information packs for tourists arriving at the airport and the land crossing at Lo Wu. Out-of-hours computer terminals provide 24-hour access to the excellent www.discoverhongkong.com website.

At the HKTB's Visitor Information and Services Centres you can pick up useful publications including the weekly *Hong Kong Diary* and the monthly *Official Hong Kong Map*. *A Guide to Quality Shops and Restaurants* is a handy (but dense) book that lists all establishments that have been accredited by the HKTB's QTS scheme, and includes special offers and vouchers that are exclusive to visitors. The centres also provide a tour-reservation service for selected tours, and stock an interesting selection of souvenirs.

### HKTB visitor centres

**International Airport:** (only accessible to arriving visitors), Halls A and B, Arrivals Level, Terminal 1, 8am–9pm daily
**Lo Wu Terminal Building:** Arrival Hall, 2/F, 8am–6pm daily
**Hong Kong Island:** Peak Piazza (between The Peak Tower and The Peak Galleria), 11am–8pm daily
**Kowloon:** Star Ferry pier, Tsim Sha Tsui, 8am–8pm daily
**Visitor Hotline** (multilingual): 2508 1234, 9am–6pm daily
Tourist information is available at www.discoverhongkong.com.

### CTS offices

**China Travel Service (CTS)** is China's state travel agency and can arrange tours, tickets and visas for travel to the mainland, although CTS offices do not provide a tourist information service.

**Hong Kong:** G/F, CTS House, 78–83 Connaught Road, Central. Tel: 2853 3533.
**Kowloon:** 1/F, Alpha House, 27–33 Nathan Road, Tsim Sha Tsui. Tel: 2315 7171.

### *Macau*

**The Macau Government Tourist Office** runs offices at the Macau ferry terminal in Hong Kong and upon arrival in Macau. There is also a **tourist information centre** on the Largo do Senado square, open 9am–6pm daily. Visitors can contact the tourist hotline (853) 2833 3000 or view the website www.macautourism.gov.mo.

### *Tourist offices overseas*

Hong Kong is the most visited city in Asia, and the HKTB has offices in Sydney, London, Paris, Frankfurt, Los Angeles, New York, Tokyo, Osaka, Seoul, Singapore and Taipei. There are also HKTB offices in Beijing, Shanghai, Chengdu and Guangzhou. www.discoverhongkong.com.

**Australia**
Level 4, Hong Kong House, 80 Druitt Street, Sydney, NSW 2000
Tel: 61 2 9283 3083
Fax: 61 2 9283 3383

**United Kingdom**
2nd Floor, 20 Orange Street, London WC2H 7EF
Tel: 44 20 7321 5380

**United States**
115 East 54th Street, 2nd Floor, New York, NY 10022
Tel: 1 212 421 3382.

## CHINESE VISAS

Visas for China are issued at the Office of the Commissioner of the Ministry of Foreign Affairs, 3/F China Resources Bldg, 26 Harbour Rd, Wan Chai; tel: 3413 2424 www.fmcoprc.gov.hk/eng/. Visa applications are made on the seventh floor. Two photos are required. A basic single-entry visa costs HK$200 but higher, "reciprocal" charges are made to citizens of 25 countries, the US and UK included. A British citizen will pay HK$360 while an American will pay HK$1,100. Visas are processed in about three days though express services are available. China visas can also be obtained through most Hong Kong travel agents, including the Hong Kong offices of the China Travel Service (CTS). The two main offices are at 1/F, China Travel Bldg, 77 Queen's Road Central; tel: 2522 0450, and at 1/F, Alpha House, 27 Nathan Road, Tsim Sha Tsui, tel: 2315 7106, 24-hour hotline 3413 2300. www.ctshk.com.

If you are planning a short trip to Shenzhen, citizens of the UK, Canada, Australia and several other nations can apply for a five-day visa on arrival when crossing the mainland border. The visa office at Lo Wu (Lohu) keeps the longest office hours and most reliable staff. Visas generally cost RMB168, but the price is hiked to more than RMB400 for British passport holders, making it more economical to apply for a regular China visa. The visa on arrival option is not open to American citizens.

If you plan on visiting Hong Kong as a side trip from the mainland, make sure that you have a double- or multiple-entry China visa.

## V

### Visas and passports

Nationals of most Western countries do not require a visa for entry to Hong Kong or Macau, but you will need one if you plan to visit mainland China.

For those taking up employment in Hong Kong, it is necessary to obtain a work permit from the Immigration Department, usually in advance of entering the territory. Your company should be able to assist with the necessary paperwork. Hong Kong residents should carry a Hong Kong identity card, which is issued by the Immigration Department.

All other visitors are supposed to carry photographic identity such as a passport with them, but it is unlikely that you will be stopped by police officers and asked to produce identification.

## VITAL STATISTICS

**Area:** The Hong Kong Special Administrative Region covers a total area of 1,103 sq km (426 sq miles), comprising Hong Kong Island, the Kowloon peninsula, the New Territories and 262 outlying islands.
**Geography:** Hong Kong lies on a latitude of 22° 15 North (similar to Kolkata and Havana) and a longitude of 114° 10 East.

**Population:** Hong Kong's population is just over 7.2 million, and population density is 6,544 people per sq km (16,948 per sq mile). Of the half a million or so non-Chinese living in Hong Kong, the three biggest groups are the 184,100 Filipinos, 153,300 Indonesians, and the 32,000 or so US passport-holders.

## W

### Weights and measures

Imperial, metric and traditional Chinese measures are all legally accepted weights and measures in Hong Kong. Distance is most often measured in kilometres. Clothes and shoes also mix Asian, European, British and US sizings.

# LANGUAGE

## UNDERSTANDING THE LANGUAGE

Hong Kong's official languages are Chinese and English. The main Chinese dialect is Cantonese, spoken by almost 90 percent of the population and an inseparable part of the sound and rhythm of the city. Mandarin Chinese *(Putonghua)*, the official language of the People's Republic of China, is increasingly important, reflecting exponential rises in tourist numbers and long-term residents from the mainland. Most Hong Kongers in customer-facing jobs can speak passable Mandarin and some have claimed this has gone hand-in-hand with an equivalent decline in the standards of English.

There are numerous dialects or varieties of Chinese that share grammatical similarities and the same basic writing form, but they are not mutually intelligible in spoken form. Of these, Mandarin and Cantonese are the most important.

Cantonese is spoken in Hong Kong, Macau and most of the neighbouring province of Guangdong, as well as parts of Guangxi. Outside China, Cantonese is the most widely spoken form of Chinese due to the history of worldwide migration from Hong Kong and its neighbouring provinces.

Hong Kong people use a standard form of Chinese when they write, or in a business situation, but speak colloquial Cantonese in everyday conversation. This language is rich in slang, and some spoken words do not have characters.

To confuse the Chinese learner further, Hong Kong (like Taiwan) uses a slightly different style of characters to the rest of China. During reforms initiated by Mao in the 1950s to increase literacy, the PRC simplified its characters. Hence the characters used on the mainland are referred to as Simplified Chinese while Hong Kong's more complex characters are called Traditional Chinese. Many Chinese can comfortably read both scripts but the way a person writes will tend to depend on which side of the mainland border they were born.

### TONES

If all this was not enough to master, many an enthusiastic linguist has been defeated by Cantonese tones. Tone is not used within a sentence to indicate stress as in many European languages; instead, each word has a distinct pitch that goes higher, lower or stays flat within each word. Among the Cantonese there is no real agreement as to how many tones there are – some say as many as nine – but most people use six in daily life (which makes Putonghua's four tones seem more accessible).

The Jyutping transliteration system devised by the Linguistic Society of Hong Kong classifies the six main tones as: 1, high falling/high flat; 2, high rising; 3, middle; 4, low falling; 5, low rising; 6, low. For the new learner, just hitting three tones to boost their intelligibility is a triumph.

Each word has one syllable, and is represented by one distinct character. A word is made up of three sound elements. An initial eg, "f ", plus a final sound eg "an", plus a tone.

Tone is an essential part of each word. A few rare words just have a final sound and a tone, eg "m" in "m goi" (thank you).

Therefore, when combined with a tone, "fan" has seven distinct and contradictory meanings: to divide (high rising 1); flour (high falling 2); to teach (middle flat 3); fragrant (high flat 1); a grave (low falling 4); energetic (low rising 5); and a share (low flat 5).

The wealth of sound-alike words (homonyms) that can be

easily mispronounced play a part in many Cantonese traditions and the development of slang. However, for the visitor or new learner tones mean that utter bafflement is a common reaction to your attempt simply to say the name of the road you wish to visit. Persevere and attempt to mimic the way a Cantonese speaker says each part of the phrase.

## PRONUNCIATION

**j** as in the "y" of **y**ap
**z** is similar to the sound in bei**ge** or jar or the zh in Guang**zh**ou
**c** as in **ch**ip
**au** as in h**ow**
**ei** as in w**ay**
**ai** as in b**uy**
**ou** as in n**o**
**i** as in h**e**

## NUMBERS

**one** jat
**two** ji
**three** saam
**four** sei
**five** ng
**six** luk
**seven** cat
**eight** baat
**nine** gau
**ten** sap
**eleven** sap jat
**twelve** sap ji
**twenty** ji sap
**twenty-one** ji sap jat
**one hundred** baak
**zero** ling
**140** jat sei ling
**235** ji saam ng

## COMMON WORDS AND PHRASES

**Good morning** zou san (joe san)
**Good afternoon** ng on
**Good night** zou tau
**Goodbye** bai bai
**Hello (on phone)** wai!
**Thank you (service)** m goi
**Thank you (gift)** do ze

*Many signs are also in English.*

**You're welcome** M sai m goi
**No problem** mou man tai
**How are you?** Nei hou maa? (neigh ho marr)
**Fine, thank you** gay ho, yau sum
**Have you eaten?** sik zou faan mei a?
**Yes** hai
**no** m hai
**OK** hou aa
**so-so** ma ma
**My name is...** ngor geeu
**yesterday** kum yut
**today** gum yut
**tomorrow** ting yut

## NOUNS

**hotel** zau dim
**key** so si
**manager** ging lei
**room** haak fong
**telephone** din wa
**toilet** ci so
**bank** ngan hong
**post office** yau jing guk
**passport** wu ziu
**restaurant** zaan teng
**bar** zau ba
**bus** ba si
**taxi** dik si
**train** fo ze

## QUESTIONS

Questions are often followed by "a"
**Who?** bin go a?
**Where?** bin do a?
**When?** gei si a?
**Why?** dim gaai a?
**How many?** gei do a?
**How much does that cost?** gei dor chin a?
**Do you have...?** yau mo ... a?
**What time is the train to Guangzhou...?** Guangzhou ge for che, gay dim hoy a?

## PEOPLE

**mother** maa maa
**father** baa baa
**son** zai
**daughter** neoi
**baby** be be
**friend** pang jau
**boyfriend** naam pang jau
**girlfriend** neoi pang jau
**husband** lou gung
**wife** lou po

## ADJECTIVES

**small** sui
**big** dai
**good** ho
**bad** mm ho
**expensive** gwai
**cheap** peng
**thin** sau
**fat** fei
**slow** maan
**fast** faai
**pretty/beautiful** leng
**hot** jit
**cold** dung
**very...** hou ...
**very cold** hou dung
**delicious** ho sick

## TAXIS

**taxi** dik si
**Please take me to** m goy chey ngor hur-ee.
**straight on** jick hur-ee
**left** hai jor bin
**right** hai yau bin

## HEALTH AND EMERGENCIES

**I have (a)…** ngo…
**headache** tau tung
**stomach ache** tou tung
**toothache** nga tung
**cough** kau sau
**fever** faat sui
**flu** gam mou
**I have a headache** ngo tau tung
**I am sick** ngo jau beng
**doctor** ji sang
**nurse** wu si
**ambulance** gau surng che
**police** ging chaat

## FOOD AND DRINK

**breakfast** zou caan
**lunch** ng caan
**dinner** maan caan
**eat** sik faan
**rice** faan
**boiled rice** baak faan
**fried rice** cau faan
**noodles** min
**vegetables** coi
**meat** juk
**beef** ngau juk
**pork** zyut juk
**lamb** joeng juk
**chicken** gai
**prawn** ha
**fish** jyu
**tea** ca
**coffee** gaa fei
**water** sur-ee
**beer** be zau
**white/red wine** baak/hung zau
**I am a vegetarian** ngo sik zaai
**My bill, please!** maai daan, m goi!
**a little** seeu seeu
**enough** gau la

## GLOSSARY

**Amah bag** – large blue, red and white bag favoured by elderly women who can carry more than their body weight inside one stripy bag, also popular with migrant workers and those moving house.
**Astronaut** – a person who lives, works or studies in a different continent to their immediate family members. A common phenomenon in Hong Kong.
**Cha Chaan Teng** – aka Hong Kong Café. Serves up comfort food that includes the local take on foreign cuisines. Milk is always of the condensed or evaporated variety.
**Chinese Tea** - green or black tea without milk.
**Chop** – self-inked stamp used for signing documents.

*Dining at Temple Street Night Market.*

**Dai Pai Dong** – literally means "big licence place", a reference to the size of the licence required by these outdoor food stalls. Outdoor seating expands simply by adding more plastic stools and fold-up tables. Serves inexpensive Cantonese fare from enormous woks in a no-frills environment.
**F.I.L.T.H.** – "Failed In London, Try Hong Kong," a derogatory reference to Britons in Hong Kong.
**Godown** – a warehouse.
**Gweilo** – white devil, foreigner.
**Hawker** – someone selling goods from a stall, sometimes licensed sometimes not.
**Helper** – always means a domestic helper or maid. The term "amah" is rarely used except in reference to holdalls.
**Lai See** – "lucky money," given at weddings and Lunar New Year.
**Junk** – traditional square-sailed Chinese vessel. The term is also used for any vessel hired for a "junk party".
**Kaido (Gaido)** – small cargo boat or ferry.
**Kowloon taxi** – a taxi whose driver claims no knowledge of streets or major buildings on Hong Kong Island.
**Legco** – Hong Kong's governing body, only partially elected.
**Lunchbox** – not filled with a packed lunch from home, but a polystyrene box of food delivered to the workplace.
**Mark 6** – the lottery, a chance to win millions for just HK$20.
**MTR** – mass transit railway – Hong Kong's train system.
**Octopus card** – pre-paid transport card, also used as a debit card.
**Sampan** – small boat, with motor at the back, usually driven by an elderly man.
**SAR** – Special Administrative Region (of China).
**Tai Tai** – housewife, a married woman, especially ladies who lunch.

# FURTHER READING

## FICTION

**Clavell, James.** *Taipan.* The rise of an influential 19th-century British merchant family in Hong Kong.
**Gao, Xingjian.** *One Man's Bible.* Nobel Prize-winning author's tale about a man in Hong Kong recalling his youth in Mao's China.
**Gardam, Jane.** *Old Filth.* Poignant and at times amusing tale of a Hong Kong judge who retires to the UK and recalls his life in the law in Hong Kong, and as a Raj orphan.
**Mason, Richard.** *The World of Suzie Wong.* An English artist falls in love with a local lass in the book that made Wan Chai famous.
**Mo, Timothy.** *The Monkey King.* A brilliant account of a dysfunctional family living in colonial Hong Kong.
**Morris, Jan.** *Hong Kong.* Wonderfully insightful text from the doyenne of modern travel writers.
**Row, Jess.** *The Train to Lo Wu.* Highly acclaimed philosophical short stories about Hong Kong.

## HISTORY AND CURRENT AFFAIRS

**Booth, Martin.** *Gweilo: Memories of a Hong Kong Childhood.* A thoroughly enjoyable memoir, amusing and affectionate.
**Chamberlain, Jonathan.** *King Hui: The Man Who owned all the Opium in Hong Kong.* This biography spans most of Hong Kong's 20th century with the adventures of a sometime playboy, brigand, gambler, smuggler, businessman, teacher and spy.
**Coates, Austin.** *Myself a Mandarin.* Evocative memoirs of 1950s Hong Kong.
**Keay, John.** *The End of Empire in the Far East.* Explores the legacy of the British Empire in Asia with some fascinating detail, and a new afterword on the remarkable development of the Chinese economy.
**Sinclair, Kevin.** *Tell Me a Story: Forty Years of Newspapering in Hong Kong and China.* Plenty of bar room tales and the inside story of how the recent history of Hong Kong unfolded, from the SAR's best-known journalist.
**Tsang, Steve.** *A Modern History of Hong Kong.* This detailed, up-to-date history of the territory has become the most authoritative general history yet published.
**Vines, Stephen.** *Hong Kong: China's New Colony.* A thorough overview of the economy, media and political set-up of modern Hong Kong.
**Welsh, Frank.** *A History of Hong Kong.* A social, economic and political history of the territory.
**Wordie, Jason.** *Streets.* A fascinating guide to the history of individual streets on Hong Kong Island.

## NATURE/WALKING GUIDES

**Spurrier, Pete.** *The Leisurely Hiker's Guide to Hong Kong.* Easy walks around Hong Kong's hills. A guide for more serious hiking is also available.
**Stokes, Edward.** *Exploring Hong Kong's Countryside: A Visitor's Companion; The Wilson Trail: Hiking Across Hong Kong; Hong Kong's Wild Places: An Environmental Exploration.* These books explore the scenic beauty of the Hong Kong countryside.
**Williams, Martin.** *Hong Kong Pathfinder.* 23 walks in rural Hong Kong.

## MACAU

**Jackson, Annabel.** *Portuguese Cuisine on the China Coast.* The best book on Macau's unique fusion cuisine, with 62 recipes.
**Porter, Jonathan.** *Macau: The Imaginary City: Culture and Society, 1577 to Present.* Recommended to anyone who is interested in learning more about Macau.

## CHINA

**Becker, Jasper.** *The Chinese.* Fine analysis of contemporary China and what makes the country tick.
**Simons, Rowan.** *Bamboo Goalposts.* The entertaining story of one man's quest to teach the PRC to love football, written by a UK-born Beijing television presenter.
**Watts, Jonathan.** *When a Billion Chinese Jump: Voices From the Frontline of Climate Change.* Dispatches by the Guardian's former China man offer a salutary take on the Middle Kingdom's acute pollution problems.

## OTHER INSIGHT GUIDES

Insight Guides publishes numerous other guides to the region, including *Insight Guide China*, city guides *Beijing* and *Shanghai, Explore Hong Kong* and *Experience Hong Kong.*

# HONG KONG STREET ATLAS

The key map shows the area of Hong Kong covered by the atlas section. An index of street names and places of interest shown on the maps can be found on the following pages. For each entry there is a page number and grid reference.

## Map Legend

| | |
|---|---|
| ==== | Motorway (under construction) |
| === | Dual Carriageway |
| ――― | Main Road |
| ――― | Secondary Road |
| ――― | Minor Road |
| ▬ ‧ ▬ | International Boundary |
| ‑ ‑ ‑ | Province Boundary |
| ‑ ● ‑ | National Park/Reserve |
| ‑ ‑ ‑ | Ferry Route |
| ✈✈ | Airport |
| ✝✝ | Church (ruins) |
| ✝ | Monastery |
| 🏰 | Castle (ruins) |
| Ω | Cave |
| ★ | Place of Interest |
| ※ | Viewpoint |
| ⌐ | Beach |
| | Motorway |
| | Dual Carriageway |
| | Main Roads |
| | Minor Roads |
| | Footpath |
| ▬▬ | Railway |
| | Pedestrian Area |
| | Important Building |
| | Park |
| ✕Ⓜ | Metro |
| 🚍 | Bus Station |
| ❶ | Tourist Information |
| ✉ | Post Office |
| ⛪ | Cathedral/Church |
| ✡ | Synagogue |

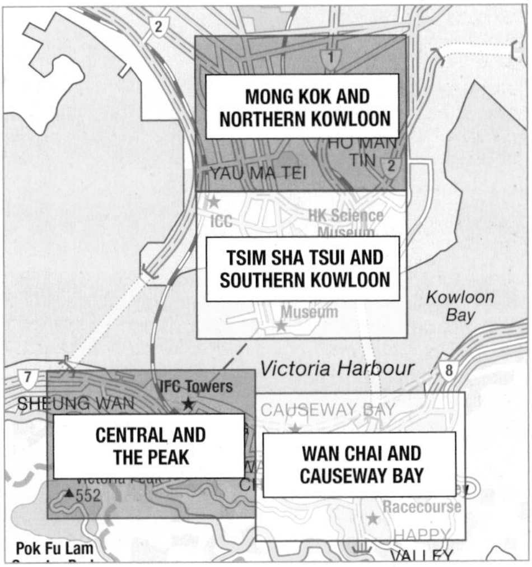

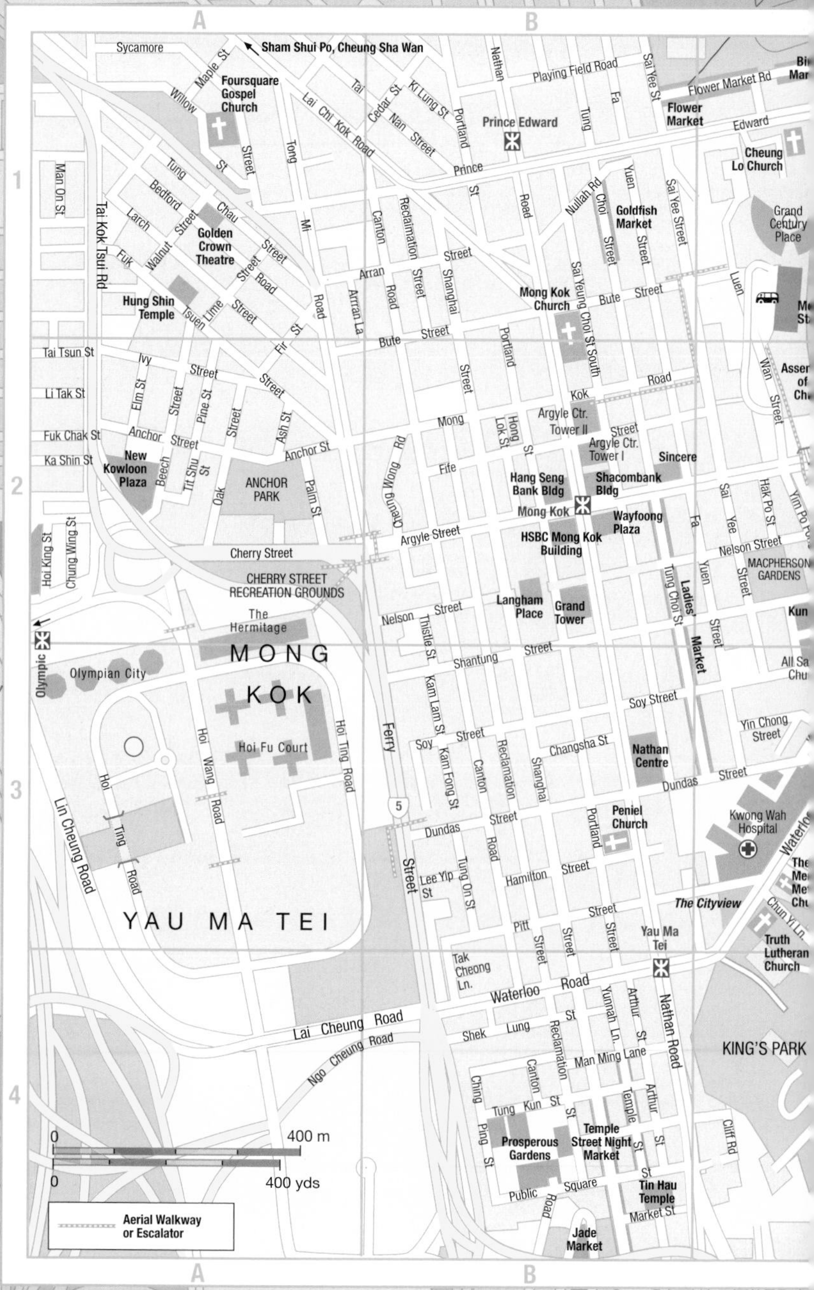
A
B
1
2
3
4
Sham Shui Po, Cheung Sha Wan
Sycamore
Maple St
Willow
Foursquare Gospel Church
Tai
Cedar St
Ki Lung St
Nan Street
Lai Chi Kok Road
Portland
Nathan
Playing Field Road
Tung
Fa
Sai Yee St
Flower Market Rd
Flower Market
Edward
Prince Edward
Prince
Cheung Lo Church
Man On St
Tai Kok Tsui Rd
Tung
Bedford
Chau
Larch
Walnut
Street
Golden Crown Theatre
Fuk
Road
Hung Shin Temple
Tsuen
Lime
Fir St
Tong
Mi
Canton
Reclamation
Arran
Arran La
Shanghai
Nullah Rd
Choi
Yuen
Goldfish Market
Sai Yee Street
Grand Century Place
Luen
Sai Yeung Choi St South
Mong Kok Church
Bute
Tai Tsun St
Ivy
Li Tak St
Elm St
Pine St
Ash St
Fuk Chak St
Anchor
Anchor St
New Kowloon Plaza
Ka Shin St
Beech
Tit Shu St
Oak
ANCHOR PARK
Palm St
Portland
Mong
Kok
Argyle Ctr. Tower II
Hong Lok St
Argyle Ctr. Tower I
Sincere
Fife
Hang Seng Bank Bldg
Shacombank Bldg
Mong Kok
Wayfoong Plaza
Cheung Wong Rd
Argyle Street
HSBC Mong Kok Building
Hak Po St
Nelson Street
MACPHERSON GARDENS
Hoi King St
Chung Wing St
Cherry Street
CHERRY STREET RECREATION GROUNDS
Langham Place
Grand Tower
Tung Choi St
Ladies' Market
The Hermitage
Nelson
Thistle St
Shantung
MONG KOK
Olympic
Olympian City
Kam Lam St
Soy Street
Hoi Fu Court
Hoi Wang Road
Hoi Ting Road
Ferry
Soy
Kam Fong St
Changsha St
Nathan Centre
Yin Chong Street
Hoi
Ting
Road
Lin Cheung Road
Dundas
Kwong Wah Hospital
Peniel Church
Lee Yip St
Tung On St
Hamilton
Waterloo
The Cityview
Chun Yi Ln.
YAU MA TEI
Pitt
Yau Ma Tei
Truth Lutheran Church
Tak Cheong Ln.
Waterloo Road
Nathan Road
Lai Cheung Road
Shek Lung St
Yunnan Ln.
Arthur St
Ngo Cheung Road
Man Ming Lane
KING'S PARK
Ching Ping St
Tung Kun St
Temple
Prosperous Gardens
Temple Street Night Market
Cliff Rd
Public Square
Tin Hau Temple
Market St
Jade Market
0
400 m
400 yds
Aerial Walkway or Escalator

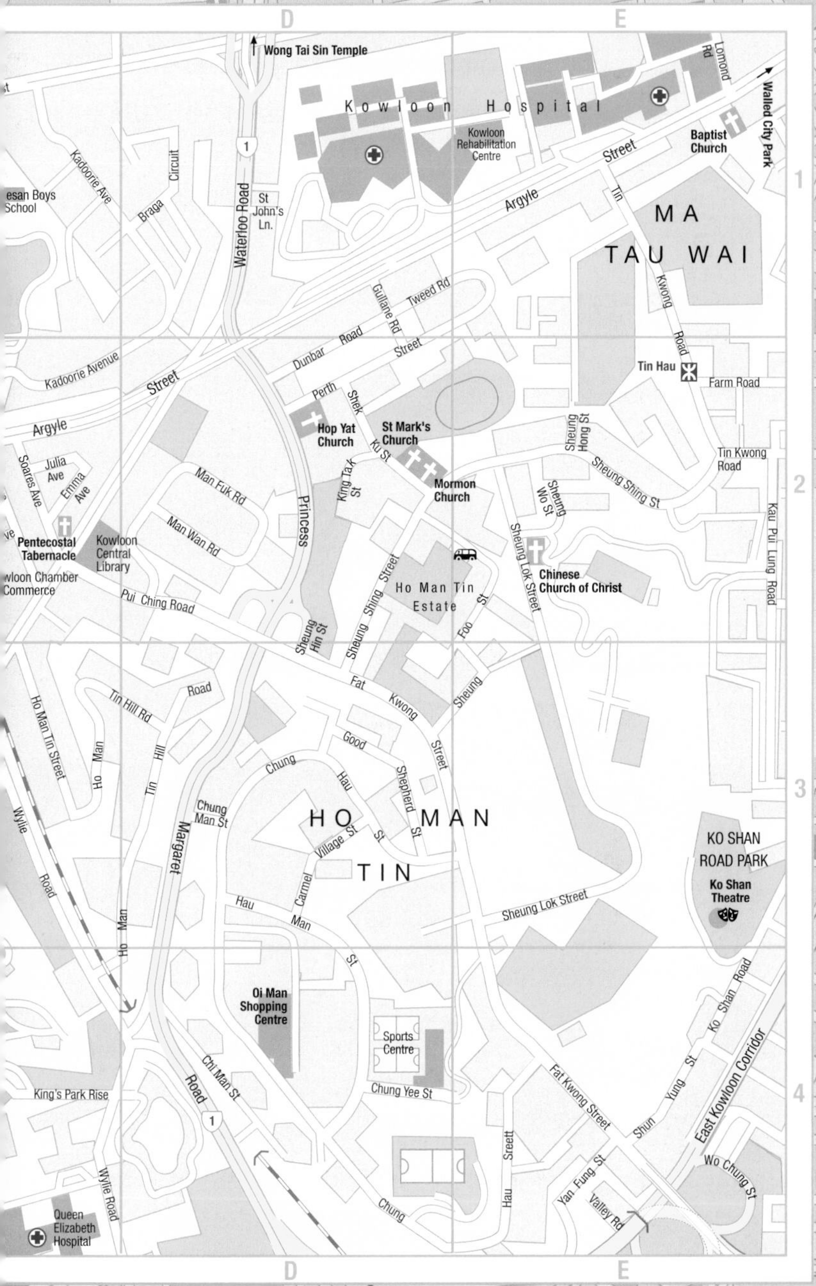
D
E
1
2
3
4
Wong Tai Sin Temple
Kowloon Hospital
Kowloon Rehabilitation Centre
Lomond Rd
Walled City Park
Baptist Church
Street
Argyle
Tin
MA TAU WAI
Kwong
Road
Tin Hau
Farm Road
Kadoorie Ave
Circuit
Braga
esan Boys School
Waterloo Road
St John's Ln.
Gullane Rd
Tweed Rd
Dunbar Road
Street
Perth
Shek
Ku St
Kadoorie Avenue
Street
Argyle
Hop Yat Church
St Mark's Church
Mormon Church
Sheung Hong St
Sheung Shing St
Tin Kwong Road
Soares Ave
Julia Ave
Emma Ave
Man Fuk Rd
Man Wan Rd
King Tak St
Princess
Sheung Wo St
Sheung Lok Street
Kau Pui Lung Road
Pentecostal Tabernacle
Kowloon Central Library
wloon Chamber Commerce
Pui Ching Road
Sheung Shing Street
Ho Man Tin Estate
Foo St
Chinese Church of Christ
Sheung Hin St
Fat Kwong Street
Sheung
Road
Tin Hill Rd
Ho Man Tin Street
Ho Man
Tin Hill
Good
Chung Hau
Shepherd St
Chung Man St
HO MAN TIN
Wylie Road
Margaret
Village St
St
Carmel
KO SHAN ROAD PARK
Ko Shan Theatre
Hau Man St
Sheung Lok Street
Ho Man
Oi Man Shopping Centre
Sports Centre
Ko Shan Road
Chi Man St
Road
Chung Yee St
Fat Kwong Street
Shun Yung St
East Kowloon Corridor
King's Park Rise
Sreett
Hau
Wo Chung St
Yan Fung St
Valley Rd
Chung
Wylie Road
Queen Elizabeth Hospital

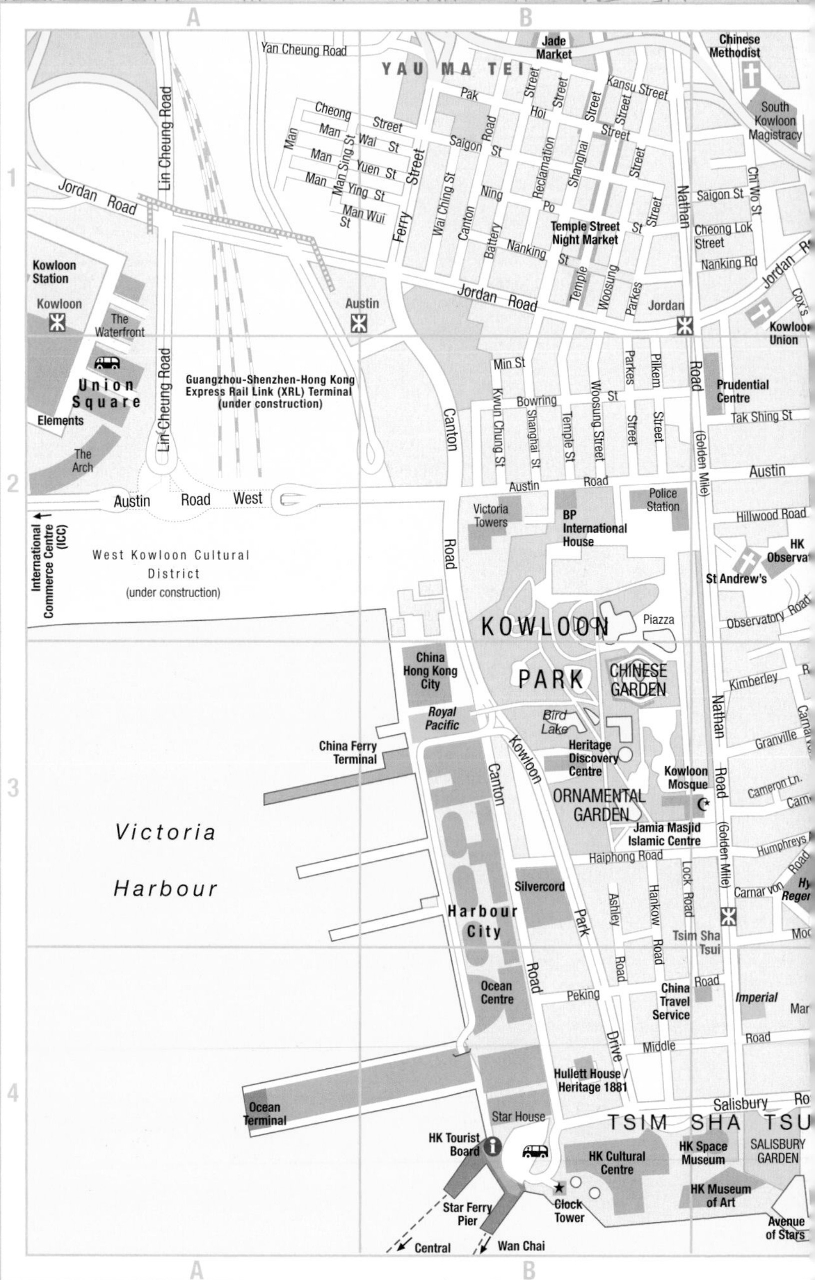

A
B
1
2
3
4
Yan Cheung Road
YAU MA TEI
Jade Market
Chinese Methodist
South Kowloon Magistracy
Kansu Street
Pak Hoi Street
Cheong Street
Man Wai St
Man Yuen St
Man Ying St
Man Sing St
Man Wui St
Ferry Street
Saigon St
Reclamation Street
Shanghai Street
Temple Street Night Market
Nathan Road
Saigon St
Chi Wo St
Cheong Lok Street
Nanking Rd
Jordan Road
Lin Cheung Road
Wai Ching St
Canton Road
Ning Po
Battery
Nanking St
Temple
Woosung
Parkes
Jordan
Cox's
Kowloon Union
Kowloon Station
Kowloon
The Waterfront
Union Square
Elements
The Arch
Austin
Guangzhou-Shenzhen-Hong Kong Express Rail Link (XRL) Terminal (under construction)
Min St
Kwun Chung St
Bowring St
Shanghai St
Temple St
Woosung Street
Parkes Street
Pilkem Street
Prudential Centre
Tak Shing St
(Golden Mile)
Austin Road West
Austin Road
Police Station
Victoria Towers
BP International House
Hillwood Road
HK Observatory
St Andrew's
International Commerce Centre (ICC)
West Kowloon Cultural District (under construction)
KOWLOON PARK
Piazza
Observatory Road
CHINESE GARDEN
Kimberley
China Hong Kong City
Royal Pacific
Bird Lake
Granville
Carnarvon
China Ferry Terminal
Heritage Discovery Centre
Kowloon Park Drive
Kowloon Mosque
Cameron Ln.
ORNAMENTAL GARDEN
Jamia Masjid Islamic Centre
Victoria Harbour
Haiphong Road
Humphreys
Silvercord
Ashley Road
Hankow Road
Lock Road
Carnarvon Road
Harbour City
Tsim Sha Tsui
Peking Road
China Travel Service
Imperial
Ocean Centre
Middle Road
Hullett House / Heritage 1881
Salisbury Road
Ocean Terminal
Star House
TSIM SHA TSUI
HK Tourist Board
HK Cultural Centre
HK Space Museum
SALISBURY GARDEN
Clock Tower
HK Museum of Art
Star Ferry Pier
Avenue of Stars
Central
Wan Chai

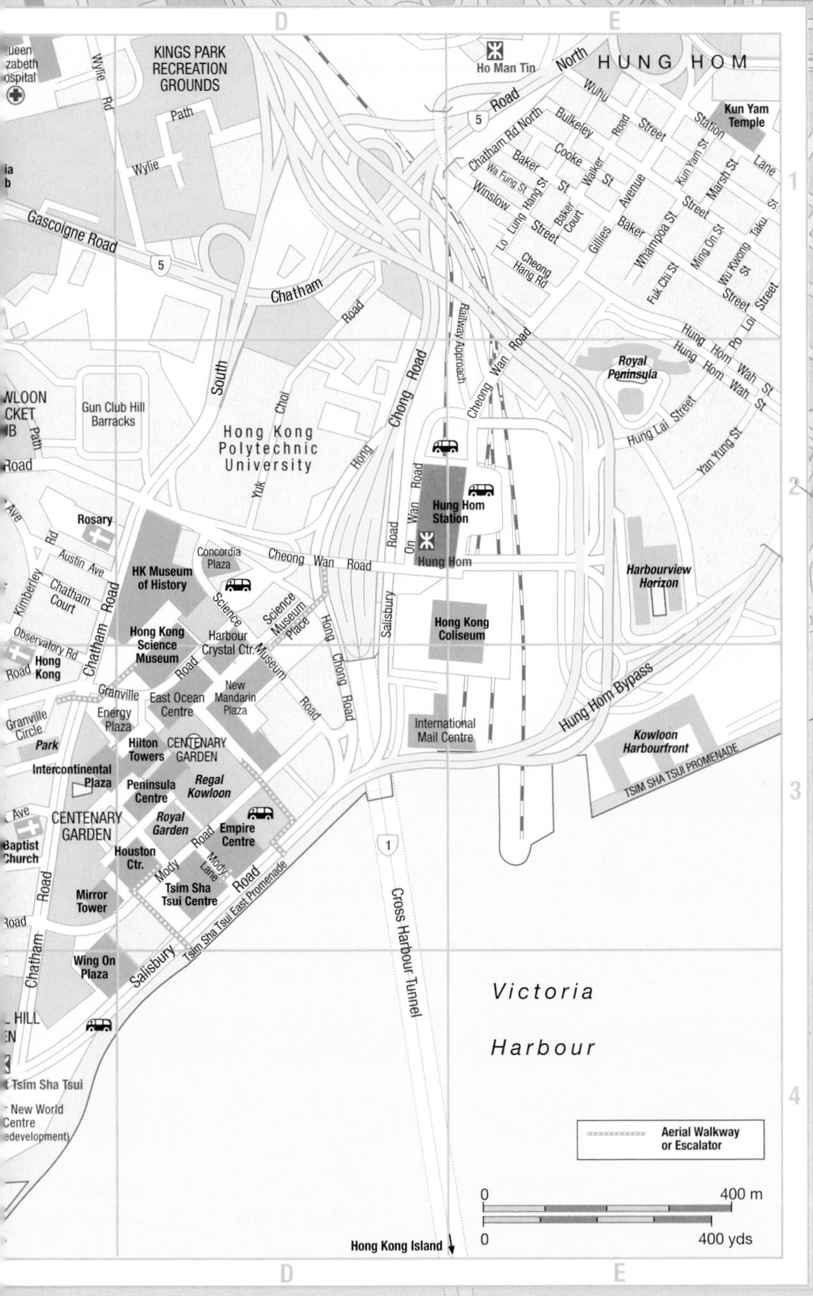
D
E
KINGS PARK RECREATION GROUNDS
Ho Man Tin
HUNG HOM
Kun Yam Temple
Wylie Rd
Path
Wylie
North Road
Wuhu
Bulkeley
Road
Street
Station
Lane
Chatham Rd North
Baker
Cooke
Walker
St
Wa Fung St
Winslow
Hang St
Lo Lung
Street
Baker Court
Gillies
Avenue
Baker
Kun Yam St
Marsh St
Street
Taku
St
Whampoa St
Ming On St
Wu Kwong St
Fuk Chi St
Street
Street
Loi
Po
Cheong Hang Rd
Gascoigne Road
5
Chatham
Road
Railway Approach
Road
Wan
Cheong
Royal Peninsula
Hung Hom Wah St
Hung Hom Wah St
Hung Lai Street
Yan Yung St
South
Chong Road
Choi
Gun Club Hill Barracks
Hong Kong Polytechnic University
Yuk
Hong
Path
Road
Ave
Rosary
Rd
Austin Ave
Kimberley
Chatham Court
Chatham Road
Observatory Rd
Hong Kong
Road
Concordia Plaza
Cheong Wan Road
HK Museum of History
Science
Science Museum Place
Hong Kong Science Museum
Harbour Crystal Ctr.
Museum
Road
Hung Hom Station
Hung Hom
On Wan Road
Road
Salisbury
Hong Chong Road
Hong Kong Coliseum
Harbourview Horizon
Granville
Granville Circle
Park
Energy Plaza
East Ocean Centre
New Mandarin Plaza
Road
International Mail Centre
Hung Hom Bypass
Kowloon Harbourfront
TSIM SHA TSUI PROMENADE
Hilton Towers
CENTENARY GARDEN
Intercontinental Plaza
Peninsula Centre
Regal Kowloon
Ave
CENTENARY GARDEN
Royal Garden
Empire Centre
Baptist Church
Houston Ctr.
Road
Mody
Mody Lane
Road
Tsim Sha Tsui Centre
Mirror Tower
Road
Road
Tsim Sha Tsui East Promenade
1
Cross Harbour Tunnel
Chatham
Wing On Plaza
Salisbury
Victoria Harbour
Tsim Sha Tsui
New World Centre (redevelopment)
Aerial Walkway or Escalator
0
400 m
0
400 yds
Hong Kong Island
1
2
3
4

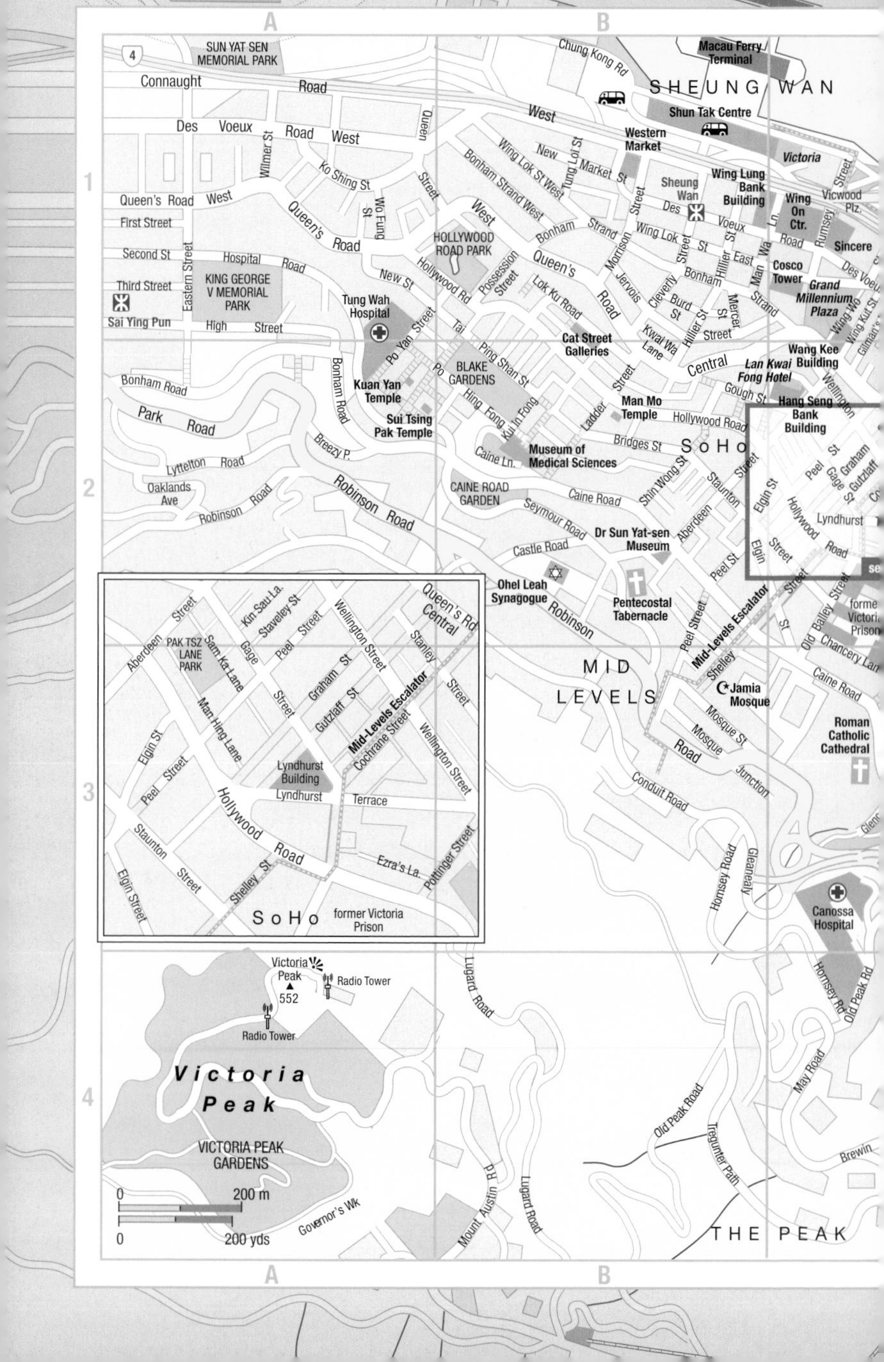
A
B
1
2
3
4
SUN YAT SEN MEMORIAL PARK
Connaught Road
Des Voeux Road West
Wilmer St
Queen Street
Chung Kong Rd
Macau Ferry Terminal
SHEUNG WAN
Shun Tak Centre
West
Western Market
Victoria
Wing Lok St West
New Market St
Tung Loi St
Bonham Strand West
Ko Shing St
Wo Fung St
Queen's Road West
First Street
Second St
Third Street
Sai Ying Pun
Eastern Street
Hospital Road
KING GEORGE V MEMORIAL PARK
High Street
HOLLYWOOD ROAD PARK
Hollywood Rd
New St
Possession Street
Queen's Road
Tung Wah Hospital
Po Yan Street
Tai Ping Shan St
Lok Ku Road
Jervois
Cleverly
Burd St
Hillier St
Mercer St
Sheung Wan
Des Voeux
Wing Lok St
Bonham Strand
Morrison Street
Man Wa Ln.
Wing Lung Bank Building
Wing On Ctr.
Rumsey Street
Vicwood Plz.
Sincere
Cosco Tower
Grand Millennium Plaza
Des Voeux
Wing Wo
Wing Kut St
Gilman's
Kwai Wa Lane
Cat Street Galleries
Central
Lan Kwai Fong Hotel
Wang Kee Building
Gough St
Wellington
Hang Seng Bank Building
Bonham Road
Kuan Yan Temple
BLAKE GARDENS
Po Hing Fong
Kui In Fong
Ladder Street
Man Mo Temple
Hollywood Road
Bridges St
SoHo
Park Road
Sui Tsing Pak Temple
Breezy P.
Caine Ln.
Museum of Medical Sciences
Lyttelton Road
Oaklands Ave
Robinson Road
CAINE ROAD GARDEN
Caine Road
Seymour Road
Shin Wong St
Staunton Street
Aberdeen
Elgin St
Peel St
Graham St
Gage St
Gutzlaff
Lyndhurst
Hollywood Road
Elgin Street
Dr Sun Yat-sen Museum
Castle Road
Ohel Leah Synagogue
Pentecostal Tabernacle
Robinson
Peel Street
Mid-Levels Escalator
Old Bailey Street
former Victoria Prison
Chancery Lan
Caine Road
MID LEVELS
Shelley
Jamia Mosque
Mosque St
Mosque
Road
Junction
Roman Catholic Cathedral
Conduit Road
Hornsey Road
Gleanealy
Canossa Hospital
Hornsey Rd
Old Peak Rd
May Road
Glen
Old Peak Road
Tregunter Path
Brewin
THE PEAK
Aberdeen Street
Kin Sau La.
Staveley St
PAK TSZ LANE PARK
Sam Ka Lane
Gage
Peel Street
Wellington Street
Queen's Rd Central
Stanley
Street
Graham St
Gutzlaff St
Man Hing Lane
Elgin St
Peel Street
Mid-Levels Escalator
Cochrane Street
Wellington Street
Lyndhurst Building
Lyndhurst Terrace
Hollywood Road
Staunton Street
Shelley St
Ezra's La.
Pottinger Street
Elgin Street
SoHo
former Victoria Prison
Victoria Peak
552
Radio Tower
Radio Tower
Victoria Peak
VICTORIA PEAK GARDENS
Lugard Road
Mount Austin Rd
Lugard Road
Governor's Wk
0
200 m
0
200 yds

D
E
1
2
3
4
Victoria
Harbour
Kowloon
Outlying Islands Ferry Piers
Pier 2
Pier 3
Pier 4
Pier 5
Pier 6
Star Ferry Pier
Pier 7
Pier 8
Hong Kong Maritime Museum
Pier 9
Pier 10
Man Kwong Street
Four Seasons Hotel
Finance Street
ifc Mall
International Finance Centre (ifc)
One ifc
Two ifc
Connaught
Hang Seng Bank Building
Central Station
Hong Kong
Harbour View Street
Man Yiu Street
The Forum
Exchange Square
General Post Office
Connaught Pl.
Central Wan Chai Bypass
(under construction)
CENTRAL AND WESTERN DISTRICT PROMENADE
CENTRAL
City Hall
Lung Wo Road
TAMAR
TAMAR PARK
Central Barracks
Tim Wa Avenue
Legislative Council
Central Government Complex
Tim Mei Avenue
Citic Building
Tamar Amphitheatre
Jardine House
Pedder St Tunnel
St George's Building
Central
Chater
STATUE SQUARE
Prince's Building
Ice House St
Old Supreme Court Building
Jackson Road
Club St
AIG Tower
Murray Rd
Lambeth Walk
Bank of America Tower
Harcourt
Road
CHATER GARDEN
Des Voeux Road C.
Pedder St
Theatre Lane
World Wide Lane
Douglas St
Douglas Ln.
Li Yuen St E.
Li Yuen St W.
Pottinger
Queen's Road Central
Shell House
New World Tower
Zetland St
Duddell St
Ice House St
Queen's Rd Central
Battery Path
HSBC Bldg
Bank St
Bank of China
Cheung Kong Centre
Bank of China Tower
Fairmont House
Cotton Tree Drive
Far East Finance Centre
Tamar Street
Admiralty
Admiralty Centre
Queensway Plaza
United Centre
Rodney St
HARCOURT PARK
May House
Queensway
HK Diamond Exchange Building
HK Central Hospital
Lower Albert
St John's Cathedral
Citibank Plaza ICBC Tower
Flagstaff House Museum of Tea Ware
Supreme Court
Government Offices
Pacific Place One
Pacific Place Three
Government House
American Embassy
Albert Road
ZOOLOGICAL & BOTANICAL GDNS
St Joseph's Cathedral
Garden Road
Peak Tram Terminus
HONG KONG PARK
Sir Edward Youde Aviary
Supreme Court Rd
Pacific Place Two
Pacific Place
The Upper House
Justice Drive
Monmouth Path
Star Street
Kennedy Road
Cotton Tree Dr.
Visual Arts Centre
Union
Hong Kong Design Centre
First Church of Christ Scientist
Macdonnell Road
Borrett Road
Bowen Road
Peak Tram Funicular
Magazine Gap Rd
May Road
Magazine Gap Rd
Magazine Gap
Tower
Aerial Walkway or Escalator

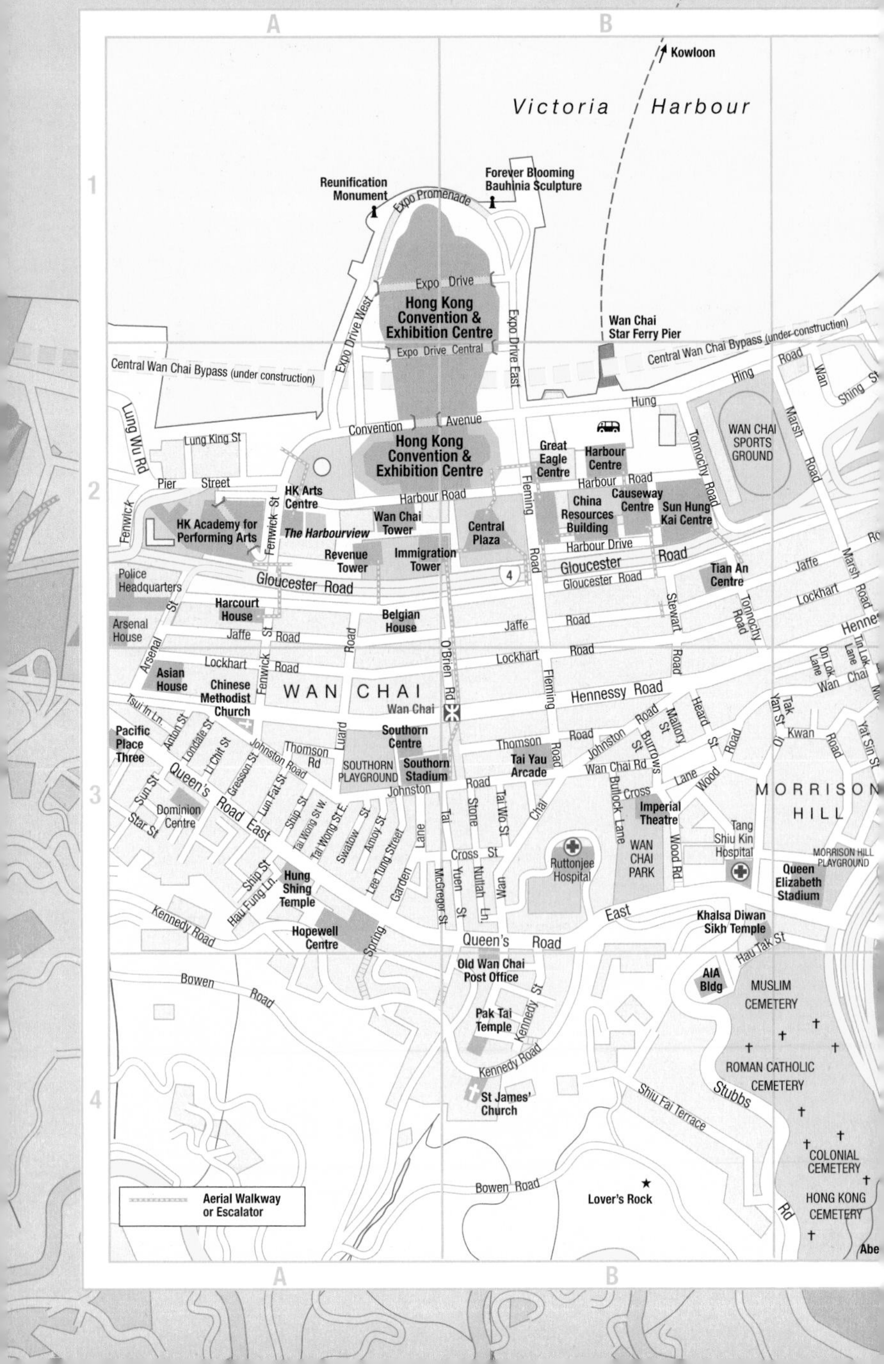
A
B
1
2
3
4
Kowloon
Victoria Harbour
Reunification Monument
Forever Blooming Bauhinia Sculpture
Expo Promenade
Expo Drive
Hong Kong Convention & Exhibition Centre
Expo Drive West
Expo Drive East
Expo Drive Central
Wan Chai Star Ferry Pier
Central Wan Chai Bypass (under construction)
Convention Avenue
Hung Hing Road
Lung Wu Rd
Lung King St
Pier Street
Fenwick
Fenwick St
HK Arts Centre
HK Academy for Performing Arts
The Harbourview
Wan Chai Tower
Revenue Tower
Immigration Tower
Central Plaza
Great Eagle Centre
Harbour Centre
Harbour Road
China Resources Building
Causeway Centre
Sun Hung Kai Centre
Harbour Drive
Fleming Road
Tonnochy Road
WAN CHAI SPORTS GROUND
Wan Shing St
Marsh Road
Police Headquarters
Gloucester Road
Tian An Centre
Harcourt House
Belgian House
Arsenal House
Arsenal St
Jaffe Road
Lockhart Road
Stewart Road
Asian House
Chinese Methodist Church
WAN CHAI
Wan Chai
O'Brien Rd
Luard Road
Hennessy Road
On Lok Lane
Tin Lok Lane
Wan Chai Rd
Tsui In Ln.
Anton St
Pacific Place Three
Landale St
Li Chit St
Gresson St
Johnston Road
Thomson Rd
Southorn Centre
SOUTHORN PLAYGROUND
Southorn Stadium
Tai Yau Arcade
Mallory St
Burrows St
Heard St
Tak Yan St
Kwan Road
Yat Sin St
Sun St
Star St
Queen's Road East
Dominion Centre
Lun Fat St
Ship St
Tai Wong St W.
Tai Wong St E.
Swatow St
Amoy St
Lee Tung Street
Lane
Tai Stone
Tai Wo St
Chai
Cross St
Bullock Lane
Cross Lane
Wood Road
Imperial Theatre
MORRISON HILL
Tang Shiu Kin Hospital
WAN CHAI PARK
Wood Rd
Ruttonjee Hospital
MORRISON HILL PLAYGROUND
Queen Elizabeth Stadium
Hung Shing Temple
Hau Fung Ln.
Garden
McGregor St
Yuen St
Nullah Ln.
Wan
Kennedy Road
Hopewell Centre
Spring
Khalsa Diwan Sikh Temple
Hau Tak St
Bowen Road
Old Wan Chai Post Office
AIA Bldg
MUSLIM CEMETERY
Pak Tai Temple
Kennedy St
ROMAN CATHOLIC CEMETERY
St James' Church
Shiu Fai Terrace
Stubbs Rd
COLONIAL CEMETERY
Lover's Rock
HONG KONG CEMETERY
Aerial Walkway or Escalator
Abe

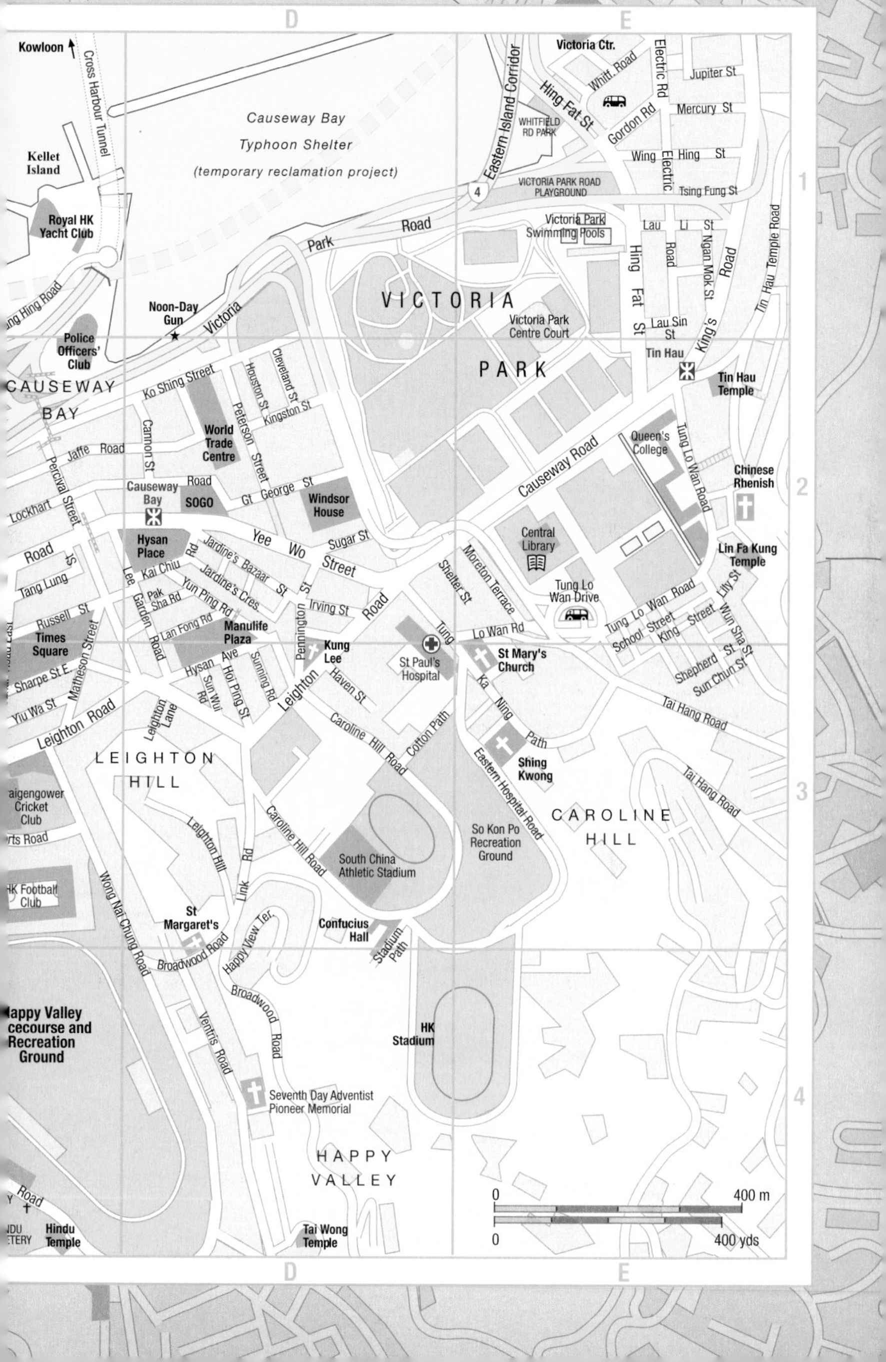
D
E
1
2
3
4
Kowloon
Cross Harbour Tunnel
Kellet Island
Royal HK Yacht Club
Causeway Bay
Typhoon Shelter
(temporary reclamation project)
Eastern Island Corridor
Victoria Ctr.
Whitf. Road
Hing Fat St
WHITFIELD RD PARK
Gordon Rd
Electric Rd
Jupiter St
Mercury St
Wing
Hing
St
Electric
Tsing Fung St
VICTORIA PARK ROAD PLAYGROUND
4
Victoria Park Swimming Pools
Victoria Park Road
Lau
Li
St
Hing Fat St
Road
Ngan Mok St
King's Road
Tin Hau Temple Road
Noon-Day Gun
Police Officers' Club
VICTORIA
PARK
Victoria Park Centre Court
Lau Sin St
Tin Hau
Tin Hau Temple
CAUSEWAY BAY
Ko Shing Street
Houston St
Cleveland St
Kingston St
Peterson Street
World Trade Centre
Cannon St
Jaffe Road
Percival Street
Causeway Bay
SOGO
Gt George St
Windsor House
Causeway Road
Queen's College
Tung Lo Wan Road
Chinese Rhenish
Lockhart Road
Hysan Place
Yee Wo Street
Sugar St
Central Library
Lin Fa Kung Temple
Kai Chiu Rd
Jardine's Bazaar St
Jardine's Cres.
Lee Garden Road
Pak Sha Rd
Yun Ping Rd
Tang Lung St
Russell St
Times Square
Lan Fong Rd
Manulife Plaza
Irving St
Pennington St
Shelter St
Moreton Terrace
Tung Lo Wan Drive
Tung Lo Wan Road
Lily St
Tung Lo Wan Road
School Street
King Street
Wun Sha St
Kung Lee
St Paul's Hospital
Tung Lo Wan Rd
St Mary's Church
Shepherd St
Sun Chun St
Sharpe St E.
Matheson Street
Hysan Ave
Sun Wui Rd
Hoi Ping St
Sunning Rd
Leighton Road
Haven St
Ka Ning Path
Tai Hang Road
Yiu Wa St
Leighton Road
Leighton Lane
Caroline Hill Road
Cotton Path
Shing Kwong
LEIGHTON HILL
Eastern Hospital Road
CAROLINE HILL
Tai Hang Road
Craigengower Cricket Club
Sports Road
Leighton Hill
Link Rd
Caroline Hill Road
South China Athletic Stadium
So Kon Po Recreation Ground
HK Football Club
Wong Nai Chung Road
St Margaret's
Confucius Hall
Broadwood Road
Happy View Ter.
Stadium Path
Happy Valley Racecourse and Recreation Ground
Broadwood Road
HK Stadium
Ventris Road
Seventh Day Adventist Pioneer Memorial
HAPPY VALLEY
0
400 m
0
400 yds
Road
HINDU CEMETERY
Hindu Temple
Tai Wong Temple
D
E

# STREET INDEX


## A

Aberdeen St 298 B2
Admiralty Centre 299 E3
AIA Building 300 B4
Albany Rd 299 C3
Albert Rd 299 C3
All Saints' Church 294 C3
Amoy St 300 A3
Anchor St 294 A2
Anton St 300 A3
Arbuthnot Rd 298 C3
Argyle Centre Tower I 294 B2
Argyle Centre Tower II 294 B2
Argyle St 294 B2, 295 C2–E1
Arran St 294 B1
Arsenal House 300 A2
Arsenal St 300 A3
Arthur St 294 B4
Ash St 294 A2
Ashley Rd 296 B3
Asian House 300 A3
Assembly of God Church 294 C2
Austin Avenue 297 C2
Austin Rd 296 B2–C2
Austin Road West 296 A2
Aviary 299 D3

## B

Baker Court 297 E1
Baker St 297 E1
Bank of America Tower 299 E3
Bank of Canton Building 299 D3
Bank of China 299 D3
Bank of China Tower 299 D3
Bank of East Asia Building 299 D3
Bank St 299 D3
Battery Path 299 D3
Battery St 296 B1
Bedford Rd 294 A1
Beech St 294 A2
Bird Market 294 C1
Blenheim Ave 297 C4
Bonham Rd 298 A2
Bonham Strand 298 B1
Bonham Strand West 298 B1
Borrett Rd 299 D4–E4
Bowen Drive 299 E4
Bowen Rd 299 D4–E4, 300 A4–B4
Bowring St 296 B2
BP International House 296 B2
Braga Circuit 295 D1
Breezy Path 298 A2
Brewin Clovelly Path 298 C4
Bridges St 298 B2
Broadwood Rd 301 D4
Bulkeley St 297 E1
Bullock Lane 300 B3
Burd St 298 B1
Burrows St 300 B3
Bute St 294 A2–B1

## C

Caine Lane 298 B2
Caine Rd 298 B2
Cameron Lane 296 C3
Cameron Rd 296 C3
Canal Rd East 301 C2–C3
Cannon St 301 D2
Canossa Hospital 298 C3
Canton Rd 294 B1–B3, 296 B1–B2–B3
Carmel Village St 295 D3
Carnarvon Rd 296 C3
Caroline Hill Rd 301 D3
Castle Rd 298 A2–B2
Cat Street Galleries 298 B2
Causeway Rd 301 E2
Cedar St 294 B1
Center, The 298 C2
Central Building 299 C2
Central Library 301 E2
Central Market 299 C2
Central Plaza 300 B2
Central Wan Chai Bypass 299 D2
Chancery Lane 298 C2–3
Changsha St 294 B3
Chater Rd 299 D2
Chatham Court 297 C2
Chatham Rd North 297 D1–E1
Chatham Rd South 297 C4–C3
Cheong Hang Rd 297 E1
Cheong Wan Rd 297 D2–E2–E1
Cherry St 294 A2
Cheung Lo Church 294 C1
Cheung Shui St 294 B4
Cheung Wong Rd 294 B2
Chi Man St 295 D4
Chi Wo St 296 C1
China HK City 296 B3
China Resources Building 300 B2
Chinese Church of Christ 295 E2
Chinese Methodist Church 296 C1, 300 A3
Chinese Rhenish Church 301 E2
Ching Ping St 294 B4
Chiu Lung St 299 C2
Chong Rd 297 D2
Chun Yi Lane 294 C3
Chung Hau St 295 D3–D4–E4
Chungking Mansion 296 C4
Chung Kong Rd 298 B1
Chung Man St 295 D3
Chung Rd 300 C4
Chung Wing St 294 A2
Citibank Plaza ICBC Tower 299 D3
City Hall 299 D2
Cleveland St 301 D2
Cleverly St 298 B1
Cliff Rd 294 C4
Clock Tower 296 B4
Club St 299 D2
Cochrane St 298 C2
Conduit Rd 298 A2–B3
Connaught Place 299 D2
Connaught Rd Central 299 C1–D2
Connaught Rd West 298 A1–B1
Conrad Hotel 299 E3
Convention Rd 300 A2
Cooke St 297 E1
Cotton Path 301 D3
Cotton Tree Drive 299 C3–D3
Cox's Rd 296 C1–C2
Craigengower Cricket Club 301 C3
Cross Harbour Tunnel 297 D3–4
Cross Lane 300 B3
Cross St 300 A3–B3

## D

Des Voeux Rd Central 298 B1–C1
Des Voeux Rd West 298 A1
Dominion Centre 300 A3
Douglas Lane 299 C2
Douglas St 299 C2
Duddell St 299 C3
Dunbar Rd 295 D2
Dundas St 294 B3

## E

East Ocean Centre 297 D3
Eastern Hospital Rd 301 E3
Eaton Hotel 296 C1
Edinburgh Place 299 D2
Edward Rd West 295 C1
Electric Rd 301 E1
Elements 296 A2
Elgin St 298 B2
Elm St 294 A2
Emma Ave 295 C2
Empire Centre 297 D3
Excelsior Hotel 301 D2
Exchange Square 299 D2
Expo Drive 300 A1

## F

Fa Yuen St 294 B1–B2
Fairmont House 299 D3
Far East Finance Centre 299 E3
Farm Rd 295 E2
Fat Kwong St 295 D3–E4
Fenwick Pier St 300 A2
Fenwick St 300 A3
Ferry St 294 B3, 296 B1
Fife St 294 B2
Fir St 294 A2
First 294 B3
First Church of Christ Scientist 299 D4
Flagstaff House Museum of Tea Ware 299 D3
Fleming Rd 300 B2
Flower Market 294 B1
Flower Market Rd 294 B1
Forever Blooming Bauhinia Sculpture 300 B1
Four Seasons Hotel 299 C1
Foursquare Gospel Church 294 A1
Fuk Chi St 297 E1
Fuk Tsuen St 294 A1

## G

Garden Rd 299 C4–C3–D3
Gascoigne Rd 297 C1
General Post Office 299 D2
Gillies Ave 297 E1
Gilman St 298 C2
Gilman's Bazaar 298 C2
Gleanealy Rd 298 B3
Gloucester Rd 300 A2–A3, 301 C2
Gloucester Tower 299 D2
Golden Crown Theatre 294 A1
Good Shepherd St 295 D3
Gordon Rd 301 E1
Gough St 298 B2
Government House 299 C3
Government Offices 299 E3
Graham St 298 C2 & A3
Grand Hyatt 300 A2
Grand Millennium Plaza 298 C1
Grand Tower 294 B2
Granville Circle 297 C3
Granville Rd 296 C3, 297 C3–D3
Great Eagle Centre 300 B2
Great George St 301 D2
Gresson St 300 A3
Guangdong Building 299 C2
Gullane Rd 295 D1
Gun Club Hill Barracks 297 C2

## H

Haiphong Rd 296 B3
Hak Po St 294 C2
Hamilton St 294 B3
Hang Seng Bank Building 294 B2, 298 C2
Hankow Rd 296 B3
Hanoi Rd 296 C3
Happy Valley Racecourse 301 C4
Happy View Terrace 301 D4–D3
Harbour Building 298 C1
Harbour Centre 300 B2
Harbour City 296 B3
Harbour Drive 300 B2
Harbour Rd 300 A2
Harbour View St 299 C2
Harcourt House 300 A2
Harcourt Rd 299 E2–E3
Hau Fung Lane 300 A3
Hau Man St 295 D3–D4
Hau St 295 E4
Hau Tak St 300 B4–C4
Haven St 301 D3
Heard St 300 B3
Hennessy Rd 300 B3–C2
Hillier St 298 B2
Hillwood Rd 296 C2
Hilton Towers 297 D3
Hindu Temple 301 C4
Hing Fat St 301 E1
HSBC Mong Kok Building 294 B2
HK Academy for Performing Arts 300 A2
HK Arts Centre 300 A2
HK Central Hospital 299 C3
HK Coliseum 297 E2
HK Convention & Exhibition Centre 300 B2
HK Cultural Centre 296 B4
HK Diamond Exchange Building 299 C3
HK Football Club Stadium 301 C3
HK Heritage Discovery Centre 296 B3
HK Maritime Museum 299 D1
HK Museum of Art 296 C4
HK Museum of History 297 D2
HK Observatory 297 C2
HK Racing Museum 300 C4
HK Science Museum 297 D2
HK Space Museum 296 C4
HK Stadium 301 D4
HK Tourist Board 296 B4
Ho Man Tin Hill Rd 295 C3–D3
Ho Man Tin St 295 C3
Hoi King St 294 A2
Hoi Ting Road 294 A3
Hoi Wang Road 294 A3
Holiday Inn 296 C4
Hollywood Rd 298 A1–C2
Hong Chong Rd 297 D2–D3
Hong Kong Church 297 C2–3
Hong Lok St 294 B2
Hop Yat Church 295 D2
Hopewell Centre 300 A3
Hornsey Rd 298 B3
Hospital Rd 298 A1
HSBC Building 299 D3
Hullett House 296 B4
Humphreys Ave 296 C3
Hung Hing Rd 300 B2
Hung Hom Bypass 297 E3

Hung Hom Railway Station 297 E2
Hung Hom Wah St 297 E1
Hung Shin Temple 294 A1
Hung Shing Temple 300 A3
Hyatt Regency 296 C3
Hysan Ave 301 D3
Hysan Place 301 D2

## I

1ifc 299 C1
2ifc 299 D1
Ice House St 299 C3
Immigration Tower 300 A2
Imperial Theatre 300 B3
Imperial Hotel 296 C4
India Club 297 C1
InterContinental Hotel 297 C4
International Building 298 C1
International Commerce Centre (ICC) 296 A2
International Mail Centre 297 D3
Irving St 301 D2
Island Shangri-La 299 E3
Ivy St 294 A2

## J

Jackson Rd 299 D3
Jade Market 294 B4
Jaffe Rd 300 A2–B2
Jamia Mosque 298 B3
Jardine House 299 D2
Jardine's Bazaar St 301 D2
Jardine's Cres. 301 D2
Jervois St 298 B1
Johnston Rd 300 A3–B3
Jordan Path 297 C1–C2
Jordan Rd 296 A1–B1
Jubilee St 299 C2
Julia Ave 295 C2
Jupiter St 301 E1
Justic Drive 299 E4–E3

## K

K-11 296 C3
Ka Ning Path 301 E3
Kadoorie Ave 295 C1–C2
Kai Chiu Rd 301 D2
Kam Fong St 294 B3
Kam Lam St 294 B3
Kansu St 296 B1
Kau Pui Lung Rd 295 E2
Kennedy Rd 299 D4–E4, 300 A3–B4
Kennedy St 300 B4
Khalsa Diwan Sikh Temple 300 B3
Ki Lung St 294 B1
Kimberley 297 C3
Kimberley Rd 296 C3
King Ming Rd 301 E1
King Tak St 295 D2
King's Park Rise 295 C4
King's Rd 301 E2–E1
Ko Shan Rd 295 E4
Ko Shan Theatre 295 E3
Ko Shing St 298 A1
Korea Centre 299 C2
Kowloon Hotel 296 C4
Kowloon Central Library 295 C2
Kowloon Chamber of Commerce 295 C2
Kowloon Cricket Club 297 C2
Kowloon Hospital 295 D1
Kowloon Mosque 296 C3
Kowloon Park Drive 296 B3
Kowloon Rehabilitation Centre 295 E1
Kowloon Union Church 296 C1
Kuan Yin Temple 298 A2
Kui In Fong 298 B2
Kun Yam 294 C2
Kun Yam St 297 E1
Kun Yam Temple 297 E1
Kung Lee Church 301 D3
Kwai Wa Lane 298 B1
Kwong Wa St 294 C3
Kwong Wah Hospital 294 C3
Kwun Chung St 296 B2

## L

Ladder St 298 B2
Ladies' Market 294 B2
Lai Cheung Road 294 A4
Lai Chi Kok Rd 294 A1
Lambeth Walk 299 D3
Landmark 299 C2
Lan Fong Rd 301 D2
Langham Place 294 B2
Larch St 294 A1
Lau Li St 301 E1
Lau Sin St 301 E1
Lee Garden Rd 301 D2
Lee Gardens 301 D3
Lee Tat St 294 B4
Lee Tung St 300 A3
Lee Yip St 294 B3
Leighton Lane 301 D3
Leighton Rd 301 C3
Li Chit St 300 A3
Liberty Ave 295 C2
Lily St 301 E2
Lime St 294 A1
Lin Cheung Road 294 A3
Lin Fa Kung Temple 301 E2
Link Rd 301 D3
Lippo Tower 299 E3
Lo Lung Hang St 297 E1
Lock Rd 296 B3
Lockhart Rd 300 A3–D2
Lok Ku Rd 298 B1
Lomond Rd 295 E1
Lover's Rock 300 B4
Lower Albert Rd 299 C3
Luard Rd 300 A3
Luen Wan St 294 C1–C2
Lugard Rd 298 A3–B4
Lun Fat St 300 A3
Lung King St 300 A2
Lung Wo Road 299 E2
Lung Wui Road 299 E2
Lyndhurst Ter. 298 C2
Lyttelton Rd 298 A2

## M

Macdonnell Rd 299 D4
Magazine Gap Rd 299 C4–D4
Mallory St 300 B3
Man Cheong St 296 A1
Man Fuk Rd 295 D2
Man Kwong Street 299 C1
Man Ming Lane 294 B4
Man Mo Temple 298 B2
Man On St 294 A1
Man Po Street 299 C1–D1
Man Sing St 296 A1
Man Wa Lane 298 B1
Man Wai St 296 A1
Man Wan Rd 295 D2
Man Wui St 296 B1
Man Ying St 296 A1
Man Yuen St 296 A1
Mandarin Orient Hotel 299 D2
Maple St 294 A1
Marco Polo Gateway Hotel 296 B3
Marco Polo HK Hotel 296 B4
Marco Polo Prince Hotel 296 B3
Mariners' Club 297 C4
Market St 294 B4
Marriott 299 E3
Marsh Rd 300 C2
Marsh St 297 E1
Matheson St 301 C3
May Rd 298 B4, 299 C4
McGregor St 300 B3
Mercer St 298 B1
Mercury St 301 E1
Metropole Hotel 295 C2
Middle Rd 296 B4
Min St 296 B2
Minden Row 296 C3
Ming On St 297 E1
The Mira Hotel 296 C3
Mody Lane 297 D3
Mody Rd 296 C3
Mong Kok Church 294 B1
Mong Kok KCR Station 294 C1
Mong Kok Rd 294 B2
Monmouth Path 299 E4–E3
Moreton Terrace 301 E2
Mormon Church 295 D2
Morrison Hill Rd 300 C3
Morrison St 298 B1
Mosque Junction 298 B3
Mosque St 298 B3
Mount Austin Rd 298 B4
Murray Rd 299 D3
Museum of Medical Sciences 298 B2

## N

Nanking St 296 B1
Nathan Centre 294 B3
Nathan Road 294 B1–B4, 296 C2–C3
Nelson St 294 B2
New Kowloon Plaza 294 A2
New Market St 298 B1
New St 298 A1
Ngan Mok St 301 E1
Ngo Cheung Road 294 A4–B4
Nikko Hotel 297 D3
Ning Po St 296 B1
Noon-day Gun 301 D1
Novotel Century Hotel 300 B2
Nullah Rd 294 B1

## O

Oak St 294 A2
O'Brien Rd 300 B3
Observatory 296 C2
Observatory Court 297 C2
Ocean Centre 296 B4
Ocean Terminal 296 A4
Ohel Leah Synagogue 298 B2
Oi Kwan Rd 300 B3–C3
Oi Man Shopping Centre 295 D4
Old Balley St 298 C3
Old Peak Rd 298 B4–C4–C3
Old Supreme Court Building 299 D2
Olympic City 294 A3
On Lok Lane 300 C3
On Wan Rd 297 D2
Outlying Islands Ferry Piers 299 D1

## P

Pacific Place 299 E3
Pacific Place Three 300 A3
Pak Hoi St 296 B1
Pak Sha Rd 301 D2
Pak Tai Temple 300 B4
Palm St 294 A2
Park 297 C3
Park Lane 301 D2
Park Rd 298 A2
Parkes St 296 B1–B2
Paterson St 301 D2
Peace Ave 294 C2
Peak Tram 299 C4
Peak Tram Terminus 299 D3
Pedder St 299 C2
Peel St 298 B3–C2 & A3
Peking Rd 296 B4
Peniel Church 294 B3
Peninsula Hotel 296 C4
Peninsula Centre 297 D3
Pennington St 301 D3–D2
Pentecostal Tabernacle 295 C2, 298 B2
Percival St 301 C2
Peregrine Tower 299 E3
Perth St 295 D2
Piazza 296 B2
Pier Rd 299 C1
Pilkem St 296 B2
Pine St 294 A2
Pitt St 294 B3
Playing Field Rd 294 B1
Po Loi St 297 E1
Po Yan St 298 A2
Police Officers' Club 301 C1
Portland St 294 B1–B3
Possession St 298 B1
Pottinger St 298 C2
Prat Ave 297 C3
Prince Edward Rd West 294 B1–C1
Prince's Building 299 D2
Princess Margaret Rd 295 D2–D3–D4
Prudential Centre 296 C2
Public Square St 294 B4
Pui Ching Rd 295 C2–D2

## Q

Queen Elizabeth Hospital 297 C1
Queen Elizabeth Stadium 300 C3
Queen St 298 A1
Queen Victoria St 299 C2
Queen's College 301 E2
Queen's Rd Central 298 B1–B2, 299 D3
Queen's Rd East 300 A3–B3
Queen's Rd West 298 A1
Queensway 299 E3 / D3

## R

Railway Approach 297 E1–E2
Reclamation St 294 B2–B4, 296 B1
Regal Kowloon Hotel 297 D3
Reunification Monument 300 A1
Revenue Tower 300 A2
Robinson Rd 298 A2–C3
Roman Cath. Cathedral 298 C3
Rosary Church 297 C2
Royal Garden 297 D3
Royal HK Yacht Club 301 C1
Royal Pacific 296 B3
Rumsey St 298 C1
Russell St 301 C2

## S

Sai Yee St 294 B1–C2
Sai Yeung Choi St South 294 B1
Saigon St 296 B1
Salisbury Rd 296 C4, 297 D3
SCAA Stadium 301 D3
School St 301 E3
Science Museum Rd 297 D2
Seymour Rd 298 B2
Shacombank Building 294 B2
Shanghai St 294 B1–B3, 296 B1–B2

Shangri-La Hotel 297 D3
Shantung St 294 B3
Shek Ku St 295 D2
Shek Lung St 294 B4
Shell House 299 C2
Shelley St 298 B3
Shelter St 301 D2
Shepherd St 301 E3
Sheraton 296 C4
Sheung Foo St 295 D3–E2
Sheung Hin St 295 D3
Sheung Hong St 295 E2
Sheung Lok St 295 E2–E3
Sheung Shing St 295 D3–D2–E2
Sheung Wo St 295 E2
Shin Wong St 298 B2
Shing Kwong Church 301 E3
Ship St 300 A3
Shiu Fai Terrace 300 B4
Shun Tak Centre 298 B1
Shun Yung St 295 E4
Silvercord Hotel 296 B3
Sincere 294 B2, 298 C1
Soares Ave 295 C2
SOGO 301 D2
South Kowloon Magistracy 296 C1
South Seas Centre 297 D3
Southorn Centre 300 A3
Soy St 294 B3
Spring Garden Lane 300 A3
St George's Building 299 D2
St John's Cathedral 299 D3
St John's Lane 295 D1
St Joseph's Cathedral 299 D3
St Margaret's Church 301 D3
St Mark's Church 295 D2
St Mary's Church 301 E3
St Paul's Church 299 C3
St Paul's Hospital 301 D3
Stadium Path 301 D4
Standard Chartered Bank Building 299 D3
Stanley St 299 C2
Star Ferry Pier 296 B4, 299 D1
Star House 296 B4
Star St 299 E4
Station Lane 297 E1
Staunton St 298 B2
Stewart Rd 300 B2
Stone Nullah Ln 300 B3
Stubbs Rd 300 B4
Sun Chun St 301 E3
Sun Hung Kai Centre 300 B2
Sun St 300 A3
Sun Yat-sen Museum, Dr 298 B2
Swatow St 300 A3
Sycamore St 294 A1

## T

Tai Hang Rd 301 E3–E4
Tai Kok Tsui Rd 294 A1
Tai Nan St 294 A1
Tai Ping Shan St 298 B1
Tai Wo St 300 B3
Tai Wong St East 300 A3
Tai Wong St West 300 A3
Tai Yau Arcade 300 B3
Tai Yuen St 300 B3
Tak Cheong Lane 294 B4
Tak Shing St 296 C2
Tak Yan St 300 C3
Taku St 297 E1
Tamar Park 299 E2
Tamar St 299 E3
Tang Lung St 301 C2
Tang Shiu Kin Hospital 300 B3
Temple St 294 B4, 296 B1–B2
Temple Street Night Market 294 B4, 298 B1
Theatre Lane 299 C2
Thistle St 294 B2
Thomson Rd 300 A3, B3
Tim Mei Ave 299 E3
Tim Wa Ave 299 E3
Times Square 301 C3
Tin Hau Temple 294 B4, 301 E1
Tin Hau Temple Rd 301 E2
Tin Kwong Rd 295 E1–E2
Tin Lok Lane 300 C2
Tit Shu St 294 A2
Tong Mi Road 294 A1
Tonnochy Rd 300 B2
Tregunter Path 298 B4
Truth Lutheran Church 294 C3
Tsim Sha Tsui Centre 297 D3
Tsim Sha Tsui East Ferry Pier 297 D3
Tsing Fung St 301 E1
Tsui In Lane 300 A3
Tung Chau St 294 A1
Tung Choi St 294 B1–B2
Tung Kun St 294 B4
Tung Lo Wan Rd 301 E2
Tung Loi St 298 B1
Tung On St 294 B3
Tung Wah Eastern Hospital 301 E3
Tung Wah Hospital 298 A1
Tweed Rd 295 D1

## U

Union Church 299 D4
United Centre 299 E3
Upper Albert Rd 298 C3

## V

Valley Rd 295 E4
Ventris Rd 301 D4
Victoria Hotel 298 C1
Victoria Centre 301 E1
Victoria Park Rd 301 D1
Victoria Peak 298 A4
Victory Ave 295 C2
Vicwood Plaza 298 C1

## W

Wa Fung St 297 E1
Wai Ching St 296 B1
Walker Rd 297 E1
Walnut St 294 A1
Wan Chai Rd 300 B3–C3
Wan Chai Sports Ground 300 B2
Wan Chai Star Ferry Pier 300 B2
Wan Chai Tower 300 A2
Wan Shing St 300 C2
Wang Kee Building 298 C2
Ward Memorial Methodist Church, The 294 C3
Waterfront Hotel, The 296 A1
Waterloo Rd 294 B4–C3
Wayfoong Plaza 294 B2
Wellington St 298 C2
Western Market 298 B1
Whampoa St 297 E1
Whitfield Rd 301 E1
Willow St 294 A1
Windsor House 301 D2
Wing Hang Bank Building 299 C2
Wing Hing St 301 E1
Wing Kut St 298 C2
Wing Lok St East 298 B1–C1
Wing Lok St West 298 B1
Wing Lung Bank Building 298 B1
Wing On Centre 298 C1
Wing On Plaza 297 C4
Wing Wo St 298 C1
Winslow St 297 E1
Wo Chung St 295 E4
Wo Fung St 298 A1
Wong Nai 300 C4
Wong Nai Chung Rd 301 C4
Wood Rd 300 B3
Woosung St 296 B1–B2
World Trade Centre 301 D2
Wu Kwong St 297 E1
Wuhu St 297 E1
Wui Cheung Road 296 A2
Wylie Path 297 D1
Wylie Rd 295 C3–C4, 297 C1
Wyndham St 299 C3

## Y

Yan Cheung Road 296 A1–B1
Yan Fung St 295 E4
Yat Sin St 300 C3
Yee Wo St 301 D2
Yim Po Fong St 294 C2
Yin Chong St 294 C3
Yiu Wa St 301 C3
YMCA International House 294 C3
Yuk Choi Rd 297 D2
Yun Ping Rd 301 D2
Yunnah Lane 294 B4
YWCA 295 C2

## Z

Zetland St 299 C3
Zoroastrian Church 301 D3

# ART AND PHOTO CREDITS

**123RF** 87TC, 124B, 169, 174, 179, 181, 190B, 223
**Alamy** 126/127T, 155TC, 182/183T
**Alex Havret/Apa Publications** 8L, 73TR, 78, 105B, 110T, 117ML, 126L, 127TC, 127M, 146B, 154TL, 167, 171B, 182MR, 190T, 202B
**Andrea Pistolesi** 147
**AWL Images** 14/15, 214
**Bigstock** 220
**Bridgeman Art Library** 33
**Corbis** 28B, 28T, 67, 79T, 85
**Dreamstime** 7T, 43, 68B, 76, 117M, 126R, 145B, 153TC, 162R, 172T, 176TL, 177, 180, 182BL, 183M, 183TC, 192/193T, 193TC, 205T, , 216T, 217B, 217T, 218, 219, 222, 224B
**Getty Images** 26B, 29T, 29B, 30, 35, 39, 40L, 40R, 42, 44, 45, 127B, 127BR, 210/211, 216B
**Glyn Genin/Apa Publications** 27T, 201B, 204B
**HKTB** 6ML, 9TR, 11T, 69, 72/73T, 75M, 79B, 133, 145T, 162L, 162/163T, 163BR, 163ML, 163MR, 171T
**iStock** 1, 4/5, 6BR, 41, 55, 68T, 71, 73BL, 74BL, 82, 86MR, 86/87T, 170, 172B, 178, 183BR, 203B, 205B, 215, 221, 224T, 225, 246
**John Ishii/Apa Publications** 77
**Kobal Collection** 81, 173B
**Las Vegas Sands Corp** 208
**Mandarin Oriental Hotel Group** 100
**Mary Evans Picture Library** 31, 32
**Ming Tang-Evans/Apa Publications** 6MR, 6ML, 7BR, 7M, 7MR, 7TR, 8R, 9L, 9BR, 10T, 10B, 11M, 12/13, 16, 17T, 17B, 18, 19, 20, 21B, 21T, 22L, 22R, 23, 24, 25L, 25R, 46/47, 48, 49L, 49R, 50, 51, 52, 53B, 53T, 54, 56, 57, 58, 59B, 59T, 60, 61, 62B, 62T, 63B, 63T, 64R, 64L, 64/65M, 65BC, 65BR, 65TC, 65BL, 66, 72MR, 72B, 72L, 74MR, 74BR, 74/75T, 75BR, 80, 83, 84, 86BR, 86BL, 87M, 87BR, 88/89, 90/91, 92, 93T, 93B, 96, 97, 98, 99B, 99T, 101, 102, 103, 104T, 104B, 105T, 106, 107T, 107B, 108T, 108B, 109T, 109B, 110B, 111, 112, 113, 114, 115, 116R, 116L, 117BR, 116/117T, 117TC, 118, 119, 120, 121, 122B, 122T, 123, 124T, 125T, 125B, 130, 131, 132, 134, 135T, 135B, 136, 136/137, 138, 139, 140T, 140B, 141T, 141B, 142, 143T, 146T, 148B, 148T, 149, 150, 151T, 151B, 152L, 152B, 152/153T, 153M, 153T, 153B, 153BR, 154MR, 154BL, 154/155T, 155B, 155BR, 156, 157, 158, 159T,159B, 160, 161, 164/165, 166, 173T, 175B, 175T, 176TR, 176B, 182MR, 184, 185T, 185B, 186, 187, 188T, 188B, 189, 191T, 191B, 192MR, 192BR, 192BL, 193B, 193BR, 194/195, 196, 197, 198B, 198T, 199, 201T, 202T, 203T, 204T, 207, 209B, 209T, 226, 228, 229, 230, 231L, 233, 236, 237, 240, 242, 243L, 244
**National Palace Museum** 73BR
**PA Photos** 36
**Peninsula Hotels** 75TC, 143B
**Photoshot** 70
**Public domain** 26T, 27B
**Starworld** 206
**SuperStock** 7B
**The Art Archive** 34

*Cover Credits*

**Front cover:** Hong Kong skyline, *Shutterstock*
**Back cover:** Lockhart Road, Wan Chai, *Ming Tang-Evans/Apa Publications*
**Front flap:** (from top) Tai Ping Shan temples *Ming Tang-Evans/APA Publications*; Little Bao, Central Hong Kong *Ming Tang-Evans/APA Publications*; Cat Street, Central Hong Kong *Ming Tang-Evans/APA Publications*; MacLehose Trail sign *Ming Tang-Evans/APA Publicationst*
**Back flap:** Hong Kong tram *Ming Tang-Evans/APA Publications*

# INDEX

Main references are in bold type


## A

Aberdeen 131
Aberdeen Harbour 132
Aberdeen Tunnel 131
Academy for Performing Arts 81, 120
accommodation 233
acupuncture 69
Admiralty 120
admission charges 234
air travel 228
A-Ma Cultural Village (Coloane) 209
Amah Rock 169
animal parts trade 68, 70, 111
antiques 108, 239
Ap Lei Chau 133
architecture 86
art galleries see museums and galleries
  the arts 80
Avenue of Stars 141

## B

Baiyun Shan 225
bakeries 62
Bank of China Tower 74
Banyan Bay 191
bargaining 217
Basic Law 39, 45
Battery Path 104
beaches
  Cheung Chau 190
  Clearwater Bay 172
  Coloane 209
  Lamma 191
  Lantau 185, 188
  Sai Kung Peninsula 174
  South coast 135, 136
Belcher, Captain Sir Edward 110
beliefs, traditional 72
Big Buddha 186
Big Wave Bay 137
Bishop's Palace (Macau) 202
Blackhead Signal Tower 142
boat people 132
Bowen Road 123
Boxer Rebellion 36
Bride's Pool 171
Britain 33, 158
British East India Company 32
Buddhism 72
budgeting 234
buses 229, 231
business 82
business hours 238

## C

calligraphy 55
Cantonese 21
  language 20
Cantonese cuisine 58
Canton see Guangzhou
  Canton Road 143
Cantopop 80, 148
Cape D'Aguilar 136, 137
Carvings 55
Casa da Mandarin (Macau) 203
casinos 204, 206, 208, 209
Castle Peak 178
Causeway Bay 100, 124
Cenotaph 100
Central District 97
Central Green Trail 115
Central–Mid-Levels Escalator 105
Central Plaza 121
Cham Tau Chau 175
Chan, Anson 42
Charles, Prince 44
Chater House 102
Chek Keng 176
Chek Lap Kok airport 38
Cheung Chau 188
Cheung Kong Centre 74
Cheung Po Tsai 135, 190
Cheung Po Tsai Cave 190
Chiang Kaishek 36
children 9, 208
Chi Lin Nunnery 159
chim sticks 158
China
  economic ties 83
  history 31
  return to 24, 39
China Ferry Terminal 148
Chinese Christian Cemetery 156
Chinese opera 77
Chinese Permanent Cemetery 133
Chinese University 170
Chiu Chow cuisine 61
Chiu Chow (people) 21
chop-makers 111
chopsticks 60
Chuen Pi, Convention of 34
Chungking Mansions 145
churches
  Chapel of Our Lady of Penha (Macau) 202
  Chapel of St Francis Xavier (Coloane) 209
  Our Lady of Carmel (Taipa) 208
  Rosary Church 148
  Sacred Heart Cathedral (Guangzhou) 222
  Santa Casa da Misericórdia (Macau) 199
  São Domingos (Macau) 199
  São Lourenço (Macau) 202
  São Paulo (Macau) 199
  Sé (cathedral) (Macau) 199
  St Andrew's Church 146
  St John's Cathedral 104
  St Joseph's Seminary (Macau) 202
cinemas 149
Citibank Plaza 101
City Hall 100
civil war, Chinese 36, 37
clans 179
Clearwater Bay peninsula 173
climate 234
Colina da Guia (Macau) 207
Colina de Penha (Macau) 202
Coloane 197, 208
Communist Party 36, 225
computers, buying 161
Confucianism 72
consulates 236
cost of living 50
Cotai 208
crafts 55
crime 51, 235
Cross-Harbour Tunnel 124
cruises 143
  Pearl River 223
Cuiheng 219
cuisine 57
cultural district 150
Cultural Revolution 37
currency 237
customs regulations 235
Cyberport 133

## D

dance 78
Daoism 72
Deep Water Bay 134, 136
Deng Xiaoping 40, 84, 215
departure tax 235
Des Voeux Road 101, 111
dialling codes 239
diet 71
disabled travellers 235
Discovery Bay 188
Disneyland 184, 188
Dom Pedro V Theatre (Macau) 202
Dongmen (Shenzhen) 217
Dongtie Ta and Xitie Ta Pagodas (Guangzhou) 223
dragon dance 79
Dragon's Back 137

## E

economy 37, 42, 45, 52

education 52
elections 39, 40, 44
electricity 236
electronic goods 161
Elliot, Captain Charles 34
embassies 236
embroidery 55
emergency telephone numbers 236
Environmental Resource Centre 122
ethnic mix 21
exchange-rate system 84
Exchange Square 99
exercise 69
expats 24, 188

## F

Fanling 172
Fa Yuen Street 151
Feiliutian Chi 219
feng shui 74
ferry services 230, 232
festivals 9, 162
- Dragon Boat Festival 162
- Mid-Autumn Festival 125, 162
- Spring Lantern Festival 162
- Tin Hau Festival 132, 174

Festival Walk 160
Filipinos 25, 100
film 81, 172
Fisherfolk's Village Lamma 191
Flagstaff House 105
floating restaurants 131, 132
food 57
foreign nationals 24
Forever Blooming Bauhinia Sculpture 121
Former Marine Police Headquarters 142
Fortaleza da Barra (Macau) 204
Fortaleza do Monte (Macau) 199
Foshan 215
Foster, Norman 100
France 35
French Mission Building 104

## G

Gage Street 105
gambling 85, 206
General Post Office 99
golf
- Hong Kong Golf Club 172
- Kau Sai Chau golf course 175
- Mission Hills Golf Club (Shenzhen) 216, 218

Government House 74, 103
Grand Lisboa (Macau) 204, 206
Grand Prix, Macau 207
Guang Ta Pagoda (Guangzhou) 222
Guangzhou 31, 225
- transport 223, 229, 231

Guia Fortress and Lighthouse (Macau) 207
gweilo 24

## H

Haizhu Qiao Bridge (Guangzhou) 222
Hakka 20, 177
handicrafts see arts and crafts 112
Hang Seng Index 85
Hap Mun Bay 175
Happy Valley 123
Happy Valley Racecourse 123
Harbour City 143
health 236
helicopter services 232
history 41
HMS Repulse 134
HMS Tamar 119
Hoi Ha 175
Hoklo 20, 132
Hollywood Road 106, 108
Hong Kong Arts Centre 120
Hong Kong Coliseum 148
Hong Kong Convention and Exhibition Centre 86, 120
Hong Kong Country Club 134
Hong Kong Cricket Club 101
Hong Kong Cultural Centre 140
Hong Kong Film Archive 125
Hong Kong Observatory 146
Hong Kong Planning and Infrastructure Exhibition Gallery 99
Hongkong & Shanghai Bank Building (HSBC) 74, 100
Hong Kong Stadium 125
Hong Kong Tourist Board 109, 237
Hong Kong University 113
horse racing
- Happy Valley Racecourse 123
- Sha Tin Racecourse 169

hotels 233
- Four Seasons 99
- Lisboa (Macau) 204
- Mandarin Oriental 100
- Peninsula 142
- Venetian Macao-Resort 206, 208
- Westin Resort (Macau) 209

hou Q (cute) 52
housing 50, 103
HSBC Building 74, 101
Huaiyang cuisine 62
Huanese cuisine 62
Huaqiang Lu (Shenzhen) 217
Hua Ta Pagoda (Guangzhou) 223
Humen 218
Hung Hom Bay 141
Hung Hom Ferry Pier 148
Hung Hom Railway Station 148

## I

immigrants 19, 22, 35
Indians 25
International Commerce Centre 99, 140, 150
International Finance Centre (One ifc and two ifc) 98
island hopping 175

## J

jade 149, 150
Japan 35, 37
Jardine House 86, 99
Jervois Street 112
Jiang Zemin 121
Joint Declaration 38
Joss House Bay 173
Jumbo Floating Restaurant (Aberdeen) 132

## K

Kai Tak airport (closed) 87, 139
Kam Tin 179, 181
Kangxi, Emperor 31
Kat Hing Wai village 179
Kau Sai Chau 175
Kennedy Town 113
Kimberley Road 146
Knutsford Steps and Terrace 146
Kowloon 139
Kowloon City 35
Kowloon Tong 160
Kowloon Walled City Park
- Kowloon Walled City Park 157

Koxinga 177
Kwai Chung 176, 177

## L

Ladder Street 110
Lamma 191
land reclamation 36, 50, 197
Langham Place 150
language 20
Lan Kwai Fong 103
Lantau 184
Lantau Peak 185
Largo do Lilau (Macau) 203
Lee, Martin 41
left luggage 237
Legislative Council (Legco) 39, 41, 44
- Legco Building 101

Lei Cheng Uk Tomb 31, 161
Lei King Wan 125
LGBTQ travellers 237
Lin Zexu 33, 218
lion dance 79, 132
Lion Rock 160
Li Yuen Street 102
Lockhart Road 121
lost property 237

Lovers' Rock 123
Lo Wu Commercial City (Shenzhen) 216
lucky numbers 75
Lui Seng Chun 151
Lu Ping 40

## M

Macau
 history 31, 34, 35, 37
 shopping 239
 transport 229
Macau Cultural Centre 205
Macau Tower 204
Mai Po Marshes 179
manufacturing 82
Man Wa Lane 111
Mao Zedong 36, 37, 221, 225
maps 237
markets 152, 239
 Aberdeen Wholesale Fish 132
 Cat Street 110
 Flower 151
 Goldfish 151
 Graham Street 106
 jade 149
 Ladies' 151
 Qingping (Guangzhou) 221
 Stanley 135
 Temple Street Night 149
 Wan Chai Street 122
 Yuen Po Street 151
Mass Transit Railway (MTR) 116
maxicabs 230
medical services 236
medicine, Chinese 67, 108, 111
metro
 Guangzhou 223
Minibuses 230
Mirs Bay 171
mobile phones 11, 240
Mody Road 147
monasteries
 Chi Lin Nunnery 159
 Po Lin 185
 Ten Thousand Buddhas 167
 Yin Hing 186
money 238
Mong-Ha Fortress (Macau) 205
Mong Kok 150
Monte Fort (Macau) 201
Moorish Barracks (Macau) 203
mosques
 Huaisheng (Guangzhou) 222
 Jamiah Masjid 107
 Kowloon 145
Mui Wo 185, 188
Murray House (Stanley) 135
museums and galleries
 Art 142
 Art (Chinese University) 170
 Coastal Defence 125
 Correctional Services 136
 Dr Sun Yat-sen 107
 Grand Prix (Macau) 207
 Guangdong Art (Guangzhou) 222
 Guangdong Folk Arts (Guangzhou) 224
 Guangdong Geming Bowuguan (Guangzhou) 225
 Guangzhou Museum of Art 224, 225
 Heritage 169
 Heritage Discovery Centre 145
 history 147
 Hong Kong Arts Centre 120
 Macau Art 205
 Macau Museum 201
 Madame Tussauds 114
 Maritime 98
 Maritime (Macau) 203
 Medical Sciences 108
 municipal (Guangzhou) 224
 Nanyue Tomb (Guangzhou) 224
 Opium War (Humen) 218
 Police 123
 Racing 123
 Railway 170
 Sacred Art (Macau) 199
 Sam Tung Uk 177
 Science 147
 Space 141
 Taipa and Coloane History 208
 Taipa Houses 208
 Tea Ware 105
 University Museum and Art Gallery 113
 Wine (Macau) 207
music 77

## N

Nanfeng Ancient Kiln (Shiwan) 219
Nanking, Treaty of 34
Nanyue Tomb (Guangzhou) 224
NAPE (Macau) 205
Nathan Road 139, 143
Nationalists (Guomintang) 36, 221, 225
New Kowloon 160
newspapers and magazines 237
New Territories 171
 99-year lease 35, 38
Ngong Ping 360 Cable Car 186
Ngong Ping Village 186
nicknames 49
nightlife 103, 216
Nina Tower 177
Noon-Day Gun 124
North Point 125
numerology 72

## O

Ocean Centre 143
Ocean Park 133
Ocean Terminal 143
octopus card 11, 230
Old Bailey Street 106
Old Protestant Cemetery (Macau) 201
Old Stanley Police Station 136
Opium Wars 31, 32, 33
O Porto Interior (Macue) 203

## P

Pacific Place 120
painting 55
Pak Sha Chau 175
Pak Tam Au 175
Palmerston, Lord 33
parks and gardens
 see also theme parks 115
 Camões Grotto and Garden (Macau) 201
 Casa Garden (Macau) 201
 Chater Garden 101
 Flora Garden (Macau) 207
 Hong Kong Park 104
 Kadoorie Farm and Botanic Garden 181
 Kowloon Park 145
 Lieshi Lingyuan (Guangzhou) 225
 Lou Lim Ioc Gardens (Macau) 207
 Nian Lin Garden 159
 Ocean Park 133
 Sai Kung Country Park 175
 Tai Tam Country Park 137
 Victoria Park 125
 Yuexiu (Guangzhou) 224
 Zoological and Botanical Gardens 103
Pat Sin Leng 180
Patten Chris 43
Peak Tower 114
Peak Tram 114, 231
Pearl River Delta 83, 217, 218
Peasant Movement Training Institute (Guangzhou) 225
Pedder Street 102
pedicabs 231
Pei, I.M. 74, 101
People's Liberation Army 22, 39, 43
pharmacies 68
phone cards 11, 240
pirates 136, 177, 190, 209
Pok Fu Lam 113
politics 40, 45, 53
pollution 45, 53, 54, 217
Ponte 16 casino (Macau) 203
population 19, 50
porcelain 55
Portas do Cerco (Macau) 205
Portuguese 31, 34, 35, 198
Possession Street 110

**postal services** 239
**Po Toi islands** 191
**Pottinger, Sir Henry** 34
**power station, Lamma** 190
**prices** 234
**Prince's Building** 102
**property market** 50
**public holidays** 234
**public transport** 229

## Q

**qigong** 69
**Qi Shan** 33
**Quarry Bay** 125
**Queen's Road Central** 102
**Queen's Road East** 122
**Queen's Road West** 111

## R

**radio** 237
**rail travel** 228, 230, 232
**Railway Clock Tower** 140
**refugees** 21, 37
**religions** 72
**Repulse Bay** 134, 136
**Reunification Monument** 121
**rock carvings** 31
**Rocky Bay** 134
**Route Twisk** 181
**Royal Hong Kong Yacht Club** 124
**Rugby Sevens** 125
**Russia** 35

## S

**safety** 235
**Sai Kung** 174
**Sai Kung peninsula** 180
**Sai Ying Pun** 111, 112
**Salisbury Road** 142
**Santo Agostinho** 201
**SARS virus** 42
**sea travel** 229, 231
**service industry** 84
**Shamian Island (Guangzhou)** 221
**Sham Shui Po** 156, 160
**Shanghainese** 21
**Sharp Peak** 180
**Sha Tin** 167
**Shau Kei Wan** 125
**Shaw Brothers Movie Studio** 172, 173
**Shek Kong** 181
**Shek O** 134, 136
**Shek Pik Reservoir** 185
**Shenzhen** 217
- **shopping** 239
- **transport** 229, 231

**Sheung Wan** 111
**Shing Mun Valley** 180
**Shiwan** 215
**shopping** 9, 152, 233
**Shunde** 219
**Sichuan cuisine** 61
**Silvermine Bay** 185, 188
**Sino-British agreement (1984)** 24, 38, 41
**Sir Robert Hotung Library (Macau)** 202
**skyscrapers** 86, 111
**social welfare** 51
**SoHo** 106
**Sok Kwu Wan** 191
**South Bay** 136
**Special Administrative Region (SAR)** 39, 197
**Special Economic Zone (SEZs)** 215, 217, 219
**Stanley** 135
**Stanley Military Cemetery** 136
**Stanley Prison** 136
**Star Ferry** 117
**Star Ferry Pier** 140
**Star House** 143
**Statue Square** 100
**Staunton Street** 114
**Stock Exchange** 99
**stock market** 85
**street signs** 232
**St Stephen's Beach** 136
**student travellers** 239
**Sun Yat-sen** 36, 221
- **Historical Trail** 97, 108
- **memorial garden** 219
- **Memorial Hall (Guangzhou)** 224
- **Memorial House (Macau)** 207
- **Monument (Guangzhou)** 224
- **Museum** 107

**superstitions** 72

## T

**taijiquan (shadow boxing)** 69, 71
**Tai Koo Shing** 125
**Tai Long Wan beach** 175
**Tai Mo Shan** 181, 180
**Tai O** 187
**Taipa** 197, 208
**Tai Po** 171
**Tai Po Nature Reserve** 170, 171
**Tai Tam** 134
**Tai Tam Reservoirs** 137
**Tang Chung Ling Ancestral Hall** 172
**Tang, David** 102
**Tanka** 20, 132
**Tap Mun Chau** 171
**taxation** 85
**taxis** 230, 231
**telecommunications** 239
**television** 237
**temples**
- **A-Ma (Macau)** 203
- **Chenjia Si (Guangzhou)** 223
- **Ching Chung Koon** 178
- **Fung Ying Sin Koon** 172
- **Guangxiao Si (Guangzhou)** 223
- **Hau Wong** 156
- **Hualin (Guangzhou)** 222
- **Hung Shing** 122
- **Kun Iam (Macau)** 207
- **Liurong Si (Guangzhou)** 223
- **Man Fat** 168
- **Man Mo** 109
- **Pak Tai (Cheung Chau)** 189
- **Pak Tai (Wan Chai)** 122
- **Pei Tu** 178
- **Tin Hau (Aberdeen)** 132
- **Tin Hau (Clearwater Bay)** 173
- **Tin Hau (Stanley)** 135
- **Tin Hau (Tap Mun Chau)** 172
- **Tin Hau (Yau Ma Tei)** 149
- **Tin Hau (Yung Shue Wan)** 191
- **Wong Tai Sin** 158
- **Yuen Yuen Institute** 177
- **Zu Miao (Foshan)** 218

**Thatcher Margaret** 38
**theatre** 77
**The Bund (Guangzhou)** 222
**The Landmark** 102
**The Lanes** 102
**theme parks** 192
- **China Folk Culture Village (Shenzhen)** 217
- **Disneyland** 184, 188, 192, see also parks and gardens
- **Ocean Park** 192
- **Splendid China (Shenzhen)** 217
- **Window on the World (Shenzhen)** 217

**The Peak** 112
**Tiananmen Square massacre** 24, 38
**Tianjin, Treaty of** 35
**Times Square** 124
**time zones** 240
**tipping** 238
**toilets** 240
**Tolo Harbour** 170
**Top Deck at the Jumbo** 132
**tourist information** 109, 241
**Tower Overlooking the Sea (Guangzhou)** 224
**trade** 31, 83
**trams** 117, 231
**Treaty Ports** 34
**triads** 52
**Tsang, Donald** 43
**Tsim Sha Tsui** 100
**Tsim Sha Tsui East** 141, 147
**Tsing Long** 178
**Tsing Ma Bridge** 176
**Tsing Yi** 176
**Tsuen Wan** 177
**Tsui Sing Lau** 178
**Tuen Mun** 177
**Tung Chee-hwa** 42, 43
**Tung Chung Fort** 187
**Tung Lung Chau** 174
**Tung Ping Chau** 171
**Tung Wan beach** 190
**typhoons** 235

## U

**Umbrella Revolution** 45
**Union Square** 150

## V

**values, traditional** 48

**Victoria Gap** 115
**Victoria Harbour** 109
**Vietnamese** 37
**Vietnam War** 37
**visas** 241
**Vital Statistics** 241

## W

**walking tours** 100
**walks and trails** 180
- **Bowen Road walk** 123
- **Hong Kong Trail** 137
- **Lantau Trail** 185
- **Lung Yeuk Tau Heritage Trail** 172
- **MacLehose Trail** 175, 180
- **New Territories** 180
- **Ping Shan Heritage Trail** 178
- **Sok Kwu Wan** 191
- **Tai Tam trail** 137
- **The Peak** 115
- **Wan Chai Green Trail** 123
- **Wilson Trail** 137, 171, 180

**Walkways** 102
**Walled City** 157, 158
**Wan Chai** 120
**weights and measures** 241
**Western District** 97
**Western Harbour Crossing** 113
**Western Market** 112
**West Kowloon Cultural District** 150
**wildlife** 183
- **Hong Kong Wetland Park** 178
- **Kadoorie Farm and Botanic Garden** 181
- **Mai Po Marshes** 179
- **Ocean Park** 134
- **pink dolphins** 188
- **Tai Po Nature Reserve** 171, 171
- **Zoological and Botanical Gardens** 103

**Wing Lok Street** 111
**Wishing Trees** 170
**Wong Shek** 175
**World War II** 36, 134, 136, 158
**Wyndham Street** 103, 107

## X

**Xiqiao Shan** 219

## Y

**Yau Ma Tei** 149
**Yim Tin Tsai** 175
**Yin and yang** 67
**Yuen Long** 178
**Yuet Kai** 168
**Yung Shue Wan** 191

## Z

**Zhou Enlai** 221, 225
**Zhuhai** 218
**Zodiac, Chinese** 163
**zoo see wildlife** 103

# ABOUT THIS BOOK

What makes an Insight Guide different? Since our first book pioneered the use of full-colour photography in travel guides in 1970, we have aimed to provide not only reliable information but also the key to a real understanding of a destination and its people.

Now, when the internet can supply inexhaustible (but not always reliable) facts, our books marry text and pictures to provide that more elusive quality: knowledge.

## The Contributors

This new edition of *Insight City Guide: Hong Kong* was commissioned and edited by **Helen Fanthorpe**.

The book has been updated by **Justyna Radomska**, and builds on the work of **Graham Bond**, a freelance travel writer and photojournalist with extensive knowledge of Hong Kong and mainland China.

Other past contributors whose work remains in this edition include **Ruth Williams**, **Edward Stokes**, **Roger Cave**, **Mischa Moselle**, **Ed Peters**, **Dinah Gardner**, **Saul Lockhart**, **Leonard Lueras**, **Philippa Conway**, **Paul Hicks**, **Suzanne Lidster** and **Angelica Cheung**.

## SEND US YOUR THOUGHTS

We do our best to ensure the information in our books is as accurate and up-to-date as possible. The books are updated on a regular basis using local contacts, who painstakingly add, amend, and correct as required. However, some details (such as telephone numbers and opening times) are liable to change, and we are ultimately reliant on our readers to put us in the picture.

We welcome your feedback, especially your experience of using the book "on the road". Maybe we recommended a hotel that you liked (or another that you didn't), or you came across a great bar or new attraction that we missed.

We will acknowledge all contributions, and we'll offer an Insight Guide to the best letters received.

Please write to us at:
**Insight Guides**
**PO Box 7910, London SE1 1WE**
Or email us at:
**hello@insightguides.com**

INSIGHT GUIDES
**HONG KONG**

*Editor:* **Helen Fanthorpe**
*Author:* **Graham Bond, updated by Justyna Radomska**
*Head of DTP and Pre-Press:* **Rebeka Davies**
*Update Production:* **Apa Digital**
*Pictures:* **Tom Smyth**
*Cartography:* **original cartography Dave Priestley and Stephen Ramsey, updated by Carte**

**Distribution**

*UK, Ireland and Europe*
**Apa Publications (UK) Ltd**
sales@insightguides.com

*United States and Canada*
**Ingram Publisher Services**
ips@ingramcontent.com

*Australia and New Zealand*
**Woodslane**
info@woodslane.com.au

*Southeast Asia*
**Apa Publications (SN) Pte**
singaporeoffice@insightguides.com

*Worldwide*
**Apa Publications (UK) Ltd**
sales@insightguides.com

**Special Sales, Content Licensing and CoPublishing**

Insight Guides can be purchased in bulk quantities at discounted prices. We can create special editions, personalised jackets and corporate imprints tailored to your needs. sales@insightguides.com; www.insightguides.biz

**Printing**

**CTPS-China**



*First Edition 1991*
*Ninth edition 2019*



**www.insightguides.com**

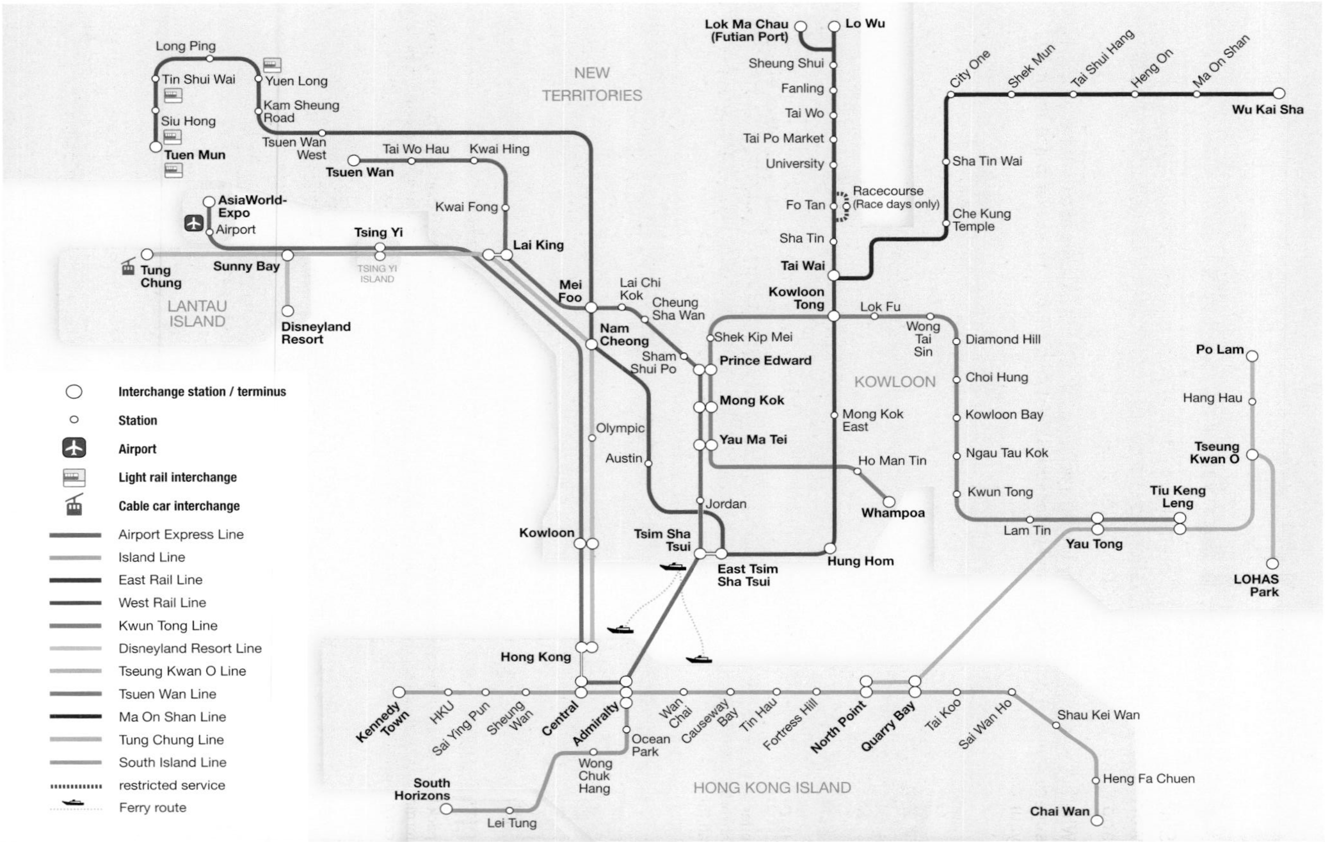

NEW TERRITORIES
KOWLOON
HONG KONG ISLAND
LANTAU ISLAND
TSING YI ISLAND
Lok Ma Chau (Futian Port)
Lo Wu
Sheung Shui
Fanling
Tai Wo
Tai Po Market
University
Racecourse (Race days only)
Fo Tan
Sha Tin
Tai Wai
Kowloon Tong
Mong Kok East
Hung Hom
City One
Shek Mun
Tai Shui Hang
Heng On
Ma On Shan
Wu Kai Sha
Sha Tin Wai
Che Kung Temple
Long Ping
Tin Shui Wai
Yuen Long
Kam Sheung Road
Siu Hong
Tuen Mun
Tsuen Wan West
Tsuen Wan
Tai Wo Hau
Kwai Hing
Kwai Fong
Lai King
AsiaWorld-Expo
Airport
Tsing Yi
Tung Chung
Sunny Bay
Disneyland Resort
Mei Foo
Lai Chi Kok
Cheung Sha Wan
Sham Shui Po
Nam Cheong
Olympic
Austin
Kowloon
Hong Kong
Shek Kip Mei
Prince Edward
Mong Kok
Yau Ma Tei
Jordan
Tsim Sha Tsui
East Tsim Sha Tsui
Ho Man Tin
Whampoa
Lok Fu
Wong Tai Sin
Diamond Hill
Choi Hung
Kowloon Bay
Ngau Tau Kok
Kwun Tong
Lam Tin
Yau Tong
Tiu Keng Leng
Tseung Kwan O
Hang Hau
Po Lam
LOHAS Park
Kennedy Town
HKU
Sai Ying Pun
Sheung Wan
Central
Admiralty
Wan Chai
Causeway Bay
Tin Hau
Fortress Hill
North Point
Quarry Bay
Tai Koo
Sai Wan Ho
Shau Kei Wan
Heng Fa Chuen
Chai Wan
Ocean Park
Wong Chuk Hang
Lei Tung
South Horizons
Interchange station / terminus
Station
Airport
Light rail interchange
Cable car interchange
Airport Express Line
Island Line
East Rail Line
West Rail Line
Kwun Tong Line
Disneyland Resort Line
Tseung Kwan O Line
Tsuen Wan Line
Ma On Shan Line
Tung Chung Line
South Island Line
restricted service
Ferry route

Pearl River Delta